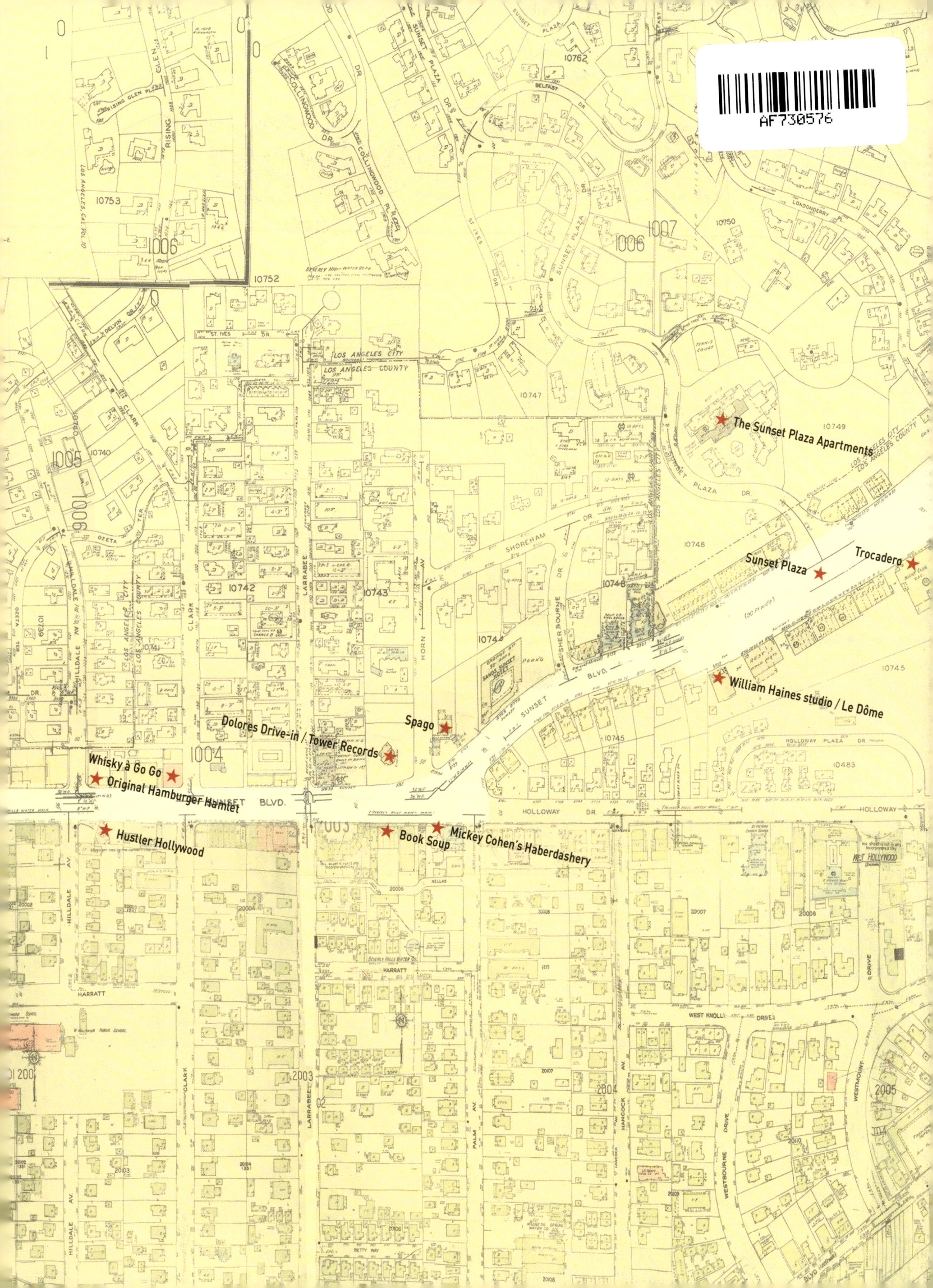
The Sunset Plaza Apartments
Sunset Plaza
Trocadero
William Haines studio / Le Dôme
Spago
Dolores Drive-in / Tower Records
Whisky à Go Go
Original Hamburger Hamlet
Hustler Hollywood
Book Soup
Mickey Cohen's Haberdashery
SUNSET BLVD.
HOLLOWAY DR.
SHOREHAM DR.
SUNSET PLAZA DR.
HOLLOWAY PLAZA DR
LARRABEE
CLARK
HILLDALE AV.
HARRATT
WEST KNOLL DRIVE
WESTMOUNT DRIVE
WESTBOURNE DRIVE
HANCOCK AV.
PALM AV.
SHERBOURNE DR
HORN AV.
LOS ANGELES CITY
LOS ANGELES COUNTY

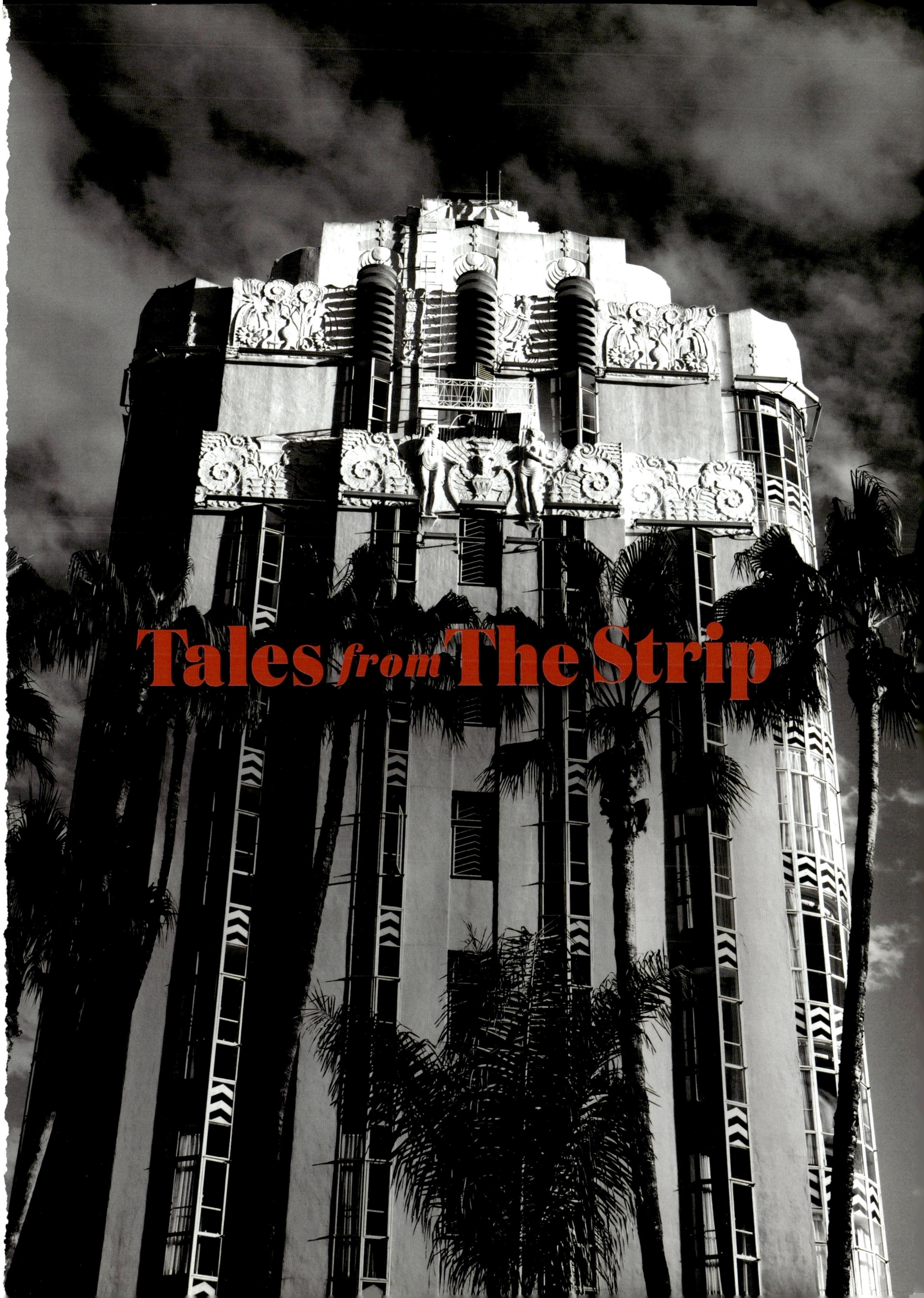

Tales *from* The Strip

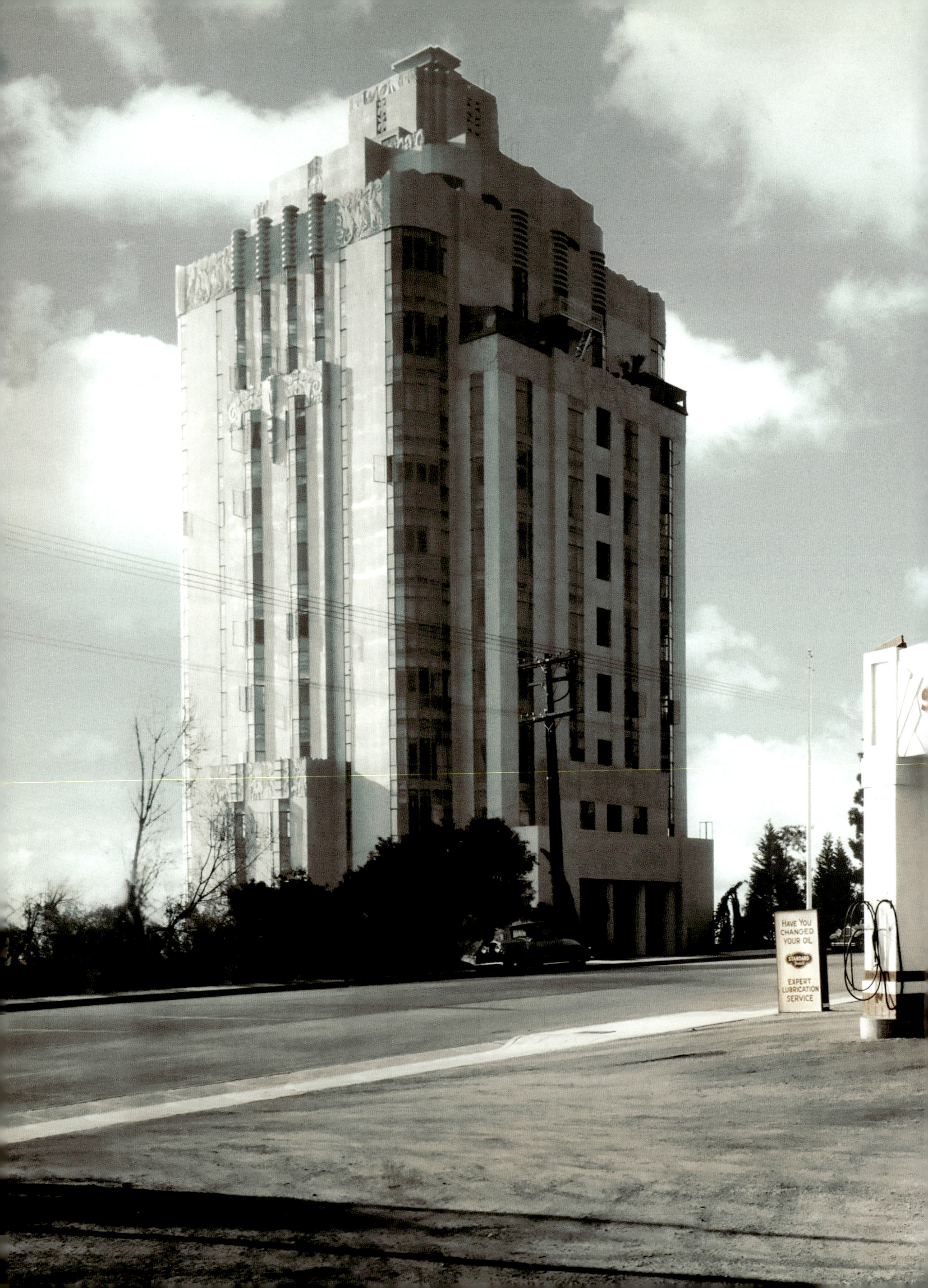
HAVE YOU CHANGED YOUR OIL
STANDARD
EXPERT LUBRICATION SERVICE

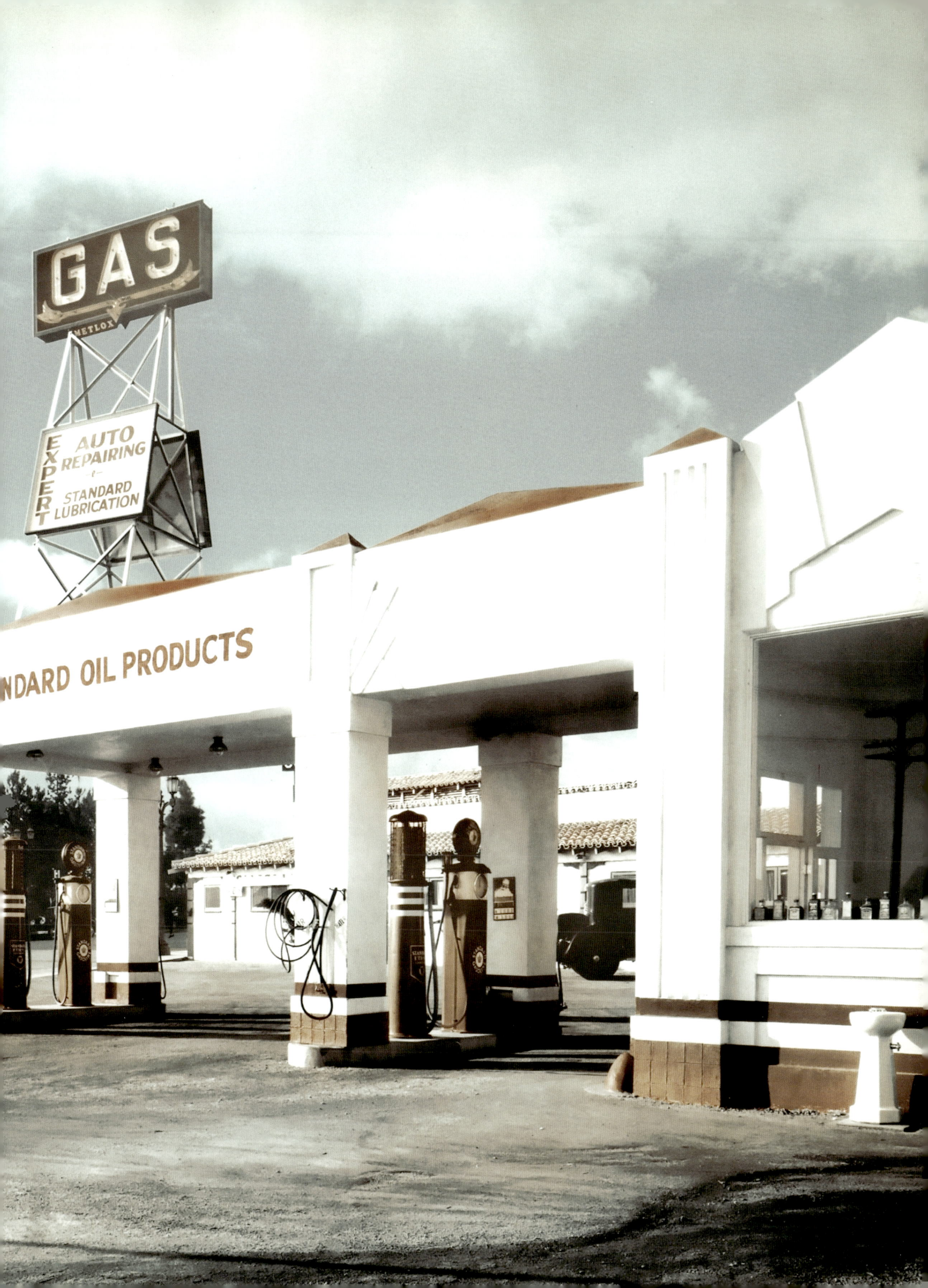
GAS
METLOX
EXPERT
AUTO REPAIRING
STANDARD LUBRICATION
NDARD OIL PRODUCTS

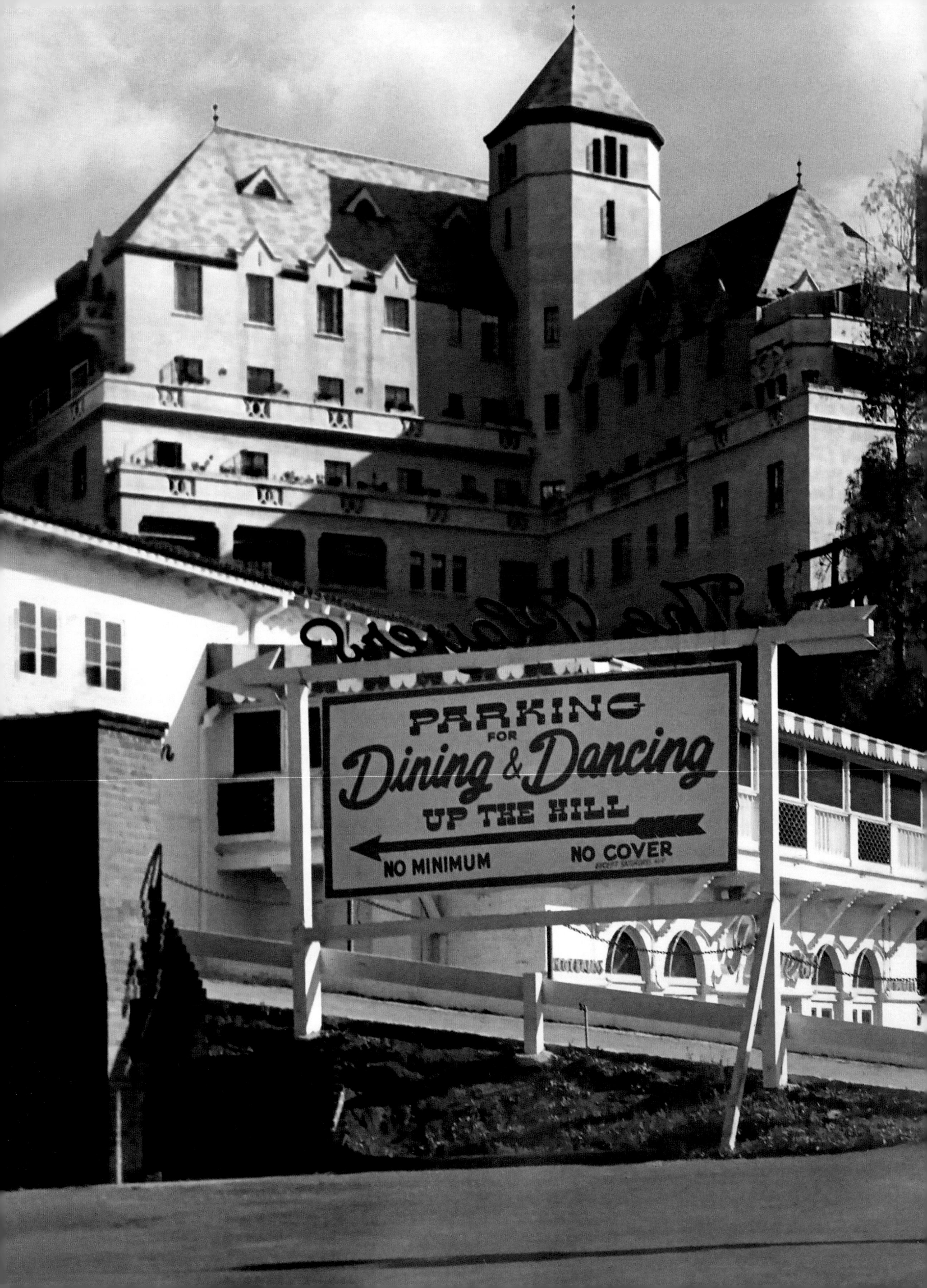
PARKING
FOR
Dining & Dancing
UP THE HILL
NO MINIMUM
NO COVER

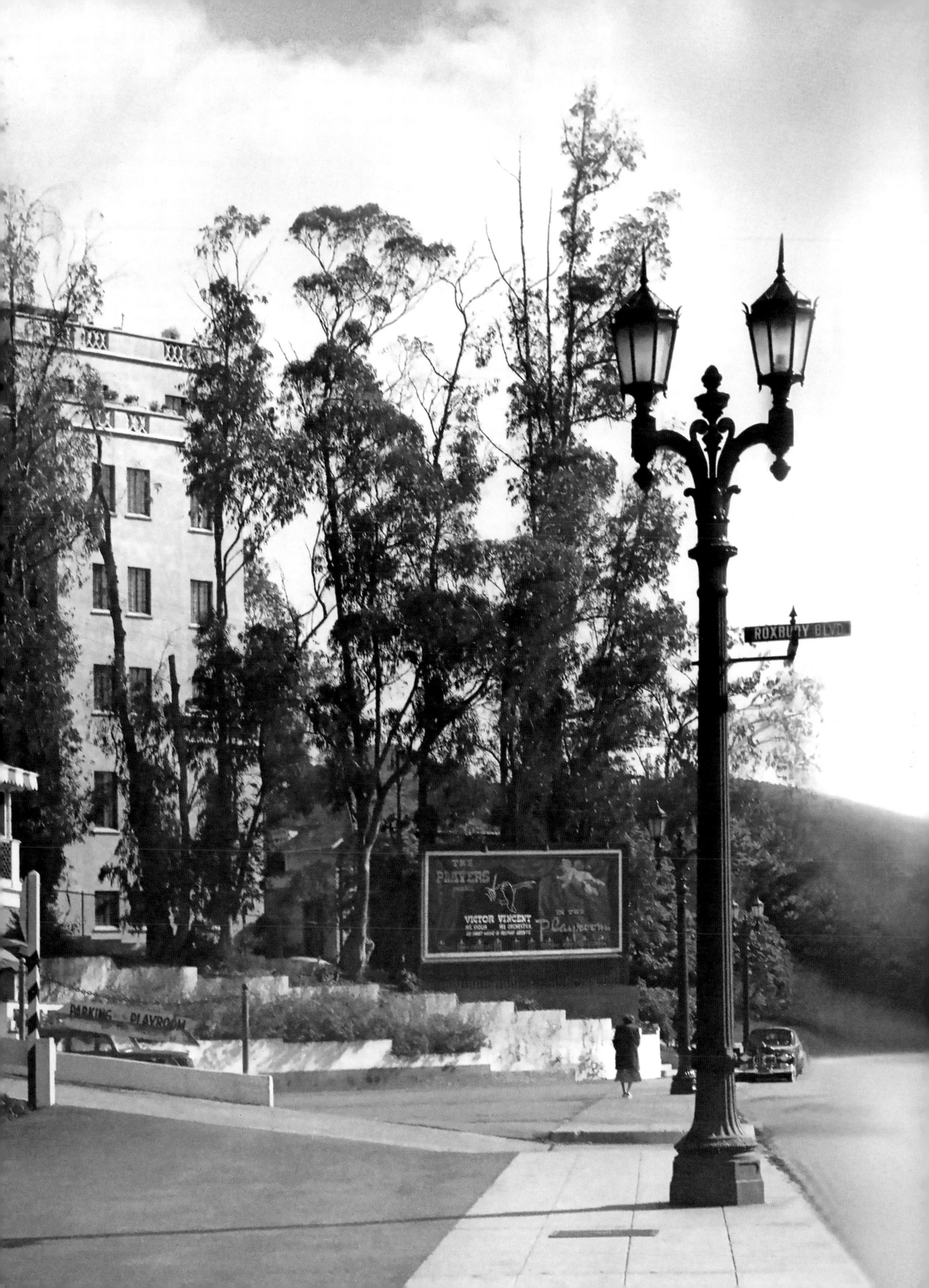
ROXBURY BLVD
VICTOR VINCENT
PARKING
PLAYROOM

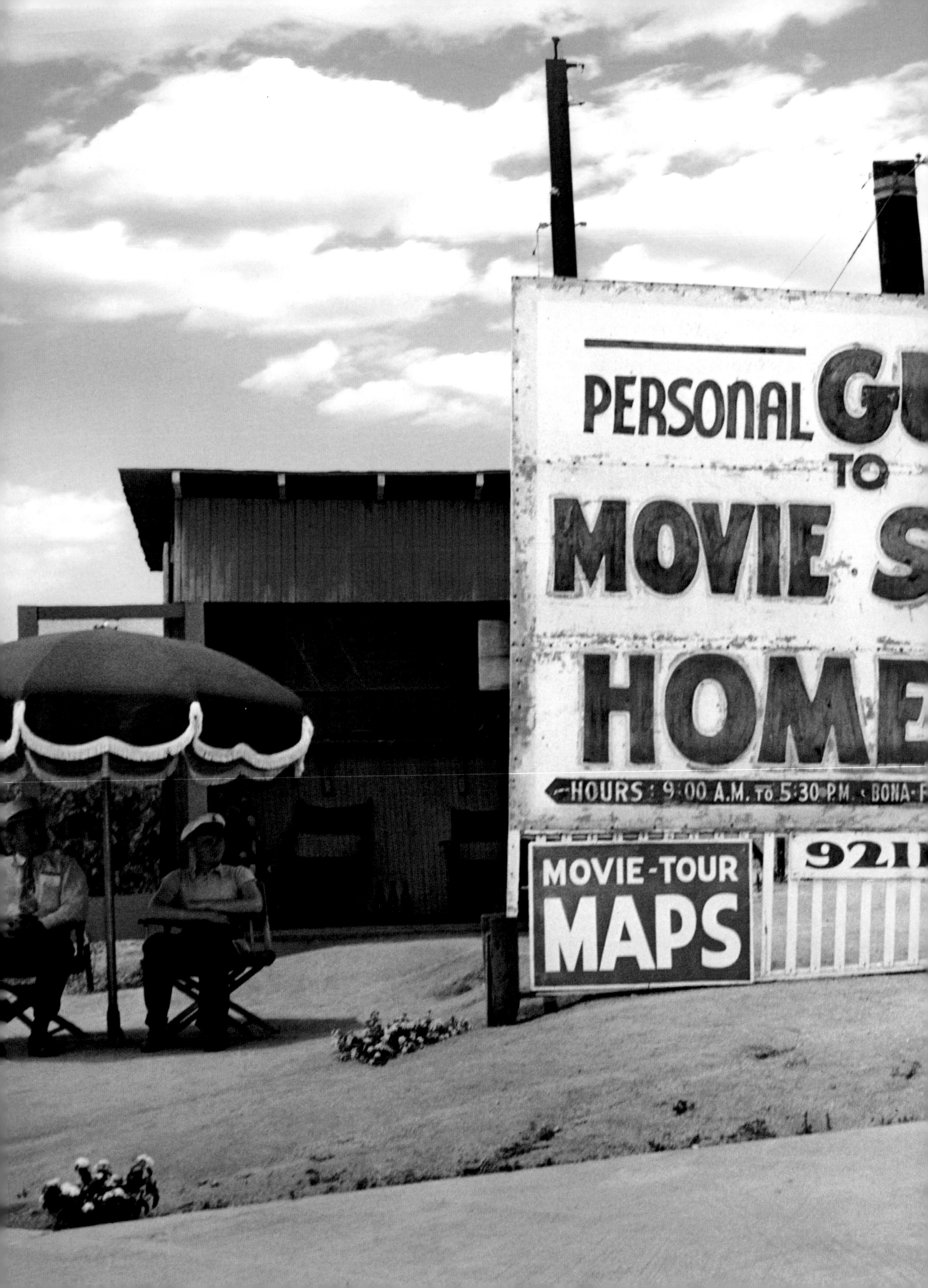

PERSONAL GU
TO
MOVIE S
HOME
HOURS: 9:00 A.M. TO 5:30 P.M. BONA-F
MOVIE-TOUR
MAPS
921

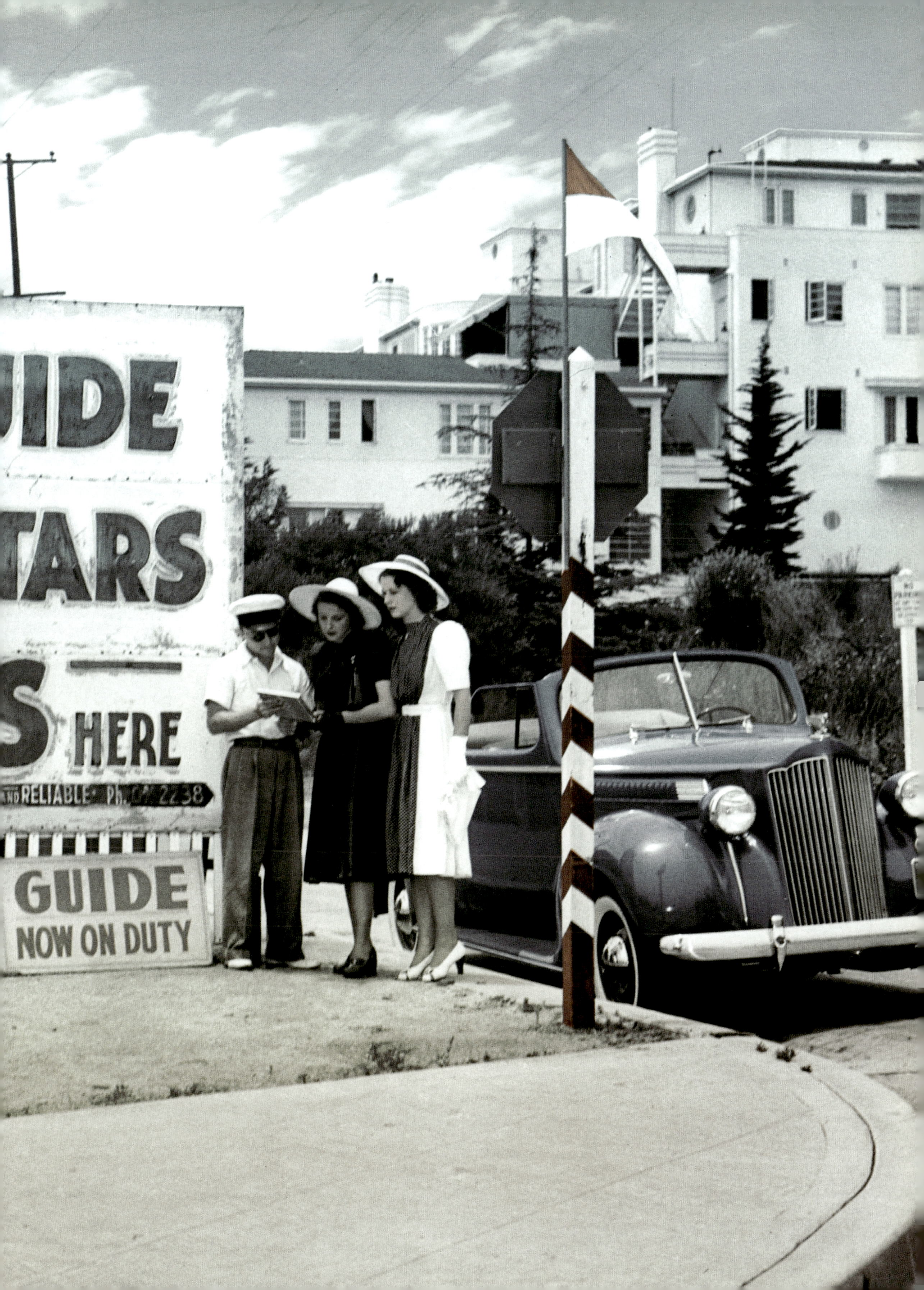
GUIDE
NOW ON DUTY

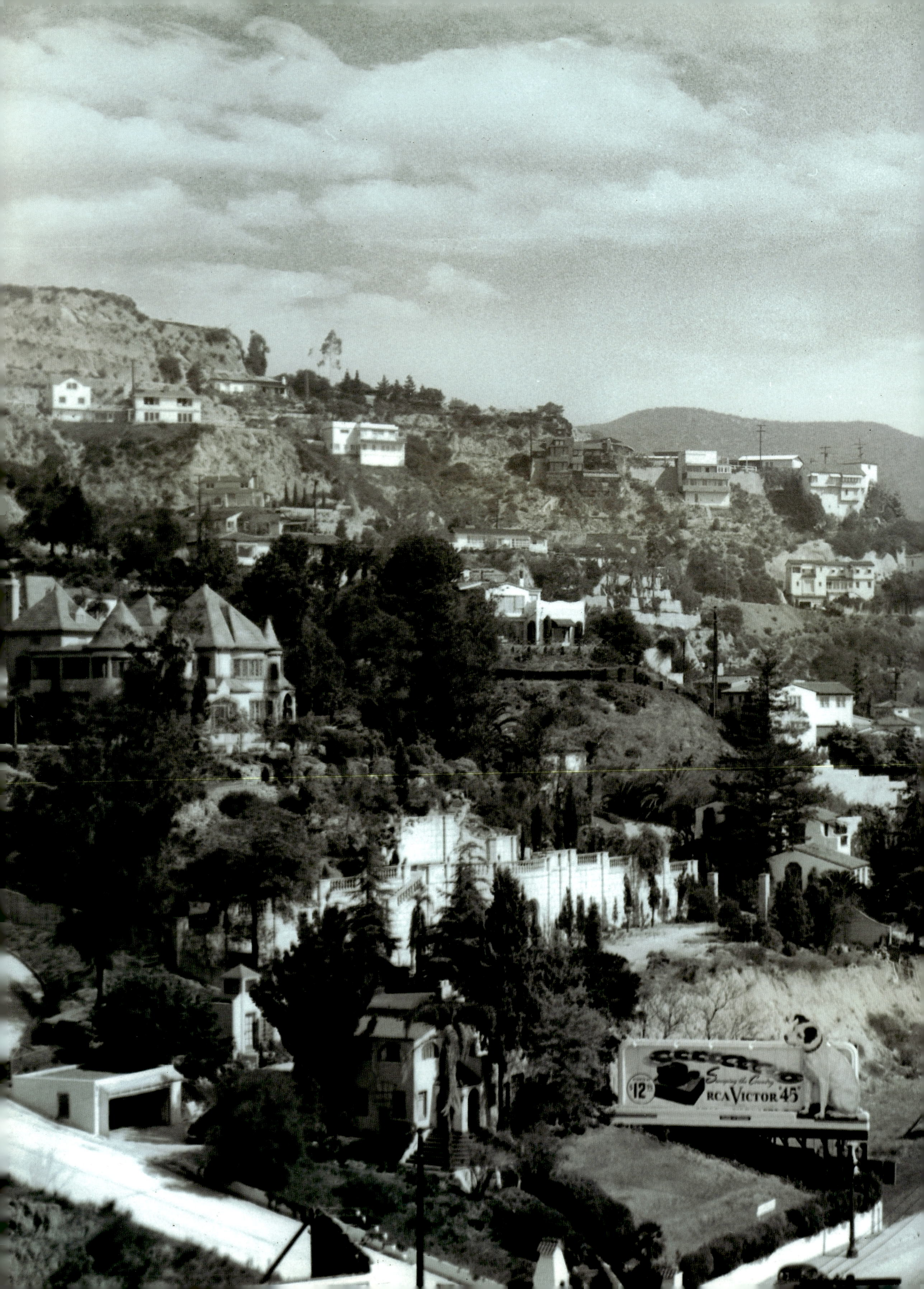
RCA VICTOR 45

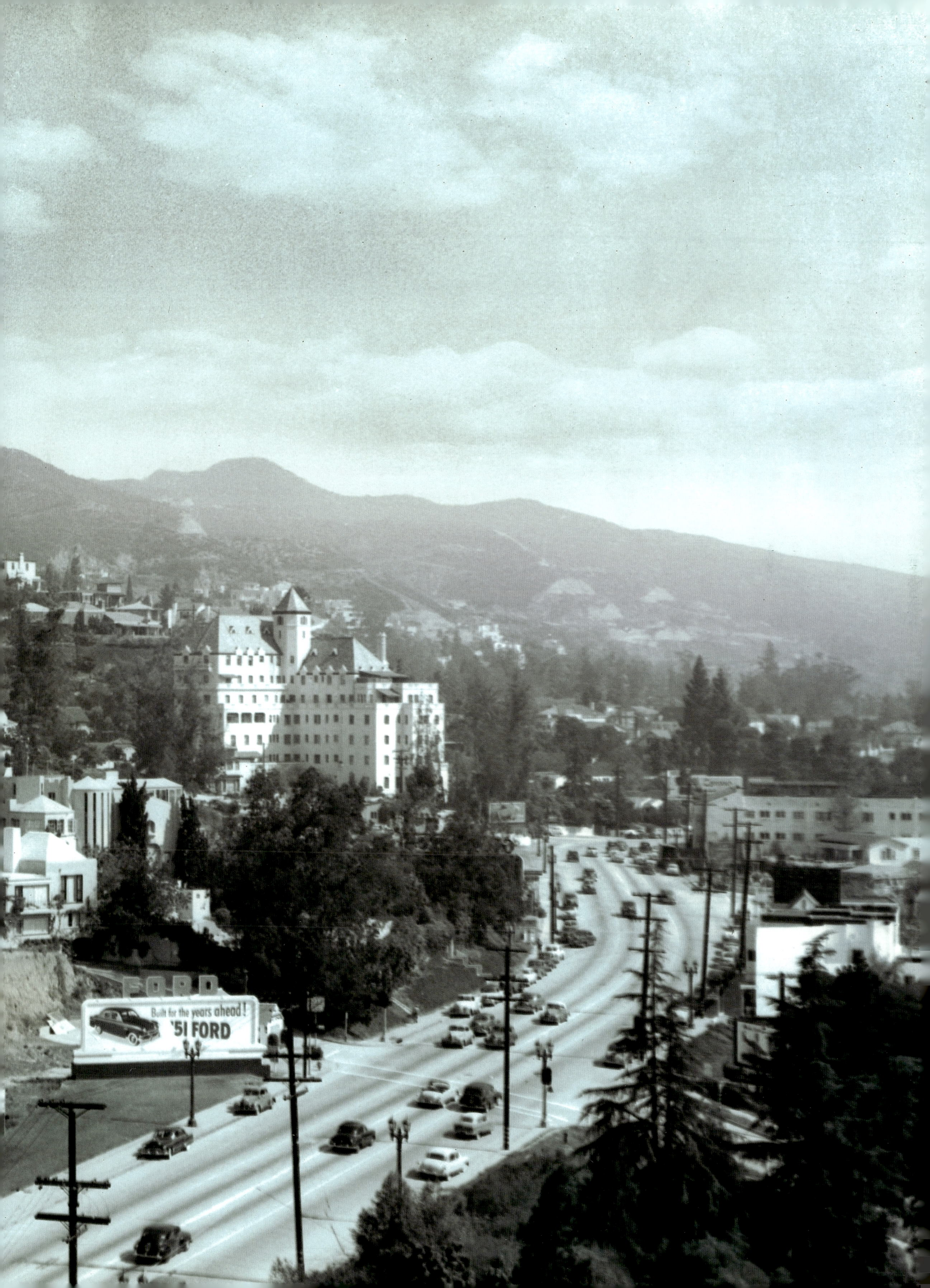
FORD
Built for the years ahead!
'51 FORD

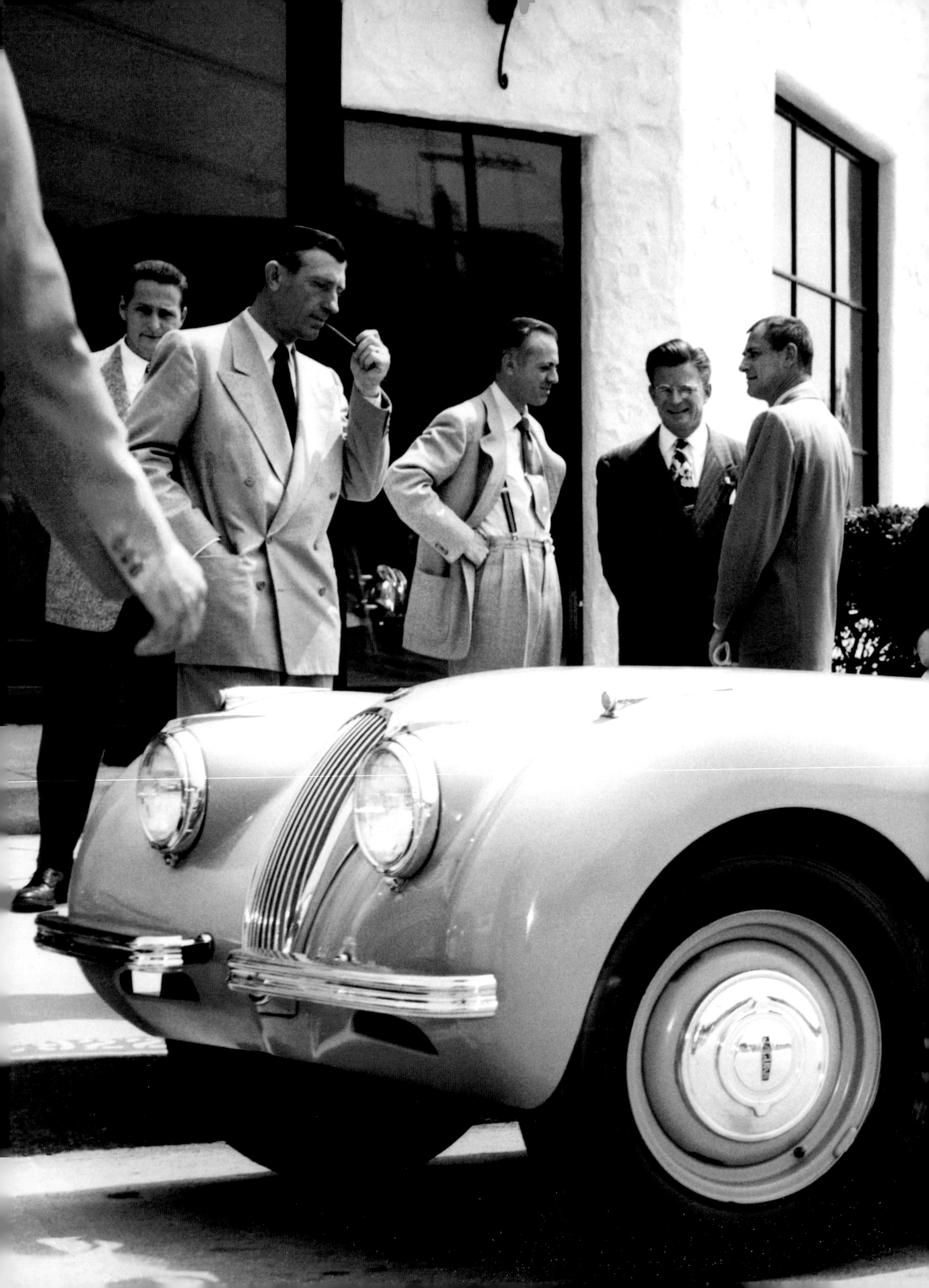

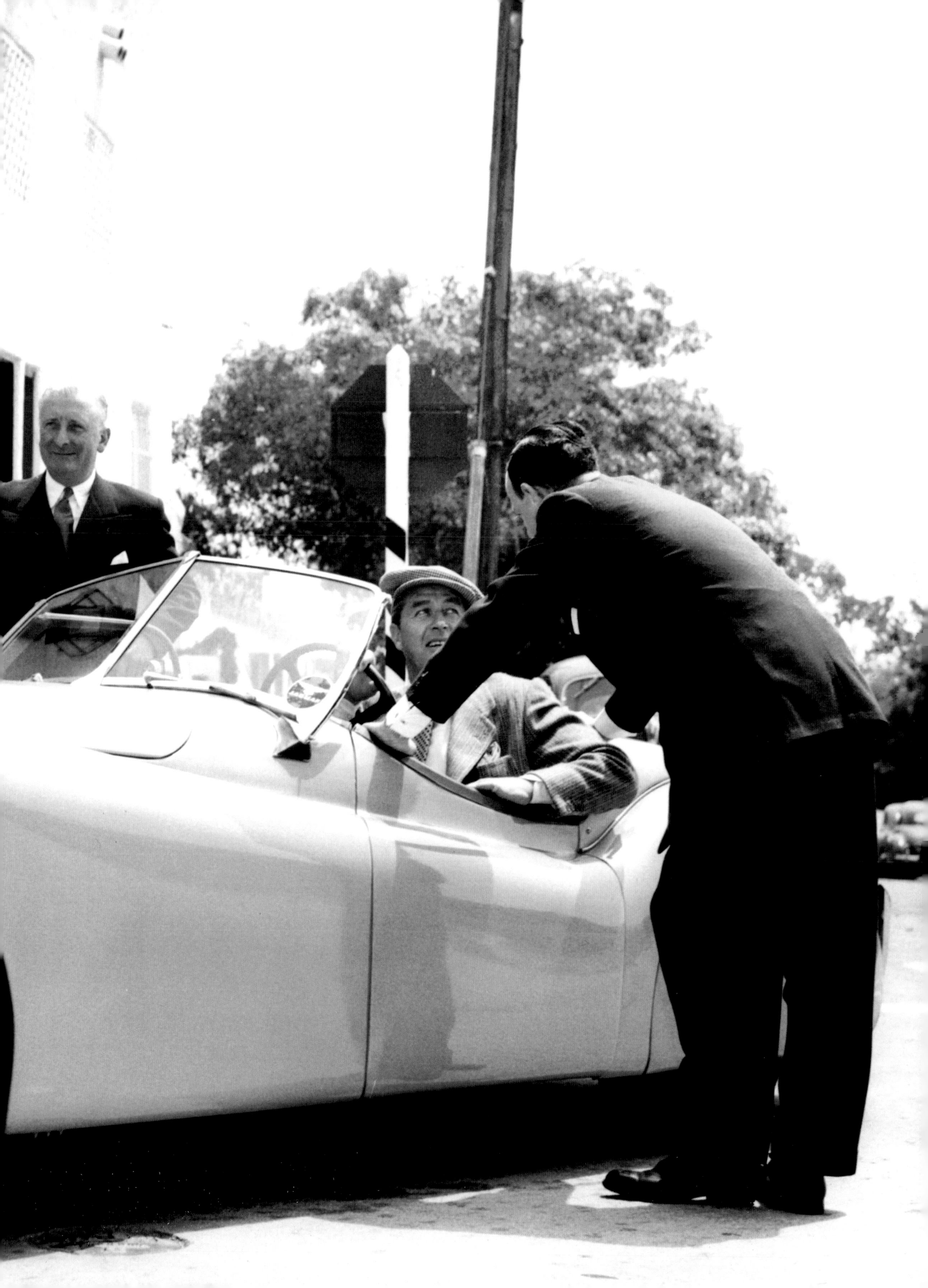

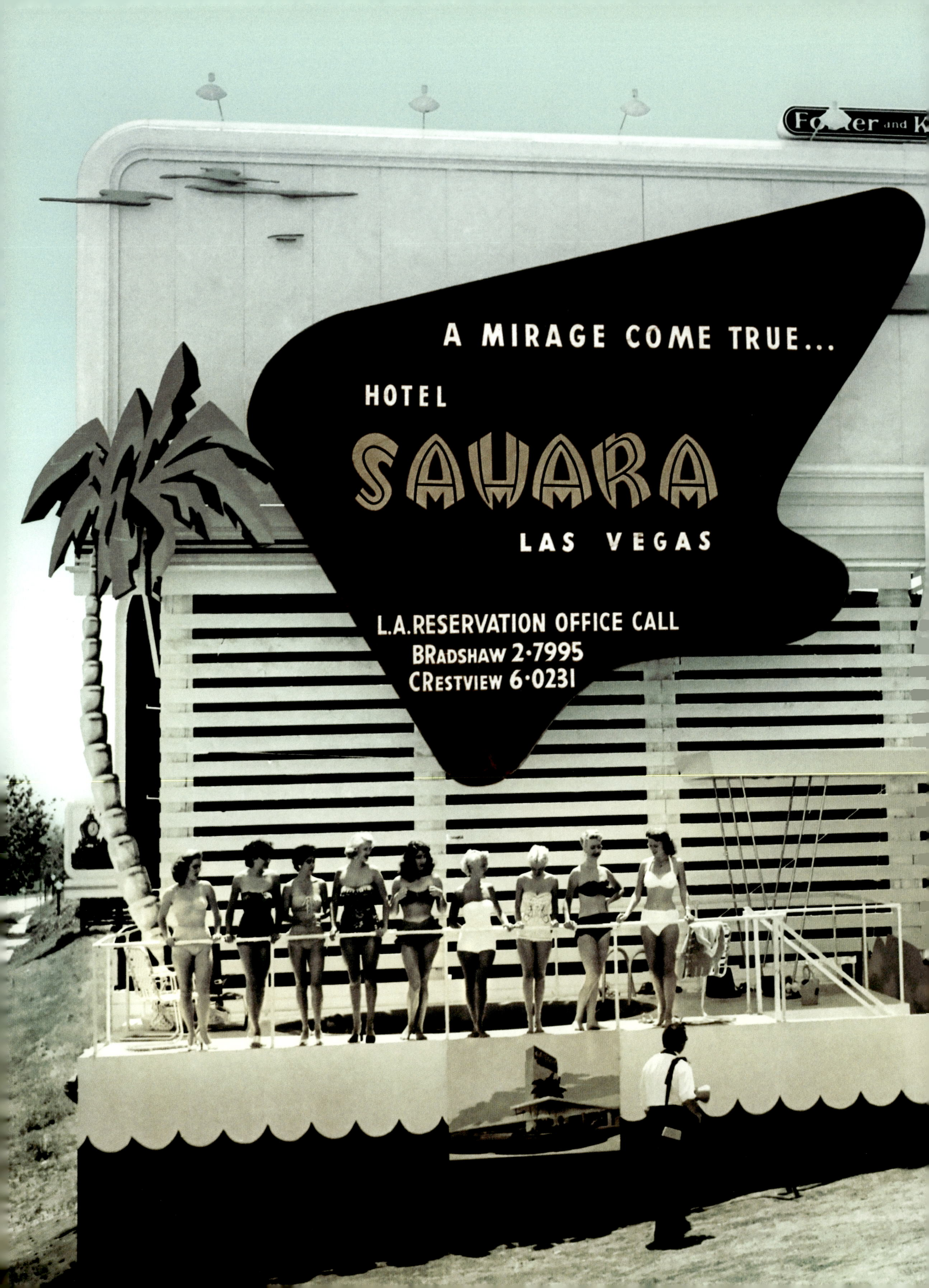
A MIRAGE COME TRUE...
HOTEL
SAHARA
LAS VEGAS
L.A. RESERVATION OFFICE CALL
BRADSHAW 2-7995
CRESTVIEW 6-0231

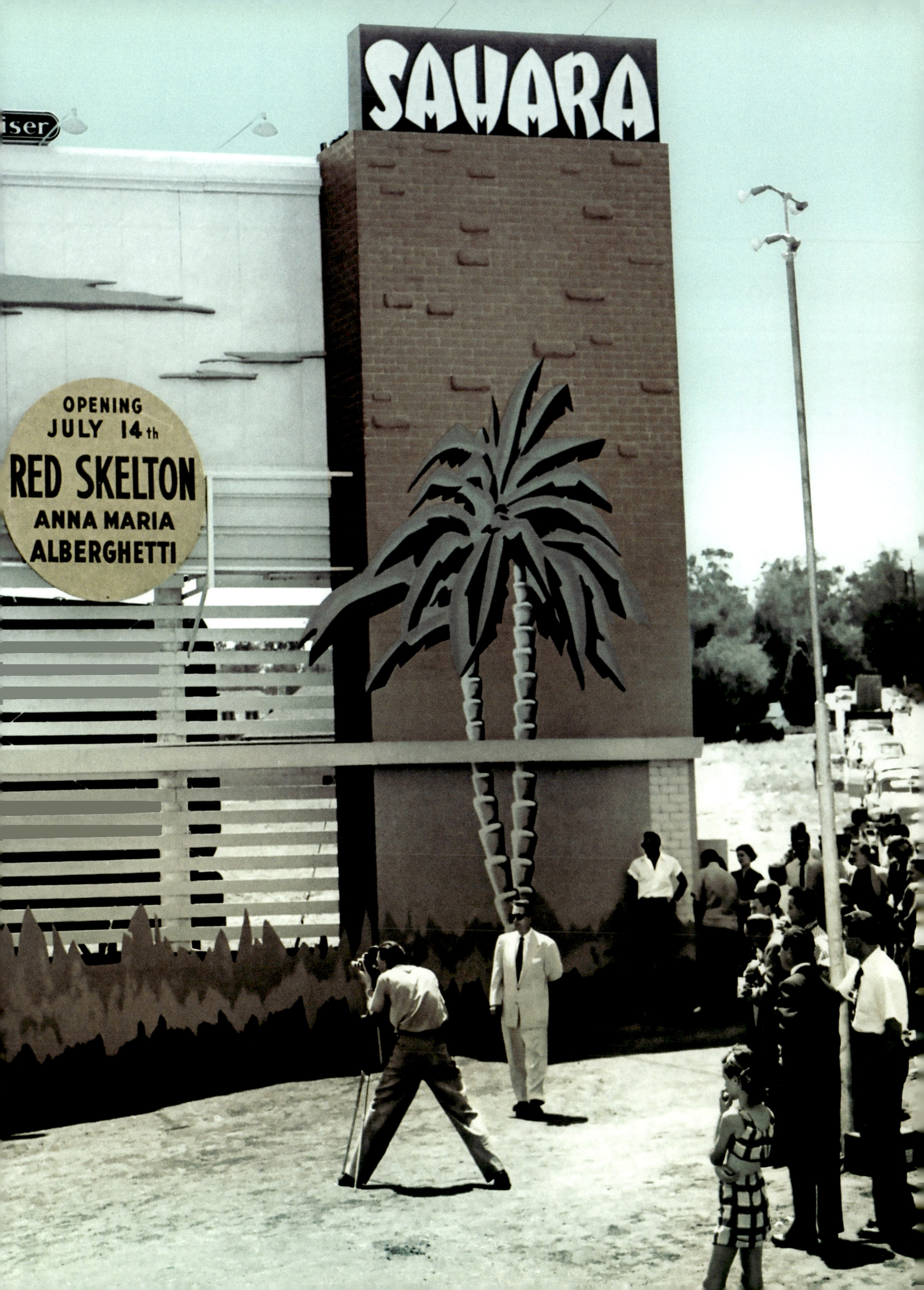
SAHARA
OPENING
JULY 14th
RED SKELTON
ANNA MARIA
ALBERGHETTI

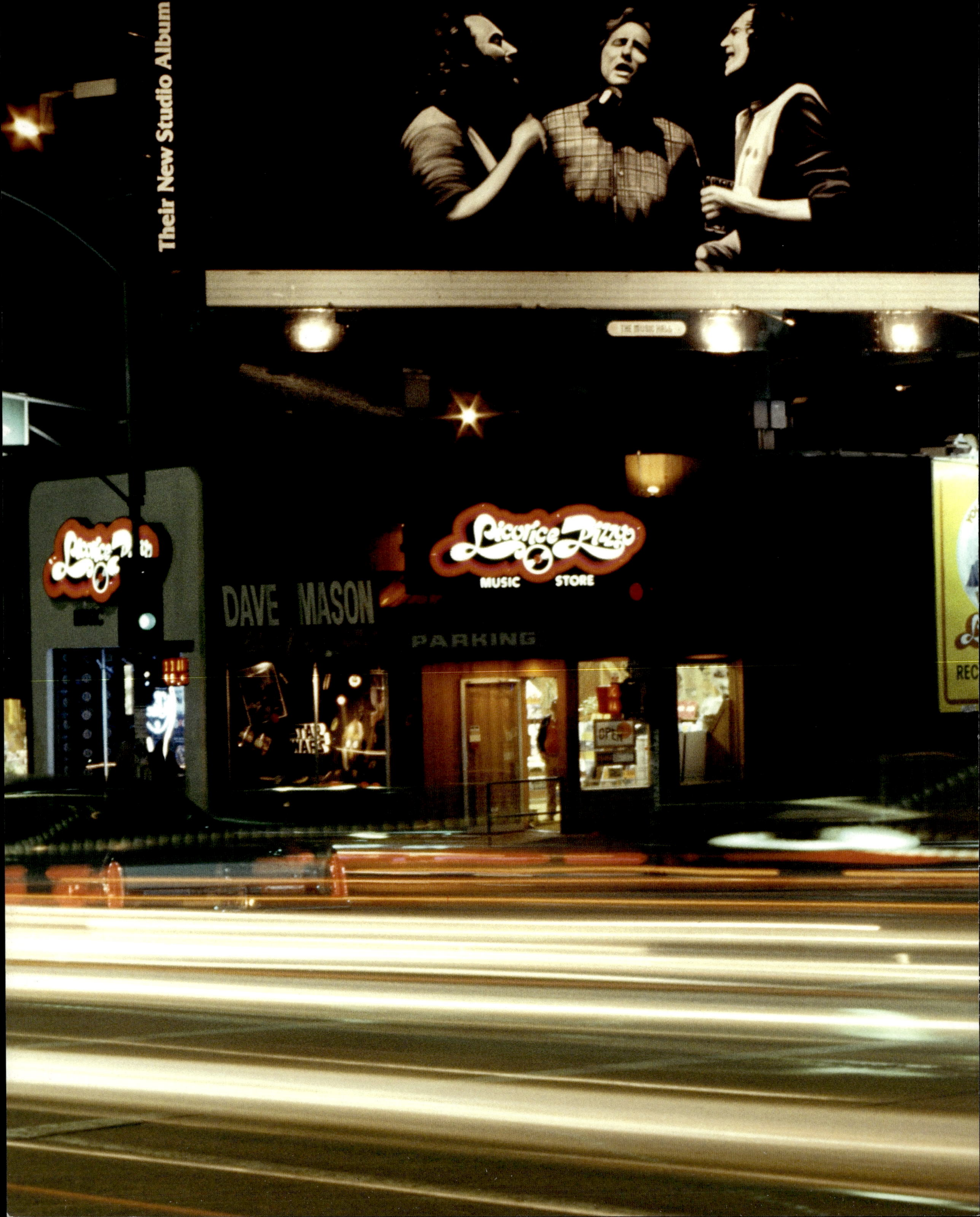
Their New Studio Album
Licorice Pizza
MUSIC STORE
DAVE MASON
PARKING
OPEN

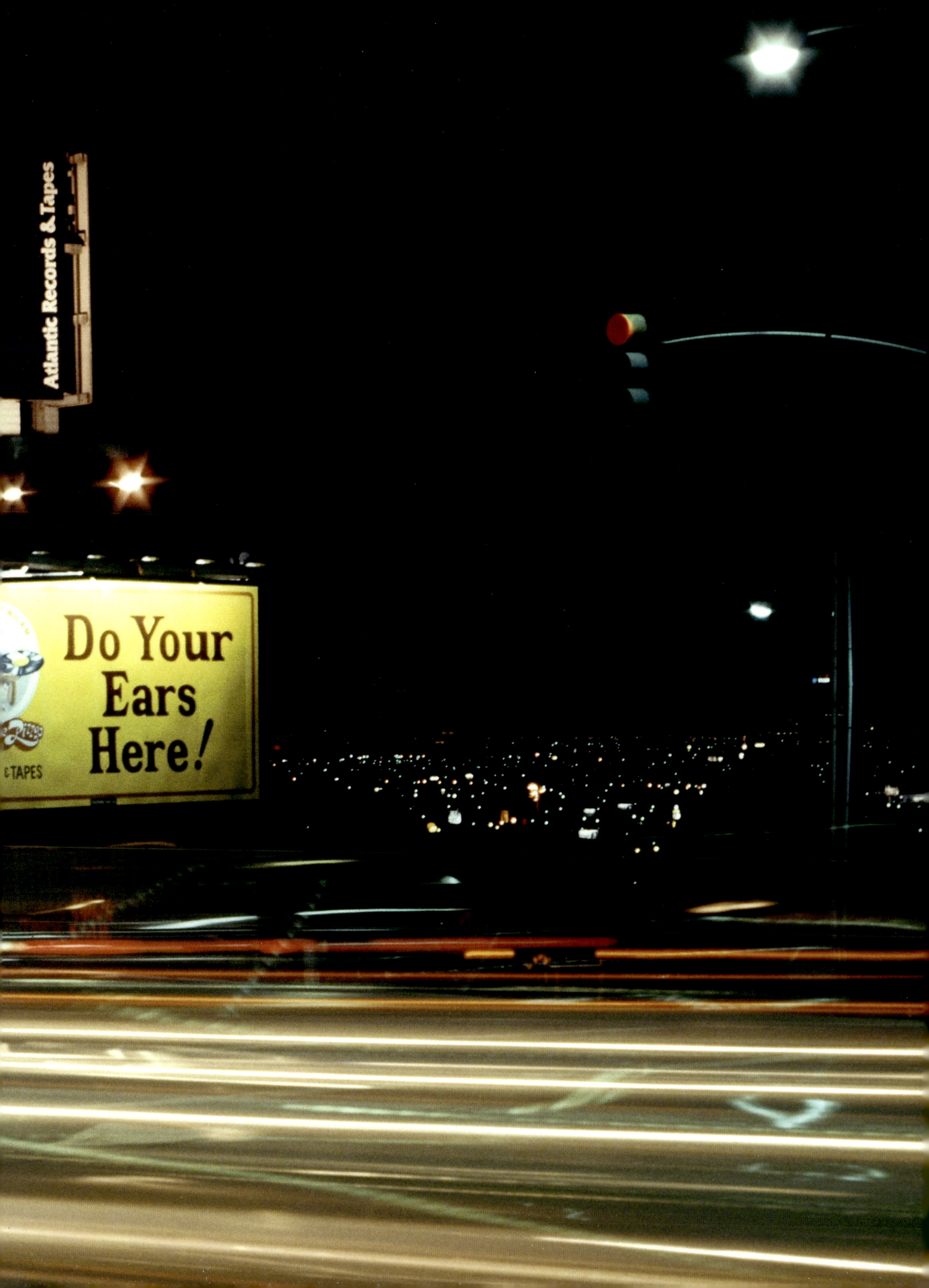
Atlantic Records & Tapes
Do Your Ears Here!
& TAPES

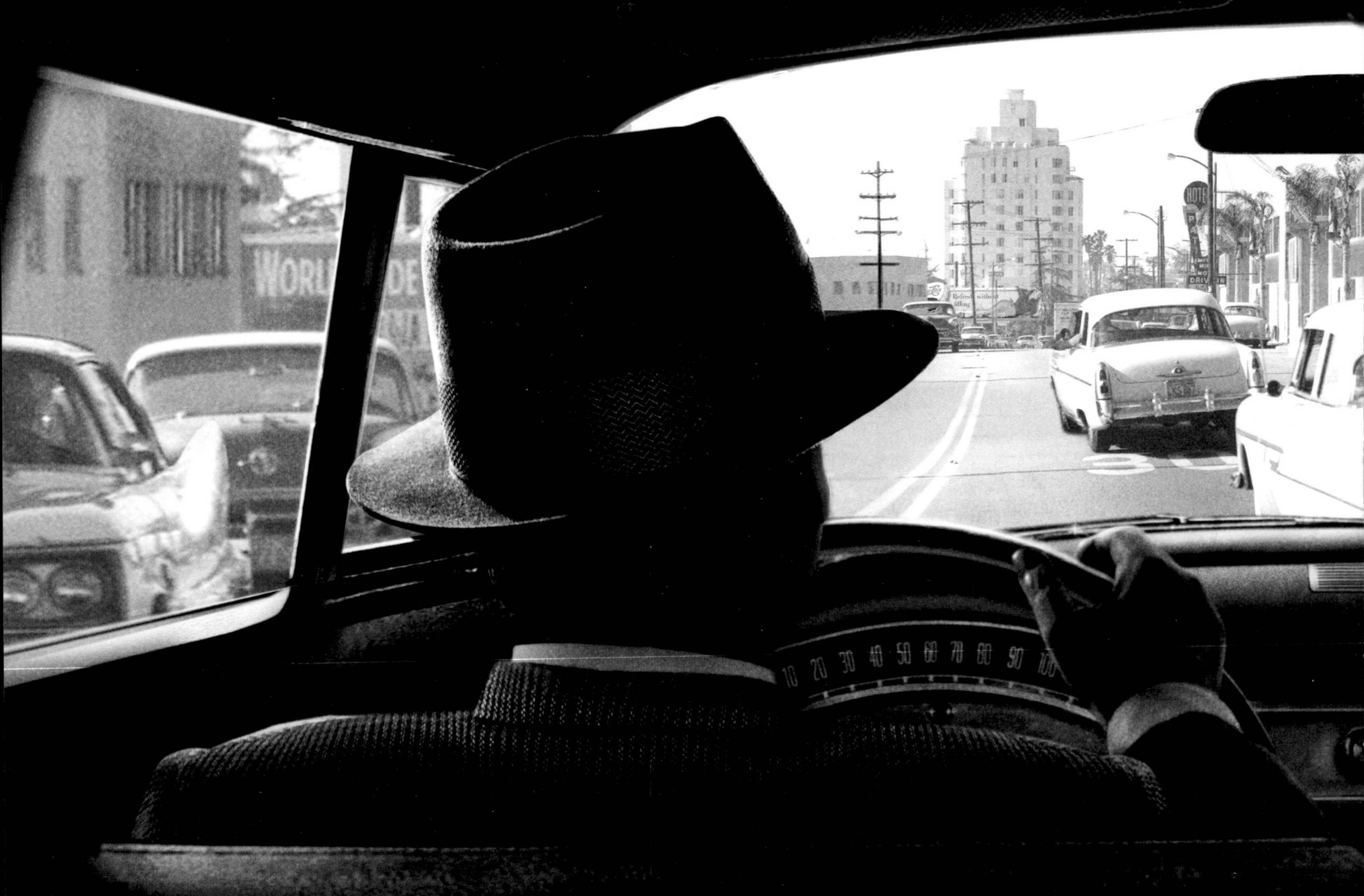
10 20 30 40 50 60 70 80 90 100

Tales from The Strip

A CENTURY IN THE FAST LANE

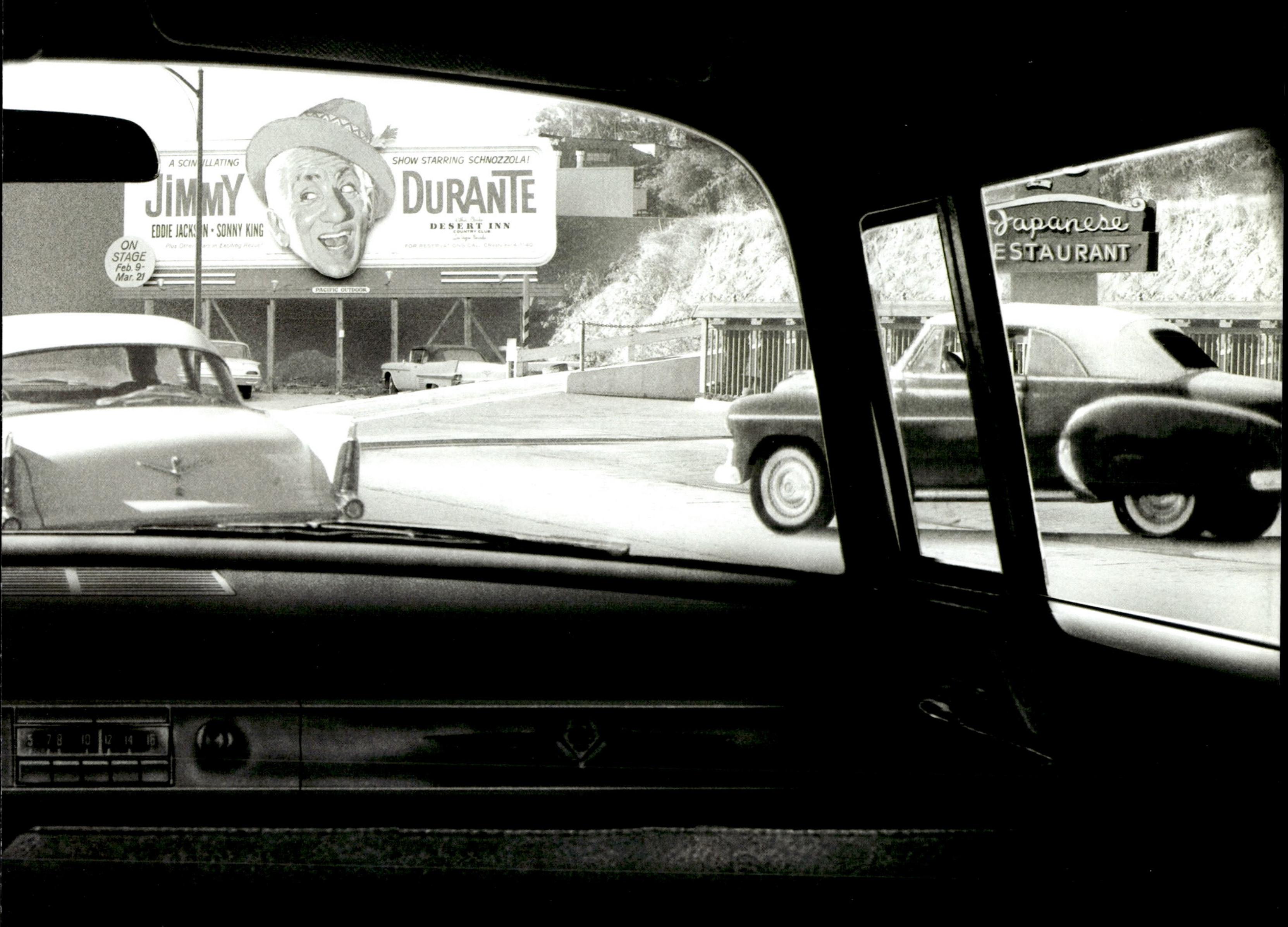

VAN GORDON SAUTER

ROBERT LANDAU FRANS EVENHUIS

Pages 2–3
With the stately Sunset Tower, which opened in 1931, on the south side of the street and a Southern California icon—a filling station—on the north, this becomes the quintessential image of the Sunset Strip. Note there's not a pedestrian in sight.

Pages 4–5
Chateau Marmont, in 1937, the grande dame of the Sunset Strip and an elegant survivor of times both plush and threadbare, stands at the eastern entrance to the Strip. Haughty, she rises above her age and a history not without graceless moments enthusiastically documented by international tabloids. One of the world's more famous hotels, the Chateau sets a tone for the Sunset Strip—an element of elegance and sophistication always appreciated, but not to preclude some of the more common, popular indulgences. Rumors were that a private tunnel allowed the patrons discreet access to the Players Club next door during club-owner Preston Sturges's reign in the 1930s and '40s.

Pages 6–7
Actresses Laraine Day (left) and Mary Howard are ready to visit the stars' homes in their 1937 Packard convertible. At one time on the Sunset Strip, uniformed guides directed fans to the homes of their favorite stars, no doubt on nearby tree-lined streets in Beverly Hills or just up a narrow lane into the Hollywood Hills.

Pages 8–9
The Sunset Strip in 1950: seen from King's Road, looking north toward the Chateau Marmont. Where were all the cars? The mind-numbing traffic? The congestion hadn't come. Yet.

Pages 10–11
The Jaguar sports car was a *de rigueur* auto for Hollywood stars. In 1950, actor Ray Milland was behind the wheel of his new XK120 at Hornburg, the Jaguar dealership at the west end of the Sunset Strip. Founder William Lyons of the Jaguar automobile empire looks on from the passenger side.

Pages 12–13
The Sunset Strip has always been a good marketing space—for movies, music, cars, Las Vegas resorts. In 1953, the Vegas Sahara displayed a billboard on the Strip with its own attached swimming pool and a covey of comely swimmers to attract a crowd. On this day, Red Skelton came by to greet visitors. Always the comedian, he ended up jumping into the pool wearing his light suit and dark tie.

Pages 14–15
Crosby, Stills, and Nash harmonize in the night sky above the Strip's "other" record store (Licorice Pizza tried to compete with Tower, a thankless battle). Emblematic of the impact of flower power, after hippies were born during San Francisco's Summer of Love in 1967, counter-culture had long overtaken the Strip by 1977 when this billboard appeared.

Published by Angel City Press
2118 Wilshire Blvd. #880,
Santa Monica, California 90403
+1.310.395.9982
www.angelcitypress.com

Tales from The Strip: A Century in the Fast Lane
By Van Gordon Sauter, Robert Landau, and Frans Evenhuis

Design by Frans Evenhuis
Cover: Photo illustration by Frans Evenhuis, Photography by Robert Landau
ISBN-13 978-1-62640-039-9 (print edition)

Library of Congress Cataloging-in-Publication Data is available

Printed in Canada

To Kathleen, who three times housed us so close to the Sunset Strip that it became my Main Street. To the five kids and twelve grandkids, each one of whom makes me optimistic about the future. And to Tefera, a man out of Africa who has never left my side in this country. –VGS

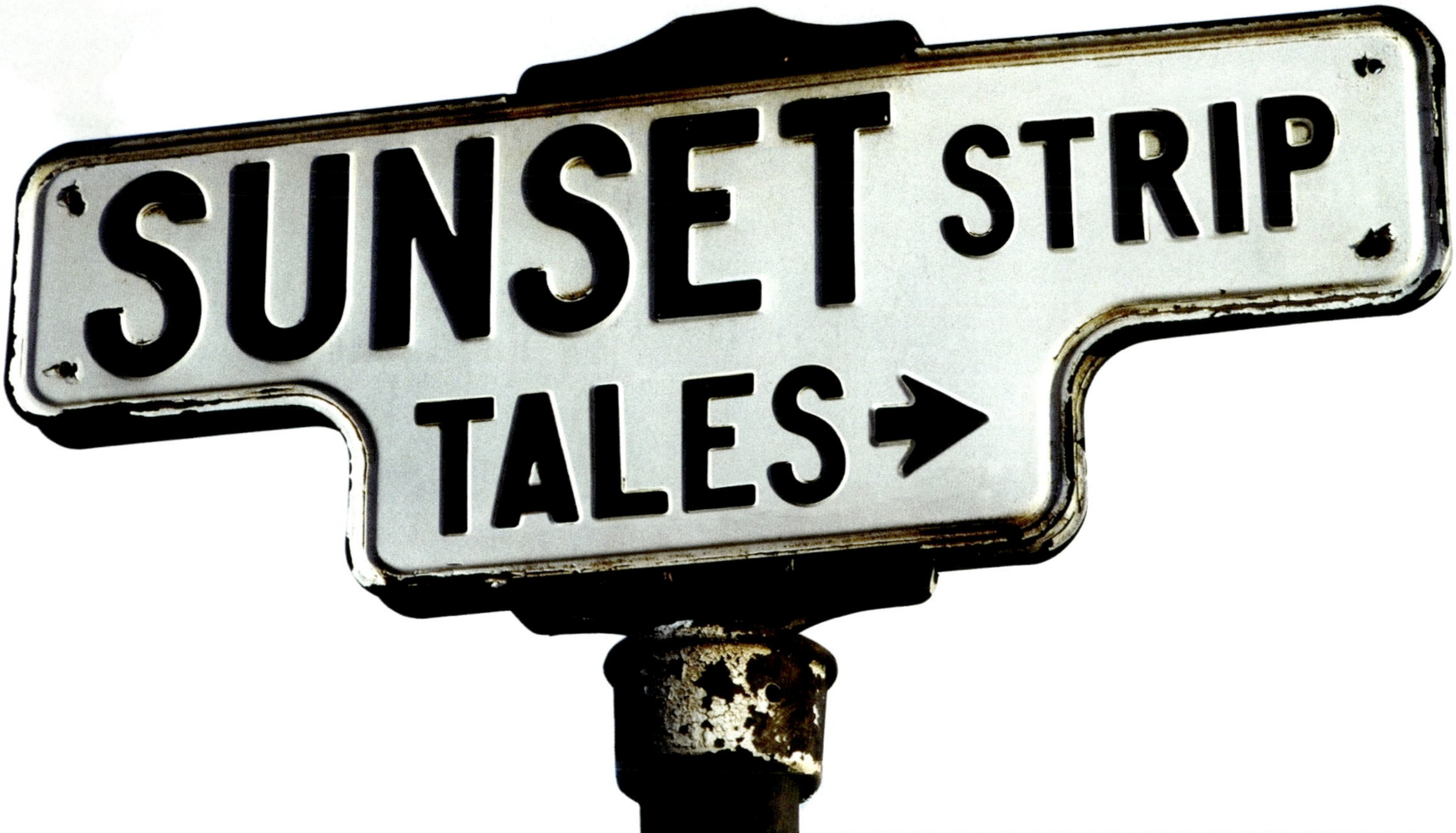

To Felix Landau, my father, with whom, in 1969 at age sixteen, I moved to an apartment one block above the Sunset Strip. There, with his encouragement, I began photographing my surroundings. Felix was one of Los Angeles's pioneer art dealers in the 1950s and '60s, and his deep appreciation of art and artists fueled my passion for books and visual imagery. –RL

To my wife Chérie. We had our first date at Le Dôme, bought records at Tower, rocked out at the Whisky, and ate pizza alongside celebrities at Spago. As the years fly by, the Sunset Strip keeps changing and most of those places have slipped away. But we're still together, going strong, and trying to remember what part of the past just disappeared. –FE

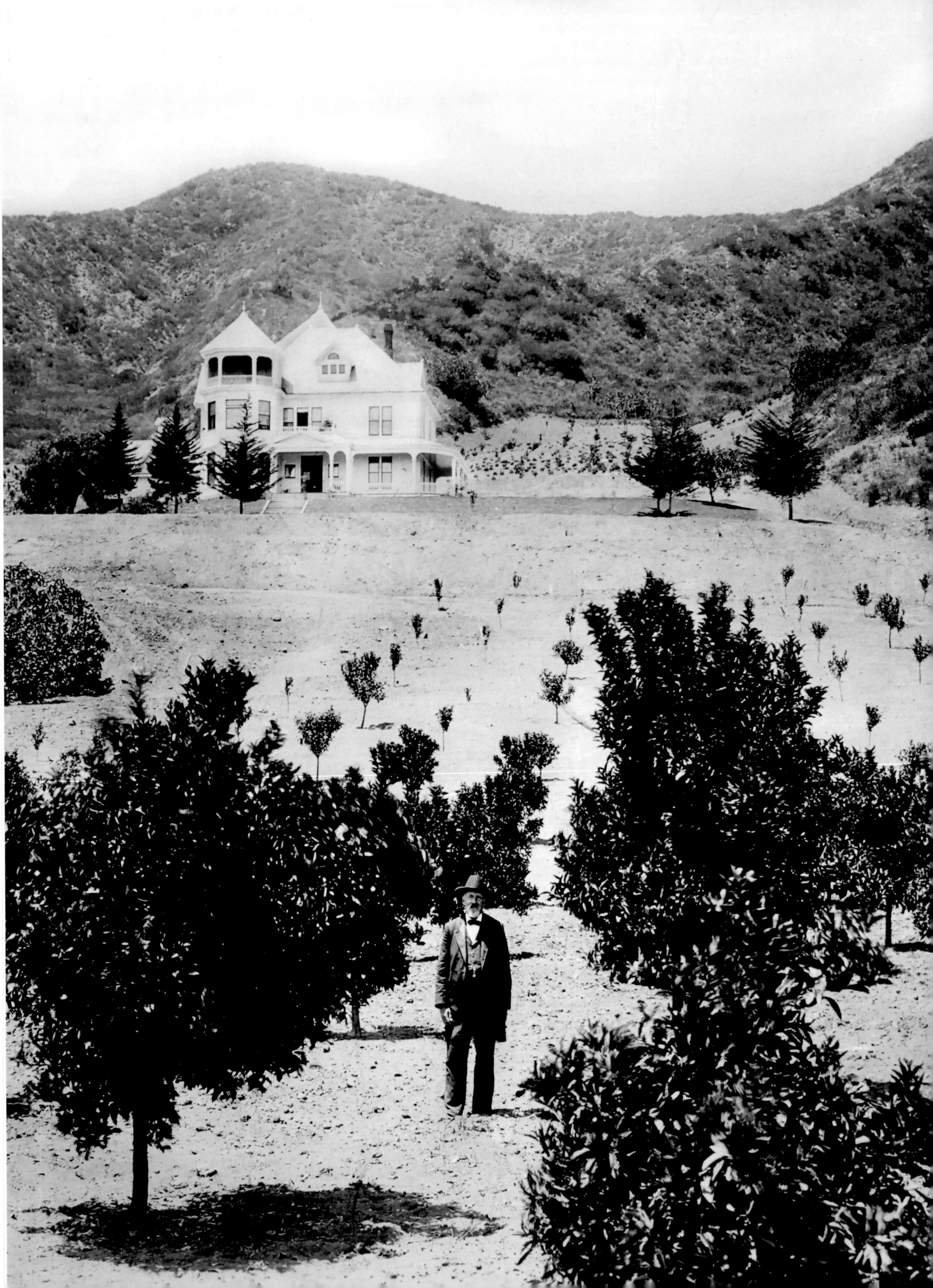

INTRODUCTION

For all its celebration and notoriety, the Sunset Strip is a stub of a street, the flamboyant two-mile stretch of the much longer thoroughfare, Sunset Boulevard, which is now part of the city of West Hollywood. The Strip has been romanticized into one of the best-known locations in the world. It has hosted movie Stars and rock Stars and punk Stars and crime Stars and literary Stars—even chef Stars. All larger than life, these Stars turned this Sunset Strip into a brand, one with a remarkable shelf life, even during periods of exhaustion and reinvention. The Strip began another transformation around 2017, one that for better or worse would define the Strip for generations.

It all began in 1888, when a now-unknown bureaucrat mapping a nascent Los Angeles was assigning names to streets or lanes or cow paths devoid of official identification. One presumes it was an arduous task, given inevitable competition between civic worthies, promotable place names like Cincinnati or Brooklyn, or topographically correct designations like Hill Street.

L.A. was a young town, filled with bluster and optimism, hardly the kind of place with a public enthusiasm for conferring street names upon novelists or philosophers or humanitarians. The town's brief history was rugged. Less than twenty years earlier, some locals tortured and lynched seventeen Chinese men in or near L.A.'s original Chinatown, a short stroll from what would become Sunset Boulevard.

In naming a path Sunset, it appears (though there are dissenters) our bureaucrat simply drew upon the direction in which the unnamed trail was advancing: to the West, toward the ocean, into the sunset. (It could have been called "Cattle Boulevard" if street names were based on its principal users.) And so Sunset Boulevard was credentialed. And began what is now a roughly twenty-four-mile route from the famed four-level Route 110 and U.S. 101 interchange downtown, all the way to the not-always-pacific Pacific Ocean.

The boulevard—itself, one of L.A.'s great streets—has no coherence and no clear organizing principle, other than its western propensity. Hardscrabble Los Angeles and moneyed Los Angeles—not to mention Beverly Hills and West Hollywood—share the thoroughfare. Sunset Boulevard can be banal and gloomy, or stunningly beautiful and creative. It has its great parks, shabby housing, and delightfully ostentatious mansions, and everything in between, all within biking distance.

Even with its jarring diversity of architecture and style and purpose, the renowned Sunset Strip hangs together. Somewhat preposterous, but understandable.

← Confederate Army veteran Charles F. Harper moved west to Los Angeles after the Civil War and earned a fortune in the hardware business. He purchased 480 acres around and to the north of what is now known as the Sunset Strip, just west of Laurel Canyon. Harper is shown here on his property in 1898, with his home in the background. One of his five sons, Arthur Cyprian Harper, who inherited the property, was mayor of Los Angeles from 1906 to 1909. Facing allegations of corruption and poor moral character, he resigned.

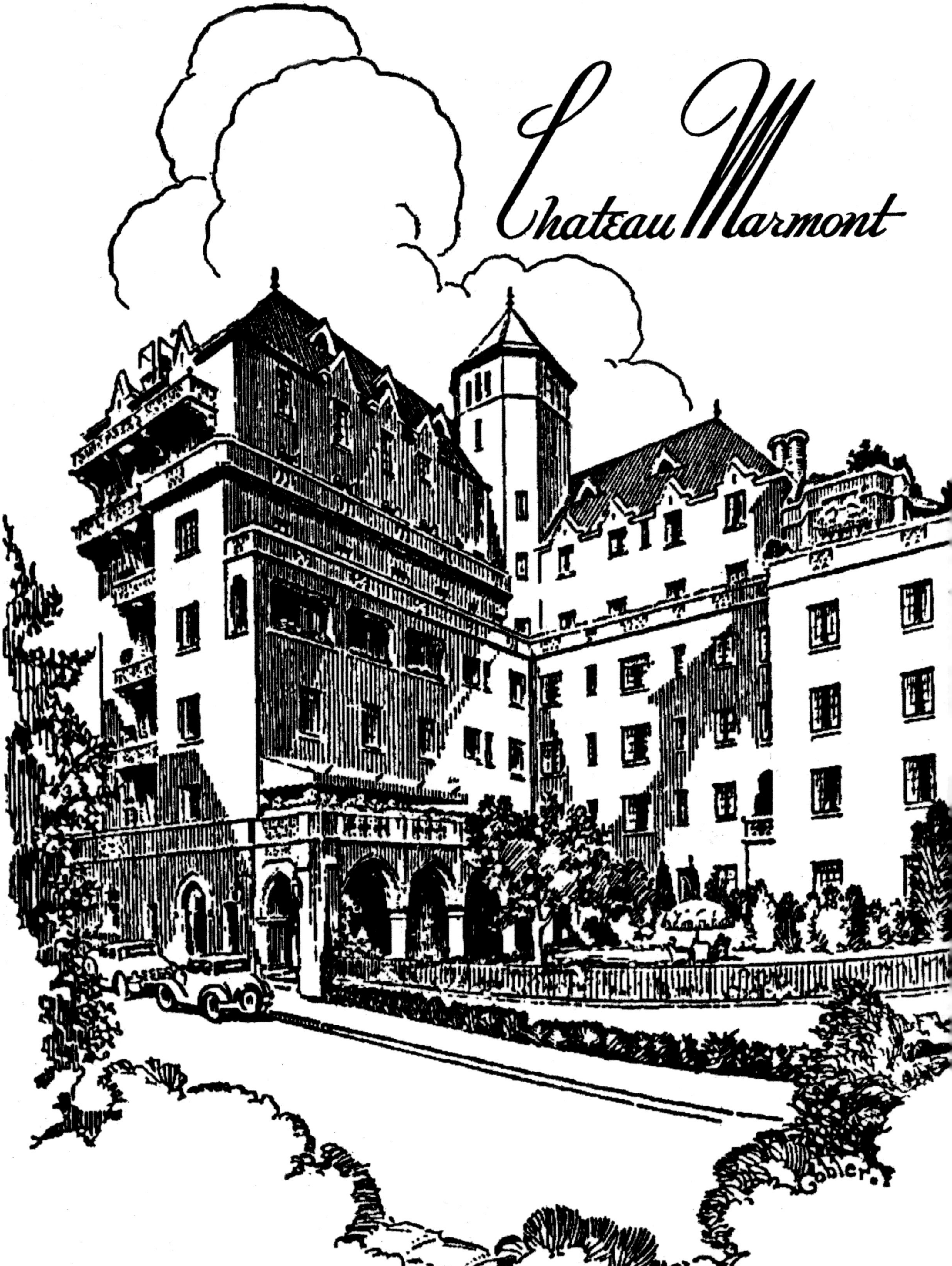
Chateau Marmont

By the early 1900s, the City of Los Angeles was rapidly expanding west from downtown, out across the basin into areas once part of the County of Los Angeles. But the city's westward expansion stalled at the northern edge of the basin, along the base of the Hollywood Hills. The city's writ and its Sunset Boulevard stopped close to a cross street now known as Crescent Heights. And for the next 1.5 miles or so, the county's Sunset Boulevard continued west until it stopped, really stopped, near the border of a smart, incredibly promising new town with clever people, adequate water, a development plan, and the stunningly good Beverly Hills Hotel. Almost from the very beginning, Beverly Hills knew what it wanted to be: decorous and prosperous.

Thus the relatively rural strip between Los Angeles and Beverly Hills fell under the dicey governance of the County of Los Angeles, where law enforcement had a somewhat cursory relationship with the law and civic morality. Not that the City of Los Angeles itself was a paragon of righteous authority.

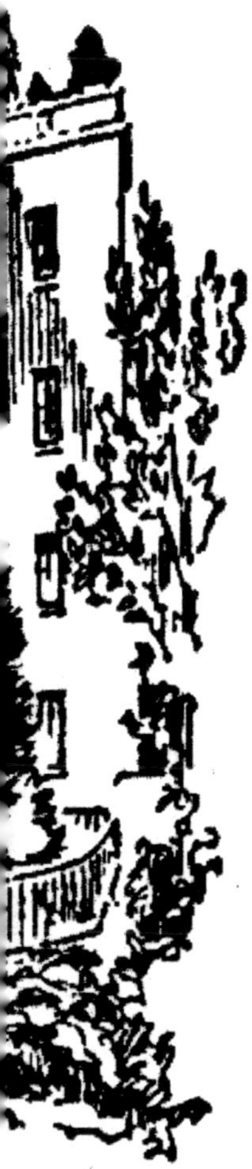

←
Shortly after the Chateau Marmont opened in 1929 as an apartment building, a newspaper lauded it as "Los Angeles's newest, finest, and most exclusive apartment house. . .superbly situated, close enough to active business to be accessible and far enough away to insure quiet and privacy."

In those early years the area around the Strip (no one really knows who first applied that term) was populated by farmers growing melons and poinsettias, barley, vegetables, and beans. But in 1918, a Russian actress bought a real estate baron's mansion there and about eight years later converted it into a hotel, the Garden of Allah. It stood at the eastern edge of the Strip, at Crescent Heights, close to the city and county border, but just inside the City of Los Angeles. Garden of Allah celebrated the libertine, and over its years, it housed some of the nation's most creative writers, musicians, actors, and filmmakers.

In the late twenties, Chateau Marmont opened as an apartment building, just across the street and a little west of the Garden. When it fell on hard times during the Depression, the Chateau was swiftly converted, with flair and imagination—it looks like one of those fairytale castles in the Loire—into a quirky hotel. While the Chateau Marmont suffered some vulgar tabloid moments, it is primarily a place where people of purpose and elegance (well, most of them could be so described) find privacy and congenial ambiance.

The two hotels anchored the eastern edge of the Strip, and as Los Angeles grew, and the film industry gained traction in nearby Hollywood, the Strip filled out with nightclubs, restaurants, hotels, stores, apartment buildings, office structures, brothels, and bars. At the same time, the business regulations for an unincorporated area of the county were more congenial to talent agents than the laws of the City of Los Angeles. So the Strip became a kind of early office park for the ten percenters.

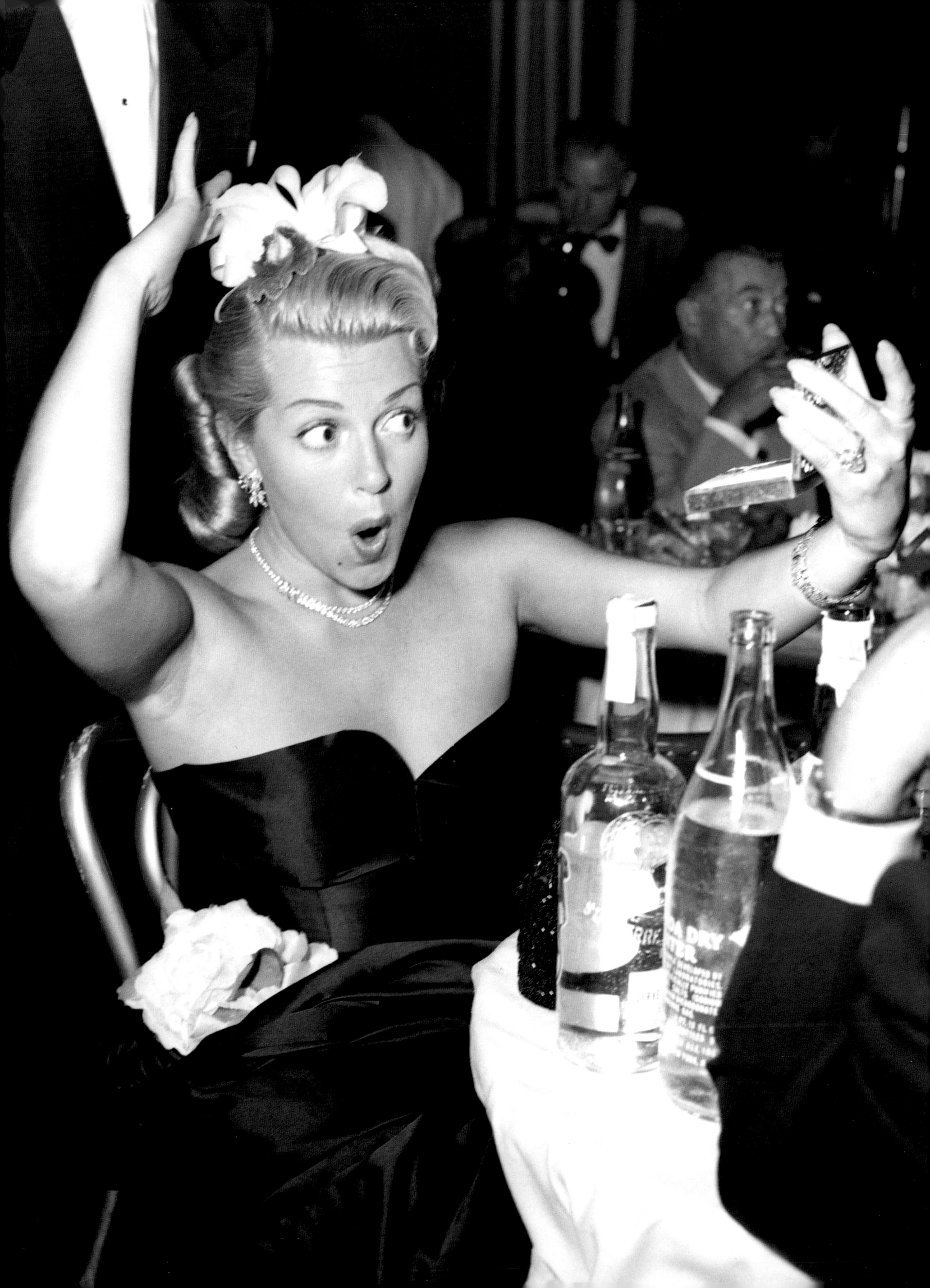

During the thirties and forties, the Strip flowered and became known to America as the center of Hollywood glamor, the playground of beautiful people. Gossip columnists, studio publicity machines, and reporters firmly embedded the Strip into the consciousness of Americans who otherwise were muddling through the Depression and its aftermath, urbanization, and the threat and, ultimately, the reality, of war. America needed diversion, and Hollywood provided it. The media defined a Strip jammed with flash and glitter, with radiant people drifting from hotel to restaurant to club, tanned by the incessant sun, garbed in the most resplendent styles, thoroughly devoid of anguish and insecurity, conditions painfully familiar to the citizenry, those fans, out there in real America.

And to spice it up, there were those rapacious gangsters hovering on the edge of the Strip, with their snarly smiles, brassy women, and conniving schemes. And their gunfire. . ..

The Hollywood Era and the public's unquestioning embrace of movie stars initially defined the street and polished a cinematic era. But the sixties gutted that world. Television altered America and its definition of entertainment. The new power brokers of Hollywood were disdainful of the self-important fogeys and their white-dinner-jacket culture. The stars had a different mindset, too, independent from the studios, disinterested in nightclubs and posturing for publicity. That old Sunset Strip elegance seemed not only outmoded but vulgar while a divisive war was waged in Southeast Asia, and political disenchantment swept the nation.

In the sixties, seventies, and eighties, musicians—young, creative, and counter-Establishment in so many ways—congregated on Sunset between Crescent Heights and Doheny to jam out classic rock 'n' roll and its many permutations. More than any other place in the country, this strip of Sunset churned with new celebrities and young, undisciplined creative types, thoroughly contemptuous of traditional American cultural mores and of its popular entertainment. Many lived up a then-rustic Laurel Canyon, just above the Strip, enjoying the close proximity of rural life and urban intensity.

Although rock 'n' roll first appeared in the fifties, introduced by such artists as Elvis Presley and Buddy Holly, a decade later Sunset Strip musicians drove the form into the mainstream of American music. The sound of the Baby Boomer culture was soon monetized. More than a few of the musicians were astute social critics, and their judgments were sometimes painfully prescient. Even Ed Sullivan had to find time slots for these countercultural ruffians.

←
No, this is not the first person ever to take a selfie. It's Lana Turner, a dedicated party girl dubbed "Queen of the Nightclubs" at the Sunset Strip's Mocambo adjusting the orchid in her hair with the assistance of the mirror in her metal pressed-powder compact, an accessory usually reserved for dusting a shiny nose. The Mocambo opened in 1941 with a Latin American theme and was an immediate success. The club remained open until 1958.

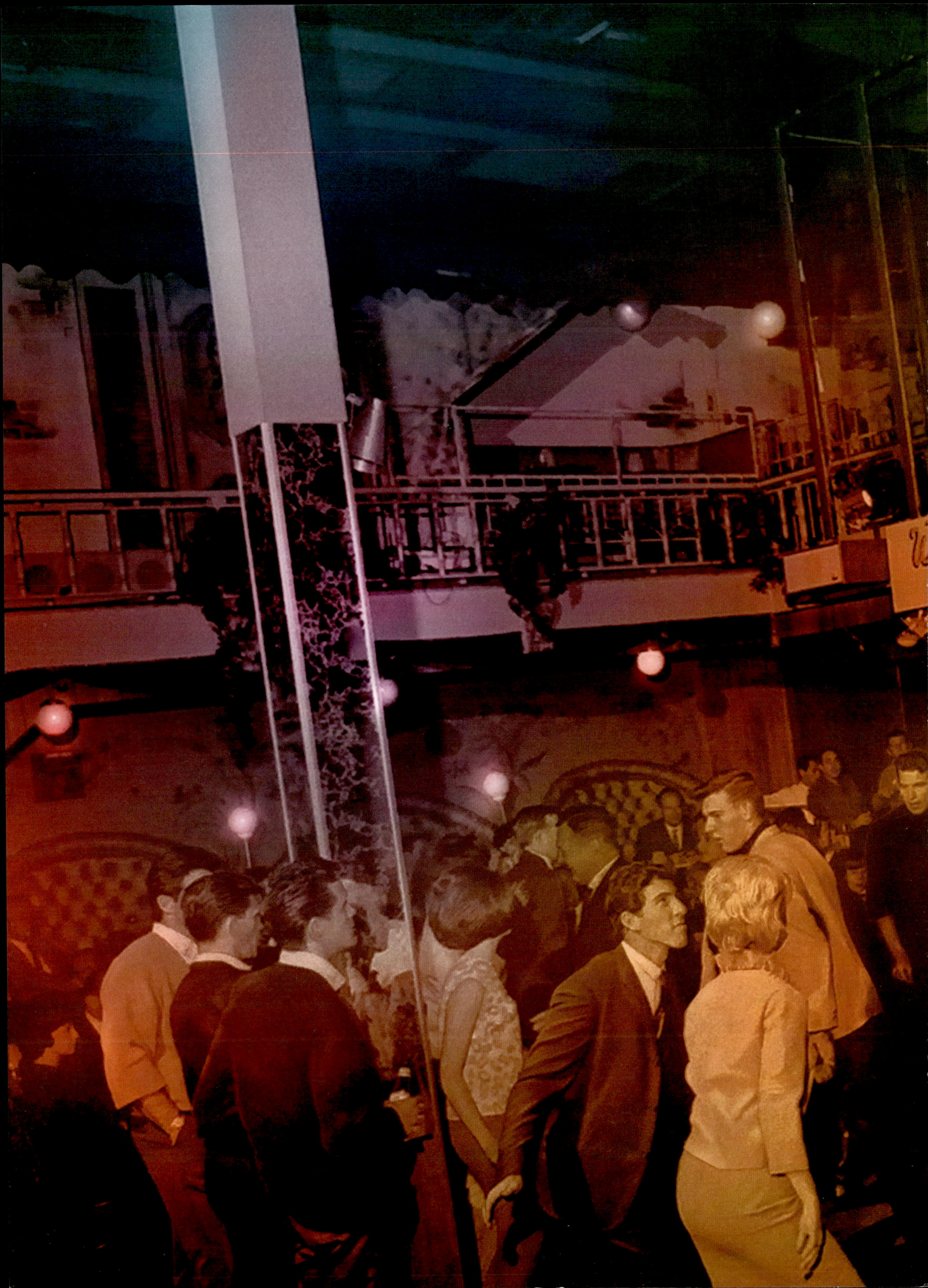

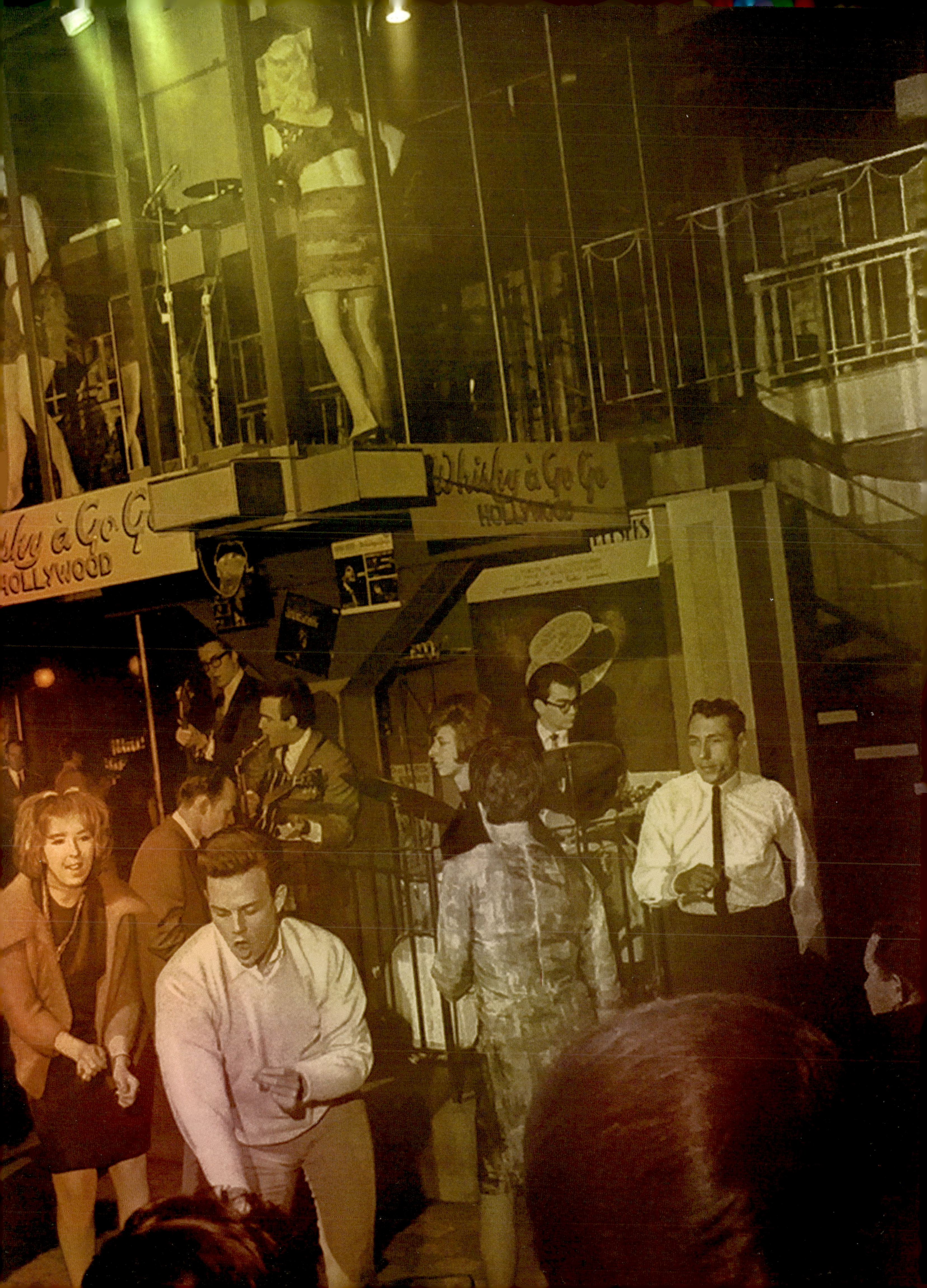
Whisky à Go Go
HOLLYWOOD
HOLLYWOOD

“The Sunset Strip is a civilization
for the broken-hearted,
the mistreated, the overlooked,
the underloved, and the doomed.”

— **KIM FOWLEY** MUSIC PRODUCER
FROM THE DOCUMENTARY *SUNSET STRIP* (2012)

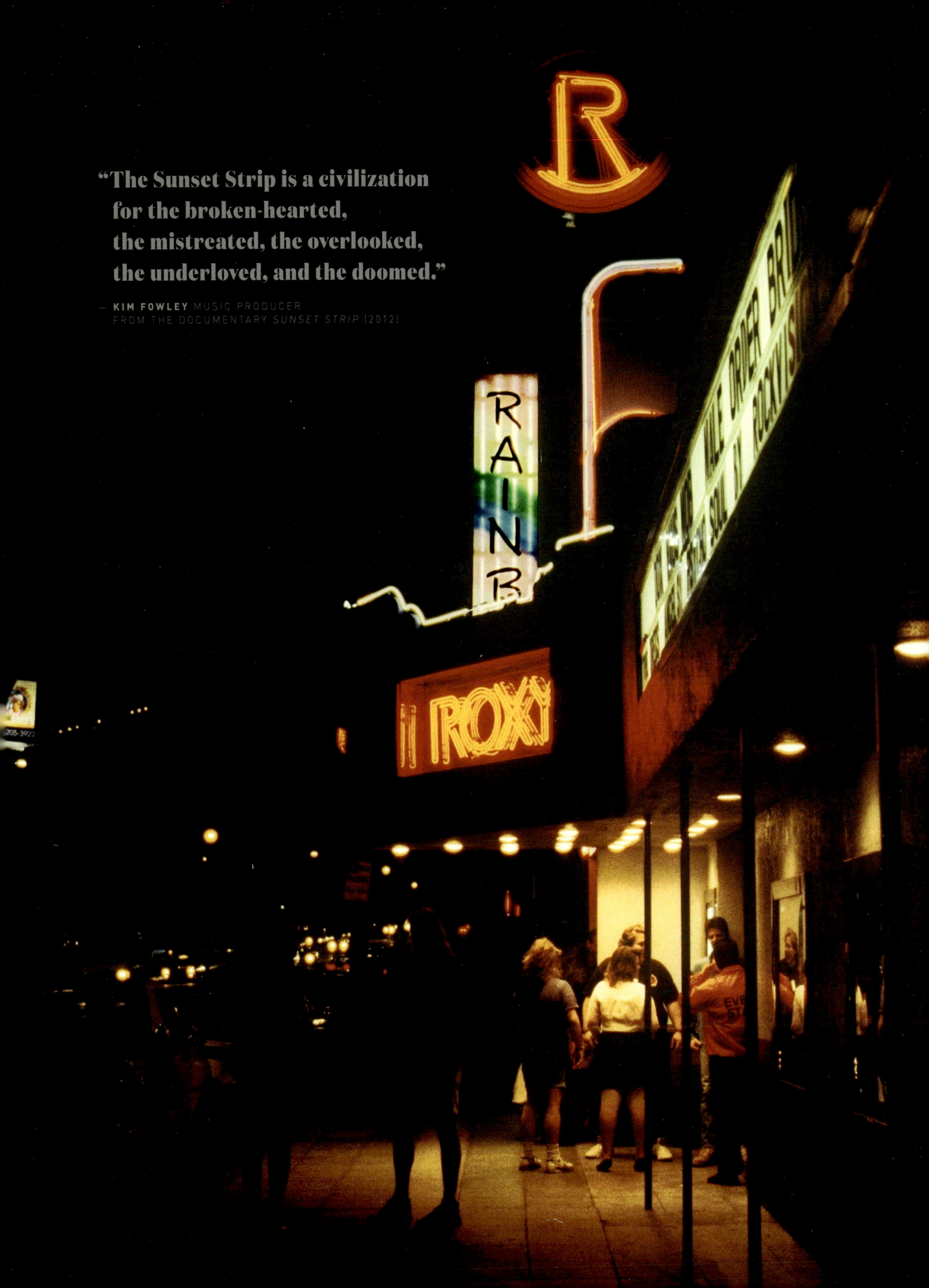

Meanwhile, scruffy young people—the fans, the wannabes, the dislocated, the disenchanted—seemed to take over the Strip, all to the horror of the traditionalists, merchants, and those who lived nearby. With no interest in plowing through clusters of groovy kids and miasmic clouds of cigarette smoke that didn't smell at all like Lucky Strikes, locals stopped patronizing familiar stores and restaurants; business plummeted. Predictably, the "it used to be so wonderful here" crowd called in their chits with the politicians and police. Curfew and loitering laws were enforced. Young people rebelled, and un-civil unrest made its way to the Strip, though the riots tended to be formulaic and not much seemed to happen or change.

What did change over the years were music styles (rock 'n' roll phases of punk, folk rock, metal, etc.). More important, voracious record buyers and large-venue concert touring infused the industry with phenomenal wealth. Music and its successful creators and entrepreneurs could live anywhere. Music didn't need a Sunset Strip. In a new millennium, there are still music clubs and event promotions on the Strip, but music—in all its incredible forms—now can be experienced almost anywhere across Los Angeles.

Nostalgia for the Sunset Strip Music Era lives on, however, providing volumes of information for the driver-announcers on the contemporary tour buses: *This is where the Doors performed as the house band. . .The Byrds were playing here when Bob Dylan come up from the audience and performed with them. . .All the great stars dropped by. . . Frank Zappa and Joni Mitchell were neighbors. . .That's the Andaz West Hollywood Hotel—used to be the Hyatt. Jim Morrison got kicked out for hanging from a window by his fingertips. One rocker rode his motorcycle down a hallway.*

← The Roxy—the literal heart of music history on the Strip—was opened in 1973 by a cabal of industry heavyweights including David Geffen, Lou Adler and Elliot Roberts and has featured some of rock 'n' roll's iconic performers. Buffalo Springfield and Crosby, Stills, Nash & Young alum, Neil Young kicked it off with a week-long appearance in the intimate setting. Genesis with Peter Gabriel, Bob Marley, Frank Zappa, Bruce Springsteen, Guns N' Roses and U2 have all played there. An adjoining watering hole on the property called On the Rox has hosted its share of high-level high jinx over the years, and is fondly remembered for visits from John Lennon and drinking buddies Harry Nilsson and Keith Moon in the early years. The club remains an important music venue, so it's common to see a long, chaotic line of fans assembling midday to attend an evening concert.

Overleaf ← Gyrating dancers on the floor of the Whisky à Go Go, the Sunset Strip nightclub that launched some of the biggest names in music history, from the Doors to Guns N' Roses. It may have been born in Paris, but the Whisky on the Strip became the world's hq for new music. The Whisky helped punk and heavy metal find their broadest audiences and credibility as important genres.

Post Music Era, the Strip settled into a fairly tame urban entertainment center.

A significant enhancement occurred in 1984 when the people of the unincorporated Strip-adjacent territory—fearing the elimination of rent control—voted to ditch the county rule, ignore merging into Los Angeles, and create their own city—West Hollywood. The movement was driven by renters, particularly the large gay population, seniors, and recent Russian-Jewish immigrants. West Hollywood not only became a major American gay residential community, it also embraced vibrant new businesses and entrepreneurs. Over time, the town found an economic and social cachet, but the Strip, along the northern edge of West Hollywood, seemed dull. Predictable. Out of date. Perhaps, God-forbid, a *has-been.*

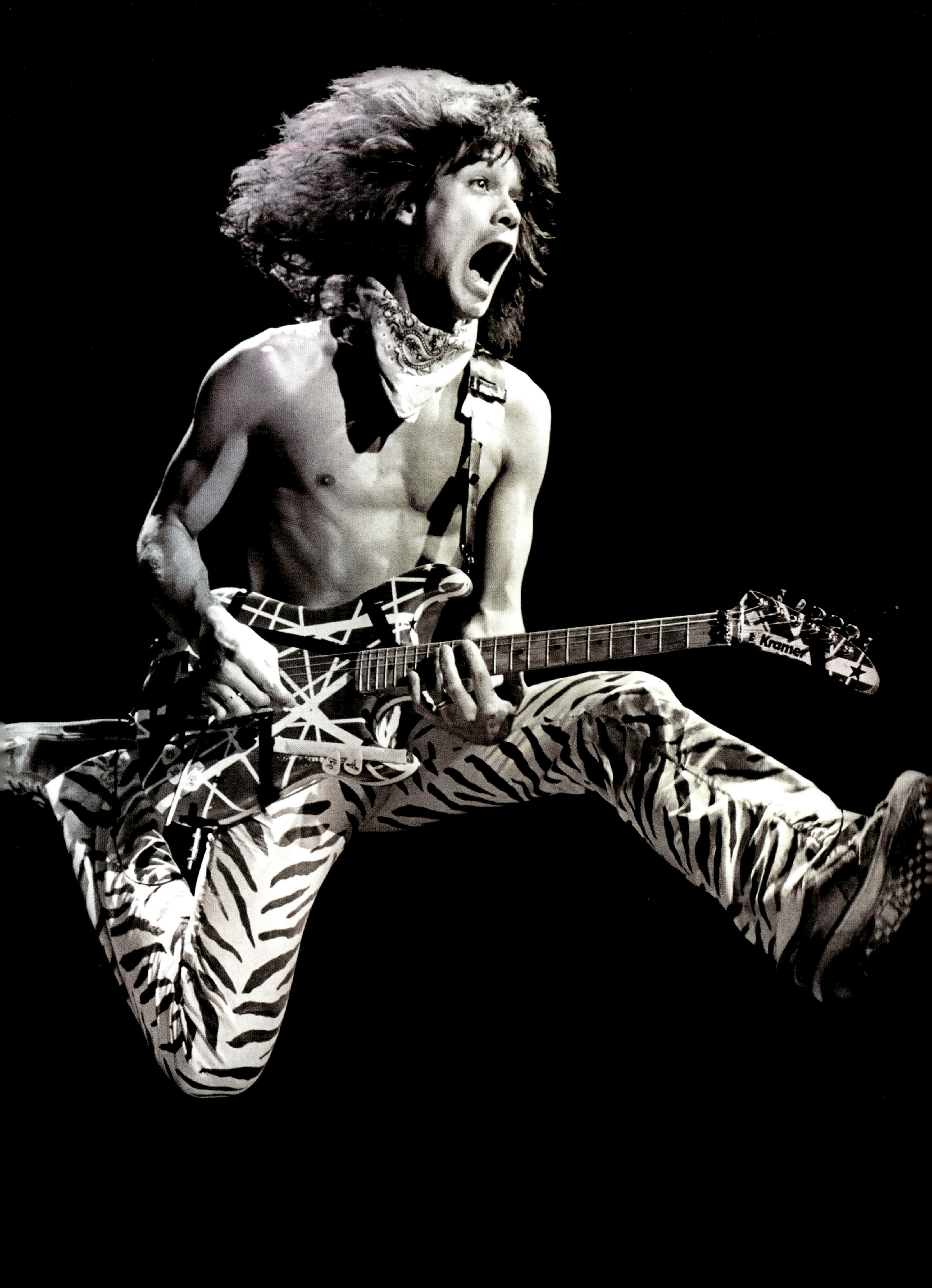
Kramer

By the late nineties, the Strip was still somewhat eclectic, jumbled, politely rambunctious. But overall, the street was less than classy and perilously more than insufferably cheesy. Moreover, some rough trade was moving onto the Strip. One night, people living in the pricey Sierra Tower on the far west end of the Strip could hear gunshots on the street. They watched people fleeing into the street from a sleazy nightclub as patrol cars came hurtling down the Strip to the scene. It wasn't a scene like New York's urban violence of the seventies, but there was a sense that violence and crime were creeping up on the Sunset Strip. And it wasn't just noticeable from the highrises. Everybody got the threatening drift.

Yes, there were stretches of success along the Strip. The expensive hotels—Marmont, Mondrian, Standard, and the Sunset Tower, not to mention boutique hotels—found their chic niches and attracted people who wanted to stay in a historic, urban setting. Sunset Plaza, central both geographically and socially on the Strip and nurtured for decades by the patrician real estate family named Montgomery, defined the upscale section of the Strip, and there seemed to be a surprisingly compatible community evolving around it. A little farther east, the classic hotel the Sunset Tower operated across the street from a faux western bar with a mechanical bucking bull, a hamburger joint housed in an old Union Pacific railroad car, and a Starbucks.

But despite the shops and eateries, the street needed to find its new "era." It was growing stale. Santa Monica Boulevard, a parallel street south of Sunset, was increasingly vigorous, attracting crowds of people to its bars and restaurants, and clever shops. West Hollywood gained recognition as an exhilarating place to live and create businesses, particularly creative businesses. All of this was away from the Strip.

Eventually, the growing appeal of West Hollywood and the congeniality of the town's enterprising management found common ground with financiers and developers and hotel operators. To them, the Strip had a presold image for entertainment, a colorful history and a superb location (nestled between Beverly Hills, Hollywood, Santa Monica Boulevard, and the upscale Hollywood hills). There emerged a shared belief that new hotels, along with condos and retail outlets and office space, would provide a powerful economic jolt to the town's best-known street, not to mention showering welcome tax revenue upon the city. Cachet and commerce were seen as the answers.

←
Eddie Van Halen in flight, in 1984, symbolic of the musicians and music that thrived on the Sunset Strip. Eddie formed the group Van Halen in staid Pasadena, hardly a community associated with rock 'n' roll. The group sold more than eighty million records, and ranked No. 7 on the VH1 list of hard-rock artists of all time.

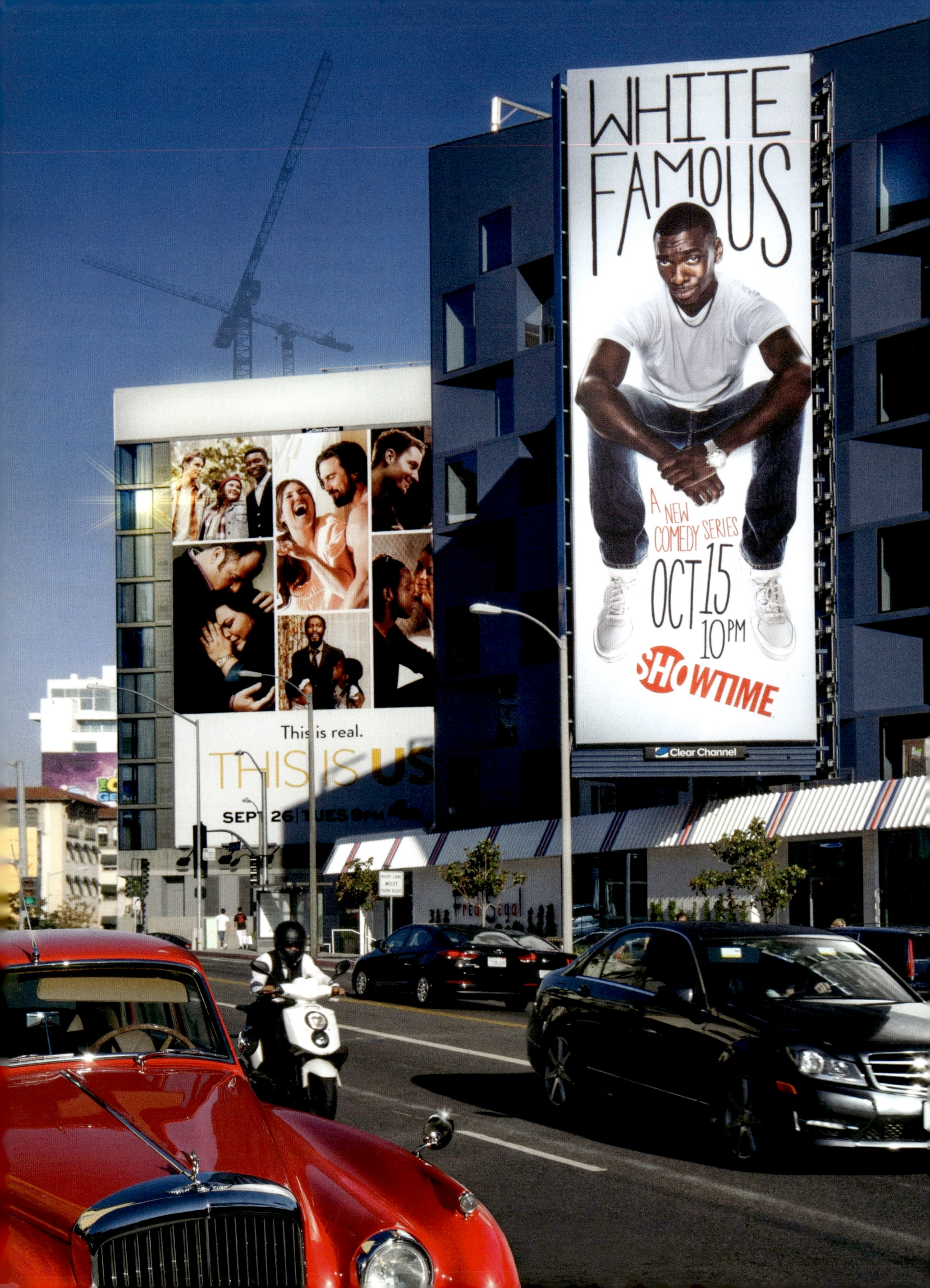

WHITE FAMOUS
A NEW COMEDY SERIES
OCT 15 10PM
SHOWTIME
Clear Channel
This is real.
THIS IS US
SEPT 26 | TUES 9PM

Seemingly overnight the construction cranes took to the sky. Two large hotel developments were in the ground. Another mammoth hotel/residential/retail/office space proposal was fronted by Frank Gehry, the world-famous architect who emerged from Los Angeles. His forget-right-angles structure would be on the site of the original Garden of Allah, on the Los Angeles end of the Strip. Other ambitious plans came over the transom to West Hollywood City Hall. Not all would get a spade into the ground, but more than enough would be built to modernize and energize the Strip—to change its appearance, personality, and economy for generations to come.

Doubters contend traffic congestion and over-commercialization will choke the Strip, forcing economic development to grind to a halt. But the Strip has never welcomed negativity. One can already imagine the dazzling profiles of the "hot new Sunset Strip" in chic travel magazines and on trendy websites.

When this book went to press, the Strip was on the verge of its new era, a new identity and a purpose capable of driving an economy for decades. In the exhilaration of the future, there will be a tendency to forget the old Strip, the one that earned the name and set the evolution in motion. The flummery of that future could erase the memory of the people and places and events of the past, the forces that created the Strip.

But the history of such a vibrant place should not be forgotten. So in these pages we retell some of the stories that forged its history.

—**VAN GORDON SAUTER** LOS ANGELES 2018

←
Aware that outdoor advertising space on the Sunset Strip generates a steady stream of passive income, developers made it a point to ask architects to include large-scale billboard space in new building designs. Entire sides of structures that were once devoted to windows with views of the Strip and the hills are now reserved for billboard display spots that can command six-figure rental fees per month in prime locations.

Garden of Allah

AKA the Garden of Carnal Abandon

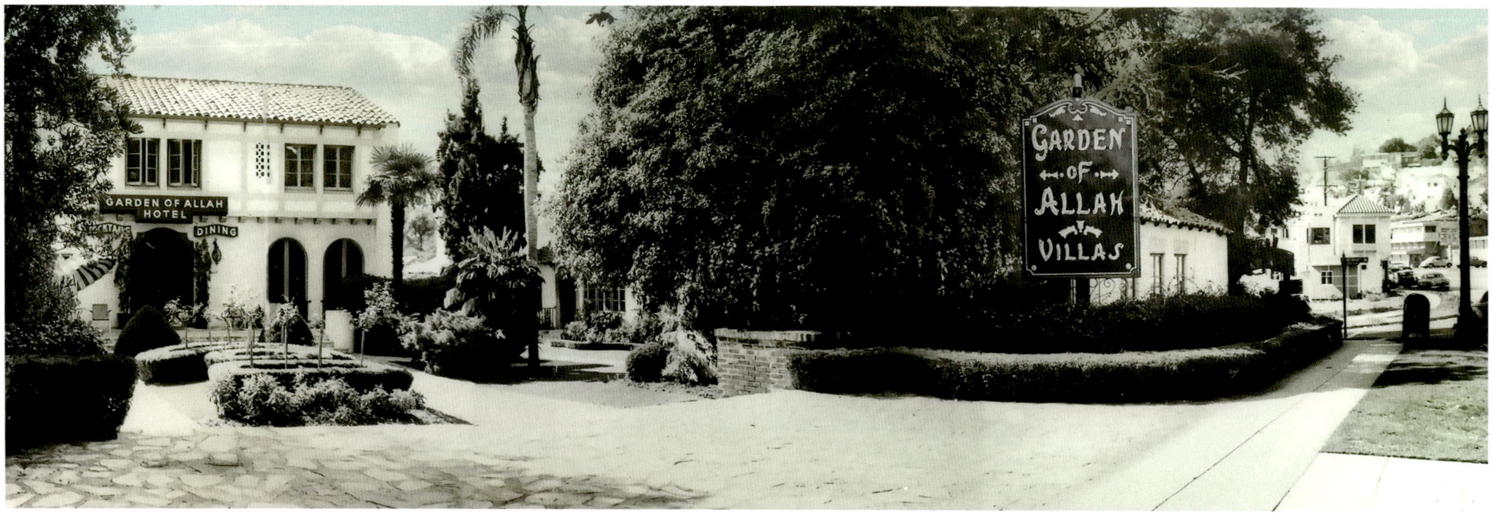

In 1954, the Garden of Allah looked, from the street, to be serene and self-satisfied, like an aging roué. But it was in decline. Its rambunctious days were over. In a few years, it would be leveled to make room for a bank.

It was unquestionably the most congenial, intellectually stimulating, and unrelentingly depraved hotel in the history of Los Angeles. If not the nation. In modern times, the name Garden of Allah would seem appropriate for one of those dreary and somewhat menacing motels farther east on Sunset, where parking lots seem filled with junkers and junkies, and the patrons are decidedly furtive—if seen at all.

But the original Garden of Allah (also known as the Garden of Carnal Abandon) was a hotel, residential community and 24/7 party center located on the Sunset Strip. Three and a half acres of prime real estate held twenty-five bungalows, a gracious main house, and a swimming pool that is reputed to have been shaped to resemble the Black Sea (a presumption lacking in documentation or even a real hint of physical representation).

In 1918 a young actress from Russia, who found meteoric success on the Broadway stage and silver screen, purchased the property on the southwest corner of Sunset Boulevard and Crescent Heights. It was then an expansive home, described as having fourteen bedrooms, set among an exotic forest of orange, lemon, and grapefruit trees, along with the popular palm and hibiscus.

Nazimova became godmother to a friend's daughter named Nancy Davis, who became the starlet who wooed a future president of the United States and eventually became known as First Lady.

Alla Nazimova, the actress, could afford it, making thirteen thousand dollars or so a week at Warner's (at a time when a movie ticket was seven cents and a gallon of gas was eight).

A native of the Crimea (thus the pool issue), Nazimova studied acting in Moscow, supporting herself as a part-time prostitute, and quickly became a major European stage star. In New York, she was luminous in plays by Ibsen and Chekhov, so much so that Lee and J. J. Shubert named a theater the Nazimova 39th Street Theatre after her. Her initial work in Hollywood was outrageously lucrative, but it ended quickly. Facing bankruptcy after some disastrous, self-financed film projects, she added the pool and two-story bungalows to her property and lurched into the hotel business in 1927. Ill-advised. Nazimova soon sold the hotel (which she had called the Garden of Alla) though eventually she returned as a permanent resident, staying there until the end of her life. Its new owners changed the spelling from Nazimova's name, Alla, to Allah, which they presumably considered more exotic and romantic. It also was the name of a successful book of the period, *The Garden of Allah* by Robert Smythe Hichens. Over the years, the Garden became a lustrous and lusty haven for visiting

→ Alla Nazimova poses in feline regalia designed by costume designer Natacha Rambova (*nee* Winifred Kimball Shaughnessy). Rambova was born in Salt Lake City to an Irish Catholic father and a mother who was the granddaughter of one of the twelve original apostles of the Mormon church. A rebellious child, she quickly abandoned Salt Lake for Hollywood, where her name was known in the set and costume design realm. She found true fame, however, as the second wife of Valentino, a union that lasted less than two years.

Overleaf → The Garden of Allah, as seen in 1937, from the north side of the Sunset Strip. The street at the lower right is Havenhurst Drive. The seven-story building at the upper left is the French Normandy Granville Towers, built in 1930 on Crescent Heights and once home to Marilyn Monroe, Rock Hudson, and David Bowie.

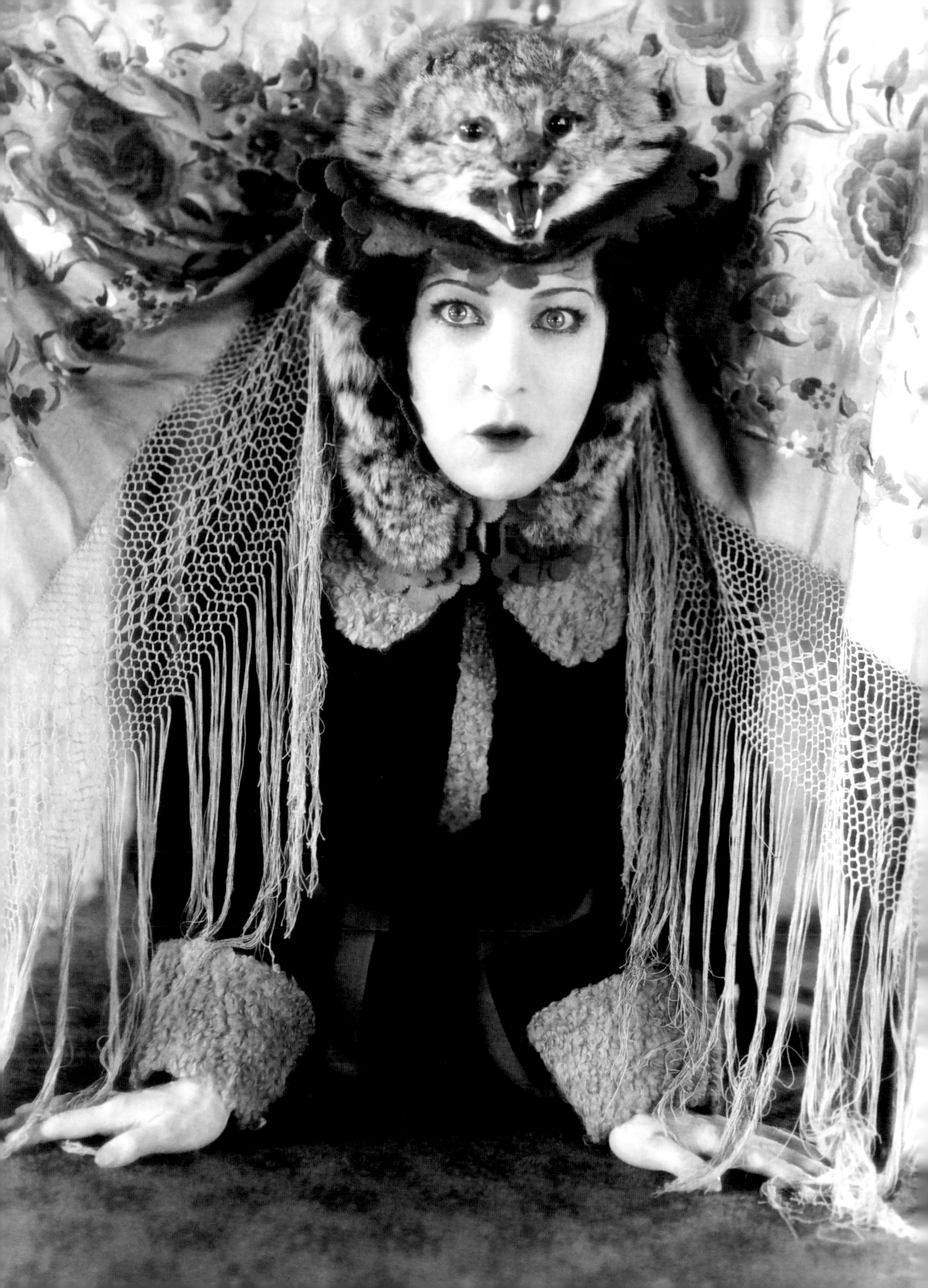

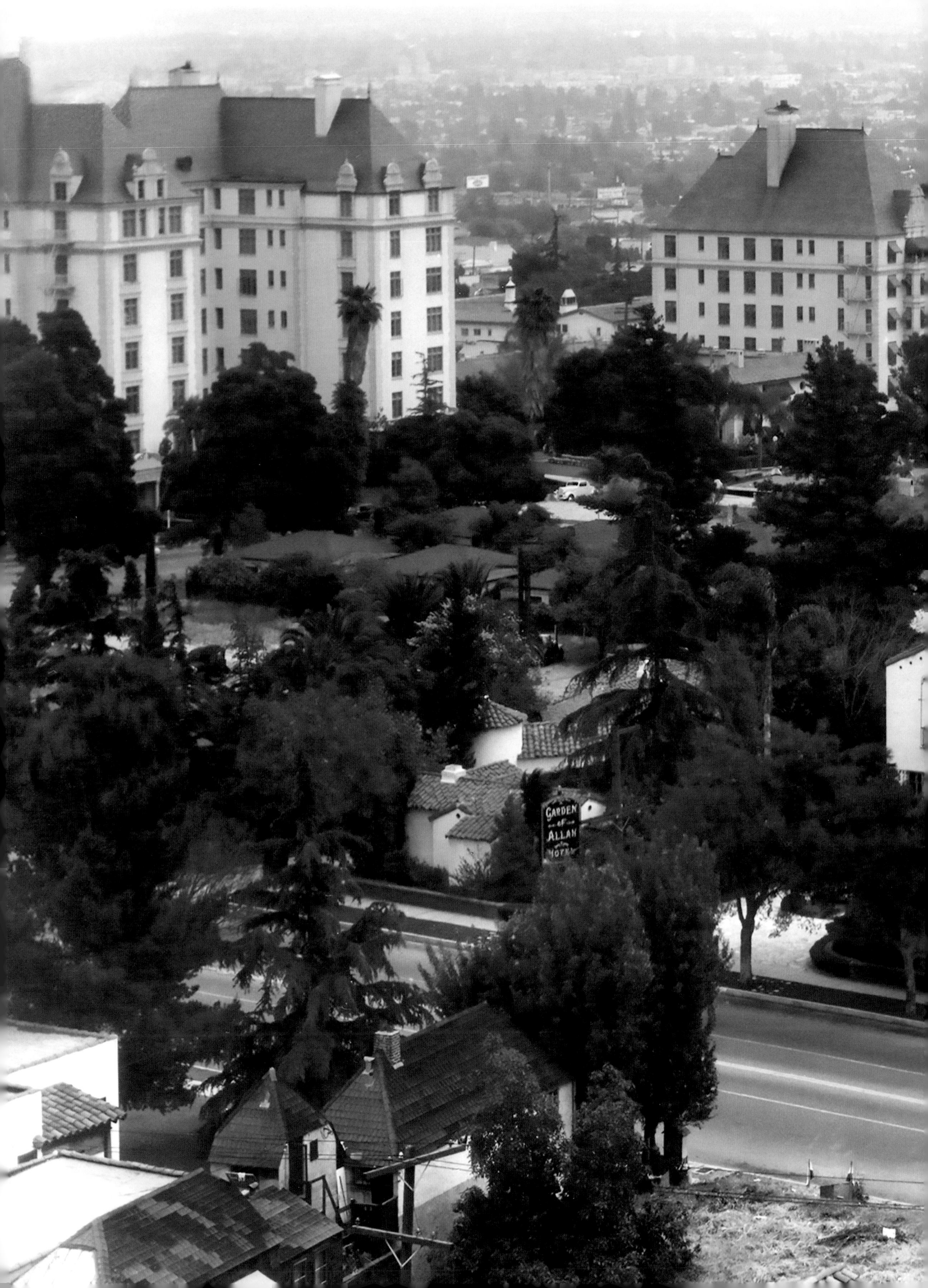
GARDEN
OF
ALLAH
HOTEL

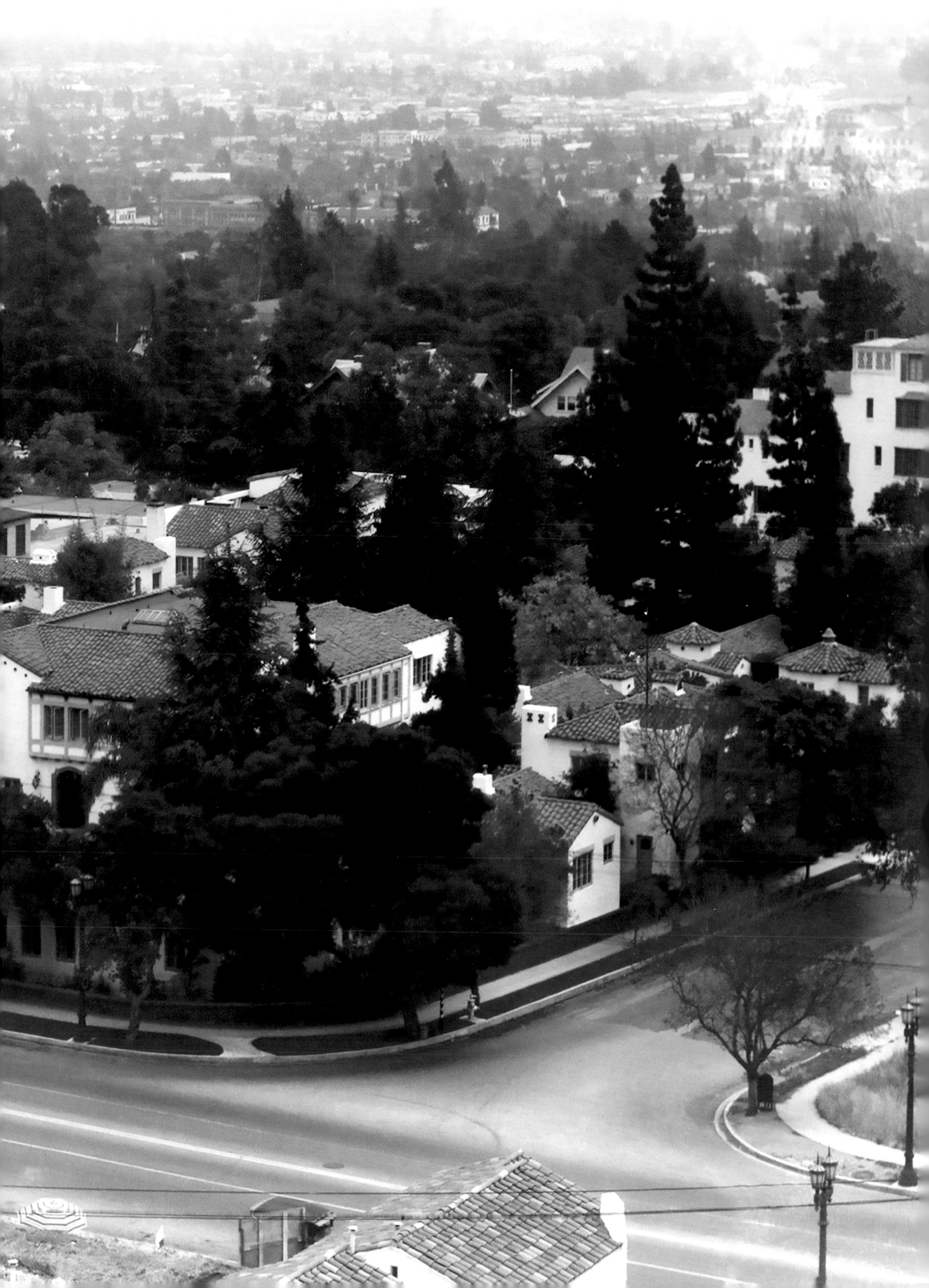

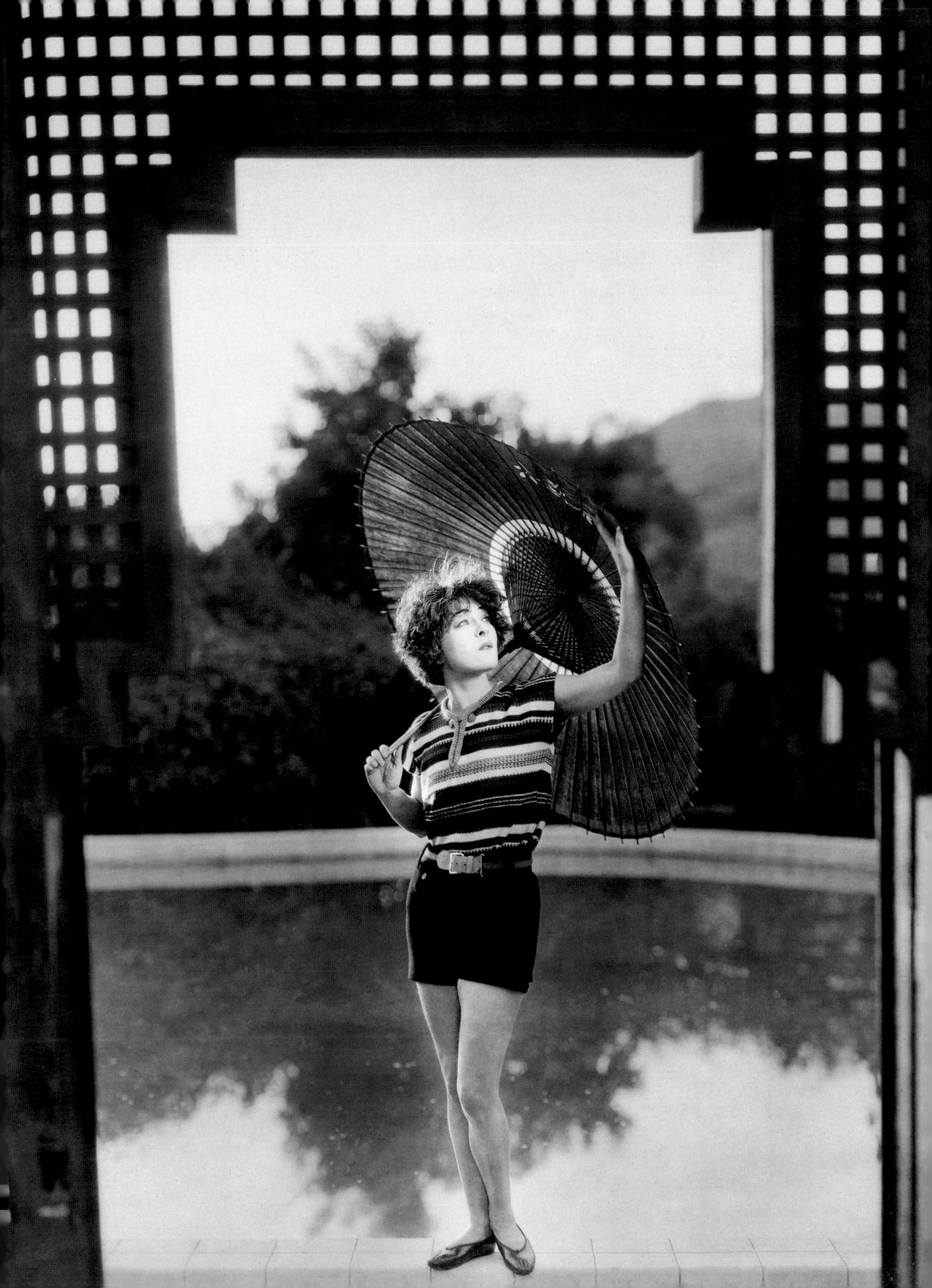

celebrities and those who considered it a kind of permanent home away from their permanent home. For some, it was a delightfully debauched commune.

The guest register listed Lauren Bacall, John Barrymore, Tallulah Bankhead, Gary Cooper, Marlene Dietrich, F. Scott Fitzgerald, Ava Gardner, Lillian Hellman, the Marx Brothers, David Niven, John O'Hara, Sergei Rachmaninoff, Frank Sinatra, Leopold Stokowski, Orson Welles, Hugh Hefner, and others among its glitterati. Along the way, Nazimova became godmother to a friend's daughter named Nancy Davis, who would of course become the starlet who wooed a future president of the United States and eventually became known as First Lady Nancy Davis Reagan.

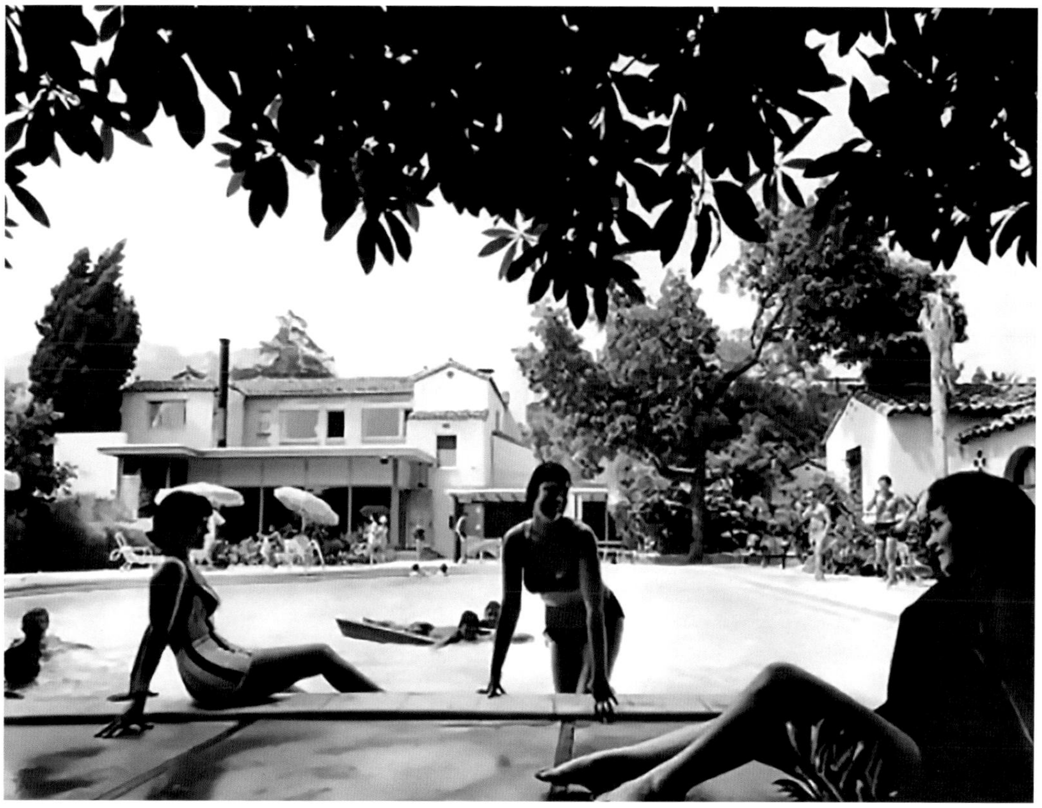

The pool was ground zero for the recreation and debauchery that fueled the Garden's libertine reputation. There is continuing debate as to whether or not the pool was shaped to resemble the Black Sea, which was bordered by Crimea (now part of the Ukraine), where Nazimova was born.

Robert Benchley, a popular writer, film actor, and Algonquin Round Table member, was a devoted guest. One of his memorable Allah moments occurred when he was walking by the pool as Tallulah Bankhead emerged nude from a swim. With great nonchalance, he reportedly gave her either a towel or a martini, though chivalry would no doubt dictate both.

Nazimova was bisexual and active with her many lesbian friends in an informal club known as The Sewing Circle. The sybaritic men of the Garden of Allah were a seeming cordial but thoroughly chaotic mix of gays, bisexuals, and heterosexuals. Most of them quite busy. Indeed, the Garden was notorious for its appallingly thin walls, which resulted in a fairly precise history of almost everyone's personal and professional endeavors.

Nazimova was bisexual and active with her many lesbian friends in an informal club known as The Sewing Circle. The sybaritic men of the Garden were a seeming cordial but thoroughly chaotic mix of gays, bisexuals, and heterosexuals.

By the early forties, the Garden of Allah was in deep decline, though it still attracted celebrities. In 1942 Frank Sinatra lived in a villa adjacent to Nazimova, and she listened to him rehearsing for his recording sessions. Gavin Lambert, in his engaging biography of Nazimova, wrote that she was frequently exasperated by Sinatra's unrelenting work on a song until it was perfect. "I think he's finally got it," she wrote in her diary as one song was thankfully completed. Then she added: "What a sexy voice."

←
A gushing public relations release says Nazimova is seen in the Garden just before taking her morning dip in her private lake. Perhaps more important at the time was her starring role in a new film, *My Son* (1925). She plays a mother whose handsome young son rejects his hometown sweetheart and begins fawning over a flapper with a checkered history.

She was also intrigued by Orson Welles, who rented the ground floor apartment of her villa for a few weeks while rehearsing a role in the radio version of Oscar Wilde's *The Happy Hypocrite*. A friend of Nazimova dropped by one day and found her with an ear to an air vent, mesmerized by his remarkable voice.

A postcard, in a kind of ironically pastoral, primitive style, depicts the very sophisticated Garden in its early years. At right is a preliminary concept for a mixed-use complex on the Garden site that would anchor the eastern end of the Strip, an initial design rendered by the renowned Los Angeles architect Frank Gehry.

Nazimova's later professional years were primarily sprinkled with character parts in films or more substantial roles in the theater. She did not easily tolerate fools and incompetents, and her personal life was unsettled. She is now recalled more for her Garden and personal life than for her performance skills.

But the Garden of Allah and Nazimova faded. She died in 1945, reportedly at the age of sixty-six. The Garden itself was razed in 1959. Contents were auctioned off and lore has it that Errol Flynn's bed attracted the highest price. The site temporarily became a bank building and then a haggard mini-mall dominated by routine fast food outlets. It cried out for a new identity.

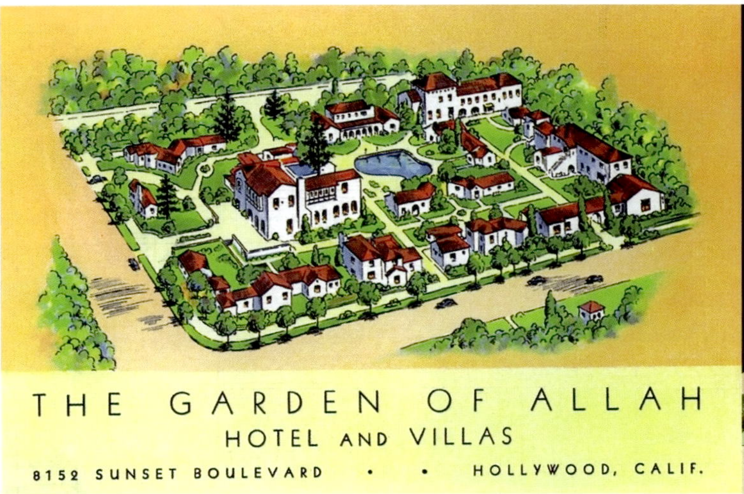

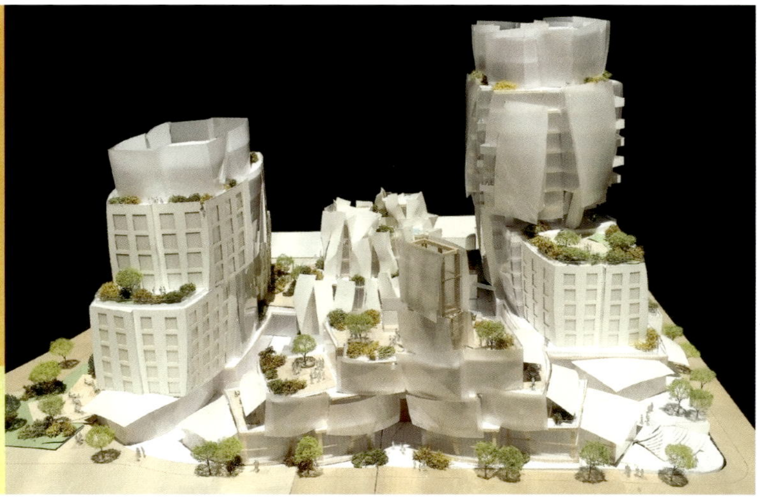

That new identity could be defined by a man who came to Los Angeles with his family from Toronto at the age of seventeen. Fascinated by the hotel and its history, he once snuck onto the property to see it for himself. That boy, Frank Gehry, grew up to become one of the most famous architects in the world. He has designed for the old Garden of Allah site a $300-million-plus community of five buildings (from three to fifteen stories) with plans for residential units plus stores, a market, a bank, a restaurant, and landscaped public spaces.

That new identity could be defined by a man who came to Los Angeles with his family from Toronto at the age of seventeen. Fascinated by the hotel and its history, he once snuck onto the property to see it for himself. That boy, Frank Gehry, grew up to become one of the most famed architects in the world.

When realized, the corner, the eastern gateway to the Sunset Strip, will have transitioned in about a century's time from a luxurious private home to the Garden of Alla(h) to a bank headquarters to a nondescript mini-mall to a formidable, ultra-chic and highly contemporary residential/shopping complex.

From Alla Nazimova to Frank Gehry. Quintessential Los Angeles. The ultimate Sunset Strip succession story.

For the romantics, however, it will always be the site of the Garden of Allah. The writer Sheilah Graham once lived nearby, as did her lover, F. Scott Fitzgerald. She best summed up the hotel in her 1970 book that was also called *The Garden of Allah*: "In the thirty-two-year span of its life, the Garden would witness robbery, murder, drunkenness, despair, divorce, marriage, orgies, pranks, fights, suicides, frustration, and hope. Yet intellectuals and celebrities from all over the world were to find it a convenient haven and a fascinating home." ■

→ The studio flacks adored the Garden as a background for publicity photos. Here in 1932, Paramount starlets Madge Evans (left) and Vicky Vola urge Max Keith to take them to lunch. Mr. Keith's disinterested expression would indicate, at the very least, that he had a full breakfast.

Overleaf →
Architect Frank Gehry's earliest designs for the Garden of Allah site featured a dramatic mix of five buildings, each three to five stories tall, with a ground-level plaza. Gehry then envisioned multi-purpose structures that would create a major architectural statement, an icon-in-the-making on the Strip.

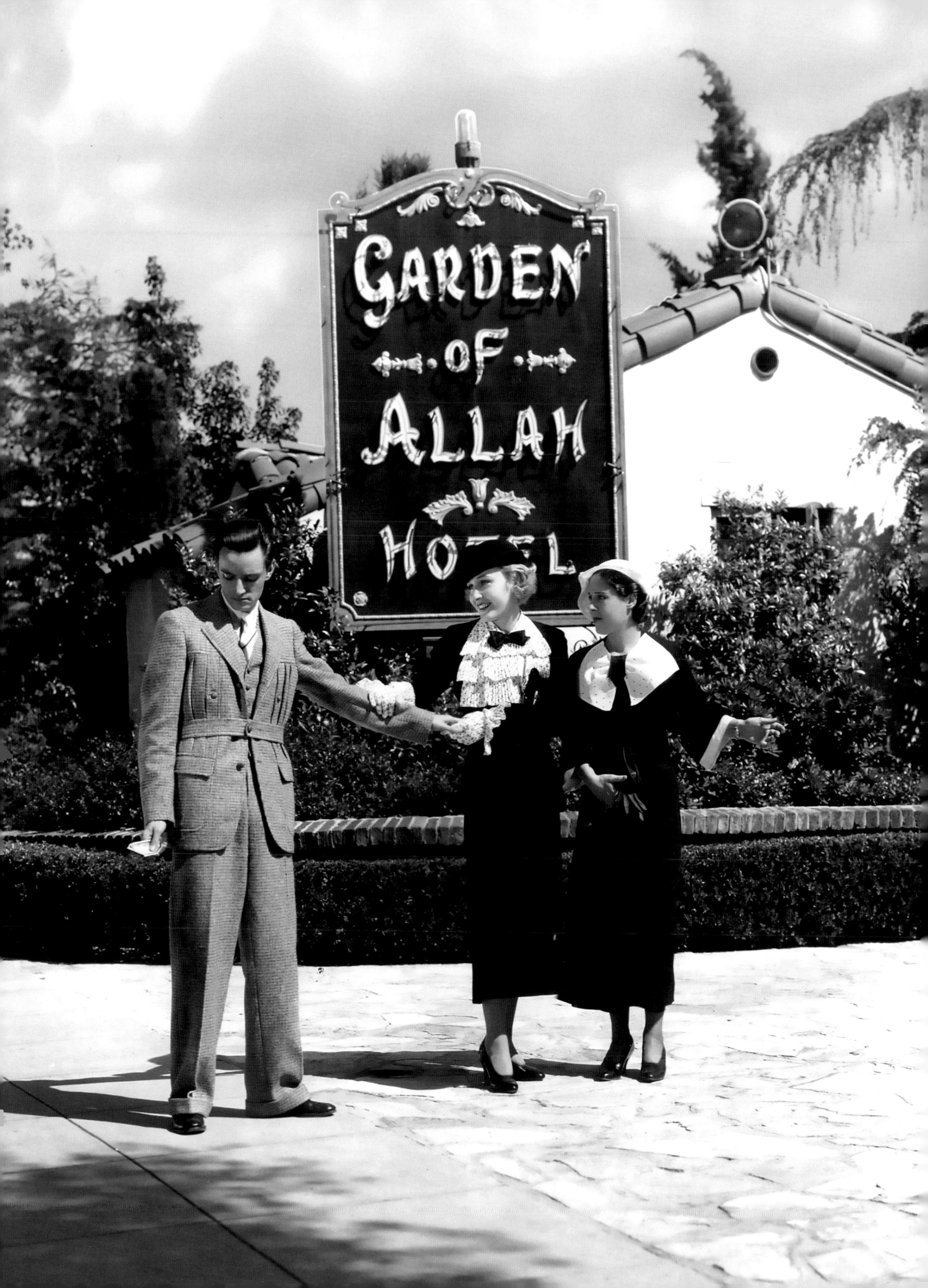
GARDEN
OF
ALLAH
HOTEL

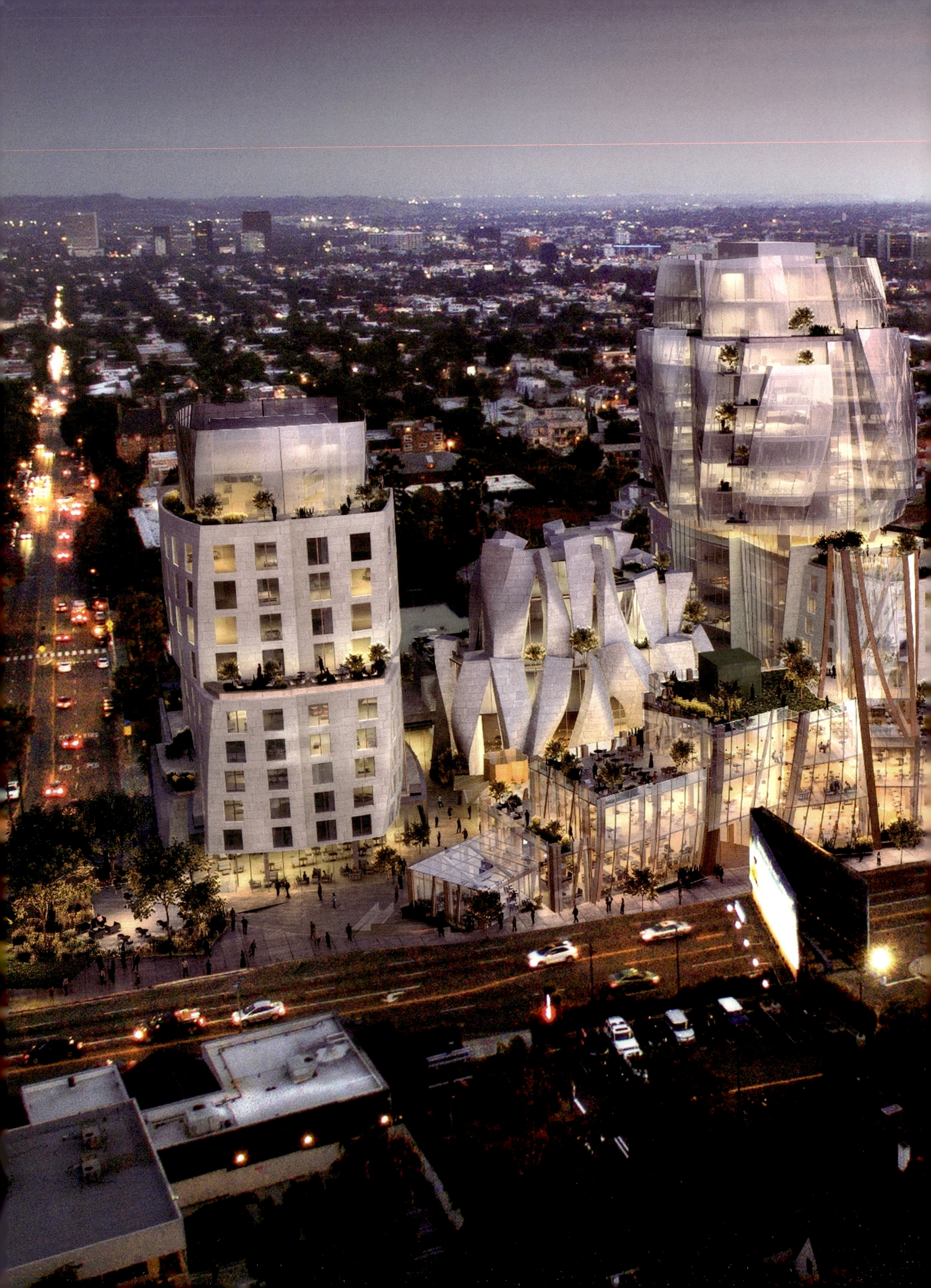

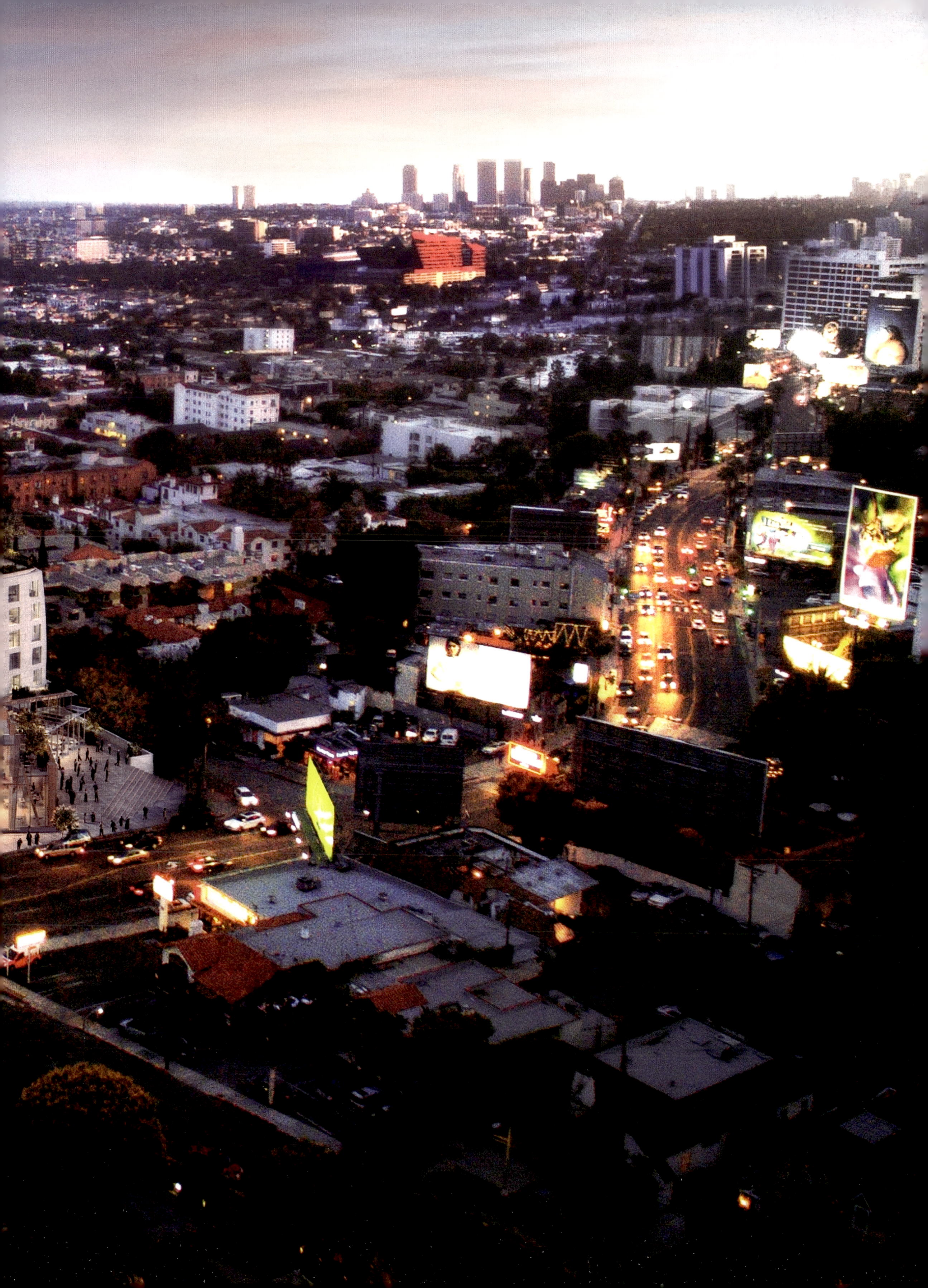

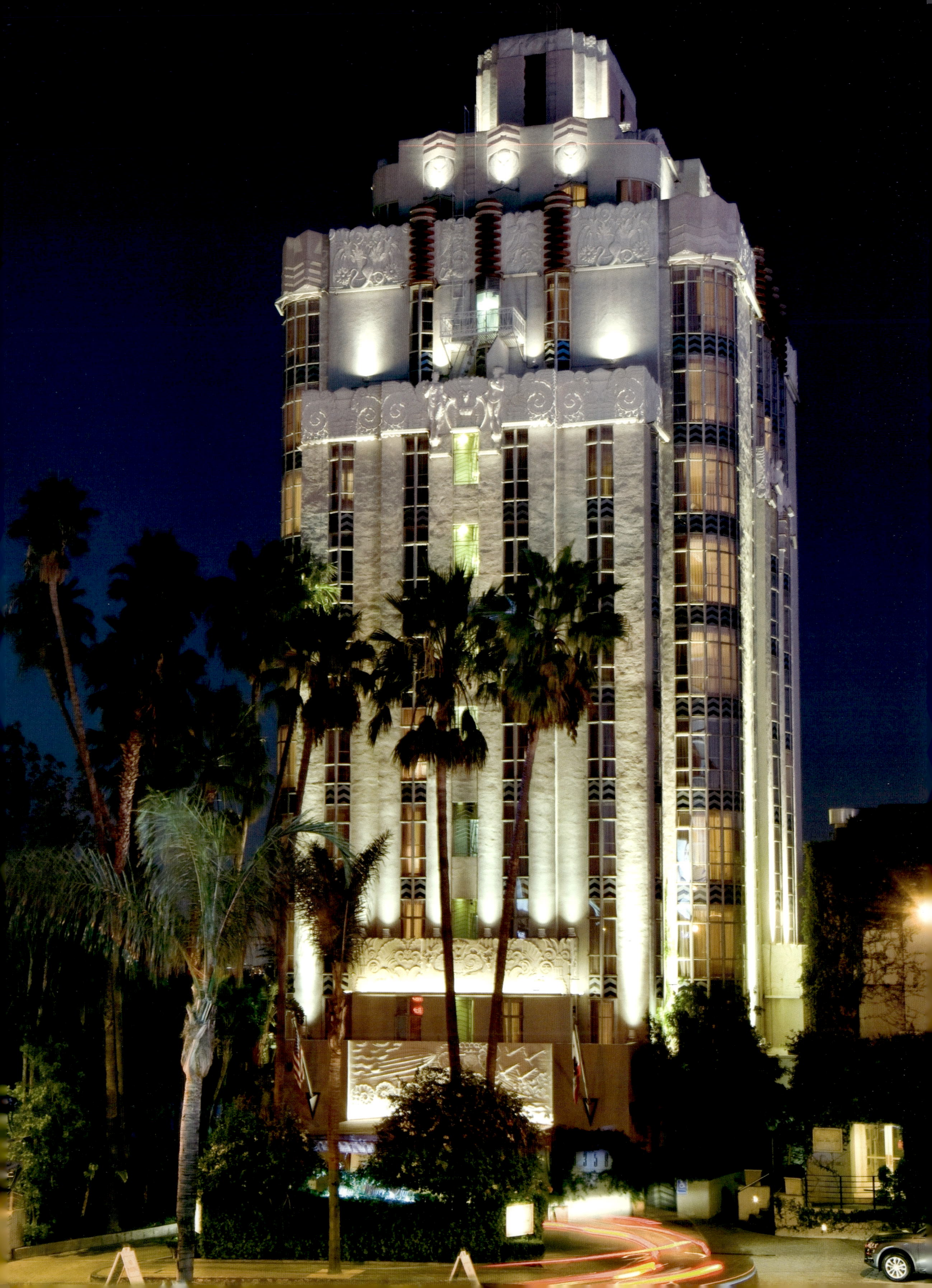

Sunset Tower

The Queen

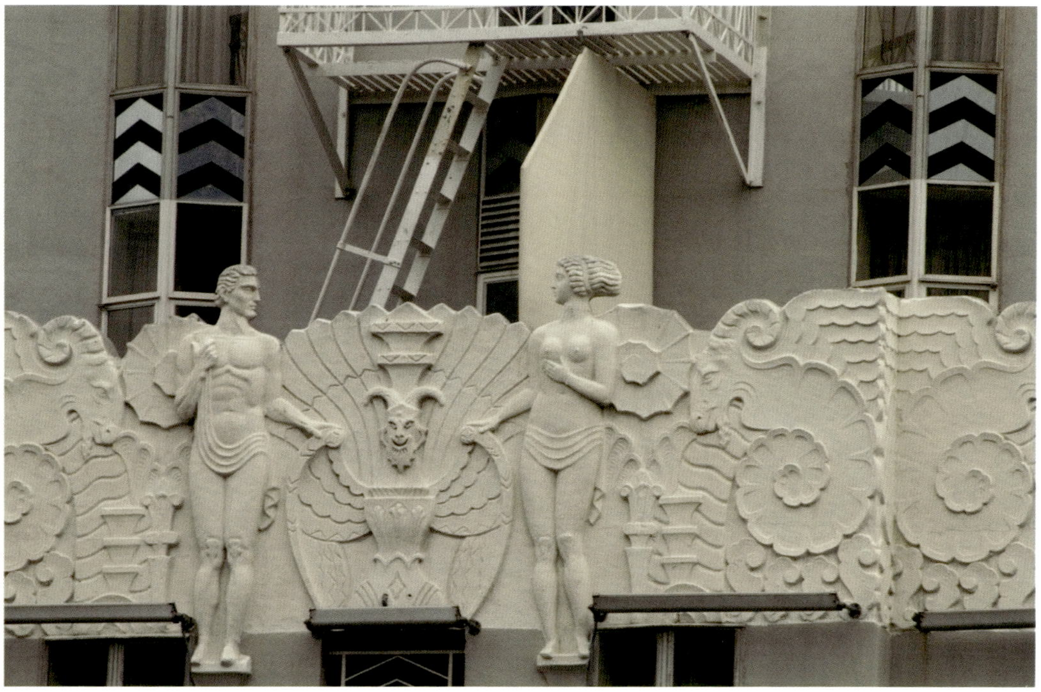

A detail of a sculptural frieze adorning the front of the building reveals the precision and elegance of the art deco style that brought such distinction to the Tower.

The Sunset Strip is a raucous, narrow gantlet formed by stores, offices, nightclubs, hotels, restaurants, noisy signage, and wearisome traffic that often makes it difficult to recognize the street's most elegant presence: a tall, cosmopolitan lady of more than a certain age, with elegant features, remarkable accessories, and great bones. The fifteen-story Sunset Tower Hotel has transitioned through many phases—both elegant and awkward—since opening in 1931 when it was the most elaborate construction on the Strip—and over the decades settled into discrete gentility. With a subtle dash of rakishness.

Along a street where name dropping constitutes an elevated form of both literature and commerce, her guest registry boasts a remarkable history of residents and visitors, from Clark Gable to Zasu Pitts, Errol Flynn to Truman Capote, Bugsy Siegel to Frank Sinatra. Modern-day tour guides even declare that penthouse-resident John Wayne once moved a cow onto a balcony to provide fresh milk for morning coffee. (Well, perhaps, for a morning capper to a rowdy all-night party?) Of the Tower, Capote once wrote, "I am living in a very posh establishment, the Sunset Tower, which, or so the local gentry tell me, is where every scandal that ever happened happened."

"I am living in a very posh establishment, the Sunset Tower, which, or so the local gentry tell me, is where every scandal that ever happened happened."

—TRUMAN CAPOTE

The Tower itself is a celebrated example of art deco modern architecture, radiant with friezes of plants, animals, Zeppelins, mythological creatures, planes, elephants, and even Adam and Eve. One observer noted that the exterior design managed to combine facets representing architecture, film, ancient history, and technology, among other themes. It covers this range without sloshing into garishness. And its sophisticated interior is an art deco tour de force.

←
The elegant Sunset Tower, like the Chateau Marmont, began as an apartment building. In February, 1938, *Screen Actors Guild Magazine* described it as "faultless. . . the ultimate in privacy." Perhaps true in concept, there were many residents for whom publicity, not privacy, was oxygen.

While the building radiates dignity, some of its occupants over the years radiated the sordid. Bugsy Siegel, the venomous gangster, resided there in the building's apartment phase and once was arrested in the Tower apartment of his good friend, Allan Smiley. Siegel, then described by the *Los Angeles Times* as a "Hollywood sportsman," was later shot to death in the Beverly Hills home of mob moll Virginia Hill while sitting on a sofa with Smiley reading the morning paper. Smiley escaped with a bullet hole in his jacket.

Life was flavorful but generally gracious in the Sunset Tower. It had convenience, comfort, and the spin of intrigue, until the cultural earthquake of the sixties. Rock 'n' roll was the sinewy soundtrack for sweeping away a lifestyle once symbolized on the Strip by dapper men with women dressed in the latest from Chanel or Adrian, all dancing to Tommy Dorsey and fueled by Champagne from the most sumptuous cellars. On the street, a burgeoning, unrelenting mob of rebellious and garish youth was rising up, elevated by the raw, emotional intensity of their music. They heard it as the fight song for their liberation from the stale ennui of American adulthood. The music that swept east from Los Angeles across the nation was the clarion of irrevocable freedom, the intoxication of drugs and sex and rightful honesty. A raw rock 'n' roll had arrived. And responsibility was not part of the baggage.

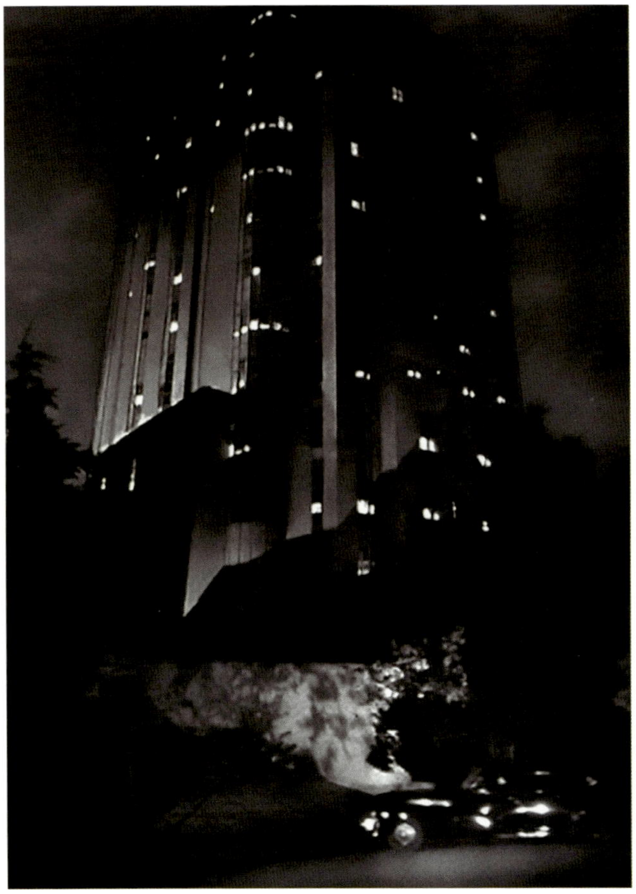

The Tower did a star turn in the 1944 film *Murder My Sweet*. Dick Powell plays the renowned Raymond Chandler detective Philip Marlowe, who visits an apartment in the Tower.

→

The Sunset Tower in the mist, 1946.

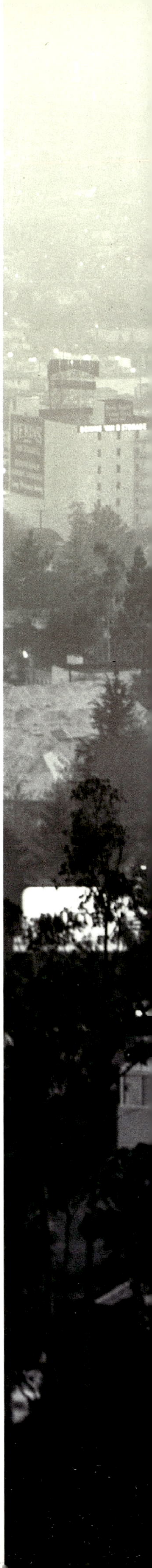

With it, Old Hollywood elite abandoned the street, if not its own identity. A younger, energized Hollywood emerged. Like its music, the scene on the Strip was loud, assertive, innovative, and at times, appallingly coarse. With that brashness came filmmaking that was new in form and content. And it quickly found its audience.

The Sunset Tower did not. A new purpose was needed for the building, which was rapidly declining into obsolescence. By 1982 the *Los Angeles Times* called it "one of the monumental eyesores in the Los Angeles basin." Actor Werner Klemperer, who played German Colonel Wilhelm Klink in television's *Hogan's Heroes*, was a resident in this phase and described the building as "Beirut West." But Klemperer was instrumental in supporting preservation laws that ultimately protected the structure.

The recovery began with the building passing through two constructive ownerships, both operating the tower as a hotel, before it was purchased by Jeff Klein in 2004. Klein, a polished, creative operator with a keen sense of branding, fashioned a hotel that deftly combines an old world charm with a sense of contemporary status. A striking and elegantly attired Catherine Deneuve might stroll into the dining room and awe producers and writers and actors who were children when she first became a luminous star. Some of them, of course, dressed like longshoremen back from a shape-up on a Red Hook pier in Brooklyn.

"This hotel is a high-end version of eclecticism," says Klein. "It isn't taking customers from the Ritz-Carlton. Customers who want a high-end corporate environment. This goes deeper. We may not have two sinks in every bathroom. We can only work with what was given to us by the original architect. But we have what the contemporary hotels can't have: a soul and a personality. Deep ones, too. People forgive us here for not having a bathtub and a shower in every room. They understand. They buy into this."

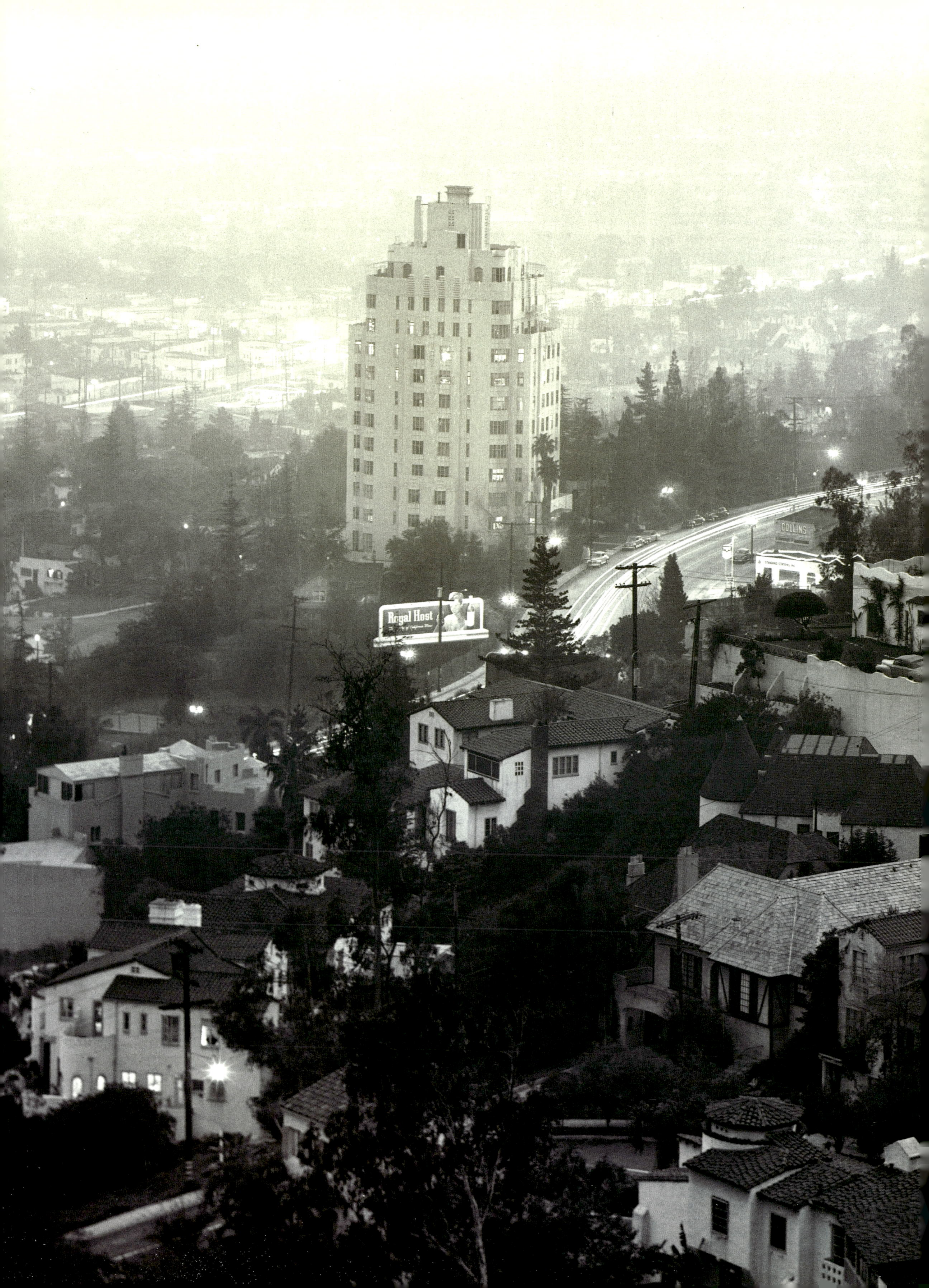
Royal Host
COLLINS

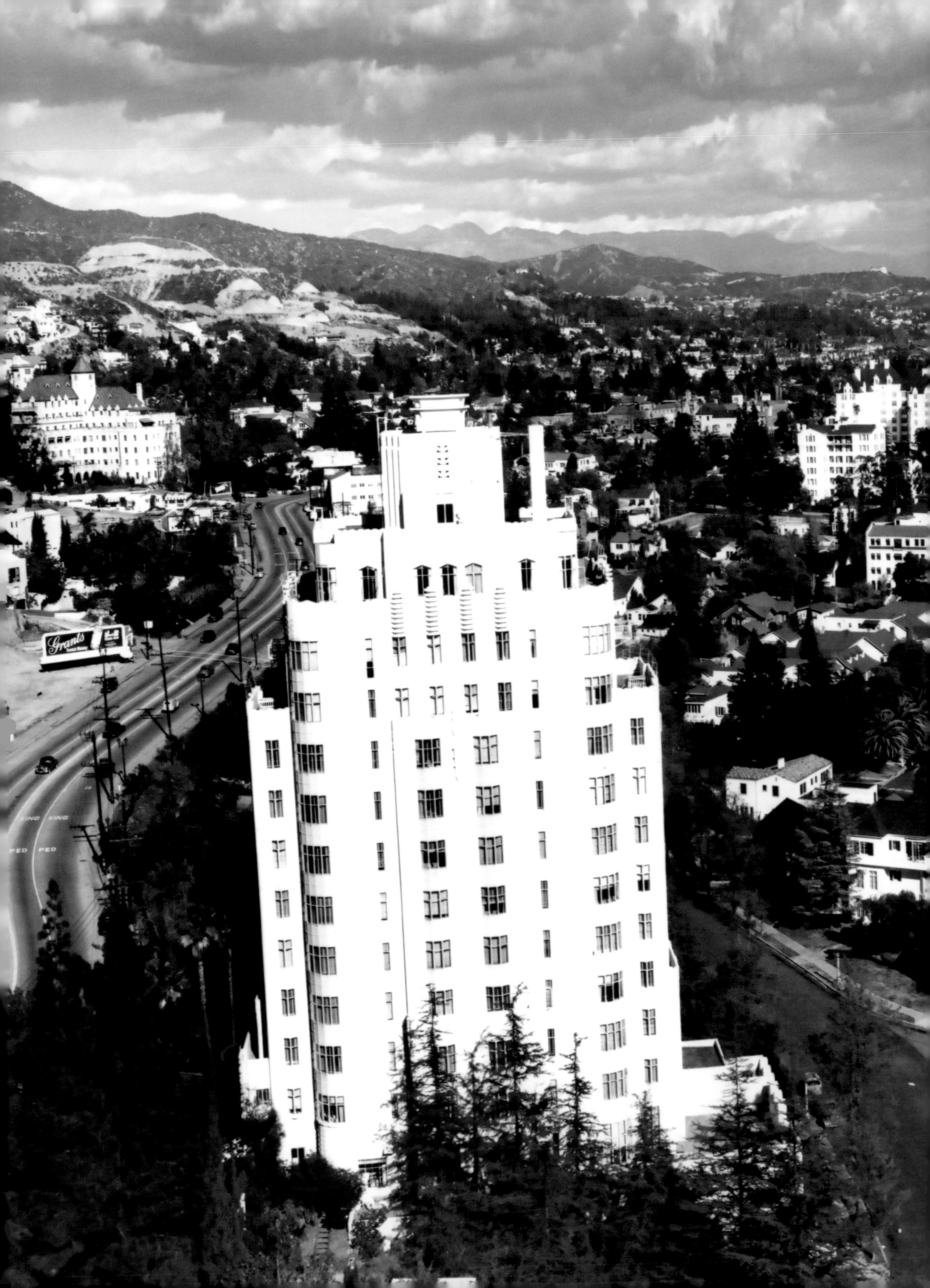
Grant's

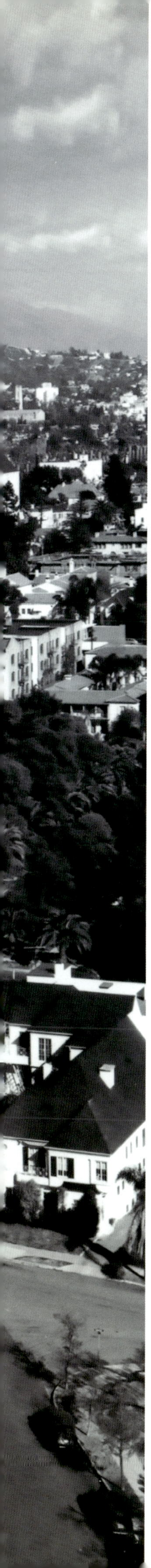

As he told the glitzy magazine *Los Angeles Confidential*, "Some hotels are geared towards everyone noticing everything, but here, it's extremely subdued. There's nothing in your face — no loud music, half-naked people, tight-fitting clothes, or fire pits. Certain people may not get us, and that's cool. I love it because (the hotel) sort of self-selects and organically screens out who belongs and who doesn't."

And that self-selected crowd also buys into another crucial element of the hotel, its restaurant and bar/pool area, at the rear of the structure, with its arresting panoramic view of the Los Angeles Basin.

When Klein purchased the hotel, the current dining area (originally the site of Bugsy Siegel's apartment) was a storage area. The remarkable view was shuttered. Now the room has an understated classicism. Nice. But more importantly, the room offers one of the three best hamburgers in Los Angeles, comfortable furniture, and Dimitri.

Who?

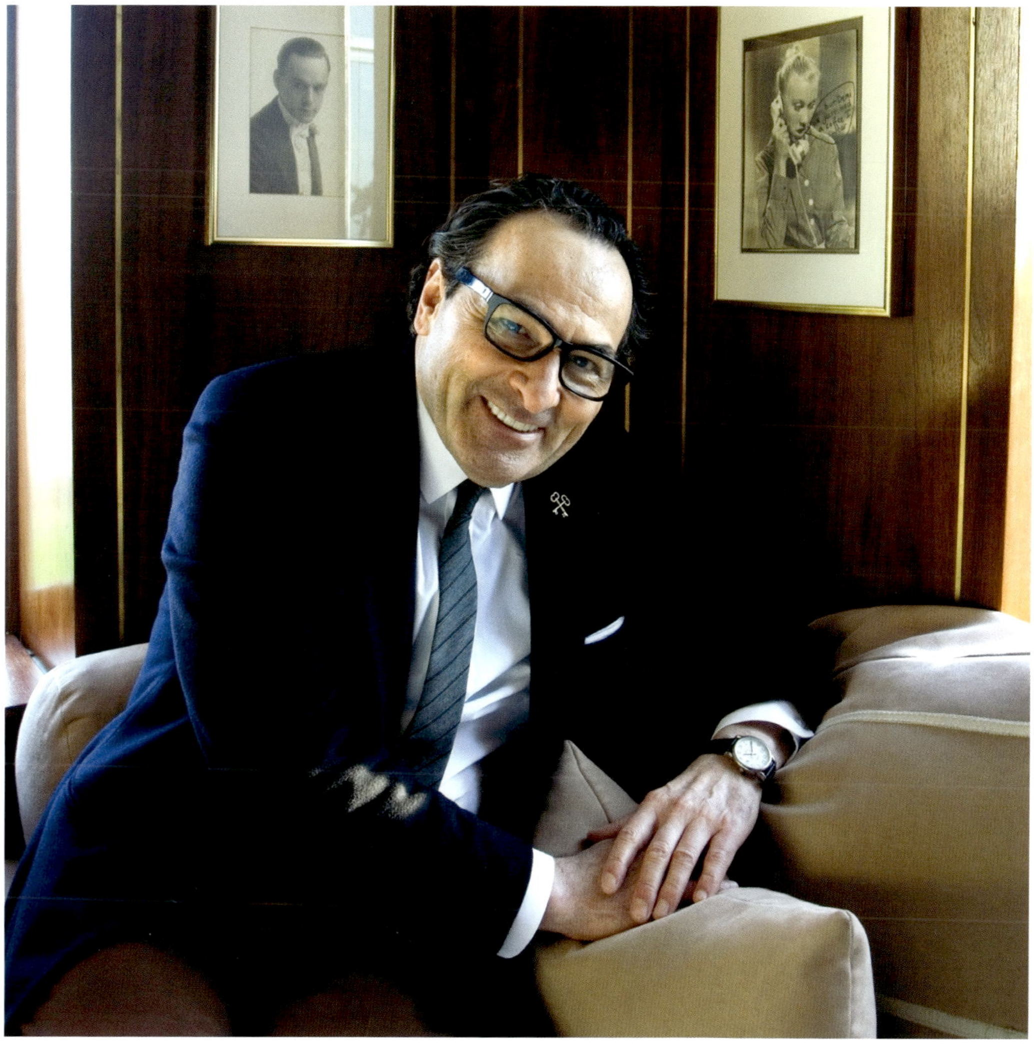

Dimitri Dimitrov, maitre d' of the Sunset Tower dining room.

Dimitri Dimitrov may be the most influential man ever to emerge from Macedonia, a landlocked, hardscrabble country in the petulant Balkans, and land in Los Angeles.

Maître d' of the Sunset Tower dining room, he's a short, wiry, and intense fellow who dominates the dining room with knowledge (he knows which celebrities prefer which tables), authority (greater efficiency can't be found on the deck of an aircraft carrier), and a surprising kindness (he insists that guests without fame and fortune be treated with the same esteem as those who have both).

← In 1949, the Sunset Tower overlooks the Sunset Strip as it winds eastward past the Chateau Marmont toward Hollywood, with the Hollywood hills and San Gabriel range in the background.

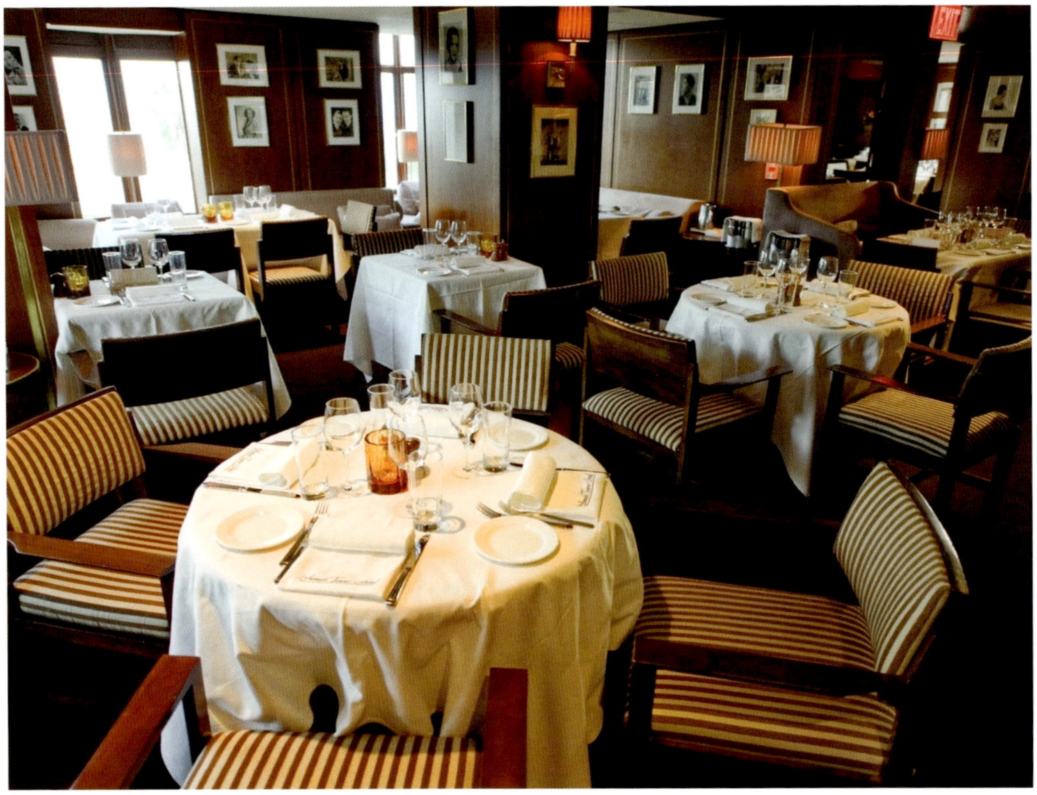

A rare view of the dining room of the Sunset Tower Hotel, at rest. This cozy space with walls now decorated with vintage portraits of classic Hollywood stars was once an apartment occupied by mobster Bugsy Siegel.

Dimitri made it to London at nineteen and got work as a busboy and apprentice waiter in a classy restaurant. "I was in awe," he recalled. "I soon couldn't imagine ever doing anything else." From there, he was off to Montreal and a chic hotel restaurant, one favored by then-Canadian prime minister Pierre Trudeau. Dimitri recalls fondly, "It had everything. Fashion. European flair. Accents."

The next move took him to "Russia." Well, a highly nostalgic Russian restaurant, Diaghilev, in a then somewhat threadbare hotel just half a block off the Sunset Strip. And it was a Russia before grim and grubby Bolshies started handing out pitchforks to the peasantry for de-privileging the layabout dukes and estate owners and lecherous monks. The music was exotic. Balalaikas and harps. Perhaps even accordions. Two themes: festive or mournful, but nothing lacking the ambiance of Mother Russia. The food seemed luscious to the longing émigrés and food fashionistas who flocked to the dark room, with its vivid flowers, ice statues, and worshipful paintings of a romanticized Moscow. And Dimitri was the house Romanov, the prince, a patrician maître d'—at once obsequious, ingratiating, endearing, intimidating, accommodating, kindly—directing the room as though conducting a herculean orchestra performing Mussorgsky in the Kiev Conservatory. Dimitri was a hit. Box office.

For Tom Ford, everything is about creating a sexy, cinematic image, whether he's directing or shaping a gown, and Dimitri does the same thing in a dining room.

As Dimitri swoons about the room, dispensing magic and benevolence, guests watch, culling vague, imperfect memories. Yes, we've seen this man, or a man just like him, in a movie, black and white. *Ninotchka* perhaps. A glorious night club, Vienna or Prague or Paris, escorting Greta Garbo and Melvyn Douglas to a table. Or maybe it was something later, in Paris. Cooper? Paulette Goddard? Maybe?

So is it any wonder that when Klein went looking for a person to organize and energize his Sunset Tower Hotel restaurant, fashion designer/movie director Tom Ford provided the answer: Dimitri. For Ford, everything is about creating a sexy, cinematic image, whether he's directing or shaping a gown, and Dimitri does the same thing in a dining room. Like Ford, his work is his life, and the performance is the reality.

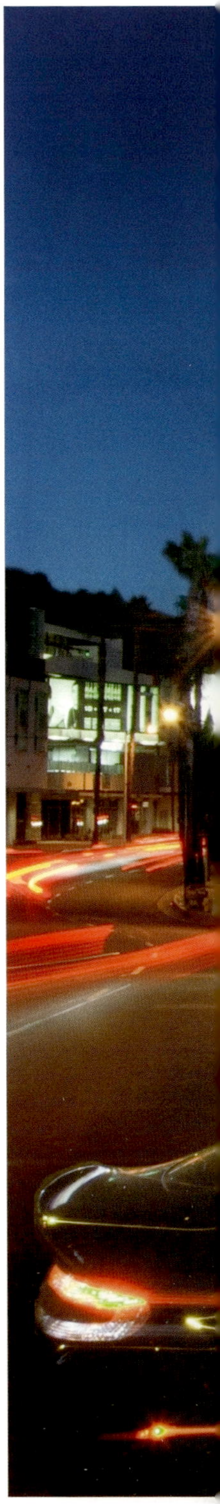

For those unlikely to visit the hotel, there is a cinematic and revealing tour in Robert Altman's 1992 film, *The Player*, a riveting drama/comedy about a reptilian Hollywood studio executive and the world in which he thrives, but not without cascading vulnerability.

One night, the executive, played to an oily perfection by Tim Robbins, pulls up to the Tower (then called the St. James Club) in his Land Rover and moves through the hotel on his way to a meeting. In the lobby, he encounters Malcolm McDowell (who dresses down the executive for his duplicity), then he meets Andie MacDowell in the bar, where they chat about Roddy McDowall. It is a running scene of tension and comedy and camp on a perfect Hollywood stage. Incidentally, Roger Ebert gave the movie four stars out of four. One suspects the venerable film critic would have done the same for this jewel of a hotel on the Sunset Strip. ■

The Sunset Tower is a Strip hotspot, not just for the rooms or the food, but for the view of L.A. by night.

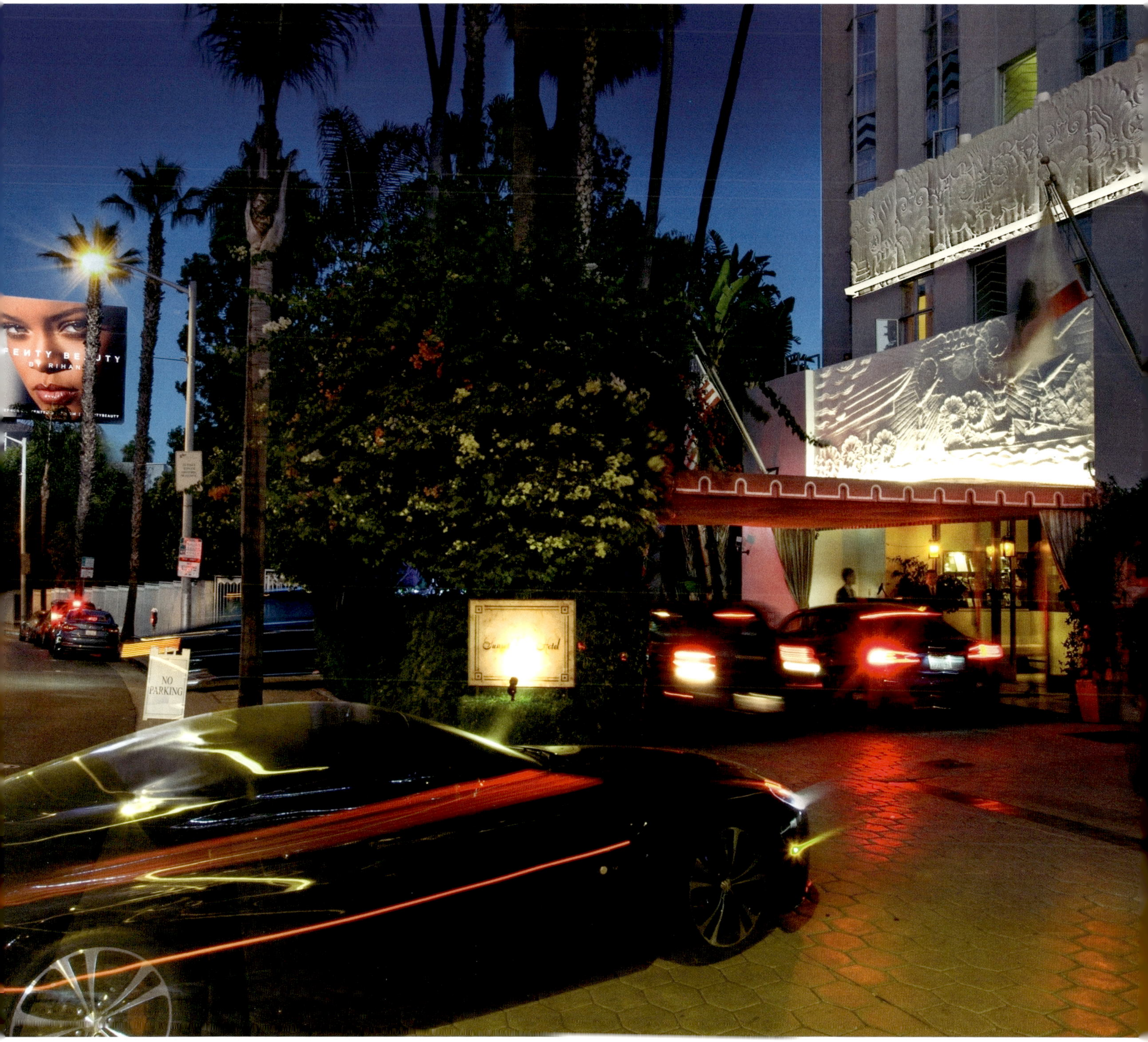

Schwab's Pharmacy

The Most Famous Pharmacy in American History

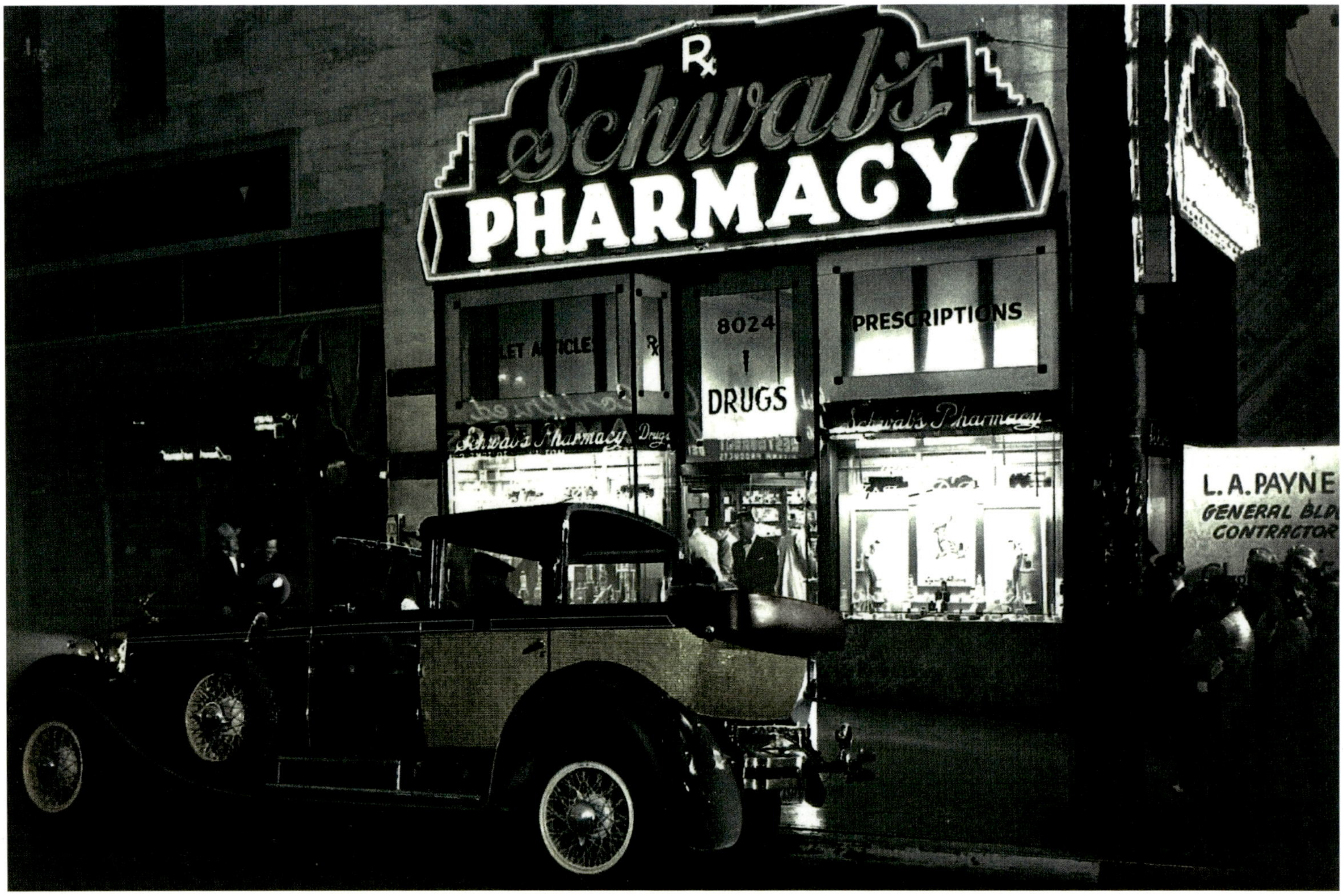

The exterior of Schwab's resembled any successful urban pharmacy across America. The only difference? There were days when you'd see Humphrey Bogart lighting up a Chesterfield or a resplendent limousine double-parked while its famous owner dashed in for a prescription. The pharmacy also appeared in films from time to time. For this scene being filmed for *Sunset Boulevard*, director Billy Wilder demanded a replica of a rare Italian luxury car—the 1929 Isotta-Fraschini 8A—parked outside Schwab's after he had the vehicle monogrammed with leading lady Norma Desmond's initials, and customized with leopard-skin, upholstered seats.

For all its medicines and elixirs and nostrums, for all the malts and cheese sandwiches and black coffees, Schwab's is best known for one thing: an audacious lie. A flagrant prevarication. And it being Hollywood, where fiction is daily translated into more convenient and lucrative fact, this should not be astonishing. Nor, it being Hollywood, is it scorned as socially reprehensible. No, Lana Turner, that hot Hollywood High School teenager turned movie star, was not discovered by director Mervyn LeRoy at the lunch counter in Schwab's Pharmacy on the Sunset Strip.

A lot went on there, but not that legendary untruth. True, however, Marilyn Monroe did fill her prescriptions there. And yes, Ava Gardner would go behind the lunch counter to make her own milkshakes. F. Scott Fitzgerald supposedly had a heart attack there while buying a pack of cigarettes. Charlie Chaplin played pinball with Harold Lloyd at Schwab's. And Humphrey Bogart did, indeed, ask Leon Schwab for something to cure a hangover. ("Stop drinking," Schwab advised.)

"That's the way a lot of us think about Schwab's. Kind of a combination office, coffee klatch, and waiting room. Waiting. Waiting for the gravy train."

—JOE GILLIS

It didn't hurt that entertainment critic Sid Skolsky called his popular column "From a Stool at Schwab's" in the movie-fan magazine *Photoplay*. Indeed, he spent a good portion of his workday perched on a stool at the soda fountain, gathering gossip and organizing his column, while a remarkable cross section of the movie business and its hangers-on paraded in and out of the drugstore.

But Lana (known then as Judy Turner) skipped a Hollywood High School typing class and went out for a Coke at a nearby hangout (variously identified as Top Hat or Pop's Top Hat Malt Shop). She was discovered there by William R. Wilkerson, the talent-smart publisher of the *Hollywood Reporter* (who, in turn, introduced her to the agent Zeppo Marx who introduced her to director Mervyn LeRoy, who cast her in her first film, *They Won't Forget* (1937)). But when Top Hat was shuttered, one of the Schwab brothers (all four were USC-grad pharmacists) reflected on the publicity and business Top Hat generated by being the place where Turner was discovered. Well, why not?, Leon concluded. And he promptly began spreading the word that the magic moment occurred at the family pharmacy.

That is not to say the Schwab boys were lying scoundrels. Far from it. The ownership was reputed to be generous and welcoming. Checks were cashed. Mail was held. There was a paging service. There was credit extended for regular patrons "on the shorts." "We've never turned somebody down who was hungry," Leon Schwab explained. "My mother told us if anyone needed, give, never turn down."

The drugstore stayed open until 1983. The block was eventually leveled, and a large, clunky building with stores, restaurants, and theaters went up in its place, just east of where the Garden of Allah stood.

The drugstore exterior is memorialized in Billy Wilder's epic film, *Sunset Boulevard* (and the interior of the drugstore was replicated on a soundstage). Screenwriter Joe Gillis (played by William Holden) is rejected by a studio and sets off to meet some friends at Schwab's. "I drove down to headquarters," he says. "That's the way a lot of us think about Schwab's. Kind of a combination office, coffee klatch, and waiting room. Waiting, waiting, for the gravy train."

Today, the only place to find a Schwab's, however ersatz, is in Florida at the Universal Studios Florida theme park in Orlando, where a small, kitschy soda fountain bears the legendary name. But nobody goes there to get discovered. ■

Among Schwab's many features—and sadly the one absent from most of today's pharmacies—was a lunch counter and soda fountain. The food ranged from corned beef and cabbage to chop suey and chocolate sundaes.

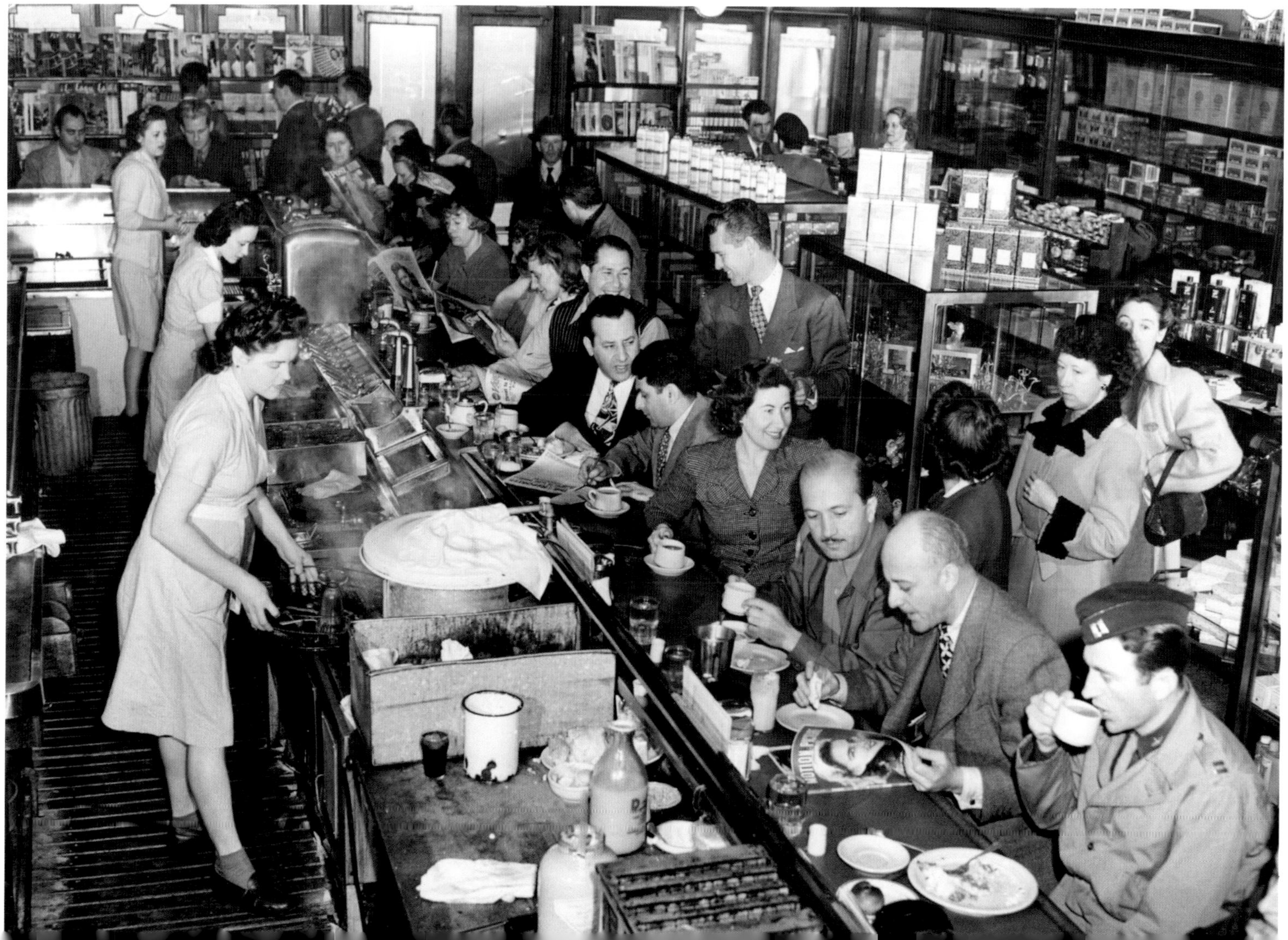

Hacienda Arms Apartments

Building in Transition: Star Digs to Saturnalia to Sushi.

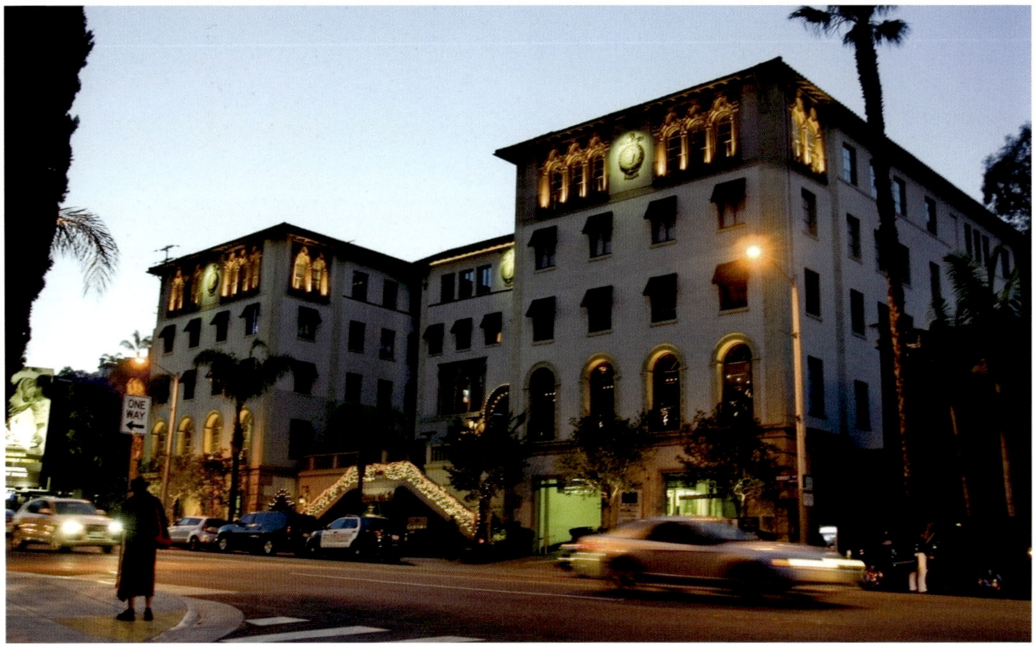

Now known as the Piazza del Sol, the once-déclassé (if not sordid) building—originally called the Hacienda Arms—has emerged as a strikingly dignified and refined address, perhaps proving that in Hollywood even buildings can have a second act.

The Sunset Strip is hardly given to subtlety and, in places, seems characterized by the almost relentless presence of tacky structures and hopelessly prosaic, outré storefronts. But then there are the buildings of traditional, uncomplicated beauty.

The Piazza del Sol (the latest in the building's history of prosy names) is one of the outstanding structures. And that's despite incredible misfortunes that have befallen it since the doors opened in 1927. Originally named (hardly for the ages) the Hacienda Arms, it offered graceful apartments designed and priced for the Stars—such as Loretta Young, Marie Dressler, and Jeanette MacDonald—and wealthy families. The academics call the design Italian Renaissance Revival, though to most civilians it is just pure "classic," with four stories, 54,000 square feet, and two graceful stairways up from the street.

The architect, Charles Sherman Cobb, a native of Albany, New York, and a Cornell graduate, isn't well remembered. But his building, now a designated historic landmark, was celebrated by the Los Angeles Conservancy for being like a "European palace." But its tasteful period was short-lived. In the 1930s, a former hooker named Lee Francis set up shop in the building and created the most elegant brothel in California (keep in mind that this was a highly competitive field in those days). The Hacienda Arms drew the predictable, priapic roués (Errol Flynn, Clark Gable, and Spencer Tracy, among them) and a large number of debauchees who avoided the Depression.

In the 1930s, a former hooker named Lee Francis set up shop in the building and created the most elegant brothel in California, a highly competitive field in those days.

Francis's enterprise undoubtedly constituted hefty paydays for the police. Francis estimated that about half her income went to ensure—through the well-established three-Cs of Champagne, caviar, and cash—the absence of police curiosity. Finally busted in the forties, Francis eventually went literary (perhaps a lateral move?) and inked a tell-all book in 1965, *Ladies on Call*, that for decades has been held in restricted stacks at fastidious libraries, and one day in 2016, the paperback was for sale on Amazon for $495. In yet

→ During a 1940 trial, Madam Lee Francis, with the aplomb of a business school professor lecturing on merchandise management, illustrates the layout of her sexual-pleasure factory and how clients were able to enter and egress her facility with minimal public exposure.

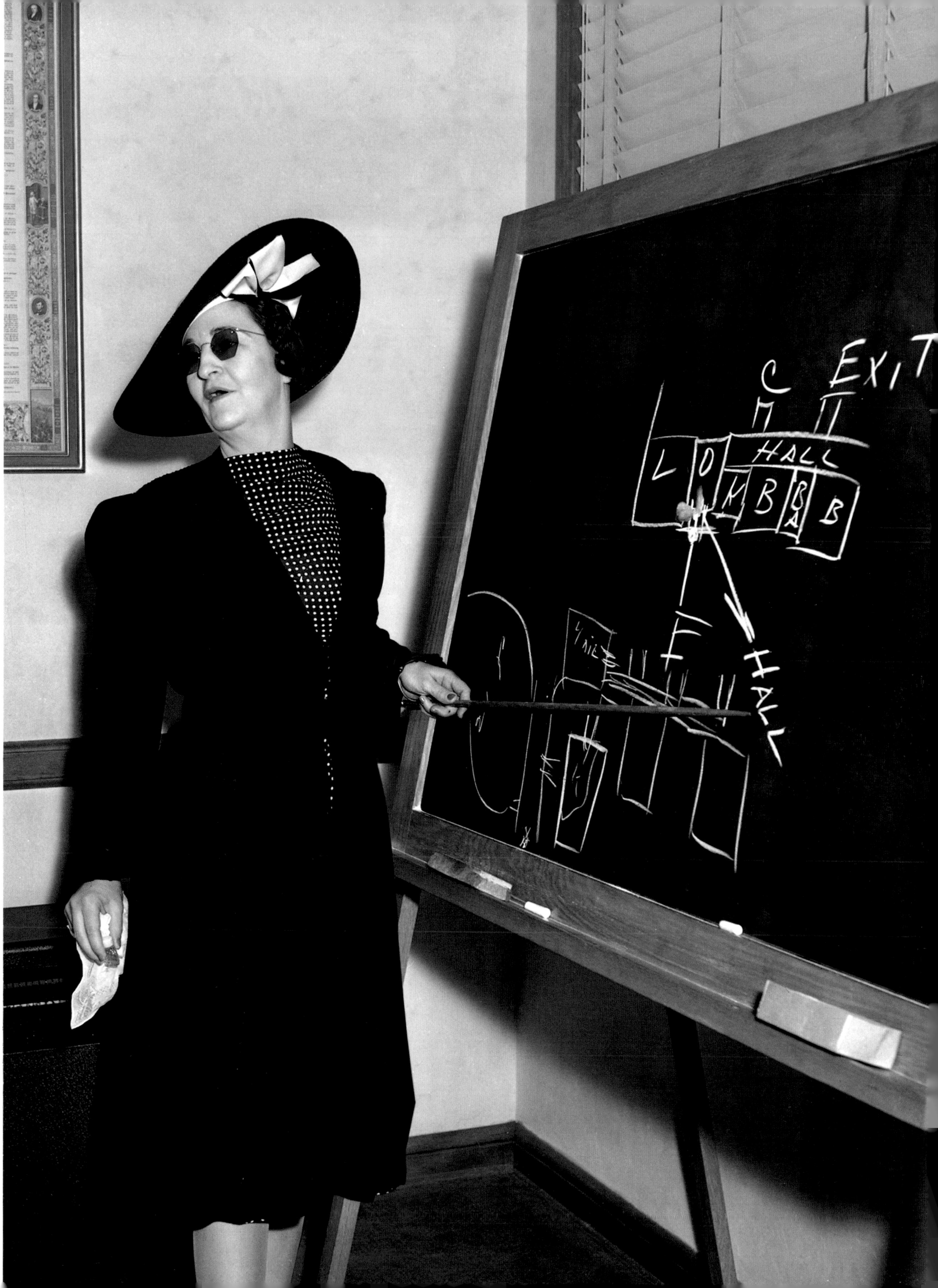
EXIT
HALL
HALL

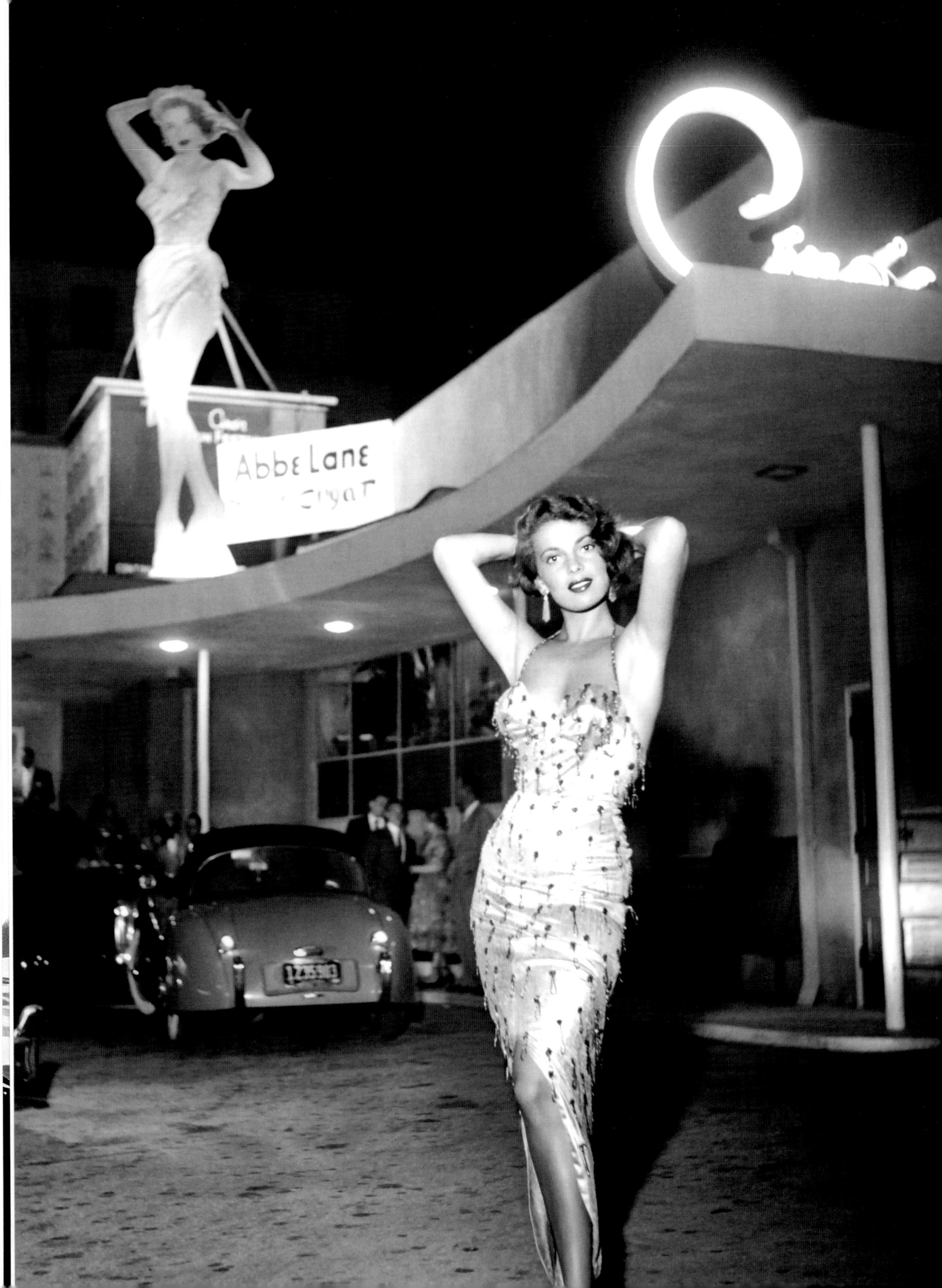
Abbe Lane

Ciro's

The Stars Came to See the Stars

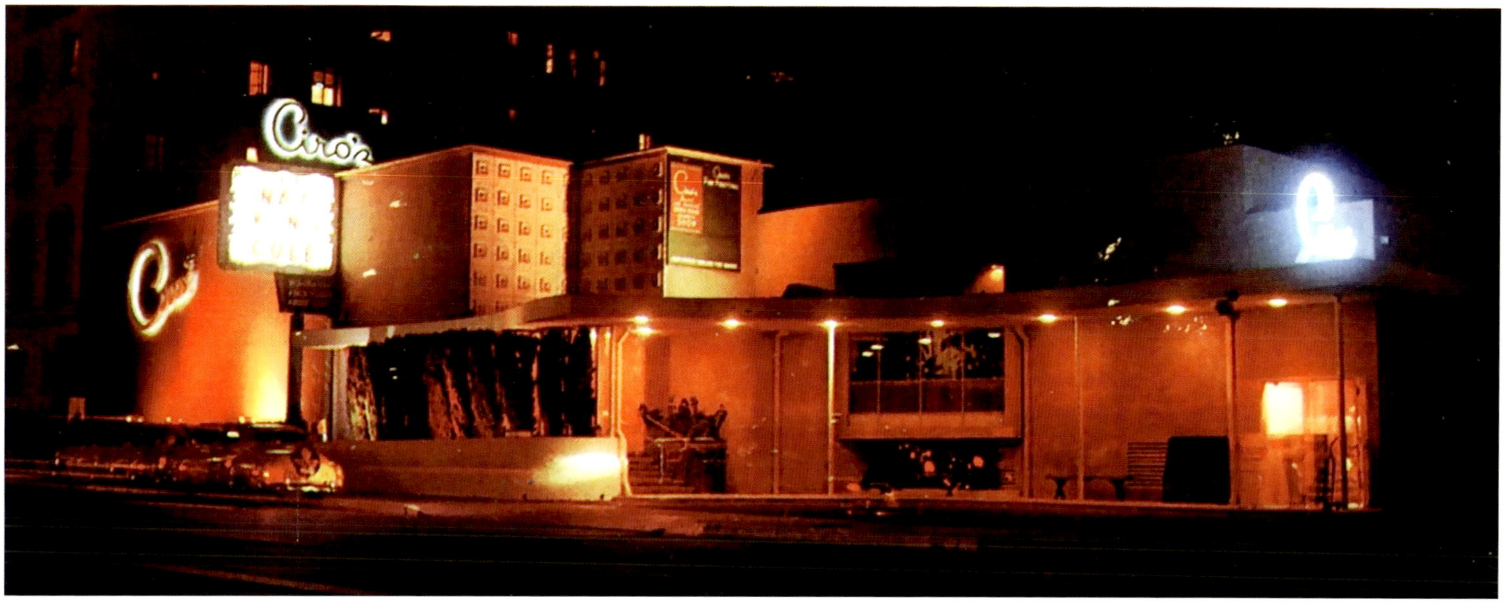

Billy Wilkerson opened Ciro's in 1940, and it continued to grace the Strip until 1959. After a brief stint as a rock 'n' roll venue in the '60s. The site went on to be occupied by the Comedy Store.

Cultural history survey question: if you could go back and spend an evening at any site in the history of the Sunset Strip, where would it be?

Music fans would argue over choices from the 1960s and '70s, and vote for various places like Whisky à Go Go, the Roxy, Gazzarri's, the Viper Room. Gamblers, whose choices are more limited, could choose between the Clover or a card game with Bugsy Siegel in the Sunset Tower. Those who seek opulent see-and-be-seen ambiance might opt for Trocadero. Libertines would no doubt favor Lee Francis's Hacienda brothel. But those who relish the glitz of epic Hollywood, the convening of its stars, the sheer self-indulgence of it all, would take Ciro's. No competition.

When Billy Wilkerson, the entrepreneur and *eminence grise* of the Strip, decided to create a nightclub, he selected a site with history. The delightfully extra-legal Clover Club casino had once operated there, until it was shut down by a perfect storm of mob conflicts, crooked police, and the bizarre possibility of political reform. It was followed by the Seville, a nightclub highlighting a glass dance floor under which schools of fish cavorted. Hollywood didn't buy into the piscine concept, and it went dark.

Ciro's was the entertainment centerpiece of Hollywood nightlife. The gossip columnists thrived on the chatter harvested at the club and their rumor-mongering spread the fascination of Ciro's far beyond the Strip.

Wilkerson envisioned a classy, luxuriant nightclub. European in style. Great entertainment. Well-turned-out guests. Facilitating the gossip and mischievous conduct and entertainment that would amuse a pleasantly well-heeled and sometimes uninhibited clientele. And he succeeded. He called it Ciro's, and over time the nightclub became a hit.

The great performers of the era took to the Ciro's stage. Pearl Bailey, George Burns, Nat King Cole, Xavier Cugat, Benny Goodman, Edith Piaf, Martin and Lewis, Al Jolson, Mae West. It was great show business—both on the stage and in the audience. One of its greatest achievements was breaking the racial barrier. When Duke Ellington played Ciro's in 1945, *Billboard* wrote it was the first of the "swank Strip spots to have gone in for a high-priced big-name Negro band." One of the most popular acts ever to perform there—initially as an opening act—was the Will Mastin Trio,

←
Singer and actress Abbe Lane poses outside Ciro's where she was performing in 1954. Notably quotable, Lane once said: "If a girl is a bad girl, she's always one type, and if she's good, she's always Peter Pan." She was married to bandleader Xavier Cugat, and got her star on the Hollywood Walk of Fame in 1960.

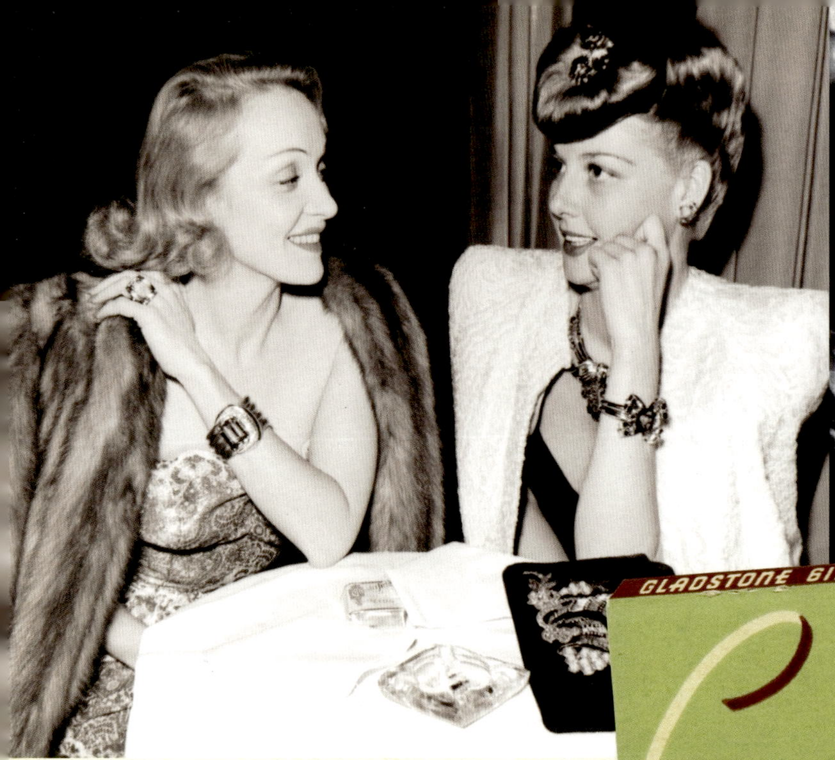

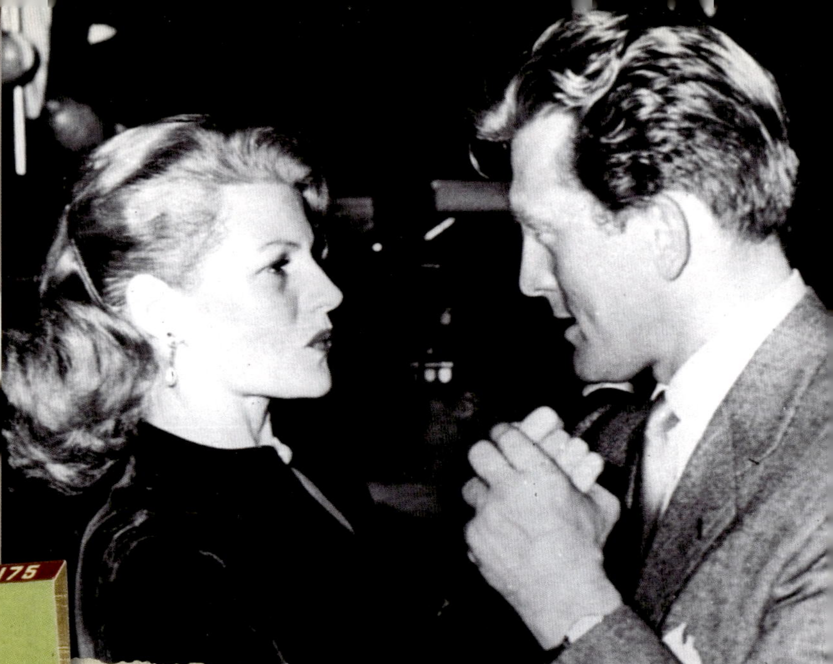

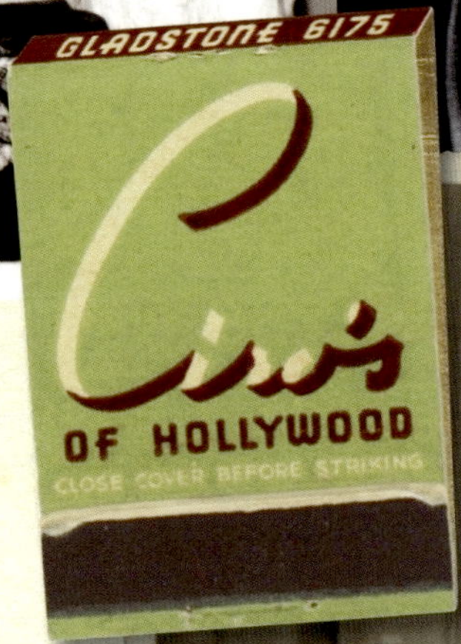

COVER CHARGE

$2.00 Per Person

BOTTLES ON TABLES

You will be charged for what you consume

. . . NOT FOR THE ENTIRE BOTTLE

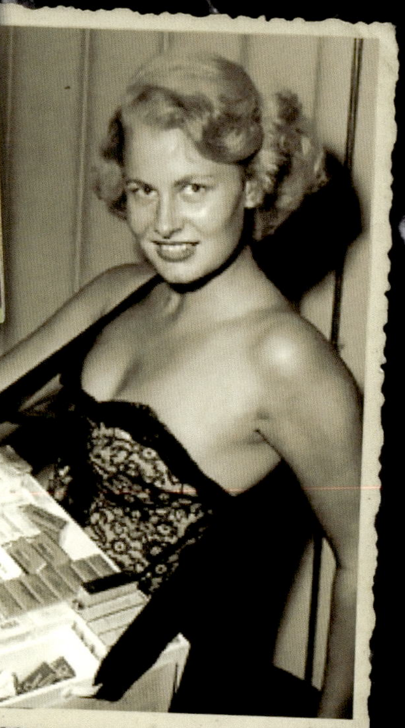

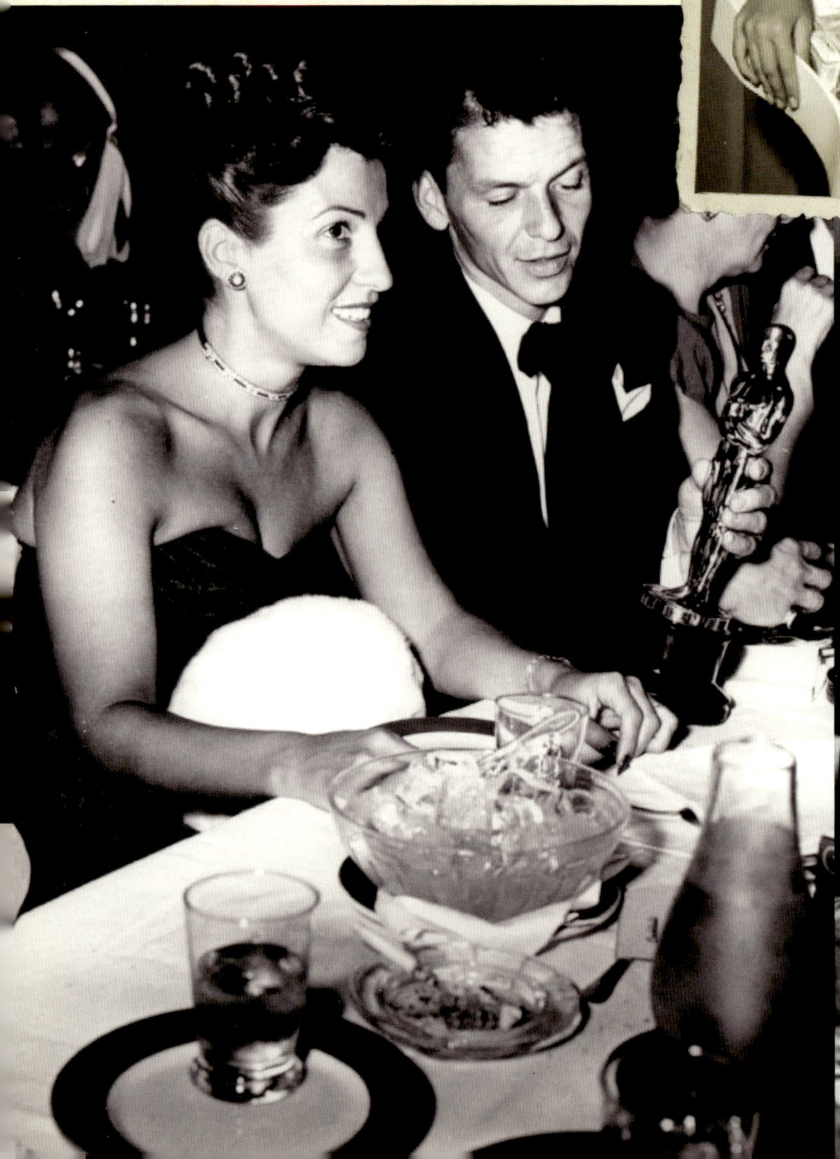

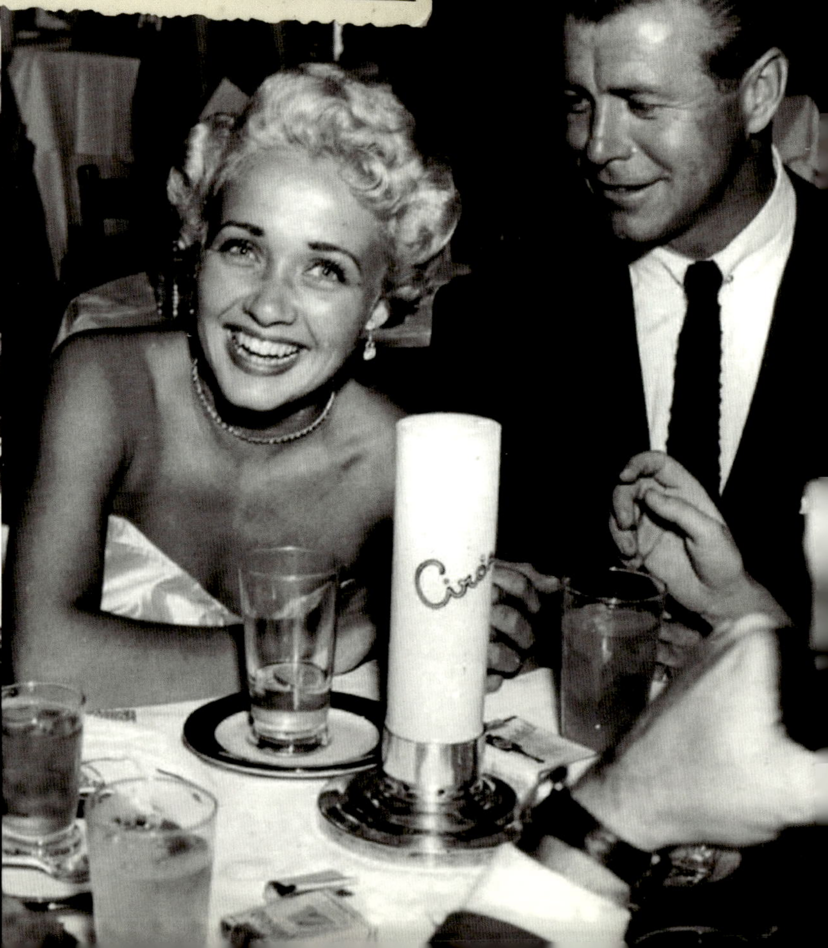

a Harlem tap-dancing troupe with Mastin, Sammy Davis Sr., and Sammy Davis Jr. The dancing, and particularly Sammy Davis Jr.'s impersonations of Sinatra, Bogart, and Satchmo Armstrong, captivated the audience and launched the young Davis's career.

Out front in the audience through the decades were the biggest names in Hollywood: Joan Crawford, Lucille Ball, Cary Grant, Judy Garland, Jimmy Stewart, Jack Benny, Humphrey Bogart and Lauren Bacall, and of course, Marilyn Monroe. The Stars came to see the Stars. Ciro's was the entertainment centerpiece of Hollywood nightlife. The gossip columnists thrived on the chatter harvested at the club, and their rumor-mongering spread the fascination of Ciro's far beyond the Strip. During an early visit to Hollywood, Jack Kennedy dined there. And before JFK, President Franklin Delano Roosevelt was not above inquiring about the intrigues at Ciro's.

On a typically difficult White House day in 1940, with Europe in turmoil, the president held his regular cocktail hour, a traditional moment of relaxation at the end of the arduous days. And this particular day would continue beyond cocktails with a major address at Constitution Hall. Among those present for drinks was Helen Gahagan Douglas, an actress, adroit California political operative, avid New Dealer, and wife of actor Melvyn Douglas. She was a White House guest of Eleanor Roosevelt and a friend of the president. Roosevelt had asked her to stay after the cocktail hour because he had an important question for her. While Roosevelt took a phone call from Winston Churchill, just designated the new English prime minister, Douglas reflected on questions she

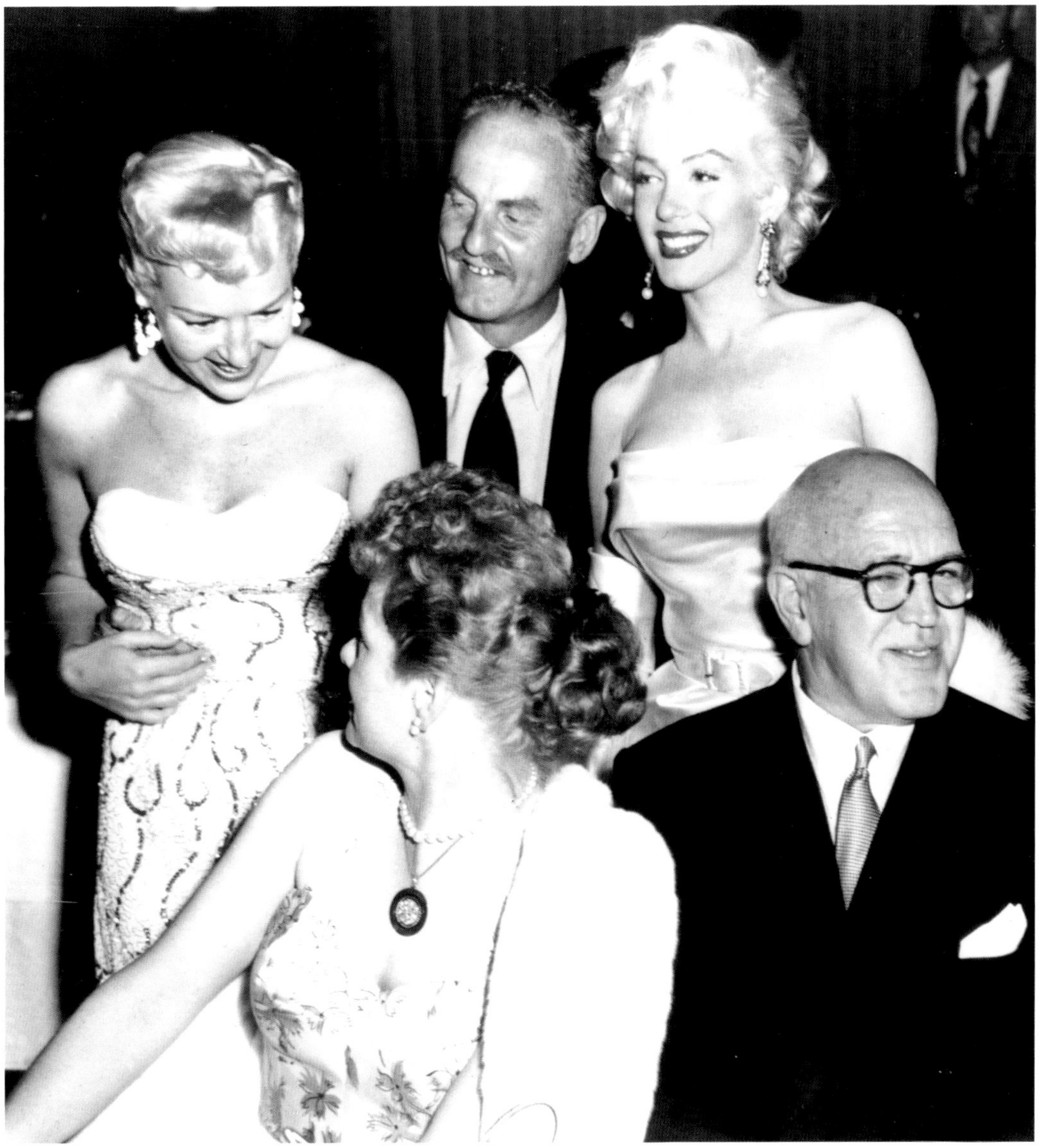

At a party for the film *Let's Make Love* (1960), clockwise from top left, Betty Grable, Darryl F. Zanuck, Marilyn Monroe, Jimmy McHugh, and Lucille Ball. McHugh may be the least familiar name, but in the music business he was legend. Among the most prolific songwriters of the 1920s through the '50s, McHugh penned hits for the likes of Frank Sinatra, Billie Holiday, Judy Garland, and Peggy Lee, among many others.

←
Opposite center, hat-check girl Margaret Barstow in 1951, and clockwise from top left, Marlene Dietrich with Ann Sheridan; Rita Hayworth dances with Kirk Douglas; Jane Powell smiles with Gene Nelson; Nancy and Frank Sinatra celebrate his Oscar-win for his role in the 1953 film *From Here to Eternity*.

a bathing mise-en-scène. Her set director reportedly spent seven thousand dollars on its staging, including a silver bathtub with a provenance (supposedly) dating back to Empress Joséphine of France (no slouch at sexuality herself, Joséphine's ex-husband Napoleon, on his deathbed, reportedly uttered three last words: France, the army, Joséphine). Her first run at Ciro's was a great success, and it is reported that Ronald Reagan and Dean Martin were there for opening night.

During the first night of a return engagement, however, St. Cyr took to the Ciro's stage with her maid, a mink coat, dress, slip, stockings, black lace bra, panties, garter belt, hat, gloves, shoes, and pearl earrings. And a large towel. At some point, behind a towel that the maid held as if it was a matador's cape (and hid the fact that she was still abiding the law and wearing a skimpy brassiere and panties), St. Cyr made her way into the tub where her sleek, glistening legs would rise and fall, etc., all contributing, among other things, to an affirmation, for some, that cleanliness is next to godliness.

The cops witnessed the show, found themselves horrified, appalled, and shocked, and promptly arrested Lili St. Cyr and charged her with "lewdly expos(ing) her body."

Alas, the Los Angeles County prudes were not convinced. The cops witnessed the show, found themselves horrified, appalled, and shocked, and promptly arrested both Hover and St. Cyr. She was charged with "lewdly expos(ing) her body" in an indecent performance (historical revisionism contends Hover arranged for the authorities to raid the club, thus generating a deluge of publicity for Ciro's).

Whatever, the resulting trial became an even larger spectacle. St. Cyr was represented by the famous and exceedingly clever criminal attorney, Jerry Giesler. Before entering the courtroom, St. Cyr defined the defense's strategy by asserting, "I didn't do anything naughty up there. My net bra and my panties covered up all the vital spots."

The courtroom was overrun by scrappy journalists and intrusive photographers. The trial was filled with hilarity and absurdity. At one point, the tubby Hover was told to define and demonstrate the difference between a bump ("a sort of pelvic propulsion") and a grind ("a circular movement of the hips where the feet don't move and the body shouldn't.").

When the time came to actually demonstrate the moves, the humiliated Hover looked at the ten women in the jury box and shyly asked: "Shall I do it in front of these ladies?" The courtroom roared as Hover bumped and ground, though he insisted neither movement was part of St. Cyr's act.

The ultimate ploy of Giesler's was to offer a full performance of the act by St. Cyr, complete with the Josephine tub and water. That was a bridge too far even for the Los Angeles judiciary, but Giesler, playing the maid, had St. Cyr (playing herself, dressed in a gray wool suit over a white blouse) demonstrate her act, particularly getting in and out of the tub.

After six days of media hilarity, the jury retired to make a decision. It returned after an hour and eighteen minutes of presumed deliberation. St. Cyr biographer (*Gilded Lili*) Kelly DiNardo wrote that St. Cyr was "perched on the edge of her chair, twist(ing) a white lace hankie in her hand," waiting for the verdict.

Not guilty, the jury agreed.

"This is a real victory for the profession," St. Cyr declared.

Giesler wanted the record to show that at no time did his defense descend into "buffoonery."

Lili St. Cyr, a true American celebrity who lived through six marriages, seven abortions, numerous arrests, public denunciation and celebration, and a successful lingerie business, died in 1999 in a Hollywood apartment with only her cats at her side. She was eighty.

It was a life that gave definition to one of her core beliefs: Sex is currency. What's the use of being beautiful if you can't profit from it? ■

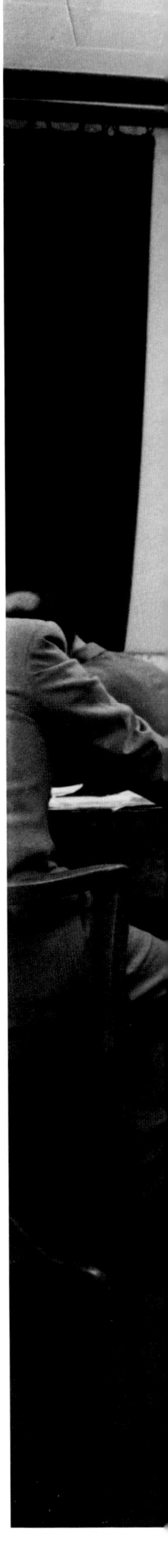

→ With attorney Jerry Giesler playing the role of handmaiden, Lili St. Cyr reveals how she would emerge from a bathtub while staying within the confines of the law. The jury deliberated and quickly concluded that Ms. St. Cyr had not violated the propriety of the City of Angels.

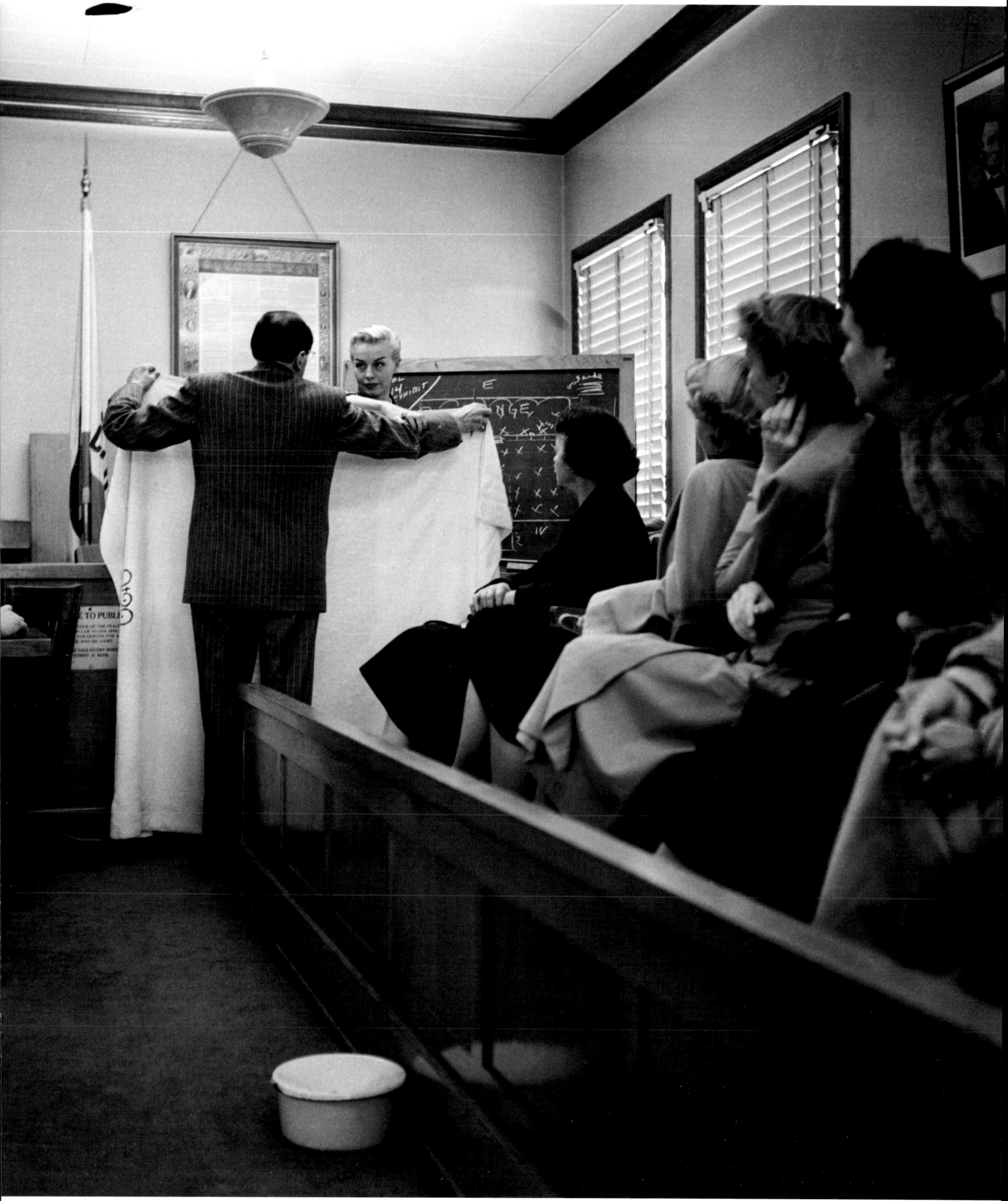

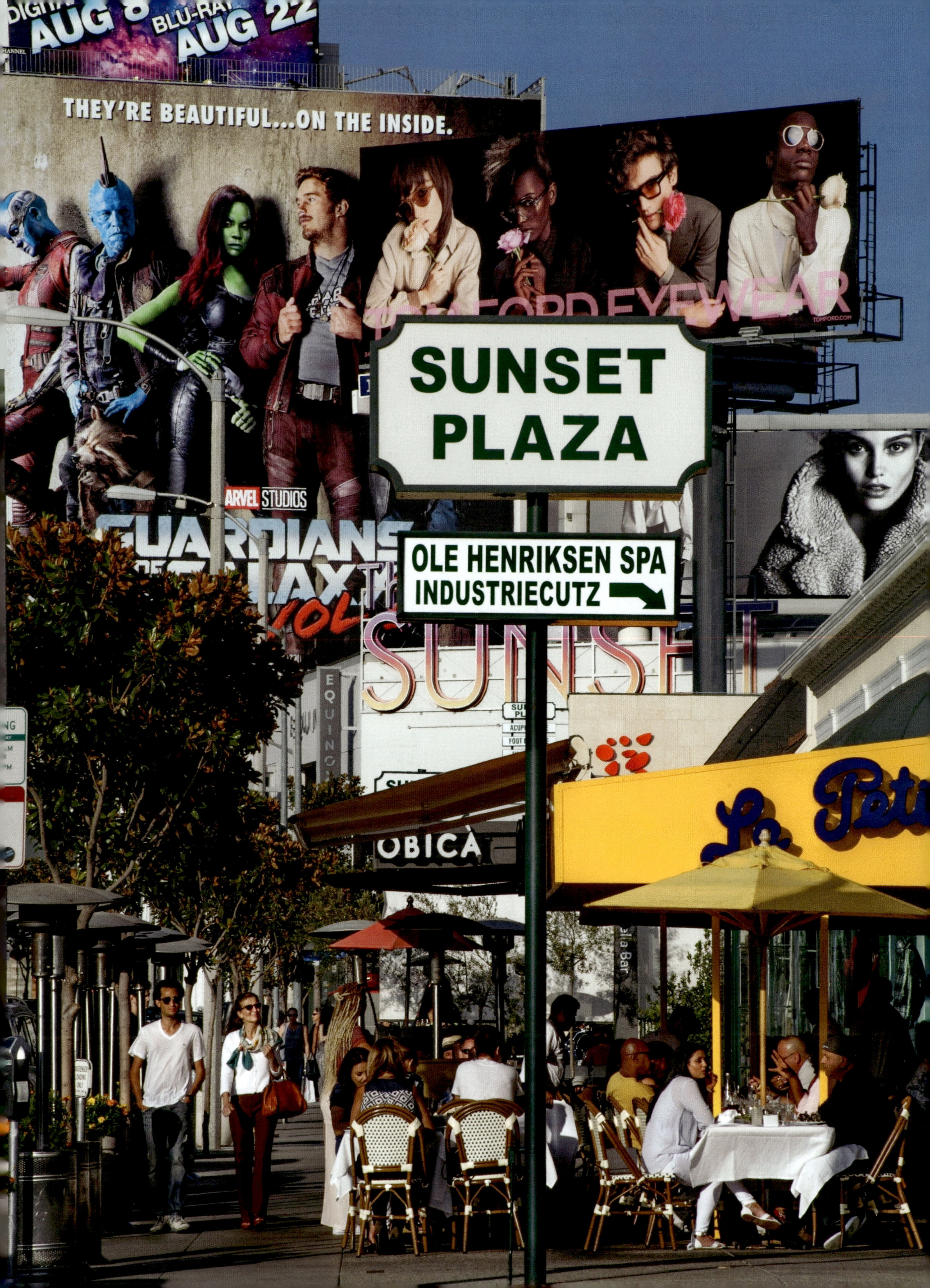
AUG 8
BLU-RAY
AUG 22
THEY'RE BEAUTIFUL...ON THE INSIDE.
TOM FORD EYEWEAR
SUNSET
PLAZA
MARVEL STUDIOS
GUARDIANS
OLE HENRIKSEN SPA
INDUSTRIECUTZ
SUNSET
EQUINOX
OBICA

Sunset Plaza

Decades of Mandated Good Taste

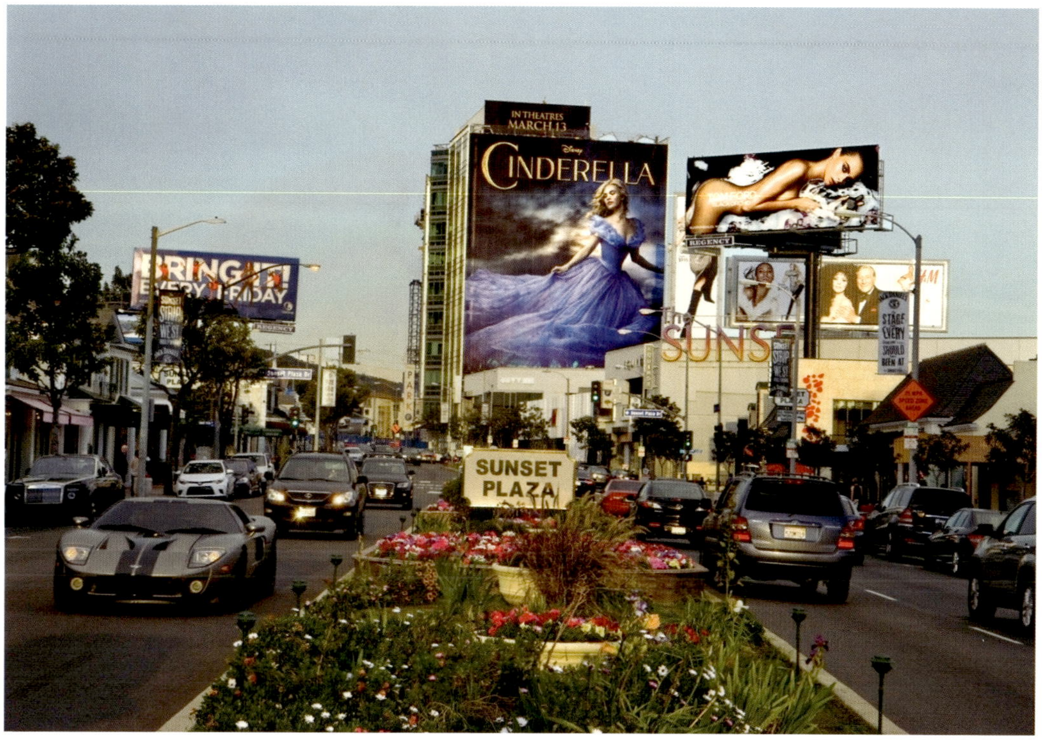

The Montgomery family has for decades made certain that its Sunset Plaza properties have a unity of architecture and that its boutiques have a certain *je ne sais quoi*. Lo be to the shopkeeper who would distract from that vibe, but even landlords can't control the preponderance of advertising that dominates the scape.

Over the decades, there has been a steady churn in the function and form of the architecture and enterprises along the Sunset Strip. If obligated to provide a descriptive term for the style, "casually spontaneous" might come to mind.

But a highly defined section along the Strip, known as Sunset Plaza, has from the beginning manifested a kind of comfortable and dignified character. The buildings are understated, handsome white structures, generally of one story, with fine stores and quality food. It is a startling departure from other segments of the Strip that seem to enthusiastically embrace the tatty.

The uniqueness of the Plaza can trace its beginning to 1892 when Belgian immigrant Victor Ponet, a successful merchant and real estate investor, purchased more than two hundred acres within the original Rancho La Brea land grant. The property embraced a section of what is now the Strip, an area known then for its avocado orchards and poinsettia fields. When Sunset Boulevard west of Los Angeles was graded to provide a more tolerable automotive experience, homes began appearing in the hills. Ponet built his gracious home around the southeast corner of Sunset and Sunset Plaza Drive. He also donated the land and money for the creation of St. Victor Catholic Church, just off the strip at 8634 Holloway Street. It was rebuilt in 1960 and is renowned for its highly creative communicants, the sophistication of its music, and a schedule of Latin masses.

After Ponet's death in 1914, his son-in-law Francis Montgomery created a commercial area on the property along Sunset. The first establishment opened its doors in 1920, and today the Plaza is a kind of gracious open-air mall, with highly personalized stores and restaurants.

When the Montgomery family wanted a shade of white for their structures, a painter spread four different shades on a wall for consideration. The family selected their favorite, which, unknown to them at the time, was known in the paint business as Montgomery White. The Montgomery family has stayed with it. And history.

←
Sunset Plaza in the twenty-first century. Towering signs and billboards speak to an advertising-driven culture, a sharp contrast to Sunset Plaza of yore.

Overleaf →
With clouds ascending in the north, a Sunset Plaza shopper retreats to her Cadillac in 1940, ready to leave the driving to her chauffeur.

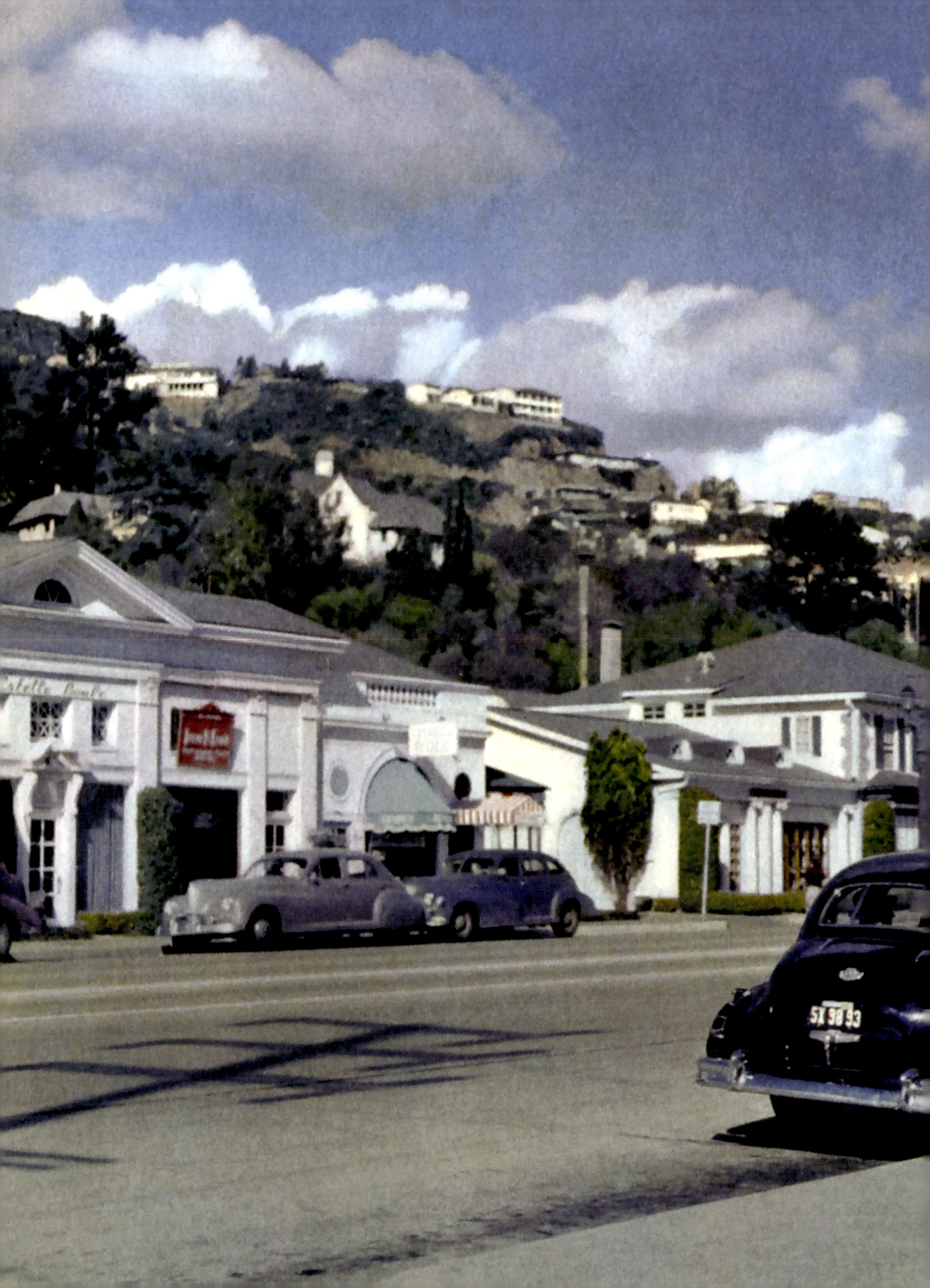
5X 98 93

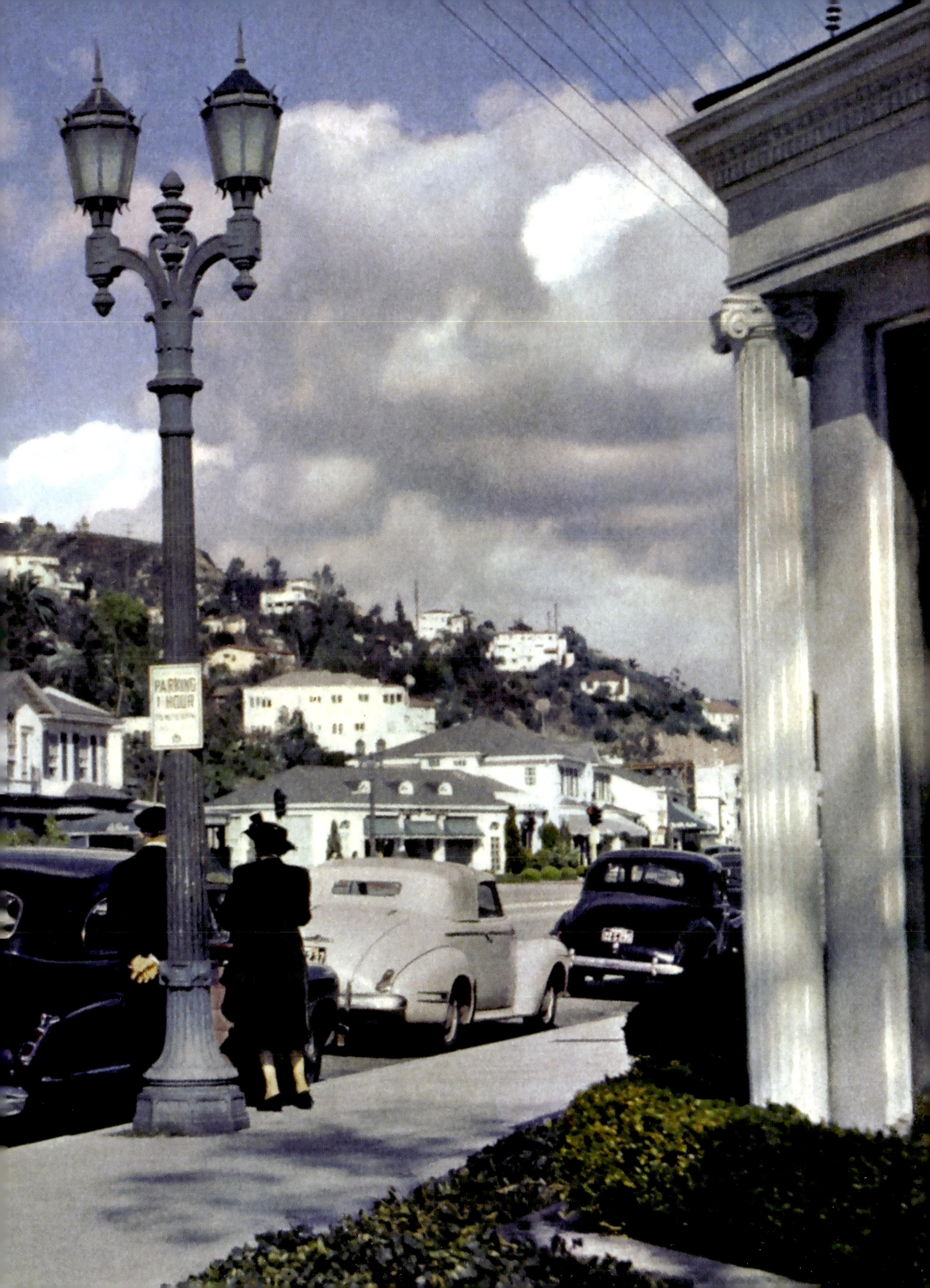
PARKING
1 HOUR

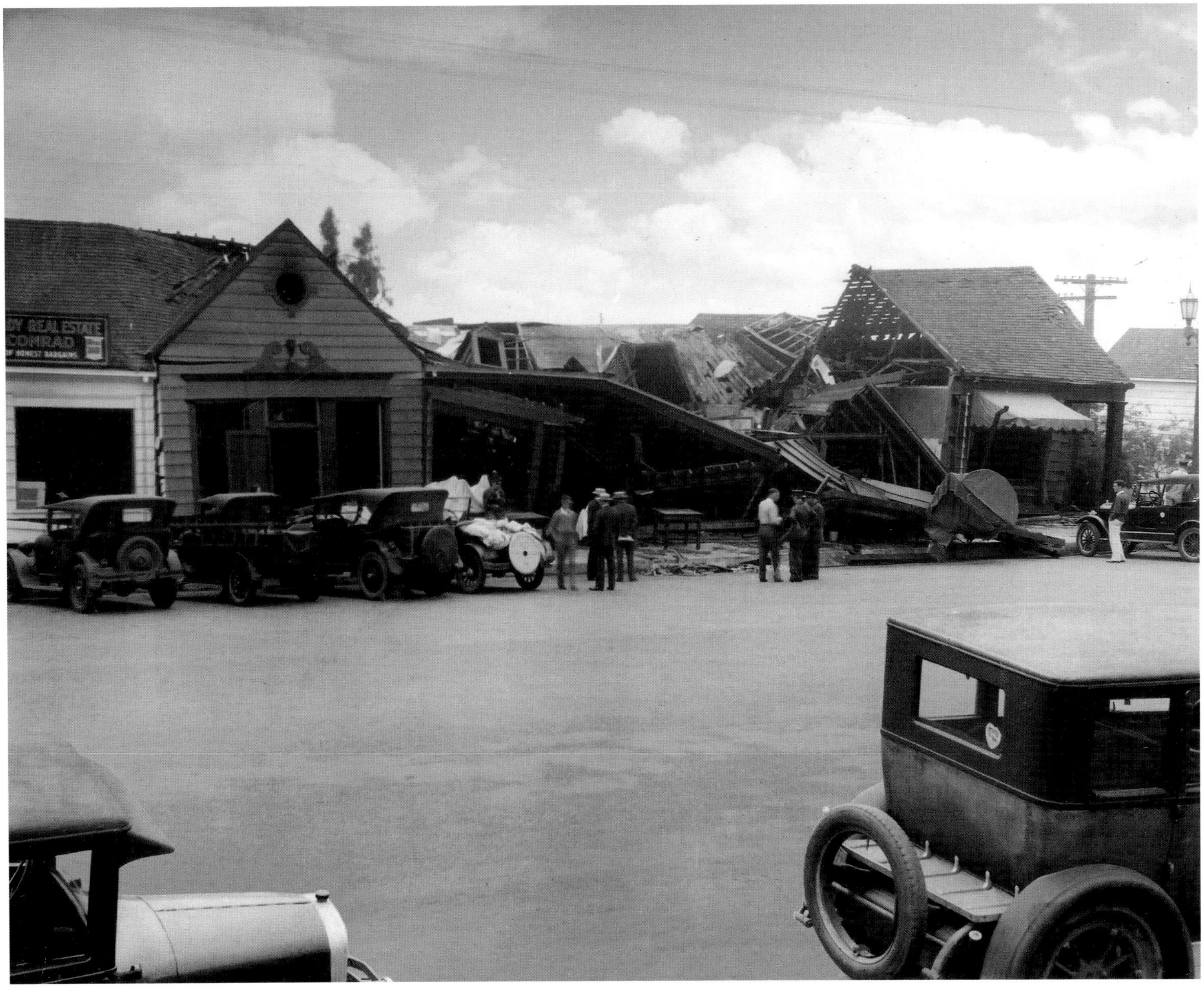

The rubble of the Russian Eagle Cafe, June 1928, drew gawkers fascinated by a blast that could have killed patrons, among them boxer Jack Dempsey and actor Charlie Chaplin. Dempsey claimed he saw smoke and, just before the blast, led the evacuation. Chaplin tried fighting the flames with a garden hose. Authorities believed it was an insurance scam gone wrong. Others attributed the blaze to a disagreement between the owners or a conspiracy between Russian cabals still fighting the revolution.

In the early days, the Plaza housed the urbane Trocadero, but also some less sophisticated places, including a speakeasy known as the Russian Eagle Café. The Russian what? Many Russian émigrés had settled in Los Angeles after the Russian Revolution. And the Russian Eagle Café, owned by—who else?—some Russians, attracted celebrities. On June 8, 1928, a massive blast shattered the café, sending customers boxer Jack Dempsey, his wife, actor Charles Chaplin, and actor Richard Dix, among others, scrambling through the debris, desperate for the exits. The building was devastated. People have attributed the blast to the café owners feuding over a woman, or a neighboring store owner bungling a kind of "Marvin the Torch" insurance ploy.

But the Montgomery family, who still manage the Plaza, say there was intrigue and hatred afoot between political factions from Mother Russia. The blast was set off by some local Trotskyites who wanted to send a message in a more emphatic form than a Western Union telegram.

The family doesn't discuss how many stores or restaurants line their Plaza, but on a recent drive along the Strip, one interested party counted more than thirty-five establishments, including at least five restaurants.

But in all the graciousness and comfort, there are times when one misses the quiet intrigue of the old Russian Eagle Café. ■

→
Ethel Schultheis leaves the stylish Sunset Plaza store Fashionette Inc. in 1937. Her husband, Herman Schultheis, who took the photo, was a highly educated German immigrant who worked in the motion picture business. An avid photographer, who traveled the world with his camera, Herman vanished in 1955 while on expedition in a Guatemalan jungle. His remains were discovered eighteen months later.

Overleaf →
A dashing and well-turned-out Clark Gable exits his stylish 1948 Lincoln convertible to visit his agent's office in the Sunset Plaza.

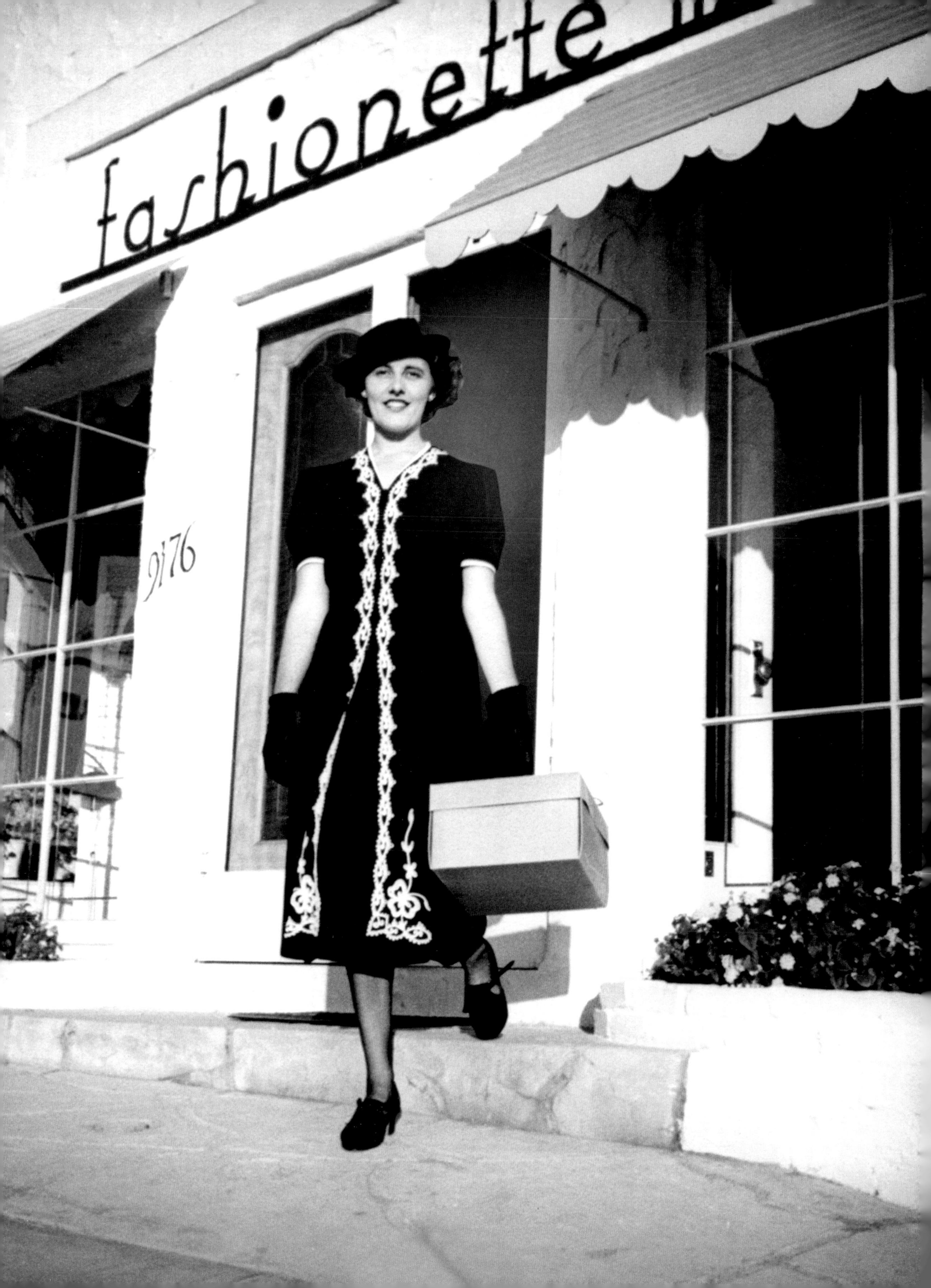
fashionette
9176

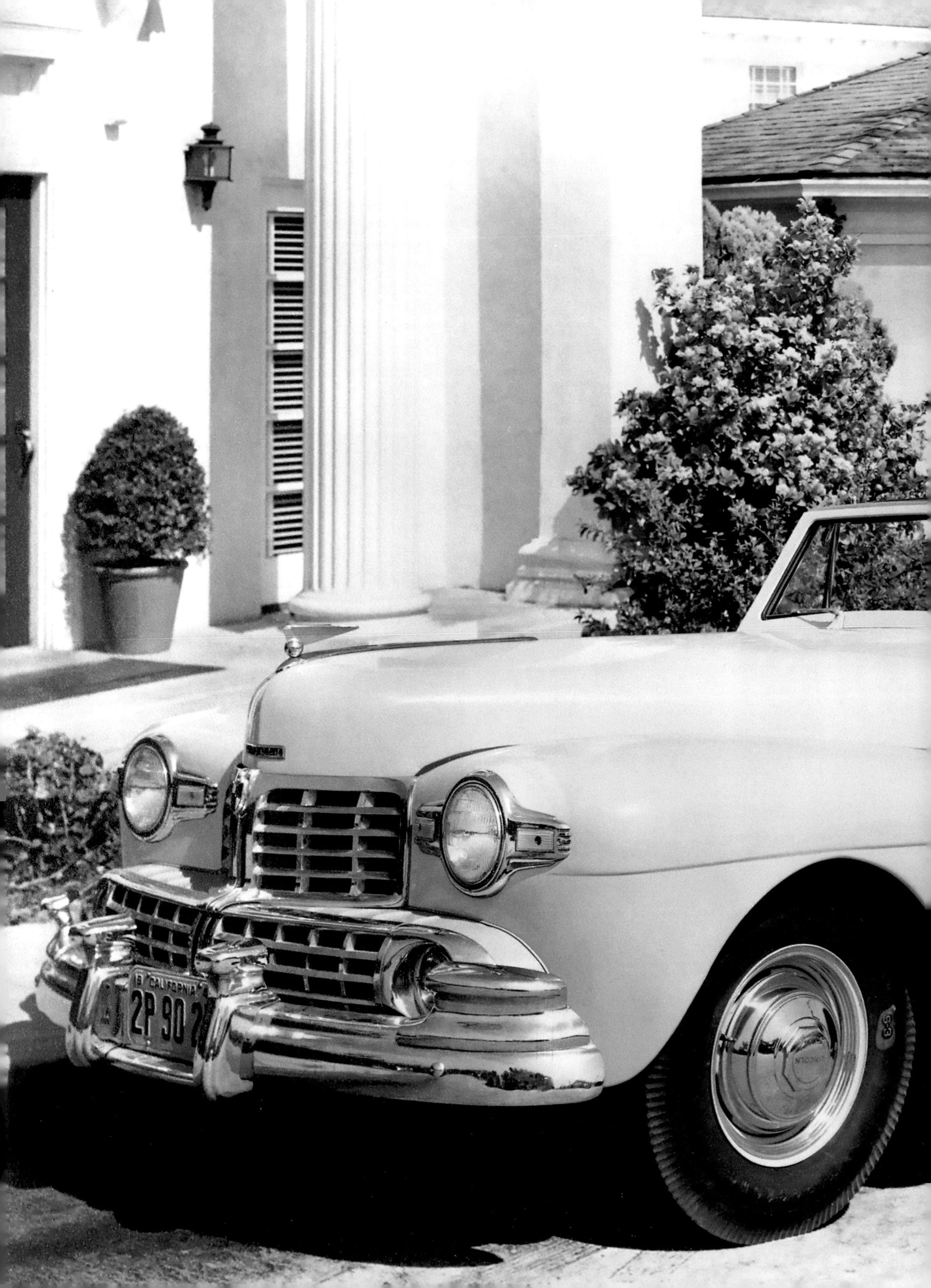
CALIFORNIA
2P 90

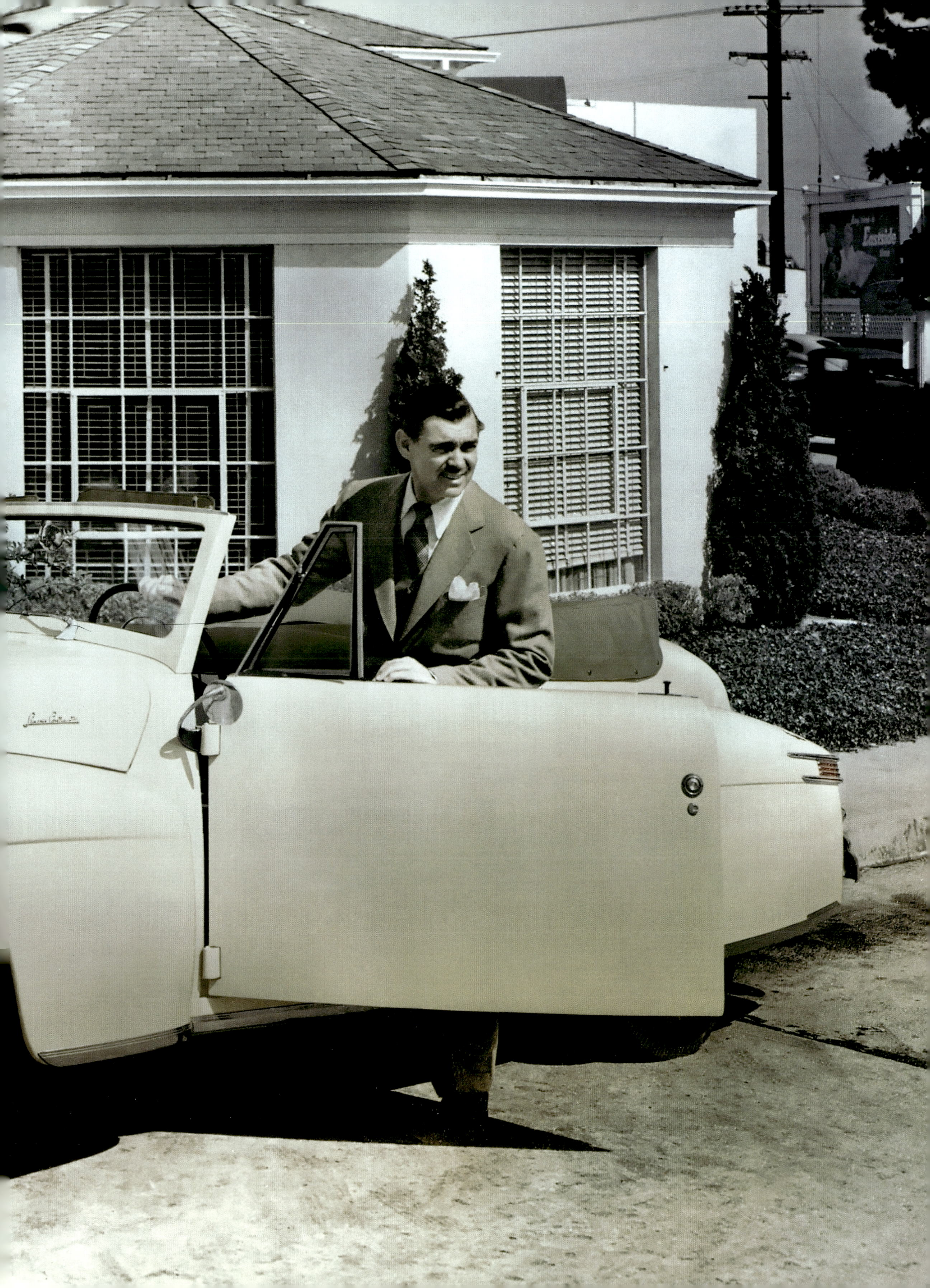

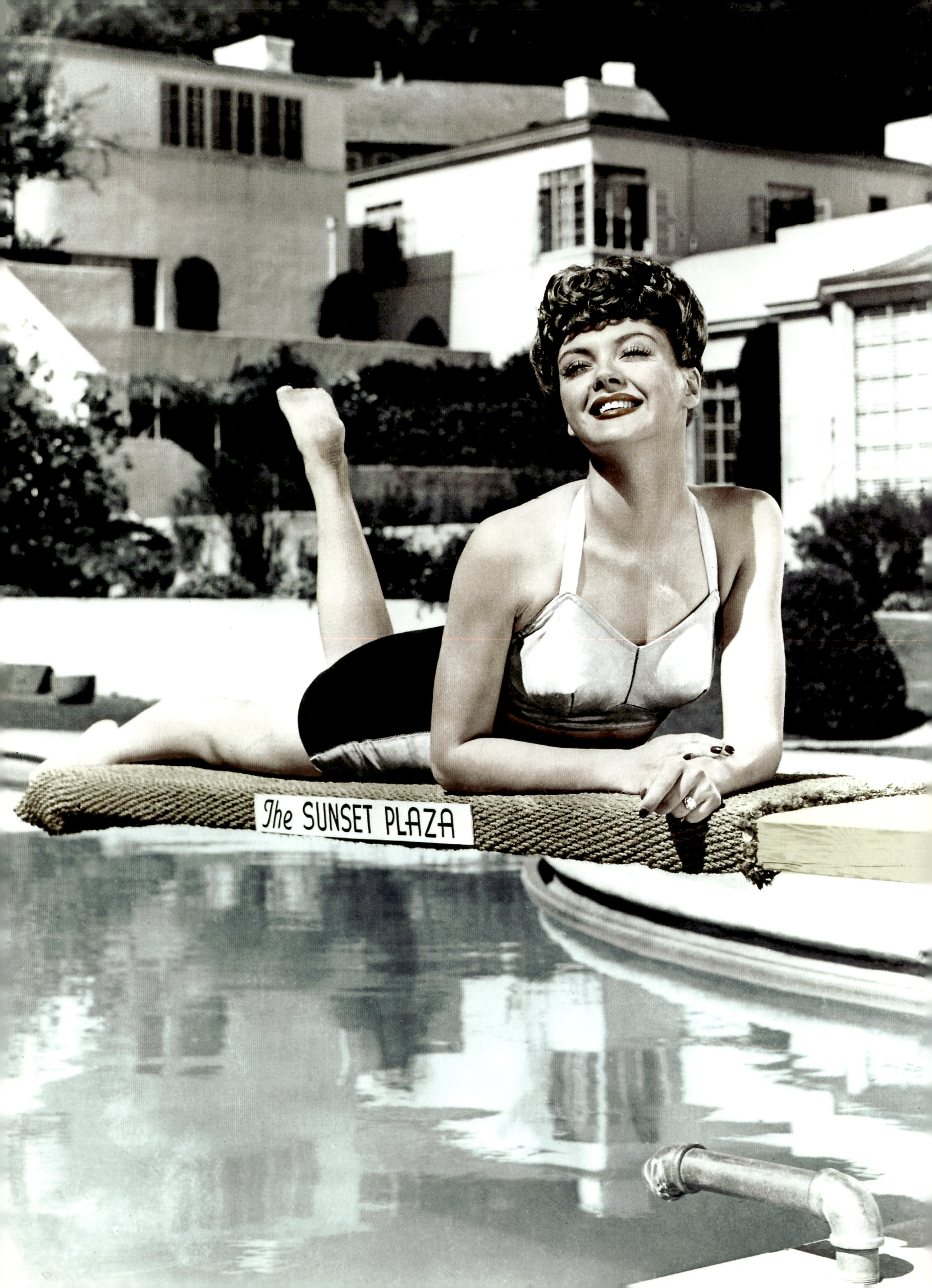
The SUNSET PLAZA

The Sunset Plaza Apartments

An Architectural Beauty and Site of Fisticuffs

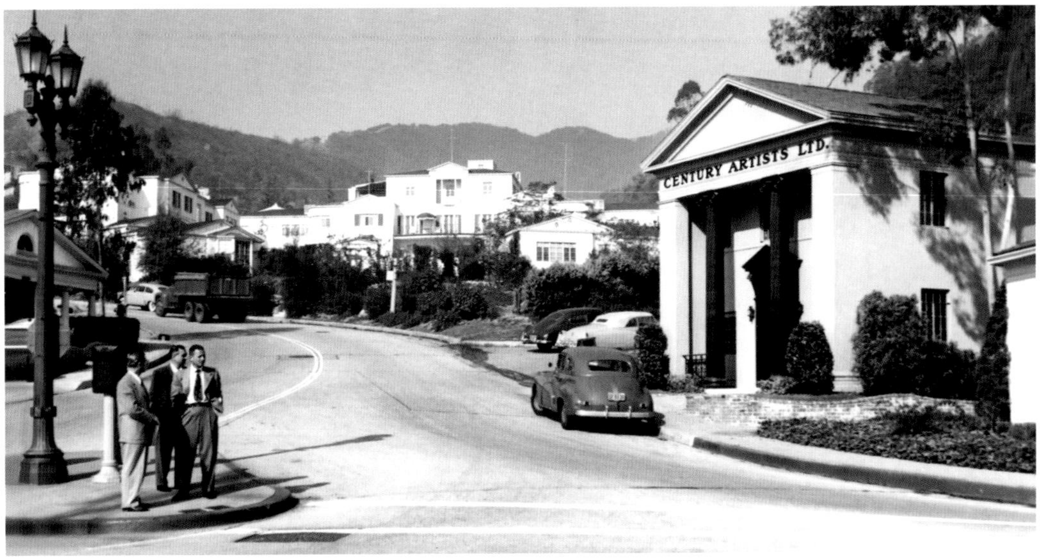

Sunset Plaza Drive as seen in 1951 looking north from the Sunset Strip. The Sunset Plaza Apartments are in the center.

Real estate in Los Angeles dotes on provenance, which in some cases has surprising economic, social, and cultural ramifications.

For several years, I lived just above the Sunset Strip in a home that was once the residence of a celebrated studio mogul. His lavish screening room had become my topsy-turvy office, with generally open French doors overlooking the adjacent property of workout paladin Richard Simmons (whose acute hearing could detect within seventy-five yards the opening of a beer can or a bag of chips, which invariably provoked a fervent but ineffectual plea that I begin treating my body with respect and justice). To cover the 0.4-mile curvy street from the Sunset Plaza area of the Strip up to my house, I passed a large, handsome apartment structure with certifiable provenance and lofty architectural regard. Now gone. Vanished. A building beloved by preservationists and fans of Hollywood history. But nonetheless, gone.

In the 1930s, a highly regarded photographer and entrepreneur named Frank S. Hoover hired the African American architects Paul Williams and L.G. Scherer to design the Sunset Plaza Apartments.

The Sunset Plaza Apartments, a sprawling, Georgian Revival apartment complex was designed by one of America's most celebrated architects. It was leveled to make way for a single family home. Yes, a single family home. This illustrates another rule of Los Angeles real estate: provenance has little to do with, and is in no way a guarantor of, permanence. In the 1930s, a highly regarded photographer and entrepreneur named Frank S. Hoover hired the architects Paul Williams and L.G. Scherer to design the Sunset Plaza Apartments on a site immediately north of the turn from the Sunset Strip onto Sunset Plaza. Over his career lifetime, Williams, an African American, became a formidable figure in L.A. architecture, designing homes for the likes of Frank Sinatra and Lucille Ball, and adding his touch to Al Jolson's tomb, the Polo Lounge of the Beverly Hills Hotel, the Tennis Club in Palm Springs, and other important buildings. Of course, Williams is always credited with designing the iconic Theme Building at LAX, which looks more like it was designed for a scene in *E.T.*, than an international airport. Whether he actually did (he didn't), is always a subject of debate, but he was certainly at the right place (working on the overall airport design, that is), at the right time. His reputation has outlived him, and it would seem that any building attributed to the drawing board of Paul Williams would be preserved. But no.

← Actress Leslie Brooks takes to the diving board, and, in an awkward pose, gives the photographer an enthusiastic smile while her left foot points up to some of the units in the Sunset Plaza Apartments. She made several movies, winning some acclaim for a femme fatale role in one of them, but basically retired after seven years and focused on raising four daughters.

Overleaf → James Dean cranes his neck as he backs into his driveway from Sunset Plaza Drive. Having recently relocated to Los Angeles for the filming of *Rebel Without a Cause* (1955), Dean drew the ire of movie execs when he informed them that he was far more interested in racing cars than in acting.

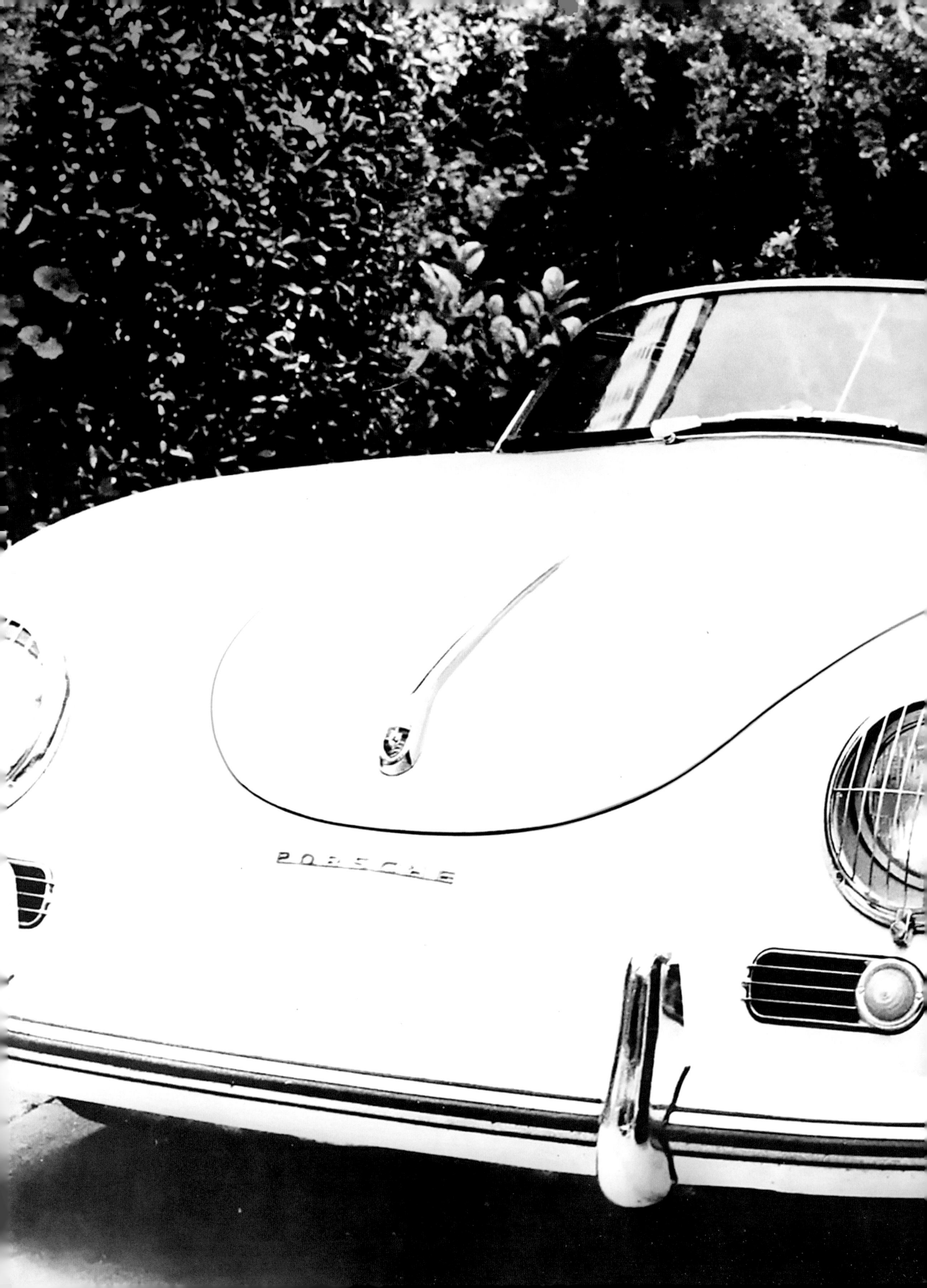
PORSCHE

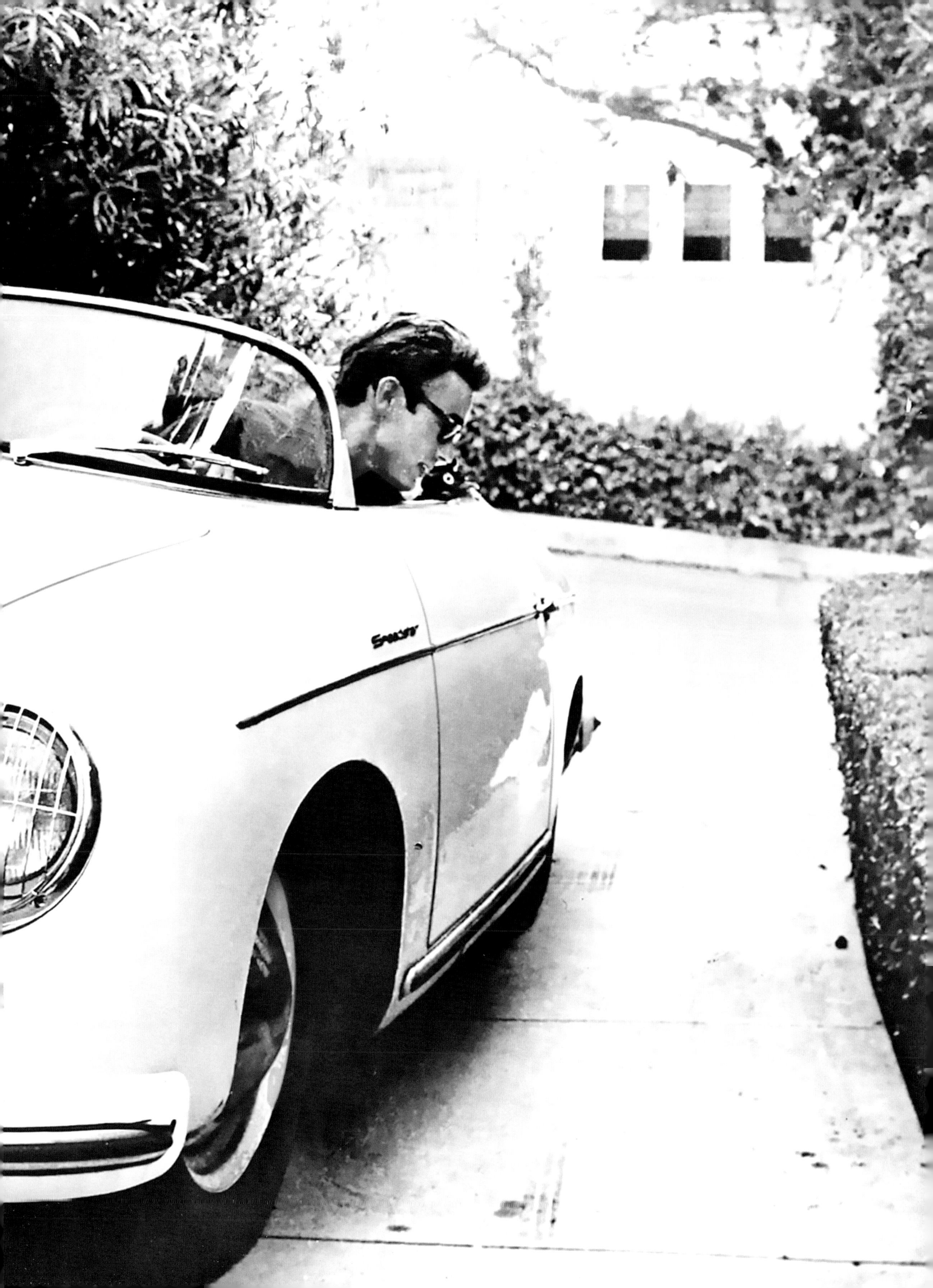

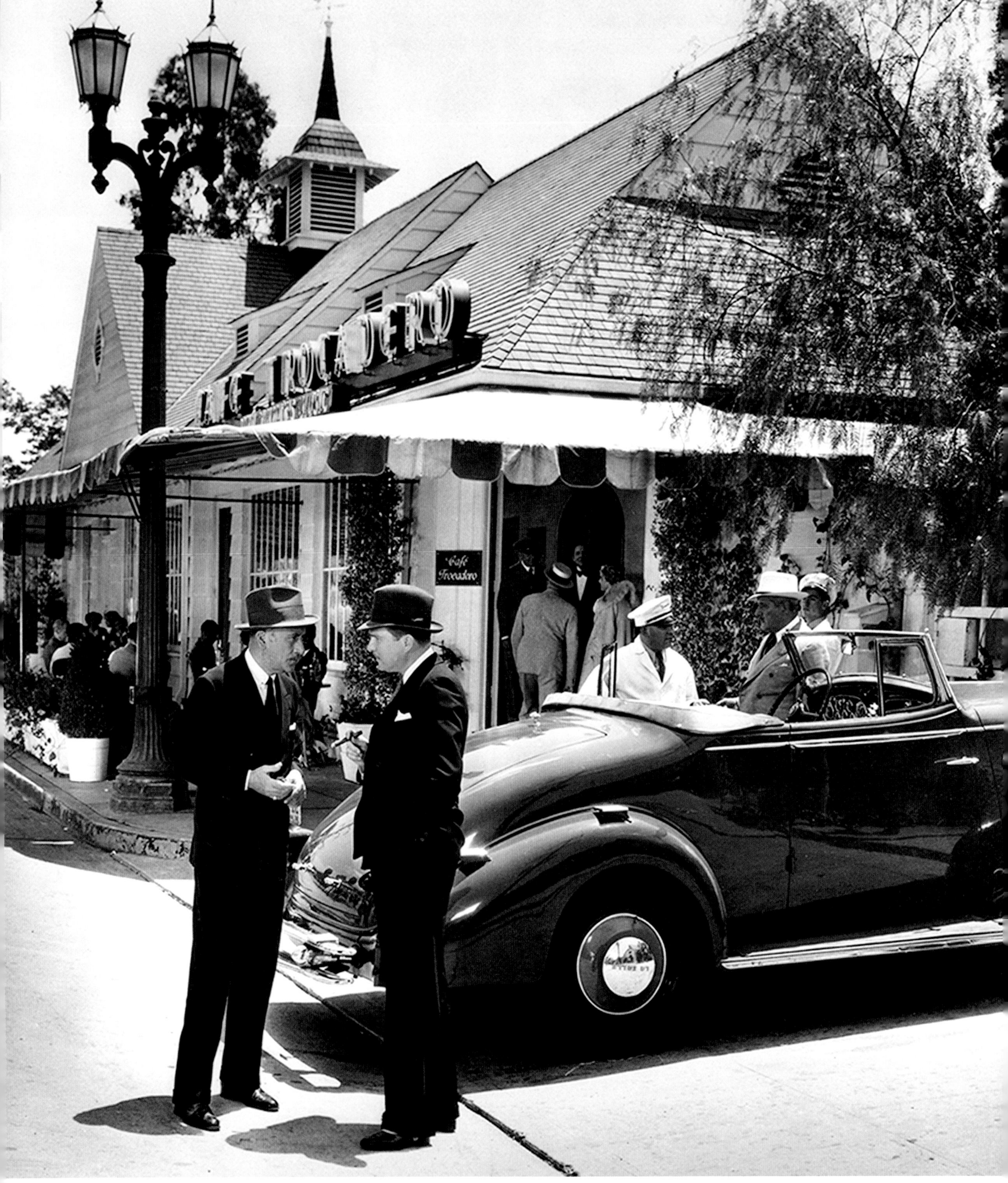
TROCADERO

• 1890 – 1962 •

Billy Wilkerson

Journalist, Impresario, and Vegas Visionary

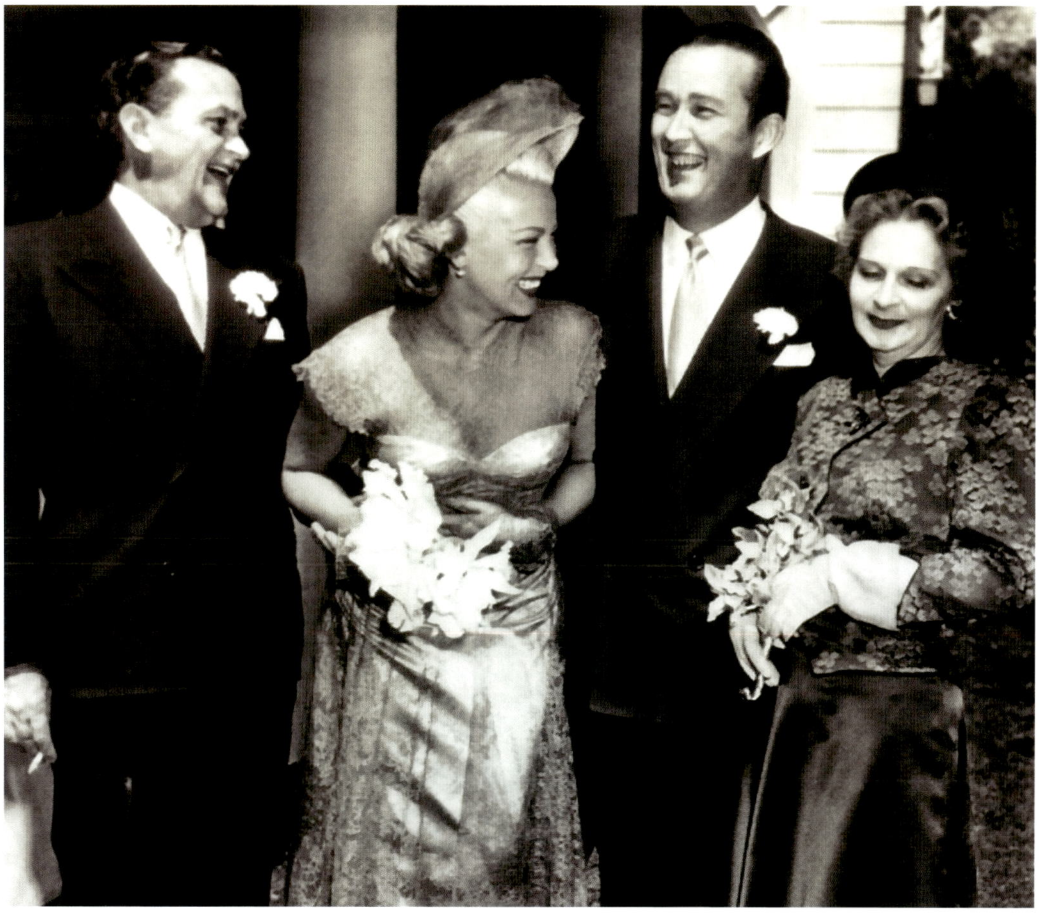

In 1948, when Lana Turner (second from left) married Henry J. "Bob" Topping (second from right), W.R. "Billy" Wilkerson (far left) was host and best man, and writer Sarah Hamilton was matron of honor. Wilkerson was the founder and publisher of the *Hollywood Reporter*. At the time, *Life Magazine* described him as an expert on marriage, having been wed five times. Over her lifetime, Turner was married eight times to seven different husbands. Topping is distinguished by his unique proposal to Turner: he dropped a diamond ring into her martini. The marriage lasted less than five years.

Fusty prudes might object to naming a school after Billy Wilkerson, but he's certainly got a legacy with the City of West Hollywood, and more precisely the Sunset Strip. Should there at least be a street near the Strip named after Wilkerson? For sure.

Wilkerson was a kid from Nashville with sharp elbows and a rough-and-tumble sense of entrepreneurship. He came to California and pioneered celebrity journalism, envisioned the future of Las Vegas before most mobsters could pinpoint Nevada on a map, and operated a couple of world-famous nightclubs on the Sunset Strip. At almost any given moment Wilkerson was on the verge of losing it all for an addiction to dice and cards. He never left home without them.

← Back in the day when suits actually wore suits, Café Trocadero on the Sunset Strip at Sunset Plaza Drive, was a popular bar and restaurant for business meetings. These two men, actors John Halliday and Creighton Hale, were suited up for their roles in the 1936 movie, *Hollywood Boulevard.* The men were actually standing on the Sunset Strip, while the nifty convertible was in a driveway that now leads down to a parking lot,with an astonishing 180-degree view of the metropolis, behind restaurants and other businesses in the Plaza.

Contrary to all other versions of the story, he discovered Judy Turner one day in 1937 at a soda fountain near his newspaper office on Sunset Boulevard. He was sipping one of his ten to fifteen daily Cokes when Judy, later renamed Lana, strolled in for a break from classes at nearby Hollywood High. The rest of the story turns into the stuff of Hollywood legend.

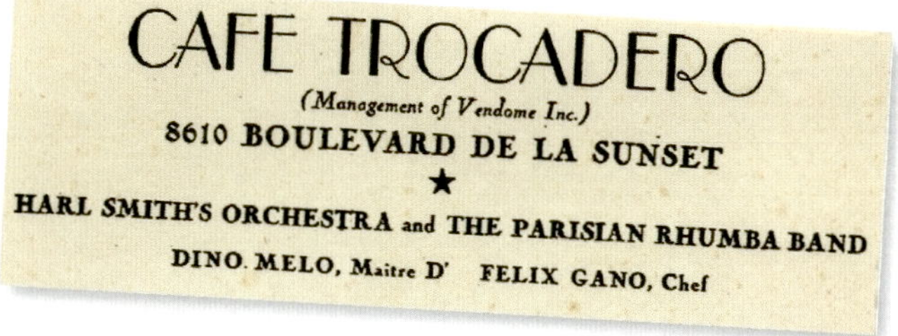

CAFE TROCADERO

(Management of Vendome Inc.)

8610 BOULEVARD DE LA SUNSET

★

HARL SMITH'S ORCHESTRA and THE PARISIAN RHUMBA BAND

DINO MELO, Maitre D' FELIX GANO, Chef

Wilkerson's father was a Tennessee gambler who, according to the *Los Angeles Times*, won the bottling rights for Coca-Cola in thirteen states. Shortly thereafter, he traded that business for an unremarkable theater, which he turned around and sold for four thousand dollars. Bad deal. There probably aren't enough digits to calculate the value of those bottling rights today.

→ Marilyn Monroe presents Billy Wilkerson, the journalist and entrepreneur, with an award for his show business newspaper, the *Hollywood Reporter*. First published in 1930, the *Reporter* survived into the twenty-first century as a digital and print journal covering all aspects of the entertainment industry.

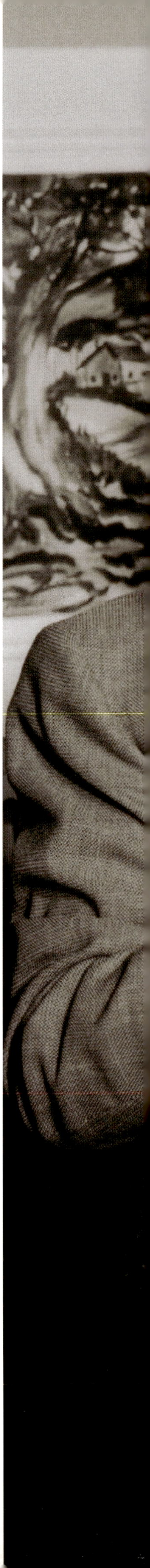

Wilkerson, who had a keener business sense than his father, hacked around New York City for a while before concluding he might draw more face cards in California. He did, but the faces weren't Kings, Queens, and Jacks, they were Hollywood royalty. In 1930 he launched the *Hollywood Reporter*, the legendary show business journal that featured famous names making deals or out on the town. He opened or ran a number of nightclubs on the Sunset Strip, most famously Trocadero (1934) and Ciro's (1940). It was Wilkerson's doing that those clubs became known to most Americans as lavish settings for the lustrous people, the Stars and the moguls who created them.

More problematic were Wilkerson's efforts to build the legendary Flamingo casino and resort on what soon became the Strip in Las Vegas. He correctly anticipated a huge postwar demand for luxurious Vegas casinos that would transcend the existing, banal-themed casinos, such as the faux cowboy joints freighted with hee-hawing "howdy partner" greetings.

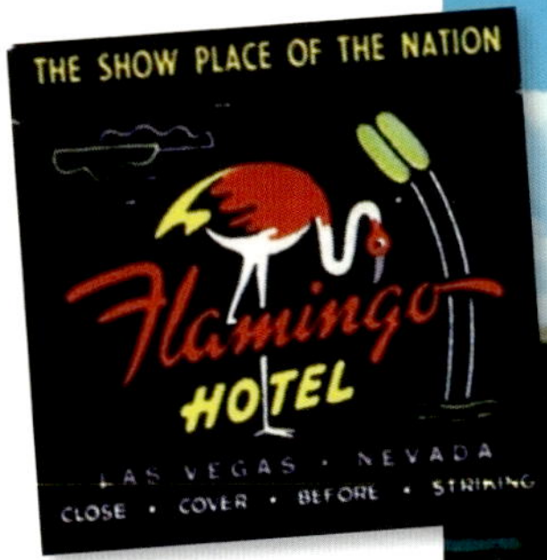

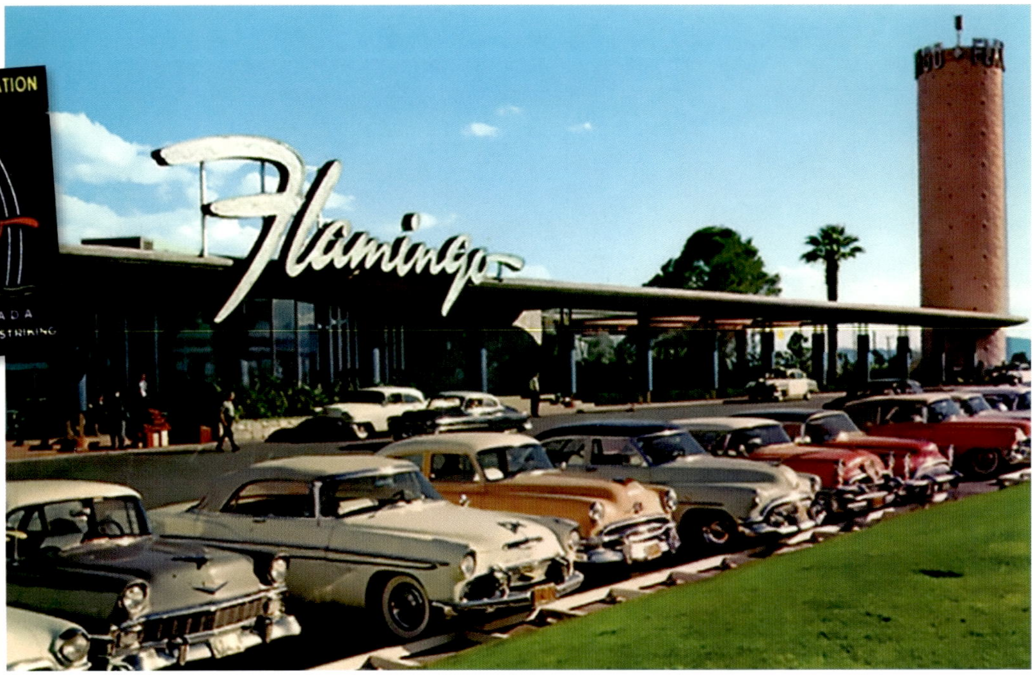

A mid-century matchbook and postcard from the early years of the Flamingo Hotel, now the oldest resort in Las Vegas. Its architecture is art deco and Streamline Moderne, an oasis in a sea of faux.

The suave Wilkerson wanted a place with Sunset Strip class and industrial-grade air conditioning. Materials costs were soaring in America's building boom, and Wilkerson was running into a critical financial shortfall. As the story goes, some private (and anonymous) investors volunteered through an intermediary to help the financially strapped Wilkerson with the costs to complete his project. He accepted without asking some key questions.

Billy Wilkerson's lawyer recalled Bugsy's message as: "I can only tell you if I don't deliver (most of your shares) to the people in the East, I'm gonna be killed. And before I go, you're gonna go first. And don't take that lightly. I'll kill ya if I don't get (it)."

Soon Bugsy Siegel infested Wilkerson's life. The psychotic hoodlum, who boasted of having killed twelve men, identified himself as the representative of those silent investors, individuals well-known to tabloid readers as the dreaded royals of American crime.

Siegel ruthlessly began muscling Wilkerson toward the door, whittling down his ownership share at every step. Wilkerson balked. But Siegel finally suggested that it would be unhealthy for Wilkerson to reject a significant reduction in his shareholder position. Actually, "suggested" doesn't capture the tenor of Siegel's pitch. Wilkerson's lawyer recalled Siegel's message as: "I can only tell you if I don't deliver [most of your shares] to the people in the East, I'm gonna be killed. And before I go, you're gonna go first. And don't take that lightly. I'll kill ya if I don't get [it]."

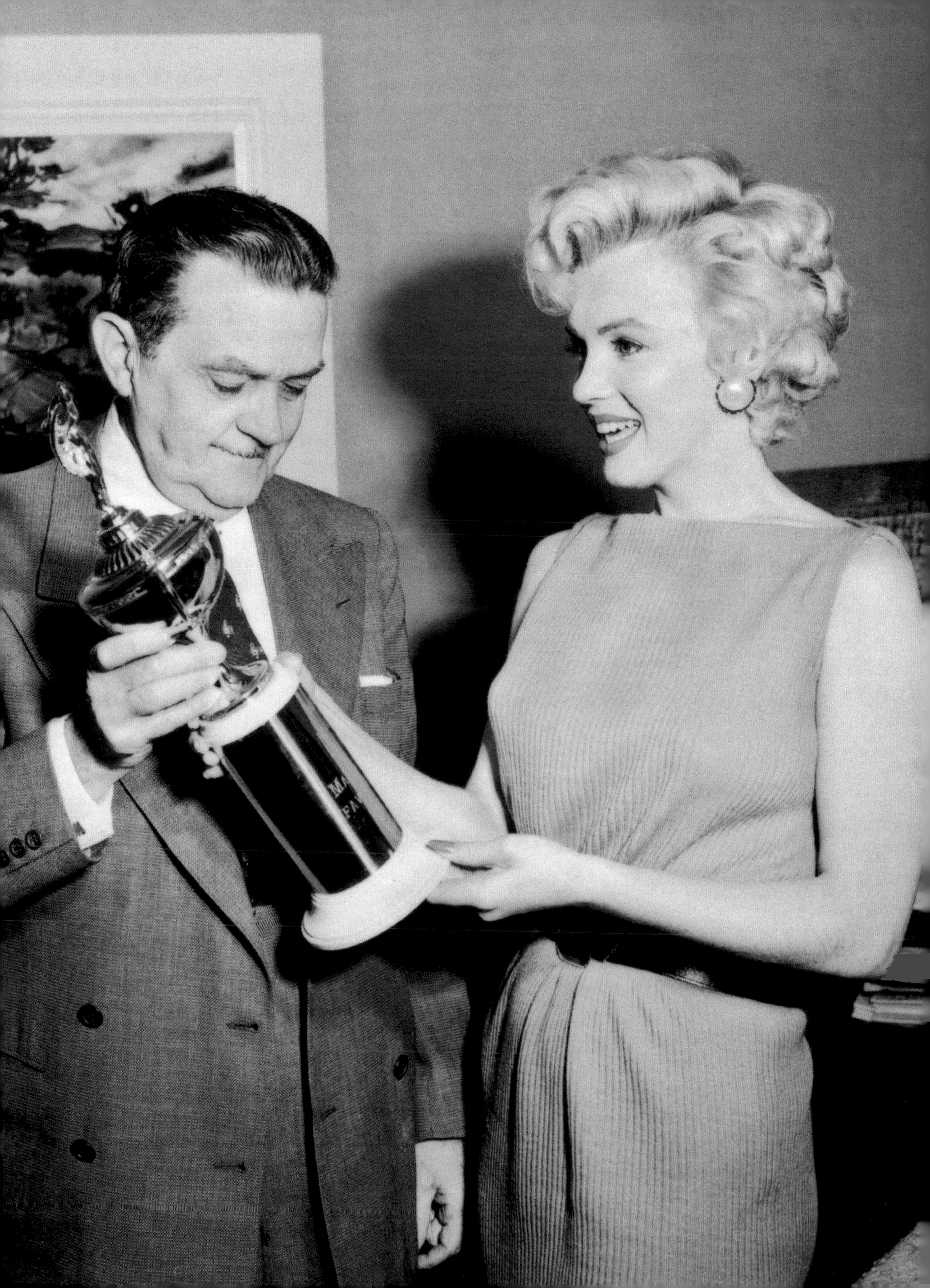

Wilkerson got the "unhealthy" message and promptly departed Vegas for New York and caught the SS *Ile de France* ocean liner, made his way to Paris and quarters at the posh Hotel George V (under an assumed name). Eventually, still under a death threat, Wilkerson capitulated to the mob and ultimately sold his remaining shares in the Flamingo for a pittance. Bugsy ultimately got even less. In 1947 his takeaway from the casino, predicated by his ill-advised chicanery in fleecing the mobsters, was nine rounds fired at him by an assassin with a carbine, all courtesy of those anonymous partners back East.

Wilkerson was at a café near his hotel, or, depending upon which report you believe, on a party boat on the Seine, when he learned that Siegel had been cashiered out of the mob. Wilkerson was soon back in Los Angeles, the ultimate bon vivant on a street with no shortage of them.

His Trocadero, on the south side of the Strip at Sunset Plaza, was a fabulous success. The stars treasured the Troc, with its Parisian motif, lavish ambiance, and Wilkerson's unfailing hospitality.

His Trocadero, on the south side of the Strip at Sunset Plaza, was a fabulous success. The stars treasured the Troc, with its Parisian motif, lavish ambiance, and Wilkerson's unfailing hospitality. Hollywood historian Martin Turnbull reports that when the stars sought even greater privacy, Wilkerson promptly created a downstairs bar called Little Troc on Sunset. Photographers and reporters were barred. Strict privacy was accorded the Saturday night high-stakes card games. Sam Goldwyn, Darryl Zanuck, Irving Thalberg, and Carl Laemmle were among the players. The likes of the quartet makes believable the Hollywood lore that a major Star was traded from one studio to another to settle an onerous poker debt piled up at the Troc.

Wilkerson was a true prince of the Sunset Strip, but his lasting legacy is the *Hollywood Reporter*. And his Troc and Ciro's remain in memory as glittering symbols of privilege and indulgence and luxury, emblematic of Wilkerson's panache and his remarkable instincts about Hollywood aristocracy and their need for a Sunset Strip. ■

Billy Wilkerson at the keyboard of a *Hollywood Reporter* linotype machine in 1936, a kind of primitive word processor that actually created and set type used by printing presses.

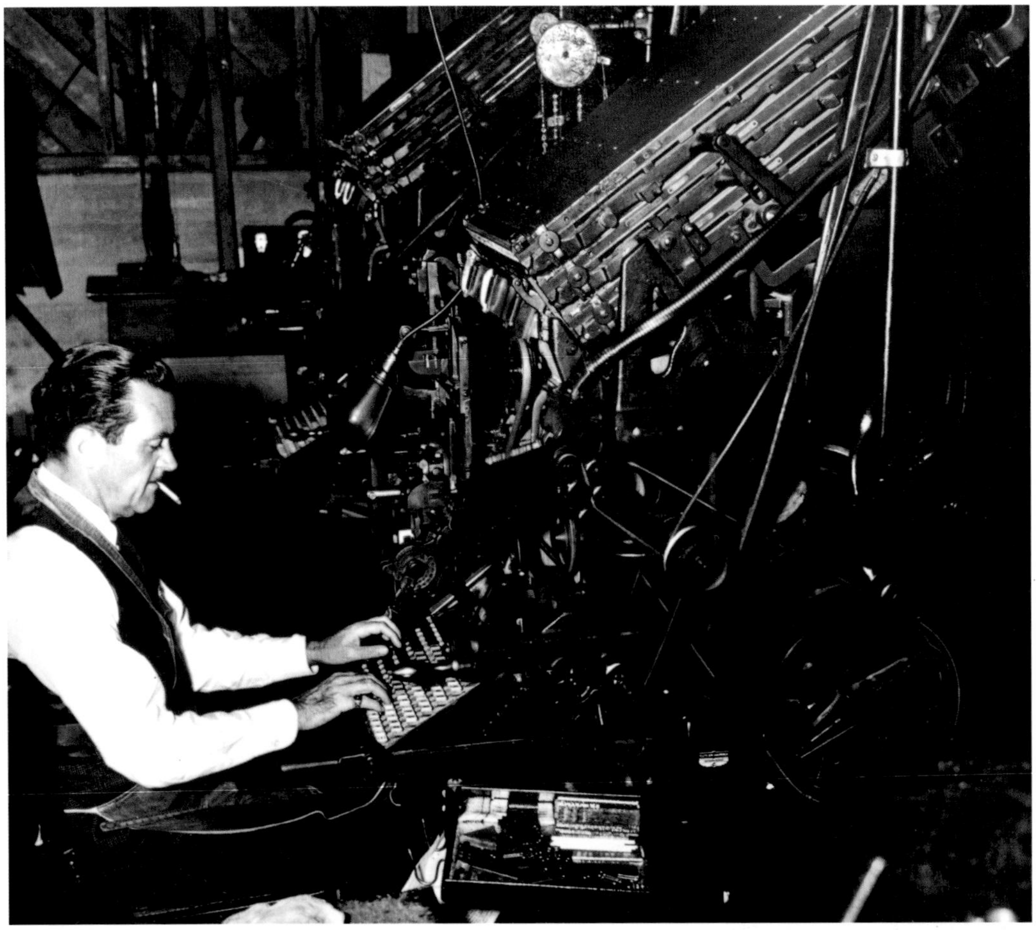

→ Schwab's Pharmacy on the Sunset Strip was frequented by actors and film workers who rarely missed an edition of the *Hollywood Reporter.* Director Edward Dmytryk was reading an edition from 1945, featuring a front-page headline about Herbert K. Sorrell, an influential labor union organizer and leader in the film industry.

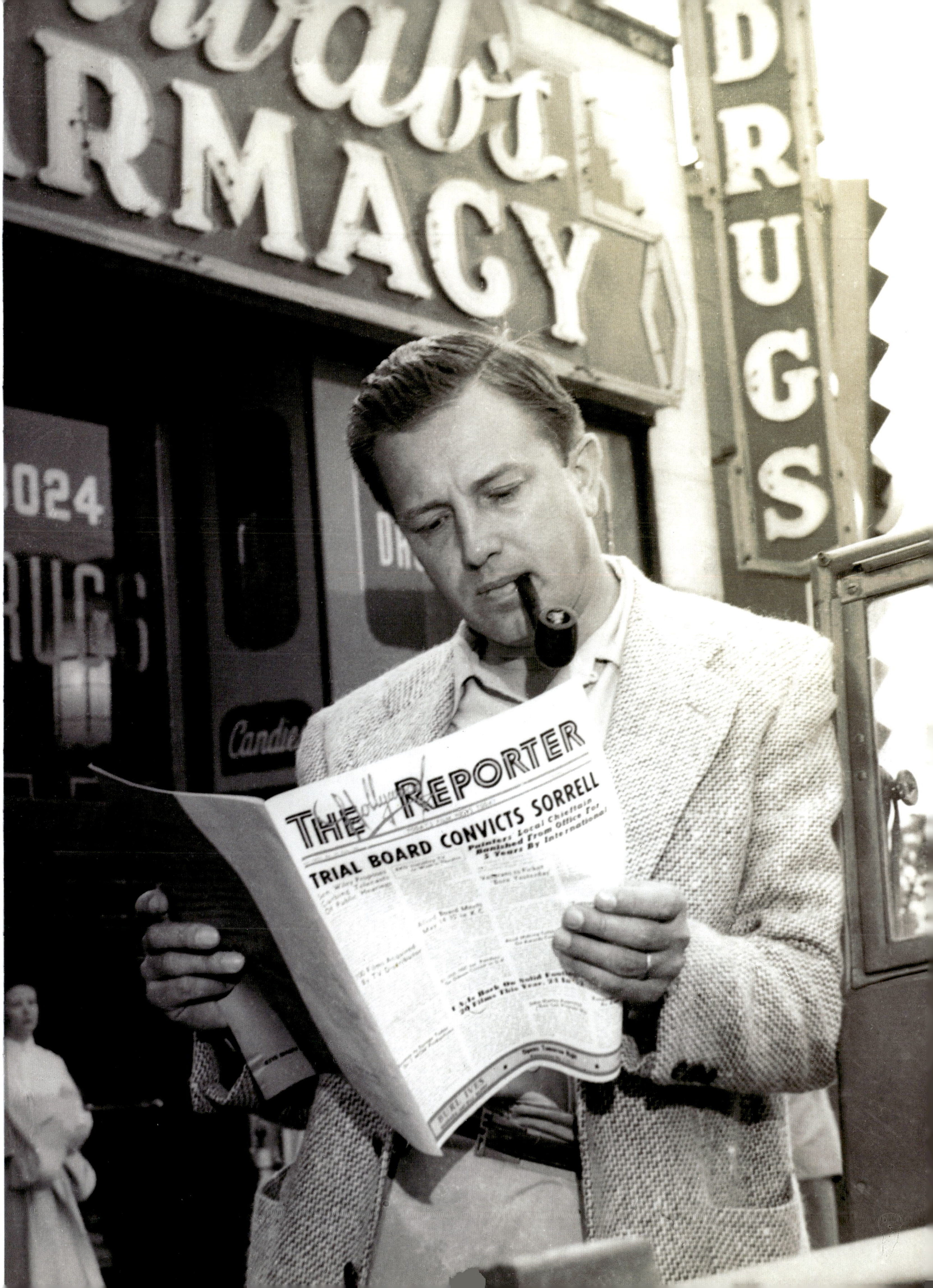

RMACY
DRUGS
3024
THE REPORTER
TRIAL BOARD CONVICTS SORRELL
Painters' Local Chieftain Banished From Office For 3 Years By International

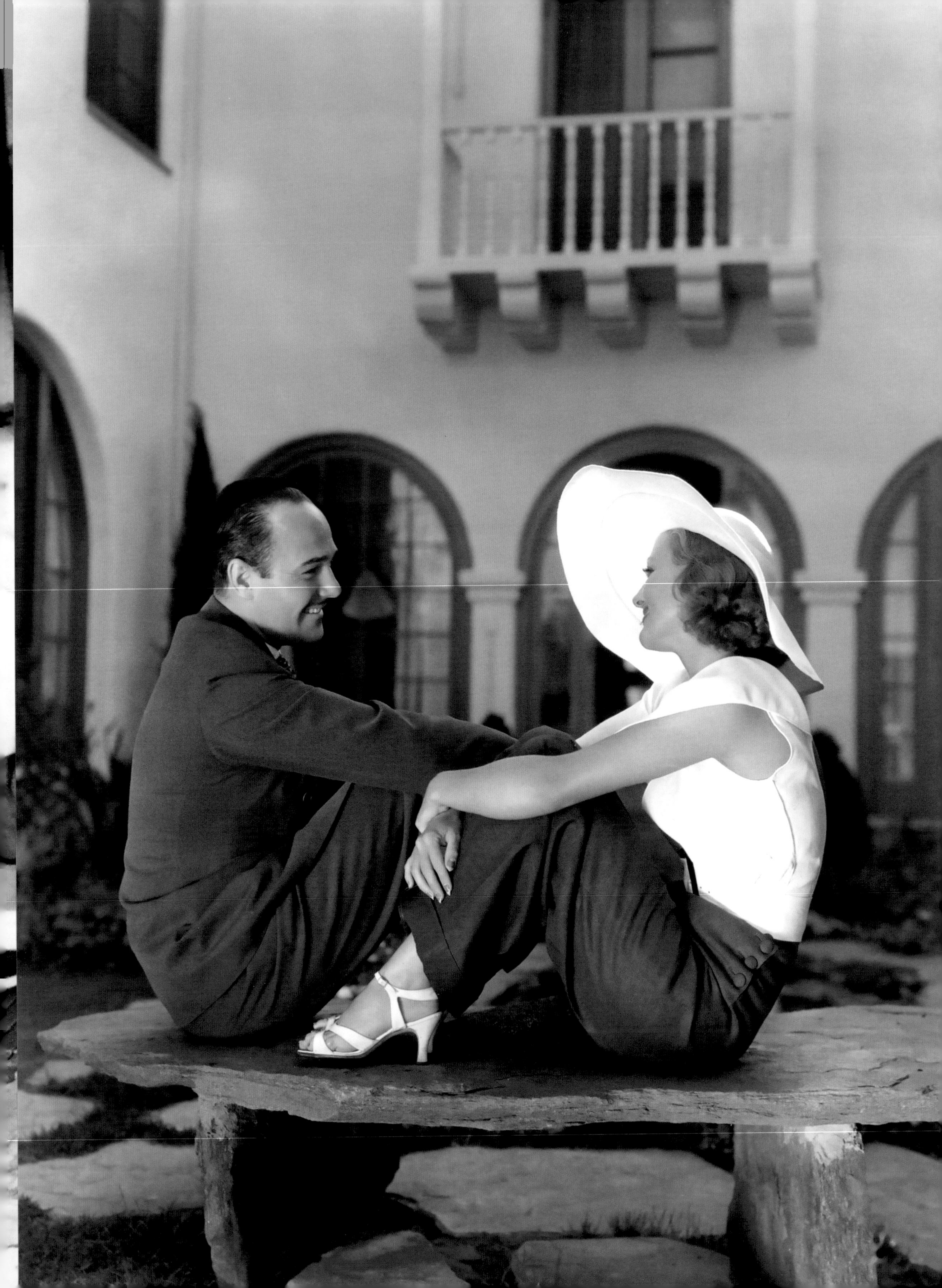

William Haines

Love and Style Transcend Film Stardom

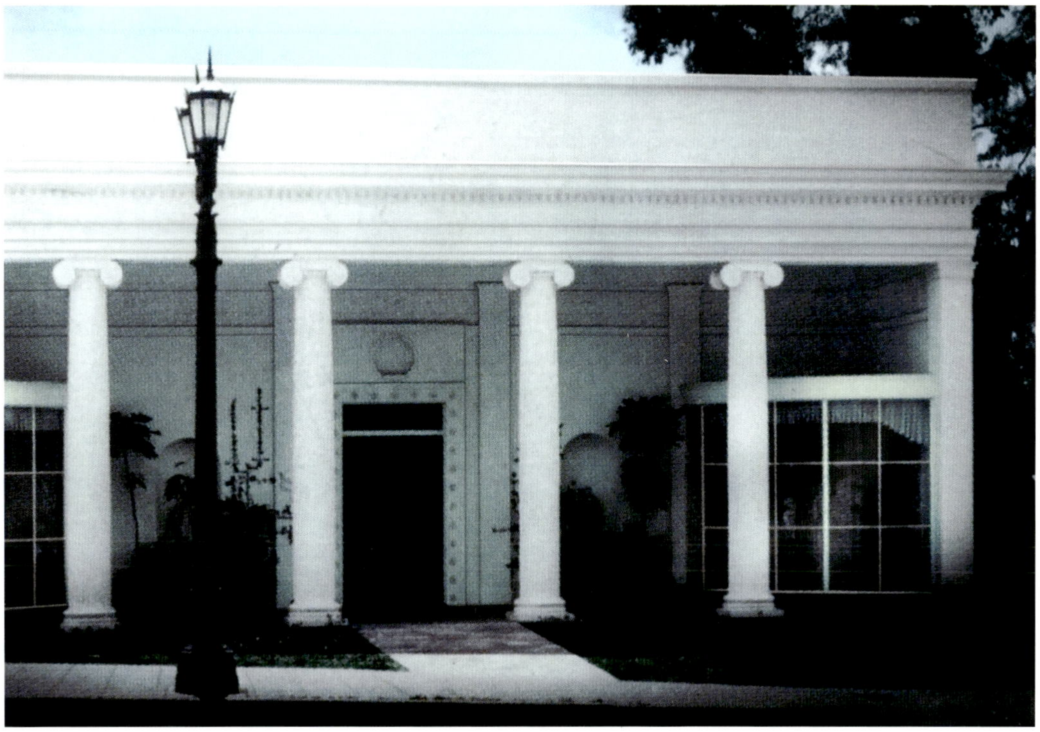

Exterior view of the Haines Studio on the Strip. The ornate façade complete with faux columns remained when the building transformed into Le Dôme restaurant in 1977.

←
William Haines and Joan Crawford, friends, co-stars on the big screen (*West Point* in 1927 was just one of the films in which they played opposite each other), and partners in style. He was the interior decorator for her residences; her sponsorship contributed to him becoming arguably the hottest designer in Hollywood.

The neoclassical structure that eventually housed Le Dôme was for many years the office and studio of one of Hollywood's most instinctively talented and personally courageous men.

William Haines had no training in acting or interior design, but became fabulously successful at both. And when told by the studio boss Louis B. Mayer to abandon the love of his life or give up his flourishing film career, he said goodbye to MGM and phased out his acting to become a famously talented and financially successful interior designer.

Born at the beginning of 1900, Haines was reared in a small railroad town in the Shenandoah Valley of Virginia. By age fourteen, he ran away with a boyfriend and created a somewhat notorious dance hall in a libertine coastal town. From there it was on to Greenwich Village, modeling and working as

Haines had a key role in the 1928 King Vidor film, *Show People*. He starred with (from left) Mae Murray, Rod La Rocque, Marion Davies, (Haines), William S. Hart, and Claire Windsor.

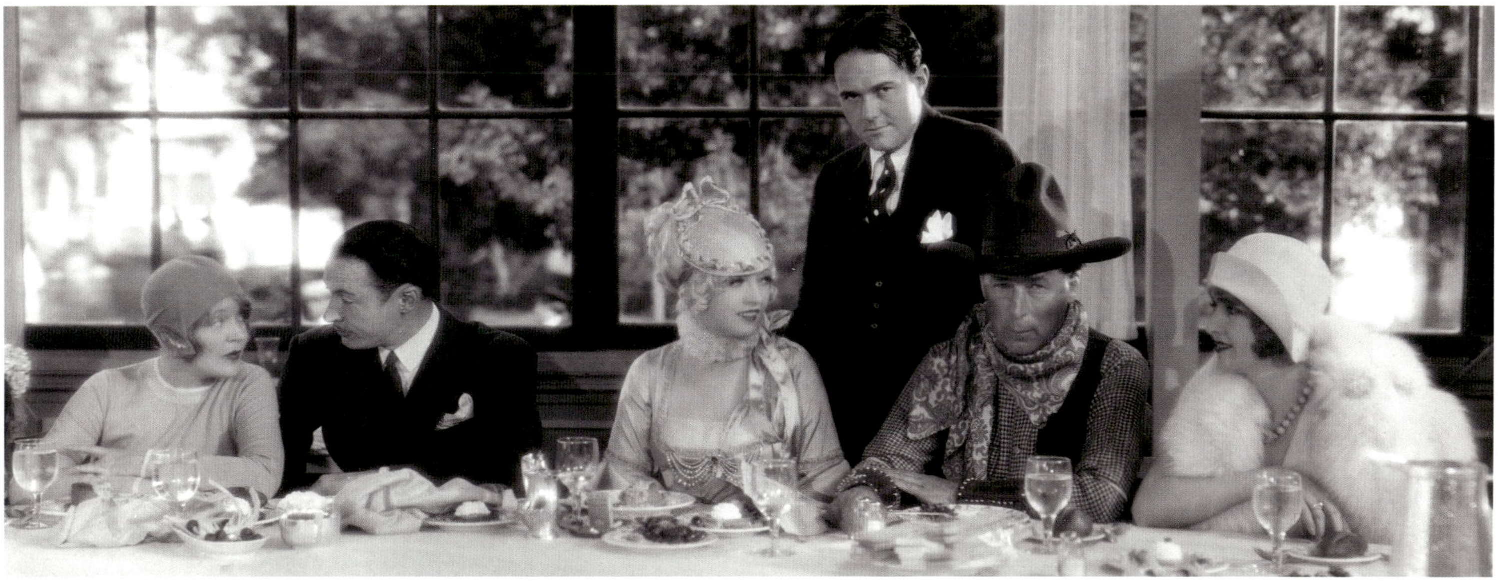

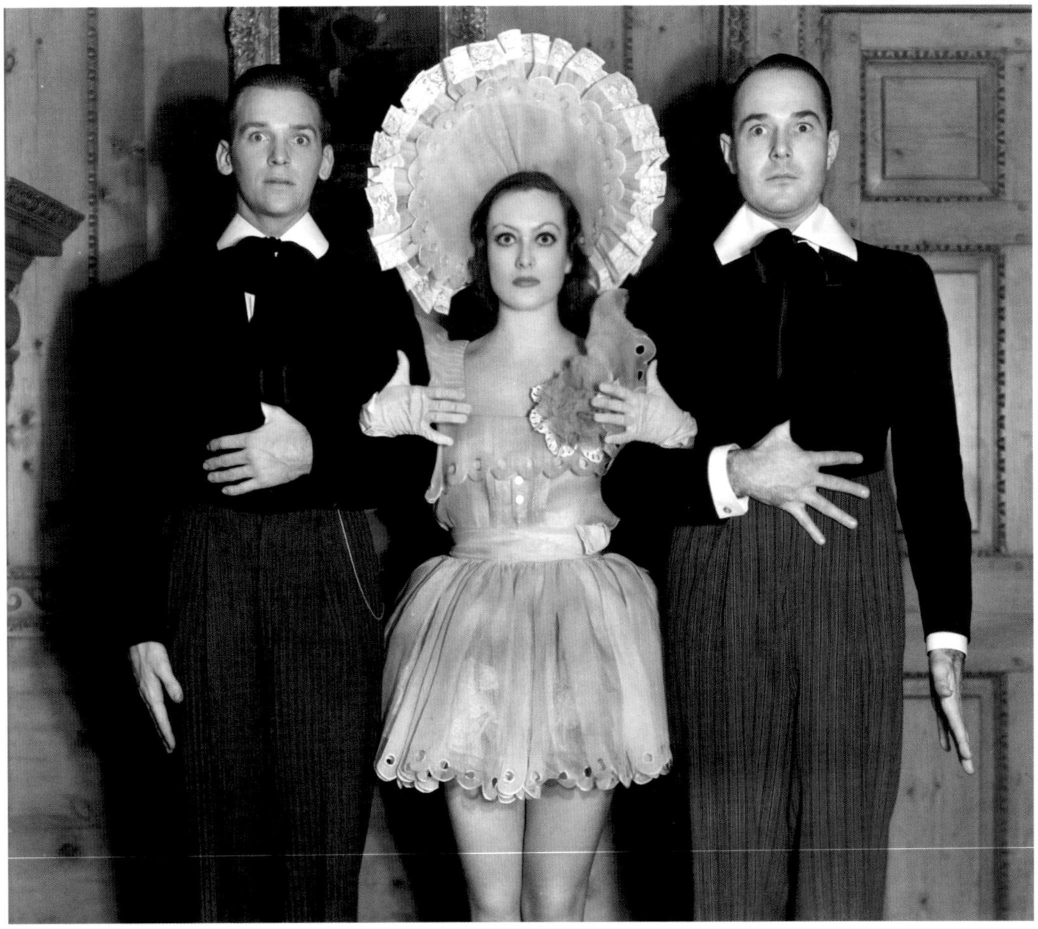

William Haines (right) joined Douglas Fairbanks Jr. and Joan Crawford (dressed as Shirley Temple) at a costume party at the lavish Santa Monica beach house of silent-film star Marion Davies, the ever-indulged mistress of press lord William Randolph Hearst. The three-story beach house had thirty-four bedrooms, three guesthouses, and two swimming pools.

a Wall Street runner. In 1922 he won a Goldwyn Studio talent contest and ended up with a forty-dollar-a-week Hollywood contract. Eight years later, a poll of film exhibitors named him the top box office attraction in the country. He had co-starred with Mary Pickford in *Little Annie Rooney* (1925) and with Marion Davies in *Show People* (1928), but most of his films didn't become the stuff of cinematic history. He turned down a cameo role in *Sunset Boulevard* that his pal Gloria Swanson had arranged.

It was well-known in Hollywood that Haines was gay, but nobody paid great attention, even though public revelation was always a threat. Some gay actors diminished their vulnerability to negative newspaper stories by entering into a "lavender marriage," a relationship of convenience that would provide a suitable cover story for the media. But after Haines got into a jam with the police, Mayer demanded he accept a sham marriage and abandon his treasured partner, James Shields. "But I'm already married," Haines declared.

When Haines got into a jam with the police, Mayer demanded he accept a sham marriage and abandon his treasured partner, James Shields.

He stiffed MGM, the salary, and the fame, and chose interior decorating. He never lacked for clients. Close friend Joan Crawford was one of his initial clients, and over the years he worked for Swanson, Frank Sinatra, Marion Davies, Walter Annenberg (doing work at both the American Embassy in London, where Annenberg was ambassador, and the family's huge Sunnyland estate in Rancho Mirage), and Douglas Fairbanks Jr. His friends and clients were undeniably loyal.

And he continued his relationship with Shields. Crawford described the pair as the "happiest married couple in Hollywood." Haines said, "I've never been divorced from show business. Many of my friends are still clients. I feel part of them. I'm still an actor who's hanging some curtains."

Haines died in 1973. After a relationship of forty-seven years, Shields decided he could not go it alone. He took his own life. The two men are interred side by side in Santa Monica's Woodlawn Cemetery. ■

→
William Haines (right), Marion Davies, and George K. Arthur sit poolside at the beach house in Santa Monica. Today, what's left of the beach house is open to the public and a modern oceanside swimming facility occupies the spot where Davies's once star-studded pool was positioned.

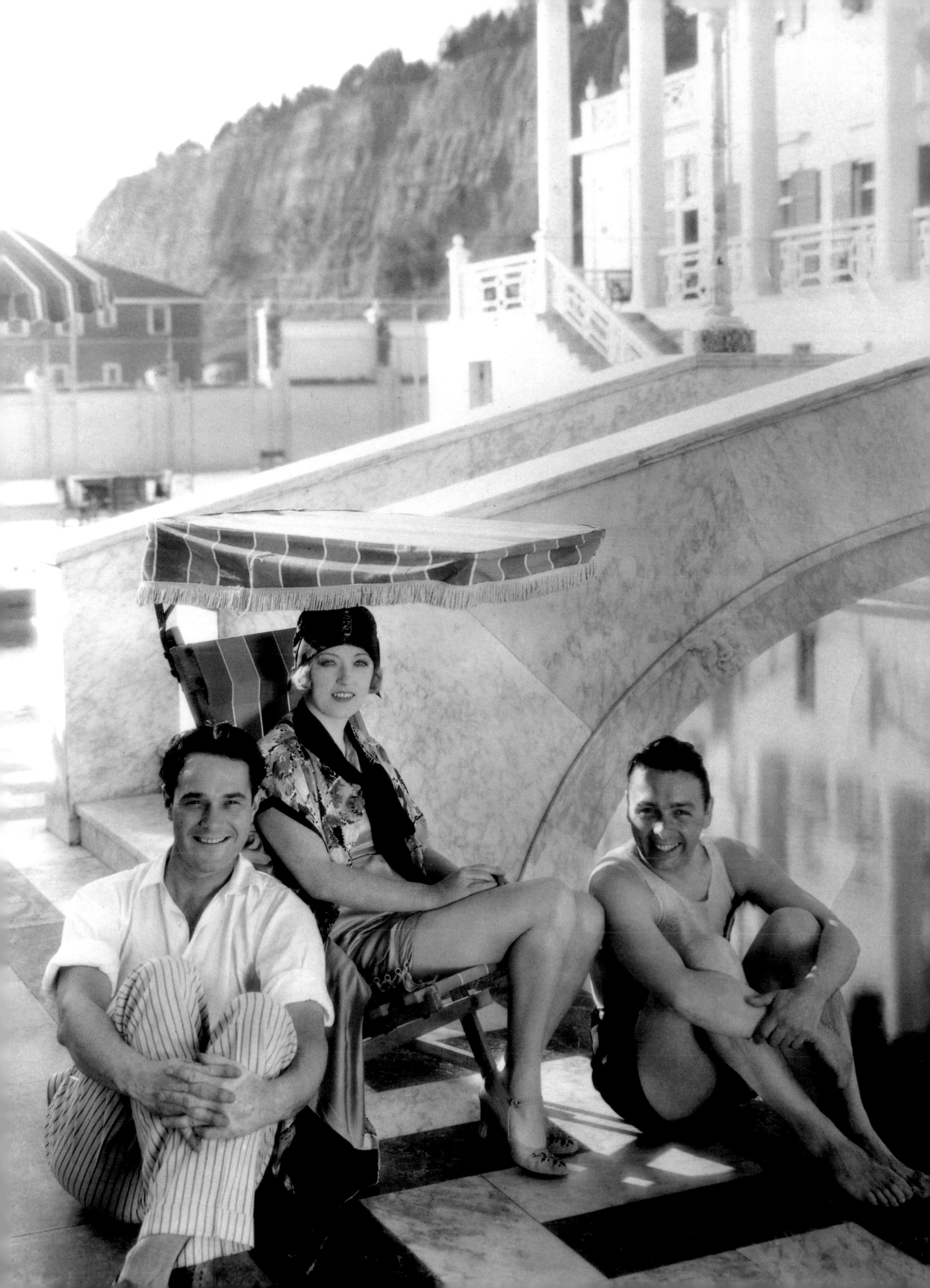

• 1896–1940 •

F. Scott Fitzgerald

The Tragic Conclusion of Brilliance

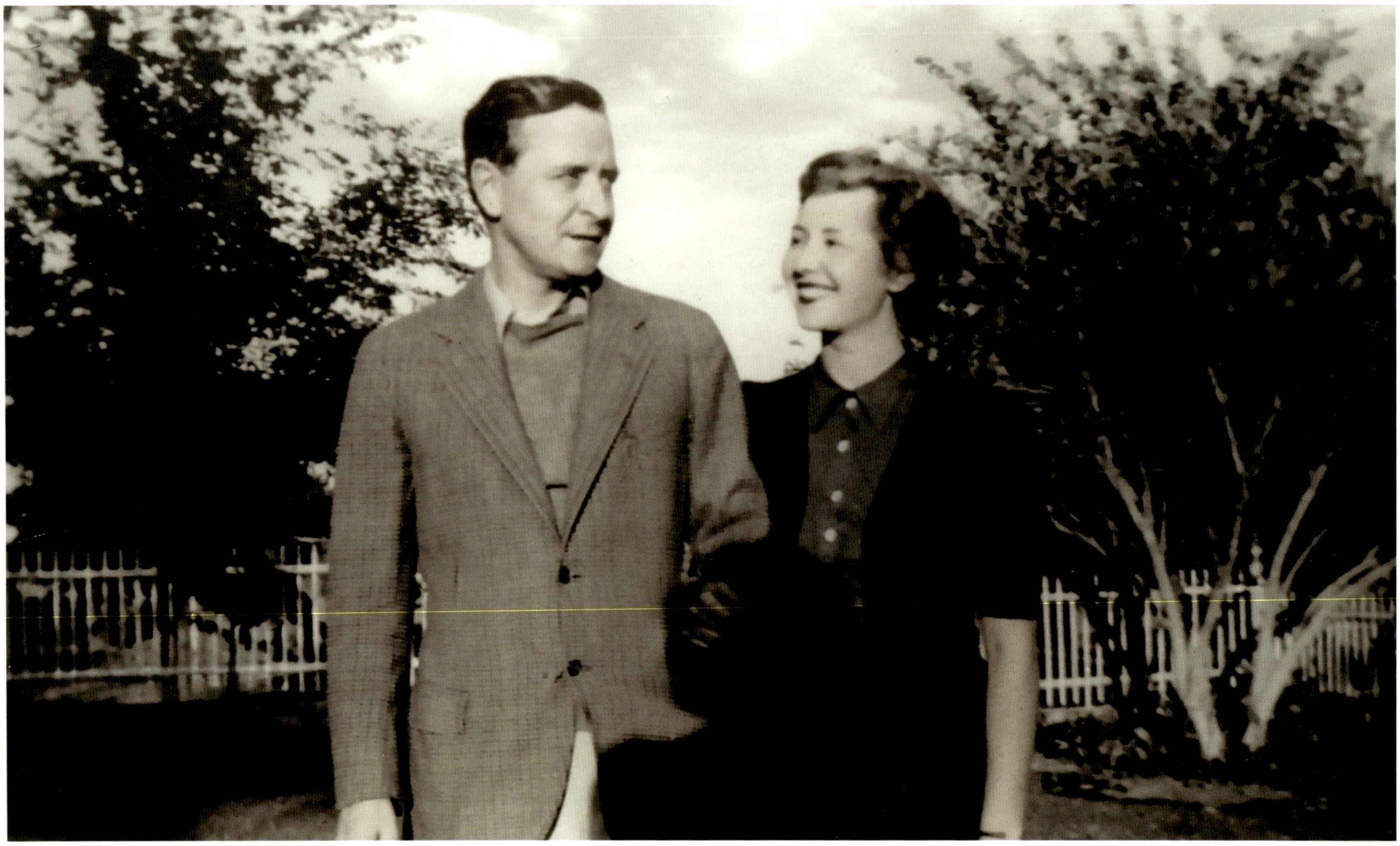

F. Scott Fitzgerald with Sheilah Graham. She was a war correspondent who became a renowned gossip columnist, admitting that she was "a fascinating flake who pulled the wool over Hollywood's eyes. . ."

It seemed the end of line for F. Scott Fitzgerald.

In late 1940, one of the great American novelists of the twentieth century was living just south of Sunset, in the apartment (1443 N. Hayworth) of his love, Hollywood gossip columnist and author Sheilah Graham. The Strip was glamour and excitement, but Fitzgerald was discouraged, his confidence fading, his skill elusive, his heart failing. He was reduced to writing schlock for Hollywood studios while struggling to resurrect his voice in a novel about Hollywood itself.

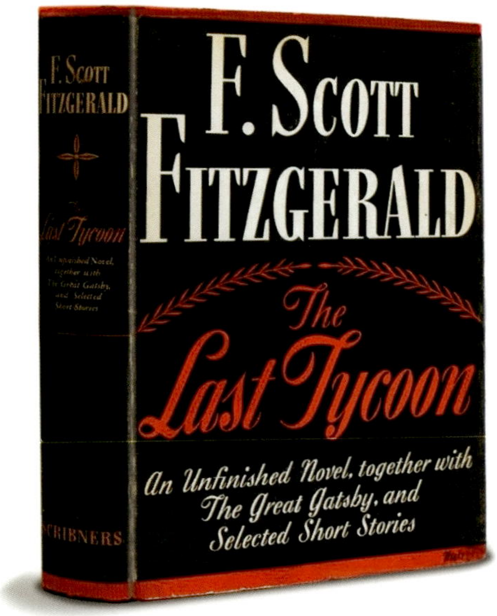

Fitzgerald had recently suffered a heart attack while standing in line to buy cigarettes at Schwab's drugstore on the Strip, across Crescent Heights from the Garden of Allah. Though physically damaged by the attack, he managed to get a grasp on his life and creativity. He cut back on the drinking. The novel was again working. Things were looking up, or so it seemed. But about a month after the Schwab's episode, while attending a movie premiere with Graham, he felt extremely dizzy. She had to help him from the theater, and he lamented that those who saw his awkward exit presumed he was just drunk again. The next day, while waiting for a doctor to arrive, Fitzgerald ate a candy bar and made some notes about the football team in his Princeton alumni magazine. He suddenly stood, gasped, and fell dead.

The Strip was glamour and excitement, but Fitzgerald was discouraged, his confidence fading, his skill elusive, his heart failing.

Billy Wilder, the director of the film classic *Sunset Boulevard*, later lamented the unproductive time Fitzgerald spent as a screenwriter. Wilder compared Fitzgerald working as a hack in the studios to being a great sculptor hired to do a plumbing job.

But the unfinished novel, known as *The Last Tycoon*, was eventually published in two different versions. In 1941, after his friend Edmund Wilson edited the manuscript and the book was released, the *New York Times* reviewed it as "the best piece of creative writing that we have about one phase of American life—Hollywood and the movies. Both in the unfinished draft and in the sheaf of Fitzgerald's notes which Mr. Wilson has appended to the story, it is plainly to be seen how firm was his grasp of his material, how much he had deepened and grown as an observer of life. His sudden death, we see now, was as tragic as that of Thomas Wolfe."

Billy Wilder compared Fitzgerald working as a hack in the studios to being a great sculptor hired to do a plumbing job.

Ironically, several days before his death, Fitzgerald attended a party for Nathanael West, author of the Hollywood novel *Day of the Locust*, another book considered to be one of the best stories of the film industry and the city that surrounds it. West and his wife were killed in a car accident the day after Fitzgerald died. That same *New York Times* review of *The Last Tycoon*, understated about its writer: "Fitzgerald's career is a tragic story, but the end is better than it might have been. And I think he will be remembered in his generation." ■

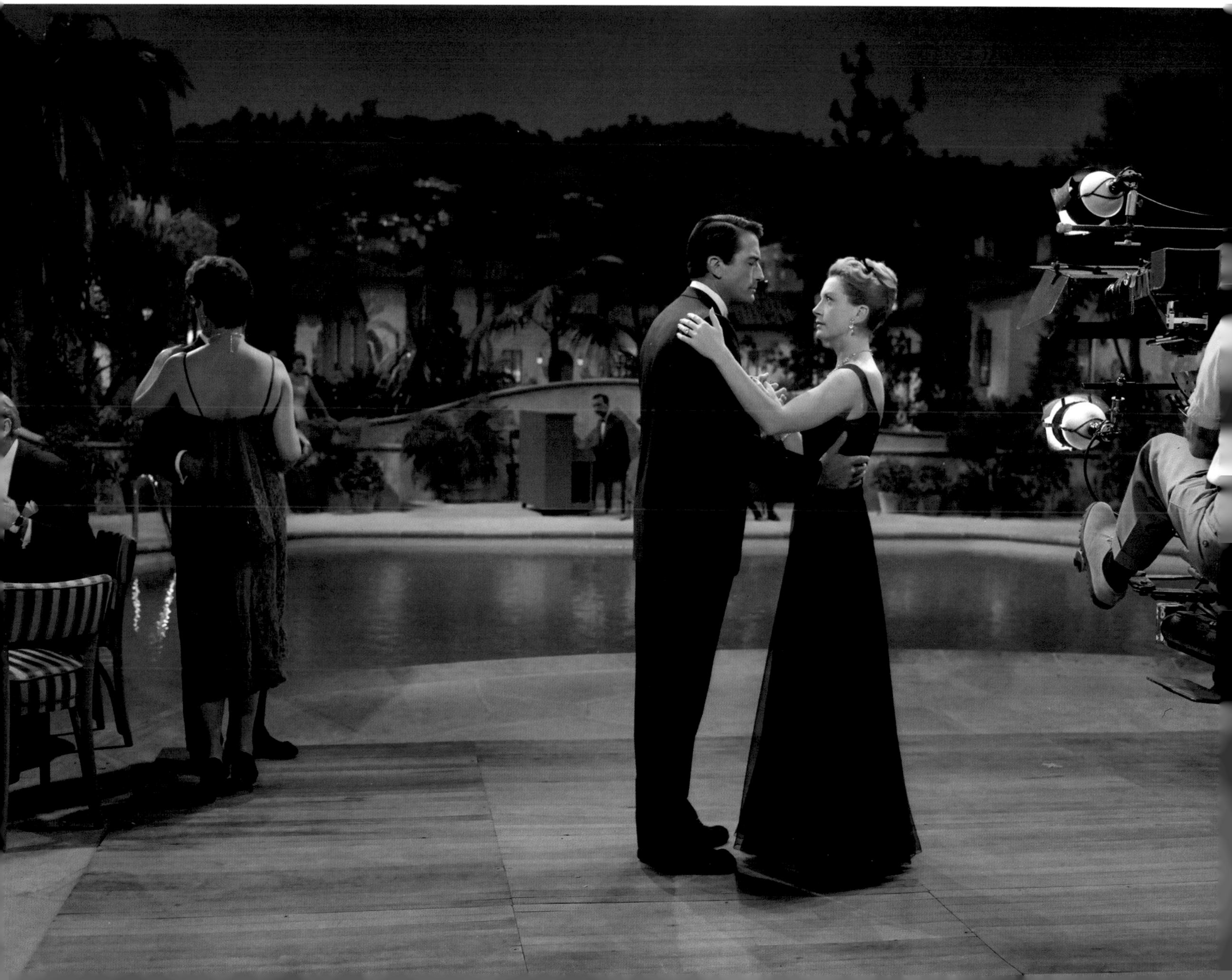

Sheilah Graham wrote *Beloved Infidel*, the story of her romance with Fitzgerald, which was adapted as a film in 1959, starring Gregory Peck and Deborah Kerr as the lovers. Here they are dancing in a set designed to resemble the Garden of Allah.

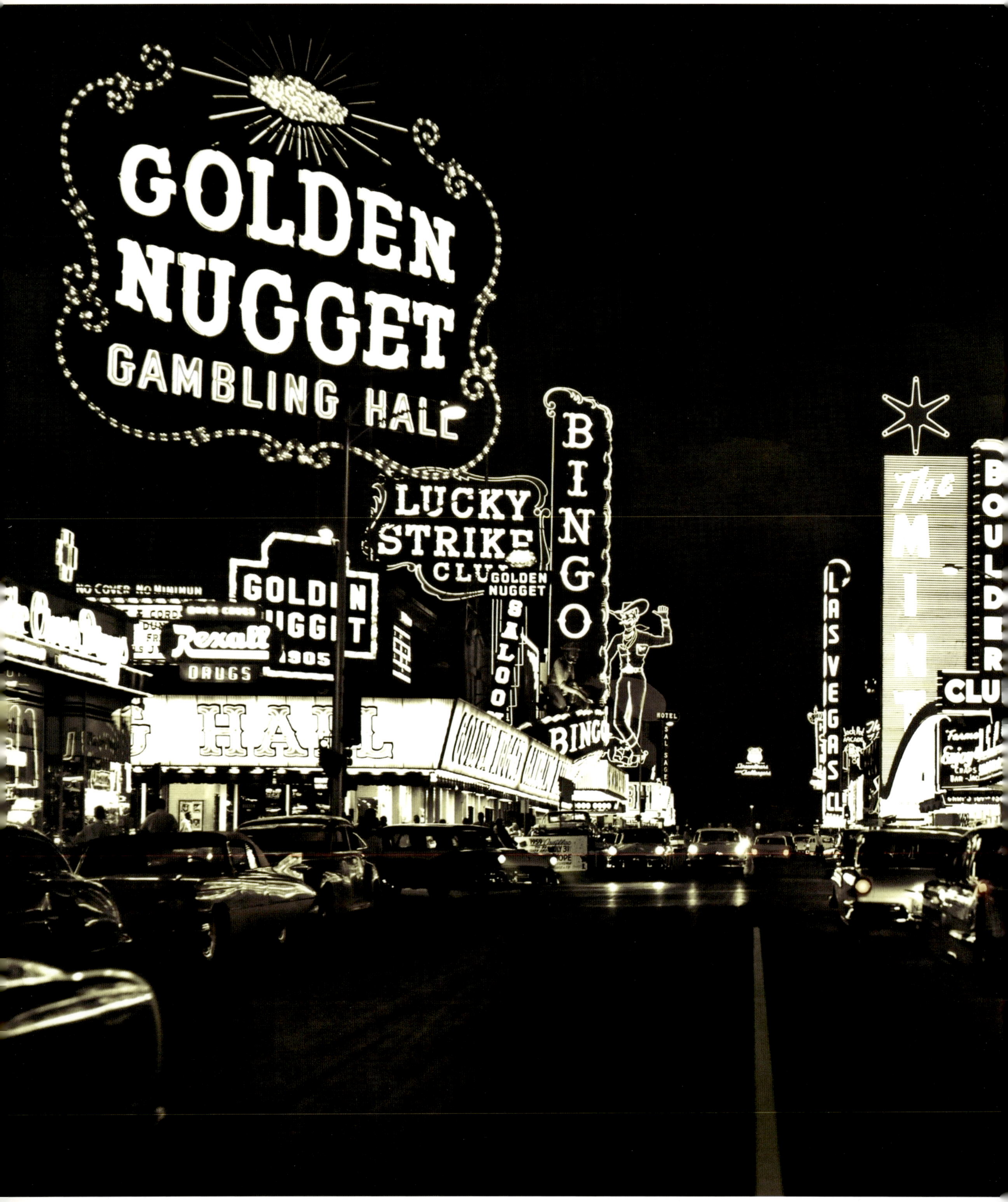
GOLDEN
NUGGET
GAMBLING HALL
LUCKY
STRIKE
CLUB
BINGO
GOLDEN NUGGET
SALOON
NO COVER NO MINIMUM
GOLDEN
NUGGET
1905
Rexall
DRUGS
HALL
BINGO
LAS VEGAS CLUB
The MINT
BOULDER
CLUB

Guy McAfee and the Two Strips

The Man Who Drew Aces

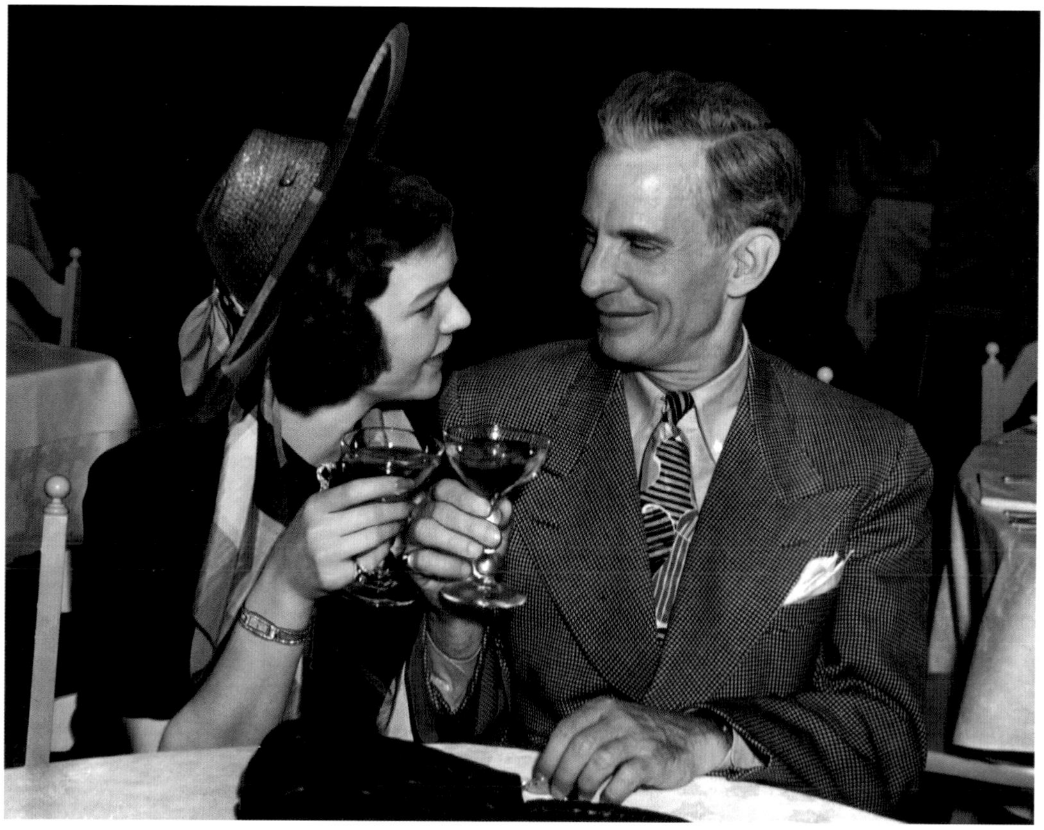

Guy McAfee and his second wife, actress June Brewster in 1937, make a toast, perhaps relating to their relocation from the Sunset Strip to Las Vegas. McAfee ran a string of Los Angeles-area gambling establishments, including the notorious Clover Club on the Sunset Strip. Threatened by a clean government movement, and confusion within the mob, McAfee took up residence in Las Vegas, where gambling was legal. Using his skills and experience as a club operator, McAfee became an important figure in the Vegas casino world.

There is no indication Guy McAfee was particularly adroit as a phrase maker, though at various stages of his life he was crafty as a corrupt public official, a corrupter of public officials and an inspired and visionary manager of gambling emporiums. But McAfee, drawing upon nostalgia or literary license, stuck two words—the Strip—to a bleak two-lane road in a forlorn desert that (1) tipped its hat to the Sunset Strip and (2) became to the world—the world—the locator, the verbal, shorthand GPS, for one of history's most singular and luminous stretches of real estate, the Strip. In Las Vegas.

He also was engaged in running—while still a leader of the "purity squad"—a number of gaming establishments, including the Clover Club, a popular, well-turned-out casino at 8477 Sunset.

An orphan from Winfield, Kansas, McAfee made his way west and became a Los Angeles fireman. Given the limited revenue potential there, he flipped over to the police department and rose to captain of the vice squad (the purity squad). Along the way he married the reported madam of a significant local brothel and was generously compensated for looking the other way as assorted gangsters, shysters, bootleggers, prostitutes, gamblers, and scoundrels raked in cash from the more uninhibited or unwise citizenry of Southern California.

← Old Las Vegas. The Golden Nugget. The Hotel Apache. Binion's Horseshoe. Just three of Fremont Street temptations luring the innocents from frugal, distant places into the belly of the beast, to throw down a week's wages on a mad chance to beat the house, to make it big, to be a player, to carry bragging rights back to those starchy villages and neighborhoods where Vegas was a wicked dream in a distant desert. A perfect place for Guy McAfee.

He also was engaged in running, while still a leader of the purity squad, a number of gaming establishments, including the Clover Club, a popular, well-turned-out casino at 8477 Sunset, on the north side of the Strip, east of La Cienega Boulevard. The Clover was popular with the show-biz crowd, a pricey diversion for celebs after dinner and dancing at the nearby Trocadero.

It was obvious to anyone who wanted to observe—the L.A. cops and the L.A. County Sheriff's Department certainly not among them—that vice was rampant throughout the city and county.

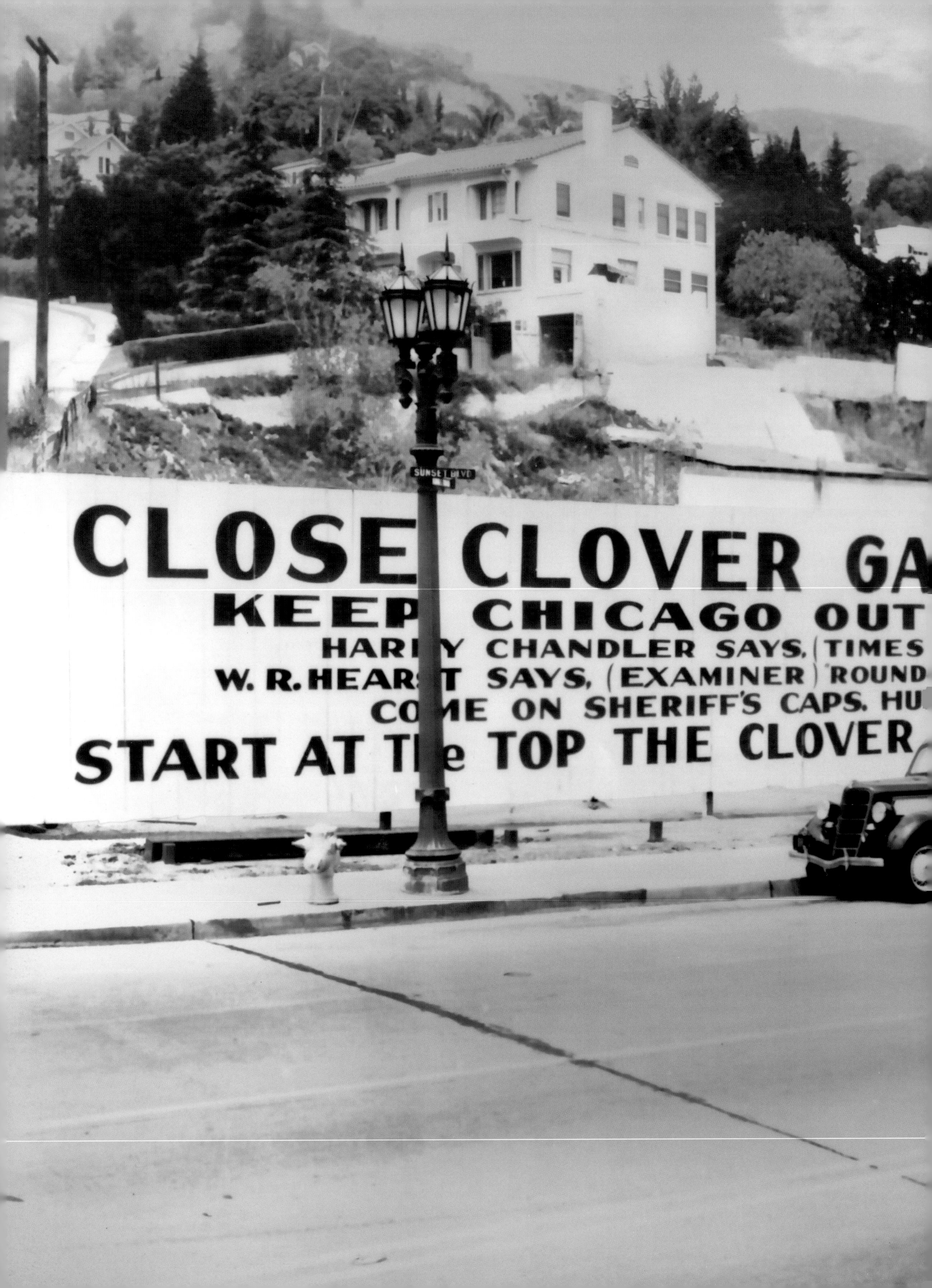
SUNSET BLVD
CLOSE CLOVER GA
KEEP CHICAGO OUT
HARRY CHANDLER SAYS, (TIMES
W. R. HEARST SAYS, (EXAMINER) ROUND
COME ON SHERIFF'S CAPS. HU
START AT THe TOP THE CLOVER

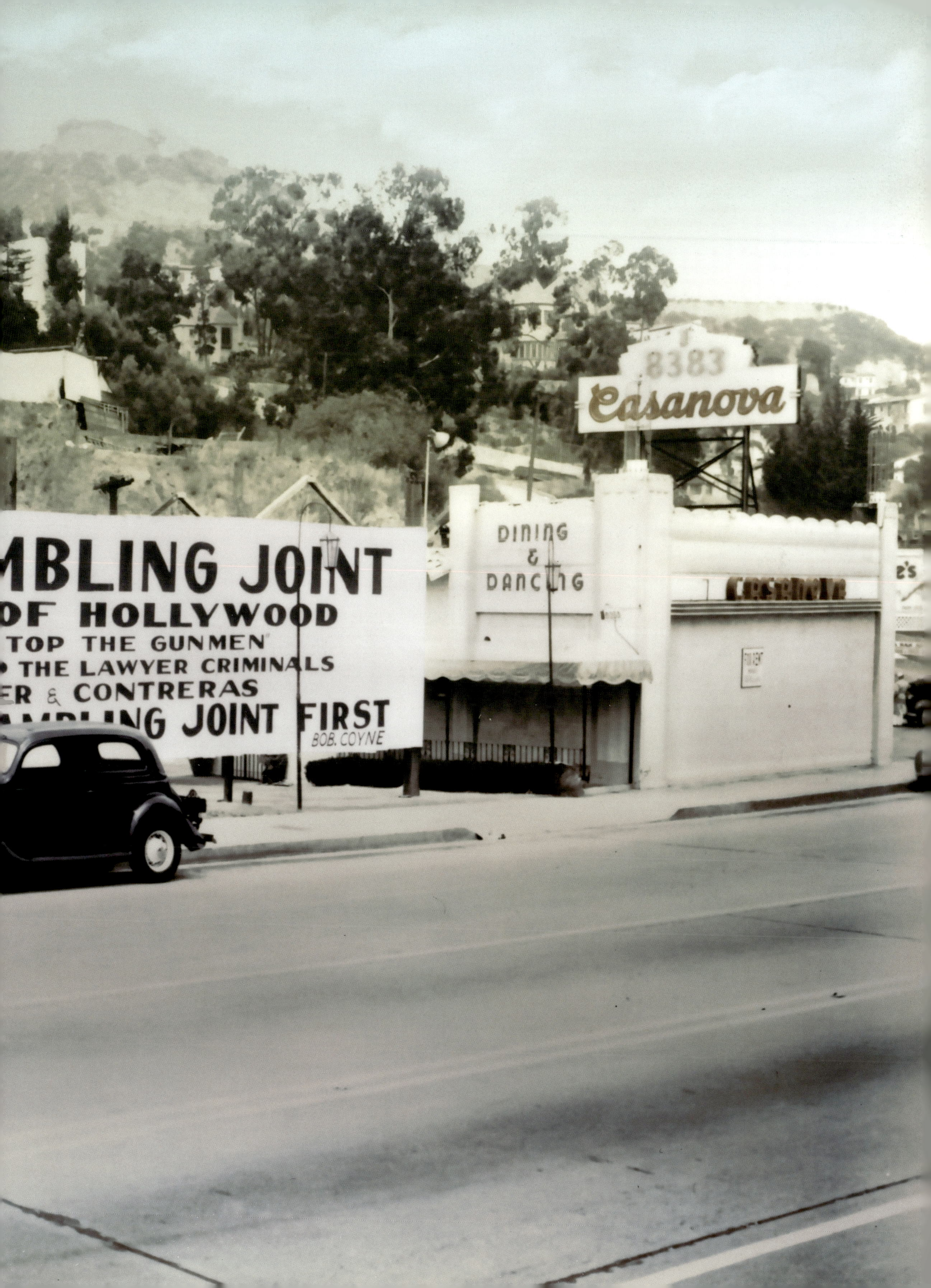
8383
Casanova
DINING
&
DANCING
MBLING JOINT
OF HOLLYWOOD
TOP THE GUNMEN"
THE LAWYER CRIMINALS
ER & CONTRERAS
JOINT FIRST
BOB. COYNE

Overleaf ←
Bursts of enthusiasm for good and honest government rolled across the city and county of Los Angeles in the 1920s and '30s. This remarkable billboard sought the jailing of Chicago-style gangsters and the padlocking of emporiums of sin, like the Clover Club. The results were mixed.

McAfee clearly established that it was easy to stay a foot ahead of the law if indeed you *were* the law.

But a reform government was ascending in the 1930s, and there were reports J. Edgar Hoover was considering a major investigation of L.A. crime and corruption. Add to that some very unpleasant tensions within the mob world. So McAfee set off for the seedy, sweaty town of Las Vegas, where casino gambling, alcohol, prostitution, and almost all other indulgences were readily available. There were estimates McAfee crossed the state border with at least a million dollars in net worth.

In 1939, McAfee opened the 91 Club, the former Pair-O-Dice Club on Route 91, the highway from Long Beach to Salt Lake City that passed through the small town of Las Vegas. He predicted it would be popular with Angelenos heading to Vegas for some legal gambling and Western ambiance. McAfee spruced up the building, added some quality décor, established a house orchestra, offered lavish steak dinners, and cranked up industrial-strength air conditioning.

And he began referring to Route 91, with a remembrance of his times in Los Angeles, as "the Strip." It caught on. And 91, known downtown as Las Vegas Boulevard, became "the Strip."

He began referring to Route 91, with a remembrance of his times in Los Angeles, as "the Strip." It caught on. And 91, known downtown as Las Vegas Boulevard, became "the Strip."

McAfee created more gambling establishments along the Strip and also in downtown Las Vegas. One of his creations was the Golden Nugget, which opened downtown (lovingly referred to as "glitter gulch") in 1946 and reflected San Francisco's Barbary Coast. A 100-foot-tall neon sign celebrated his club as "the world's largest casino." Decades later, the Golden Nugget was purchased by the ultimate modern-day Vegas impresario, Steve Wynn.

McAfee is remembered as a hard man with a sardonic sense of humor who mellowed in later years. But he is primarily remembered today as a major figure in the emergence of Las Vegas and its Strip as the world's greatest entertainment center. He died at age seventy-one in 1960. His obituary was carried on the front page of the *Las Vegas Review-Journal*. ■

Dressed in a tuxedo to conduct a raid on the Sunset Strip's Clover Club in 1936, Captain George Contreras (right) of the Los Angeles County Sheriff's department examines a pile of chips. His colleague, Captain Hunter, chose less formal attire for the event.

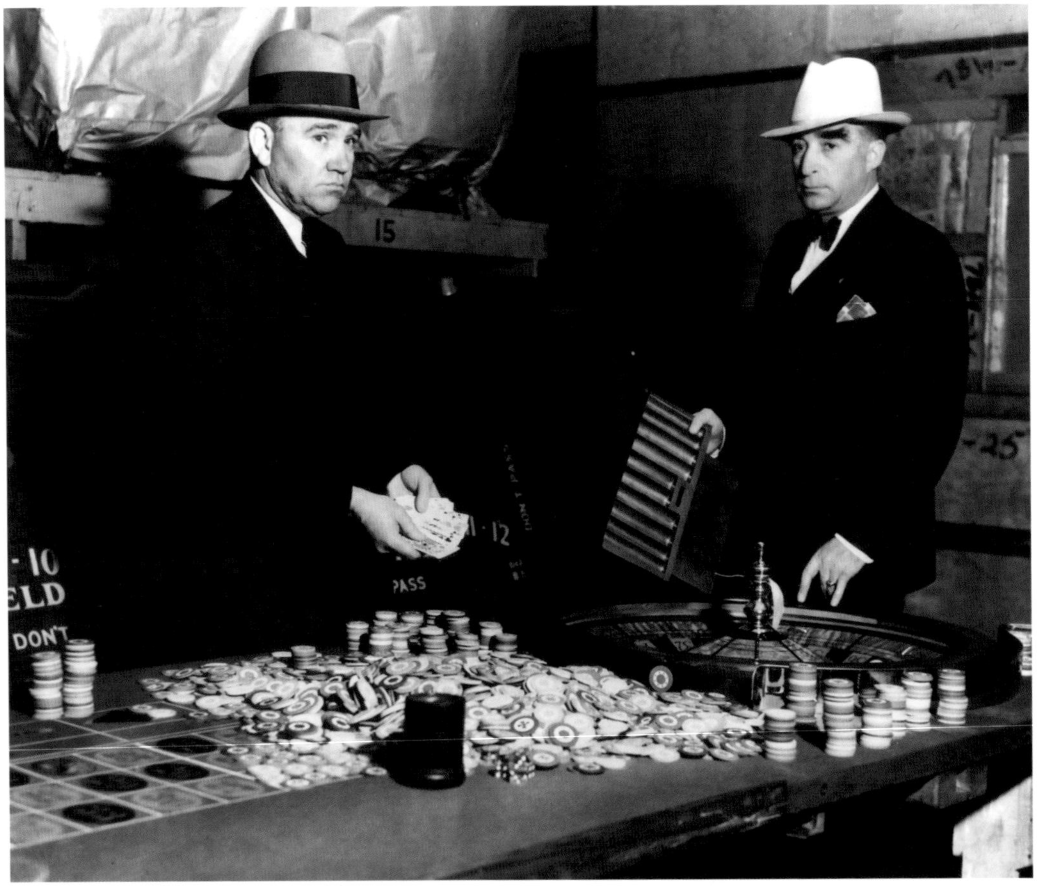

→
Why is this man laughing? Guy McAfee, an orphan from an obscure Kansas village, made his way to the Sunset Strip and then on to Las Vegas as a highly effective casino executive and owner. His death in 1960 merited front page newspaper coverage in Vegas.

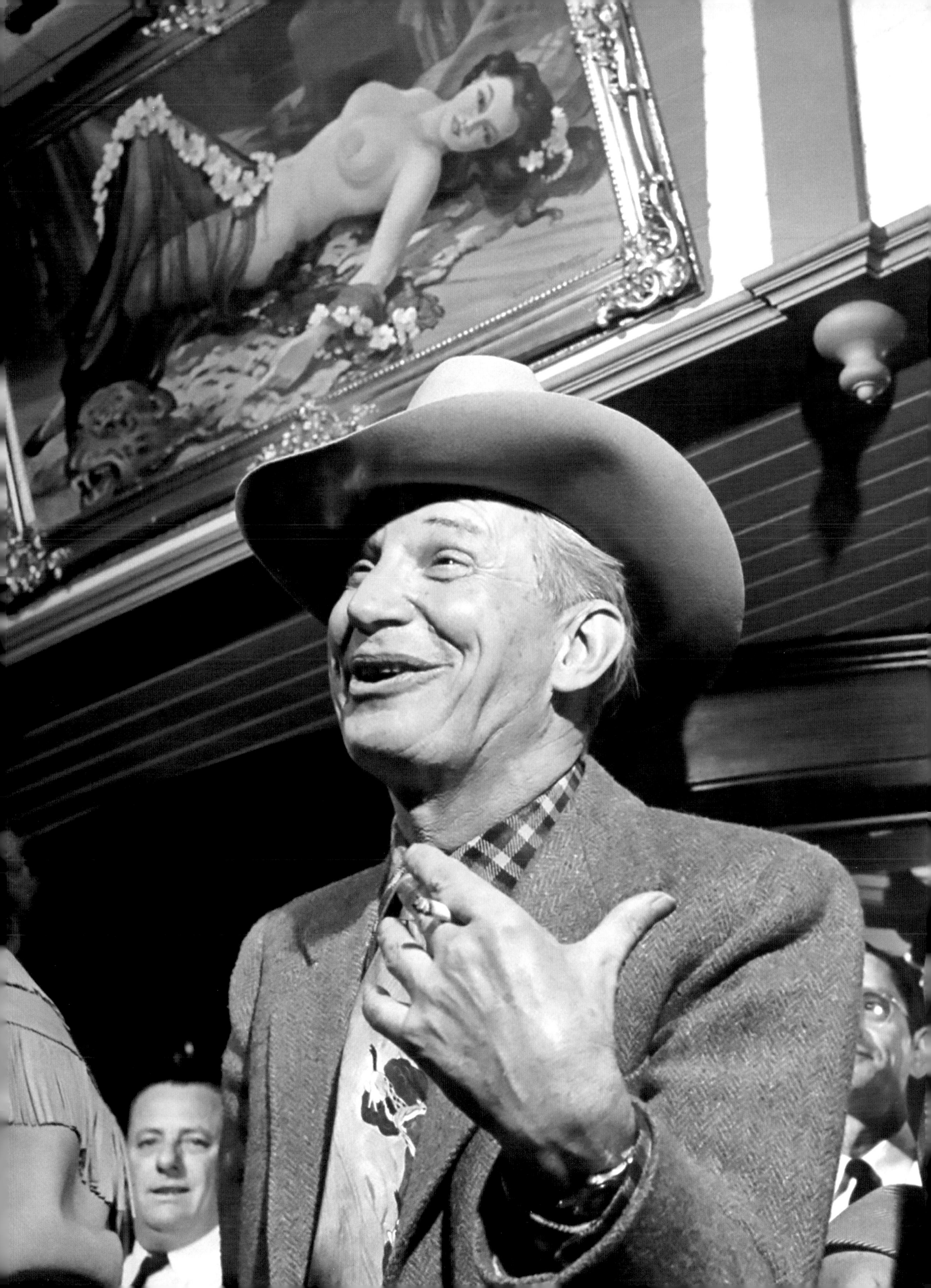

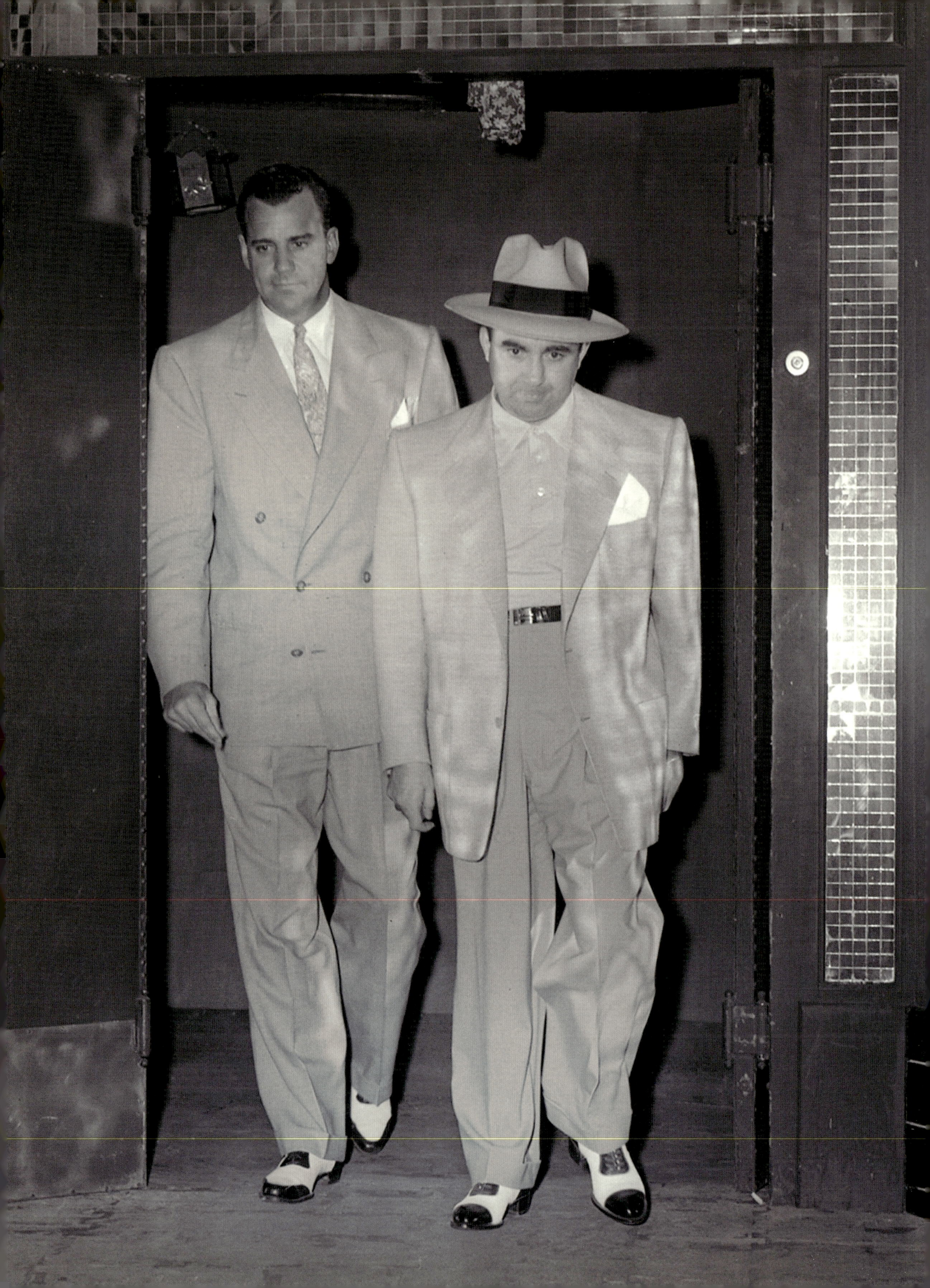

Mickey Cohen

Chaos, Corruption, and a Haberdashery

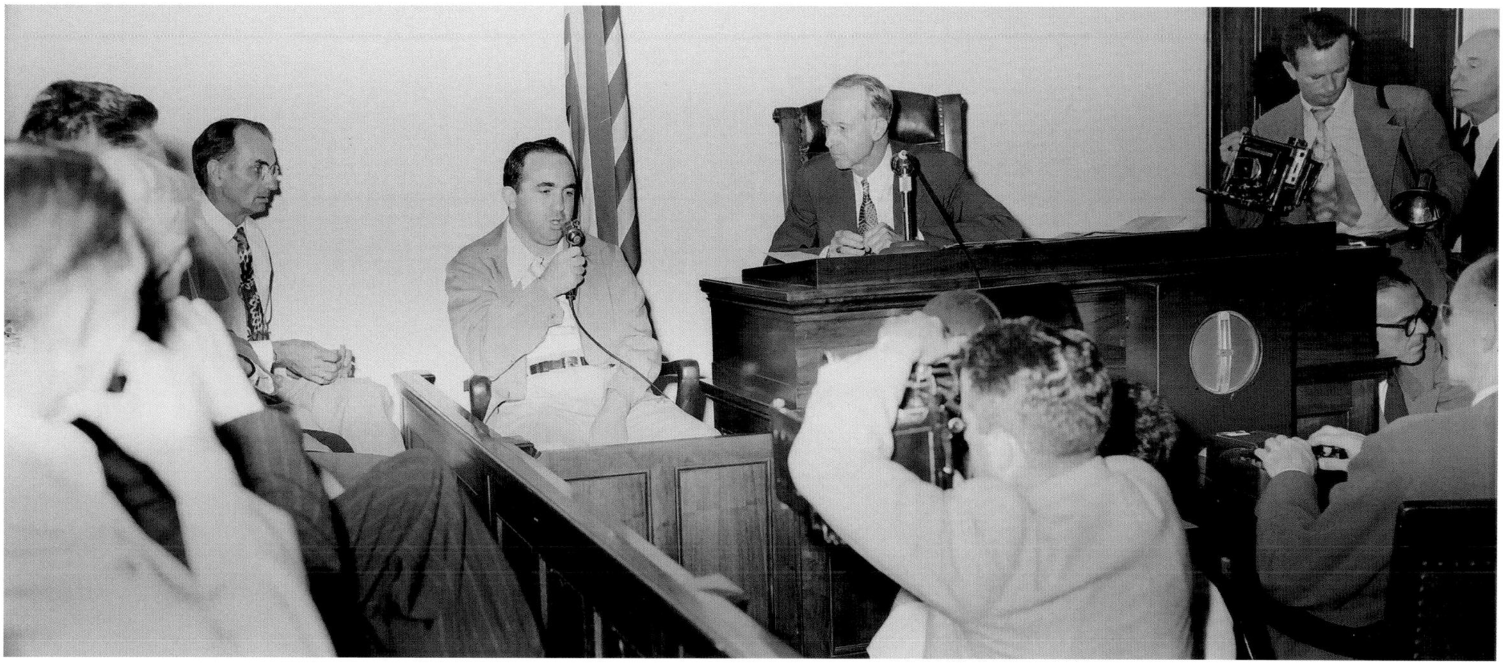

Cohen spent so much time in courtrooms that he should have qualified for an honorary license to practice criminal law. In those years, photographers enjoyed remarkable access to legal and police proceedings, so local newspapers thrived on Mickey's flamboyant presence. The publicity contributed to his public recognition, and in many cases, approval.

Until it found a home on the Sunset Strip, the mob never seemed to have an address in Los Angeles.

As Midwesterners flooded into Los Angeles in the early decades of the twentieth century, the town took on the tone of western Iowa, priggish and abstemious and industrious. The newcomers could have been models for Grant Wood's *American Gothic*, plain and a tad grumpy, but hard workers, very Protestant. Though in L.A., they were well tanned year-round.

At the opposite extreme, long-established Southern California mobsters were very Mediterranean. Mercurial. Street tough. Catholic. There was no large, local immigration pool for quality Mafia recruiting. So the local mob family sagged into the minor leagues.

For years the mafiosi back East considered the City of Angels alien and inhospitable. A lot of orange groves and Hollywood poseurs and starchy Masons going to lodge meetings. And the local mob guys were, well, somewhat hopeless.

Besides, who could generate enthusiasm for managing a crime franchise days away by train?

L.A.'s economic potential grew irresistible, however, and the mob eventually determined Benjamin "Bugsy" Siegel to be its change agent in the City of Angels—the glossy, corporate-turnaround guy. Quickly muscling aside the flummoxed Italians, Siegel generated big dollars while dating all the pretty women and chumming about with dimwitted Hollywood types. The locals were furious. A Beau Brummel from New York was ordering them around with the approval of the Sicilians back East.

Bugsy wasn't a particularly nice guy, or, as they eventually discovered back East, a particularly honest guy.

So when Siegel took a carbine slug in the face at the home of his girlfriend, legendary mobster courier and fellatrix Virginia Hill, there were few mourners. It was a no-name funeral. And to the horror of the Italians, Meyer Harris "Mickey" Cohen, the ex-prizefighter and vicious hoodlum, stepped into the void.

← Mickey Cohen, short, and Harry Cooper, long, en route to Sherry's, a Sunset Strip restaurant known for its rakish, late-night crowd. Cooper, a former wrestler, was a special agent from the California attorney general's office, assigned to serve as a bodyguard for Mickey. A gun battle ensued, leaving another man dead. Cohen and Cooper survived. Ironically in 2014, the rap-music tycoon and one-time NFL player Suge Knight was attending a private party in a club at the same Strip address when he was shot six times. Suge survived. There is no indication Suge was under the protection of the attorney general's office.

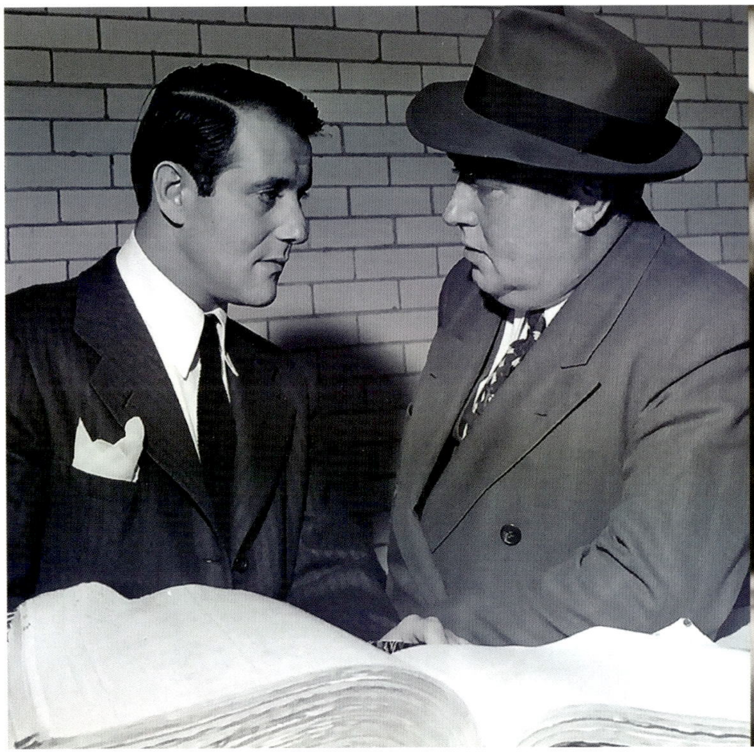

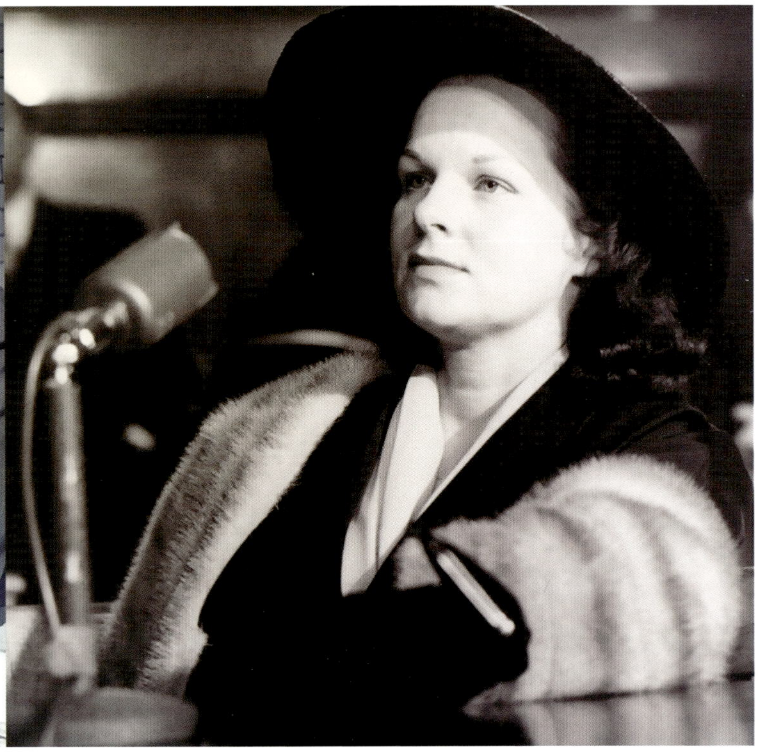

Ace criminal defense attorney Jerry Giesler (right) advises gangster Bugsy Siegel, just one of his big-name West Coast clients. Celebrities involved in legal debacles were frequently heard to shout the anguished cry, "Get me Giesler." Marilyn did when she divorced Joe.

Virginia Hill (sometimes known as the Flamingo because of her long, skinny legs) was a mob insider. She played many roles for many mobsters and has the distinction of being played on television by Dyan Cannon and on the big screen by Annette Bening. Her death was ruled a suicide, though many feel she was erased by the mob because she knew far too much.

And in no time, the Sunset Strip became Mickey's Main Street.

Cohen presented himself as a sometimes legitimate businessman, a Babbitt haberdasher with a five o'clock shadow, who sometimes lost his temper. But his friends. He had a lot of unsavory friends, low-level, sycophant gangsters given to crude speech, violent conduct, and unquestioning devotion to Cohen. Some of them died in shootouts honoring that devotion.

Many in the media pinched their noses and bought variations of his image. Rancid, but great copy. Many in the law enforcement and political communities smiled broadly and also bought into Cohen's façade. For cash, clout, and perverse camaraderie.

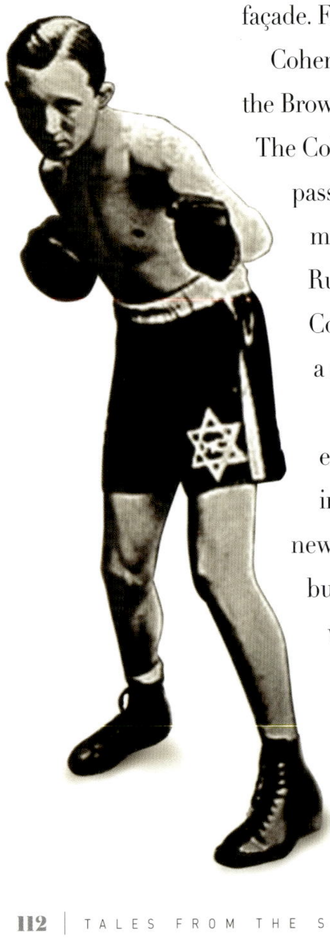

Cohen had begun his march to the Sunset Strip as a young boy when his mother, Fanny, set off from the Brownsville section of Brooklyn to create a better life for her family in the California sun.

The Cohens settled near the historic Breed Street Shul, a center for the large Jewish population that passed through Boyle Heights (L.A.'s version of Manhattan's lower east side) on its way to the more amiable neighborhoods west of downtown. Fanny Cohen ran a pharmacy/grocery in a Russian neighborhood (she was born in Kiev). Brad Lewis, in his entertaining and informative Cohen biography, *Hollywood's Celebrity Gangster*, wrote that God-fearing Fanny Cohen also had a still on the property so she could make and sell hooch.

Despite his mother's efforts, Mickey Cohen rejected religion and rectitude. From an early age he was a head-busting crook. At one point, as a newsboy, he muscled his way into dominating the best street corner in Los Angeles for selling one of the popular local newspapers. He walked about with a cash roll that frequently contained more than four hundred bucks. With cash and his fists, Mickey began to define a life. He entered the ring at age twelve while simultaneously developing skills with dice and cards. A critical moment in Mickey's life occurred with a conversation between his mother and a neighborhood butcher:

"Mrs. Cohen, you must be proud of your boy's boxing (success)," said the butcher

"What's this 'boxing'?" she responded. Before long, Mrs. Cohen was railing against Mickey's ring activities. And when his mother decided to remarry, Mickey said goodbye to mom and set off on his own. At fifteen, he headed to Cleveland (there are indications

←
Mickey Cohen had a lackluster boxing career but tried to curry favor with the fans by wearing a Star of David on his trunks. His mother's attempts to lead him into the faith proved futile.

→
A seemingly dejected Mickey Cohen leaves the office of a bail bondsman, presumably after a negative—and expensive—engagement with law enforcement.

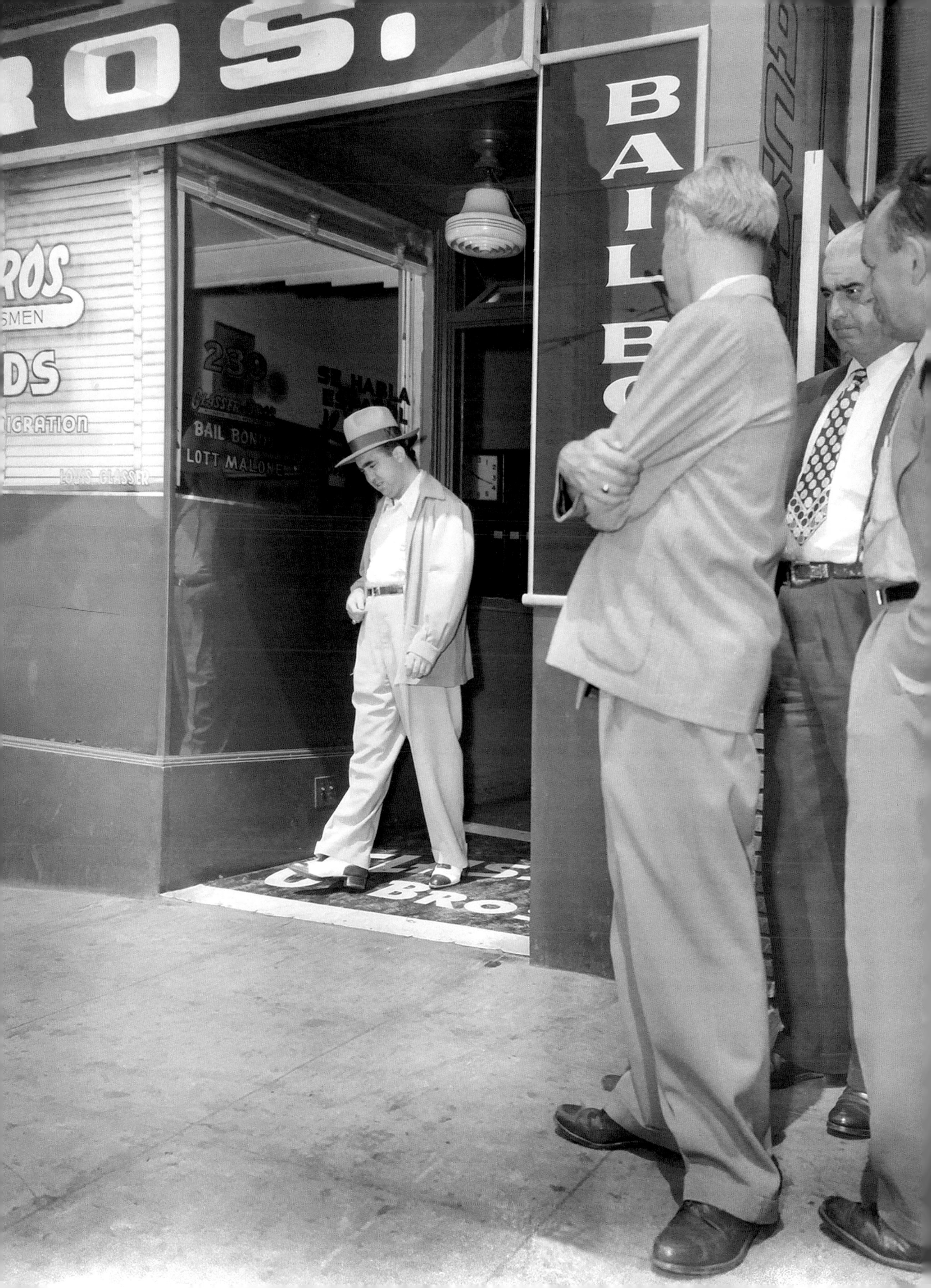

ROS.
BAIL BO
SE HABLA
BAIL BONDS
LOTT MALONE
LOUIS GLASSER
IGRATION

he may have hopped a freight) to join an older brother who was a part-time fight promoter. His brother got Mickey to New York City and the legendary Stillman's Gym on 8th Avenue. Cohen was a tenacious fighter, but was not keen on training. As a germophobe, Cohen may have been appalled by the grubby conditions. Owner Lou Stillman used to say that "the golden age of prizefighting was the age of bad food, bad air, bad sanitation, and no sunlight." He presumably kept the place like that for the fighters' own good. "If I clean it up, they'll catch a cold from the cleanliness." But the gym was used by champions from Jack Dempsey to Joe Louis to Rocky Marciano. Mickey, who boxed in satin shorts that bore the Star of David, was now what they call "an opponent." That was the nice way to say he was undistinguished.

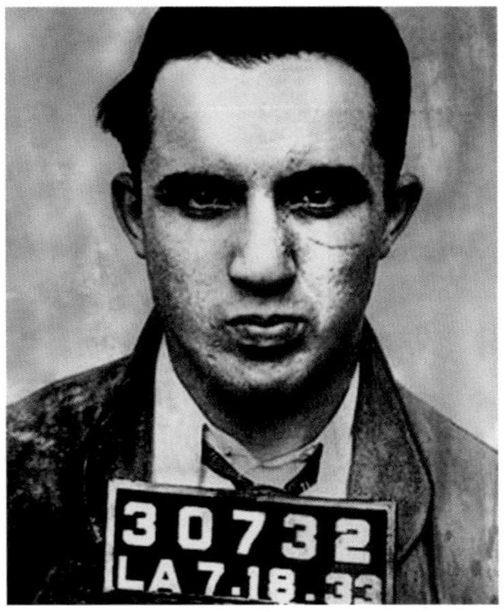

A seasoned criminal by age nineteen, Mickey Cohen provides a surly, intimidating glare for his first West Coast mugshot after being arrested by Los Angeles police for suspicion of robbery. Nothing ever came of the charge.

But again, Mickey augmented his legitimate but trivial ring income with far more lucrative work as a holdup artist and pain applicator for the mob. His reckless endeavors both awed and alarmed the racketeers as he burnished his villainy skills in New York, Cleveland, and Chicago (the Ivy League of higher mayhem). Eventually, the mob sent him to Los Angeles to assist Siegel (and perhaps to report back on his conduct). Along the way there was great collateral damage.

Cohen years later told journalist Mike Wallace that "I killed nobody that didn't deserve killing. In all of these here killings there was no alternative. You couldn't call them cold-blooded killings—it was either my life or theirs."

Cohen years later told journalist Mike Wallace that "I killed nobody that didn't deserve killing. In all of these here killings there was no alternative. You couldn't call them cold-blooded killings—it was either my life or theirs."

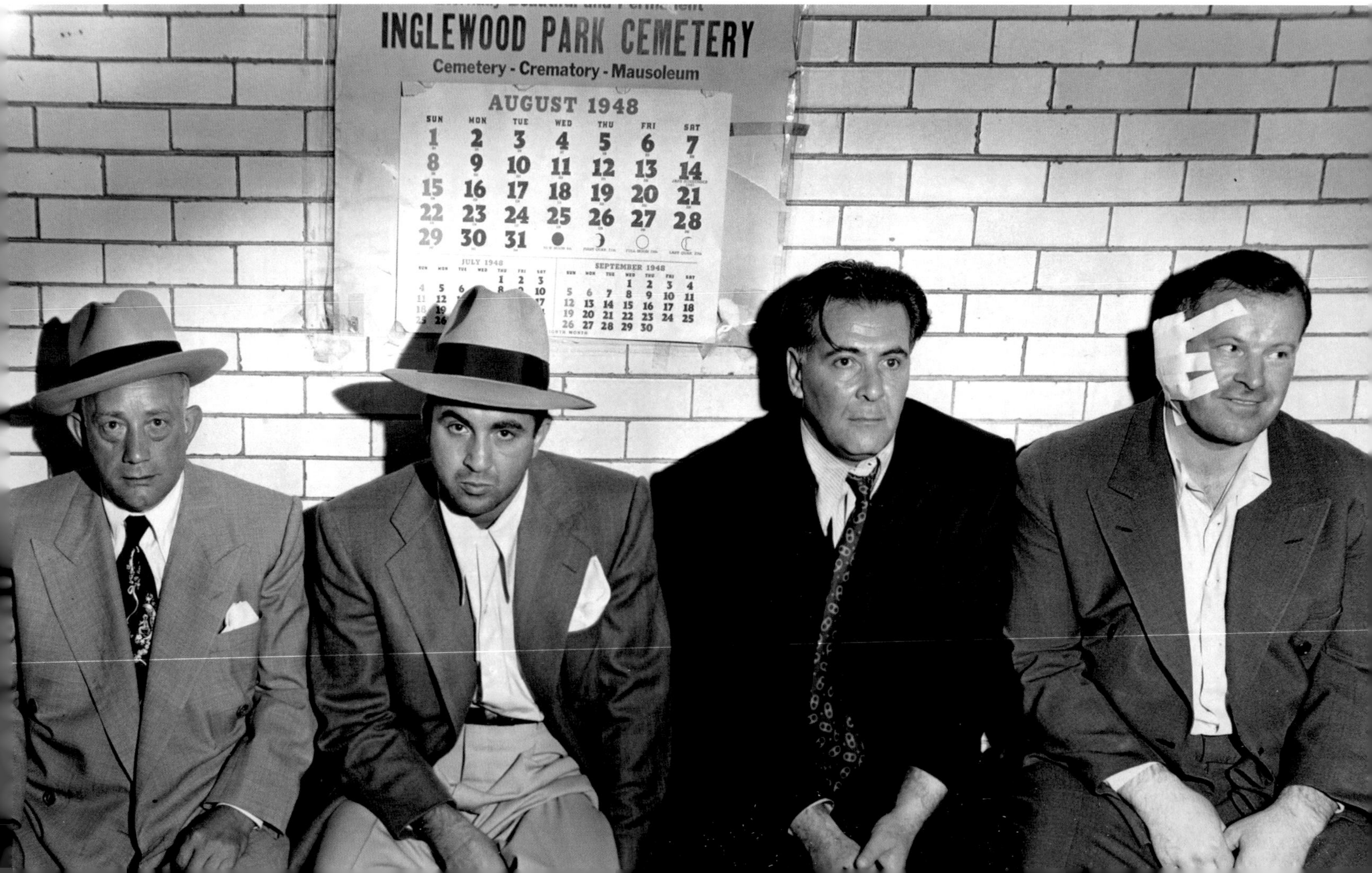

A forlorn Mickey and his gang sit in a sheriff's station after they survived an assassination attempt at Mickey's store. Cohen's top mob lieutenant, Harry Rothman, was killed by a point blank blast of a shotgun. The gang survived, but they were arrested for suspicion of murder. Left to right, Mike Howard, Cohen, Sol Davis, and Jimmy Rist were all released with no charges. As they left, Cohen declared, "I'll know who done it in half an hour."

He quickly became a murderous dandy and national celebrity, casually fronting the store's jackets and ties while directing a broad array of lucrative criminal endeavors and civic corruption. All while surviving some astonishing shootouts and a bombing generally initiated by the bungling locals.

Cohen lacked Siegel's sophistication and good looks. He was about five foot five, weighed around 145, and had a face dominated by a badly flattened nose. In the vernacular of the day, he had a "gutter face." His shop, which also served as a primary office, was Michael's Exclusive Haberdashery (which became the site of a striking office building just east of Book Soup, near the intersection of Sunset and Palm). While perhaps hyperbole, it was once said that every shirt, jacket, pants, and pair of shoes in the store were in Cohen's size.

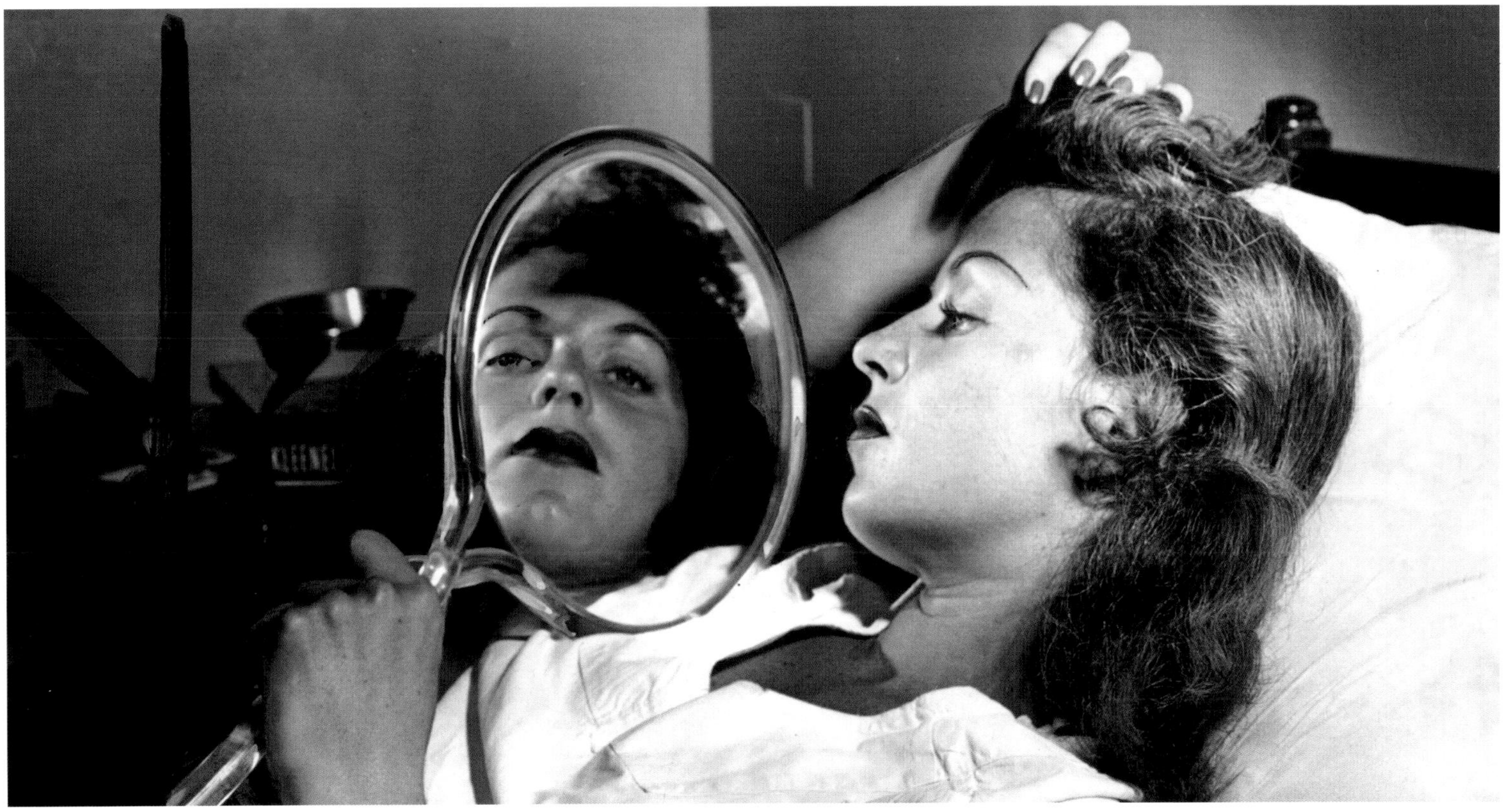

Dee David was in Mickey Cohen's party when the shooting broke out in front of Sherry's restaurant. She was seriously wounded but recovered. David is shown primping in her hospital bed for a photographer. At the time, she was variously identified as a "bit actress," "an aspiring actress," "a secretary in a doctor's office," or "a popular social companion." In the original *Los Angeles Times* article about the shooting, she was simply called "a blonde," a description that could cause outrage in modern times. In 1955, she shot and wounded a Mafia heavy in "a business dispute"—but served no time.

In 1948 hit men laid siege to Cohen's store. One of the two attacking gunmen was so fearsome that he buried more bones than could be found in the dinosaur room of the Natural History Museum of Los Angeles. One gunman, wearing a dashing white Panama hat and armed with a shotgun, immediately killed Mickey's dear friend and employee Hooky Rothman. The blast literally blew off his face. Cohen's two other henchmen were subsequently wounded, but the boss was nowhere to be seen. The shooters, unable to locate their true target, fled. Cohen, a cleanliness freak who washed his hands fifty to sixty times a day, was in the bathroom when the shooting started. "I fell to the floor," he said, "and put my feet up against the toilet door."

A major Sunset Strip shootout occurred July 21, 1949 just before 4 a.m. outside Sherry's Restaurant, a stylish and popular destination on the north side of Sunset just west of Wetherly. As Cohen's large and eclectic evening entourage exited to the sidewalk, two gunmen were hidden in a vacant lot across the street, next to a building owned by Bing Crosby. Cohen was, predictably, in the washroom cleaning his hands.

The gunmen opened fire—slugs and shotgun pellets whizzed across Sunset Boulevard. An agent from the California State Attorney General's office (with the seemingly implausible assignment of "protecting" Cohen) was hit in the stomach. A piano player got winged in the ear. A starlet, Dee David, who was accompanying Mickey, took rounds in her stomach and groin. One of the

Overleaf →
The gunmen had this view of the restaurant as Cohen and his party departed. Cohen was credited with bravery. . . though there is debate whether he returned fire. He drove a more seriously wounded colleague to the hospital. Bullet holes can be seen in the light-colored sedan parked at the sidewalk. It is not clear if the holes were caused by bullets from the Cohen group (if they returned fire at all) or some remarkably inept aim by the attackers. The gunmen split before the cops arrived, leaving behind only expended shells and half-eaten sardine sandwiches.

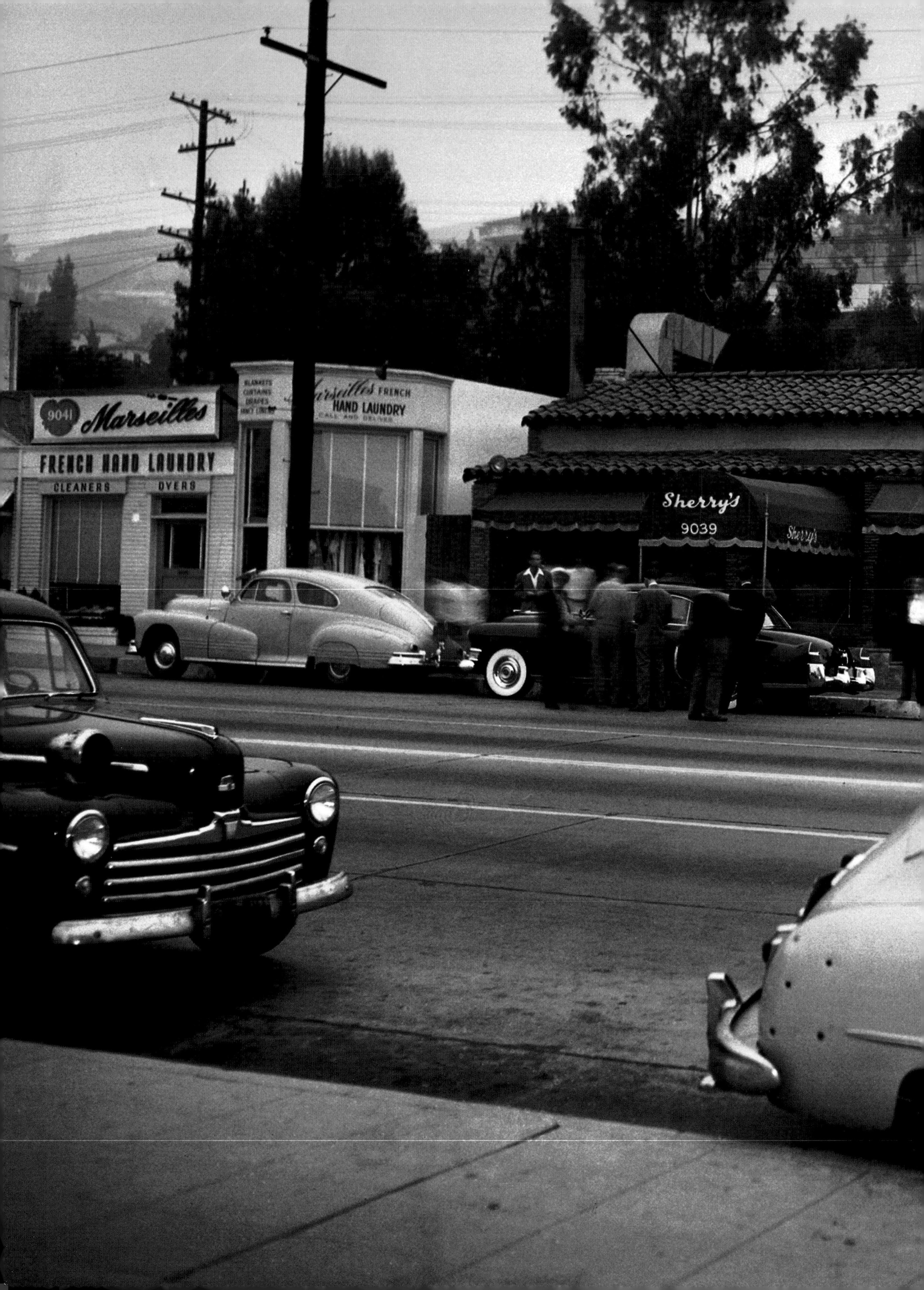
9041
Marseilles
FRENCH HAND LAUNDRY
CLEANERS
DYERS
BLANKETS
CURTAINS
DRAPES
Marseilles FRENCH
HAND LAUNDRY
Sherry's
9039
Sherry's

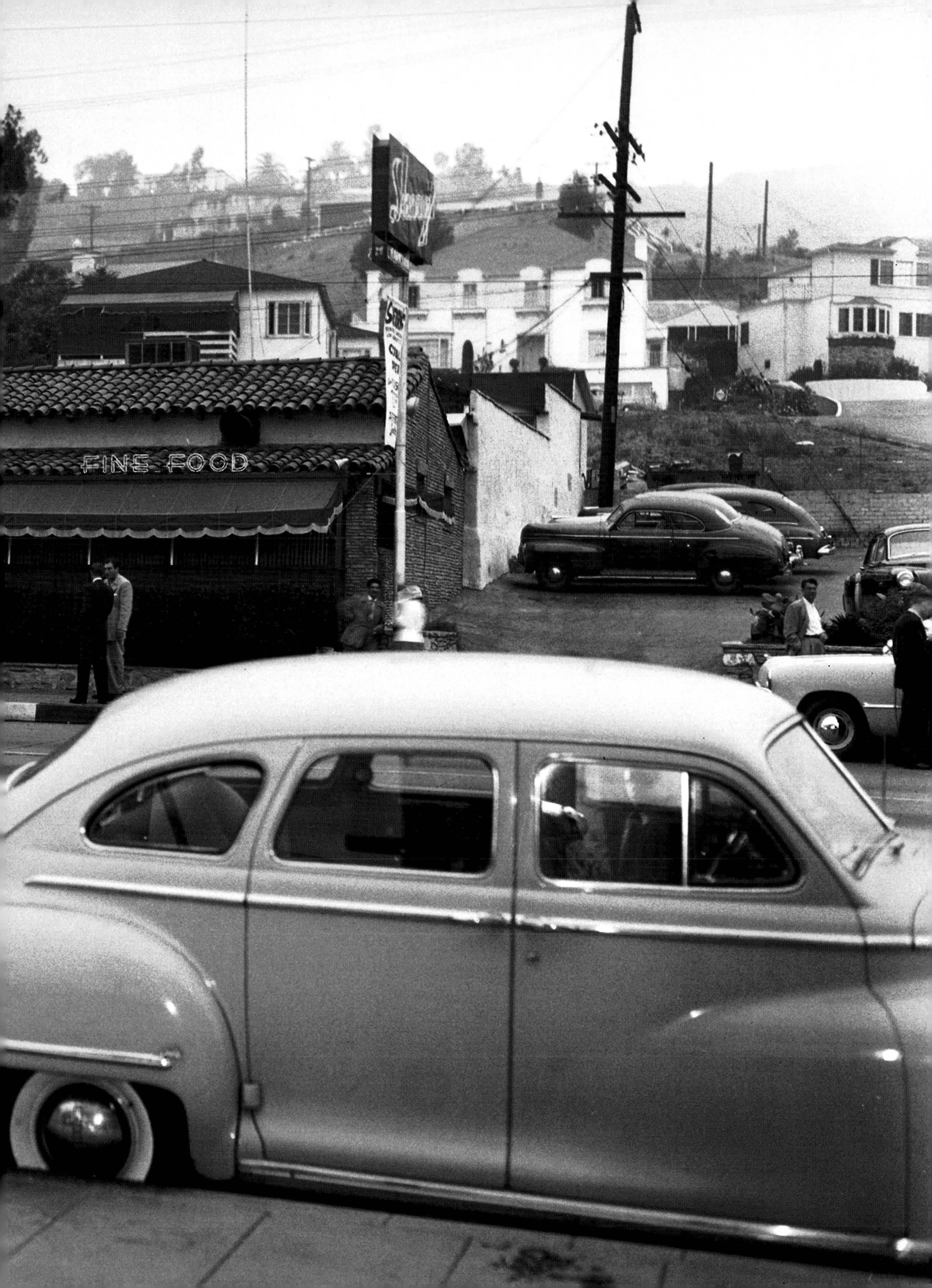
FINE FOOD

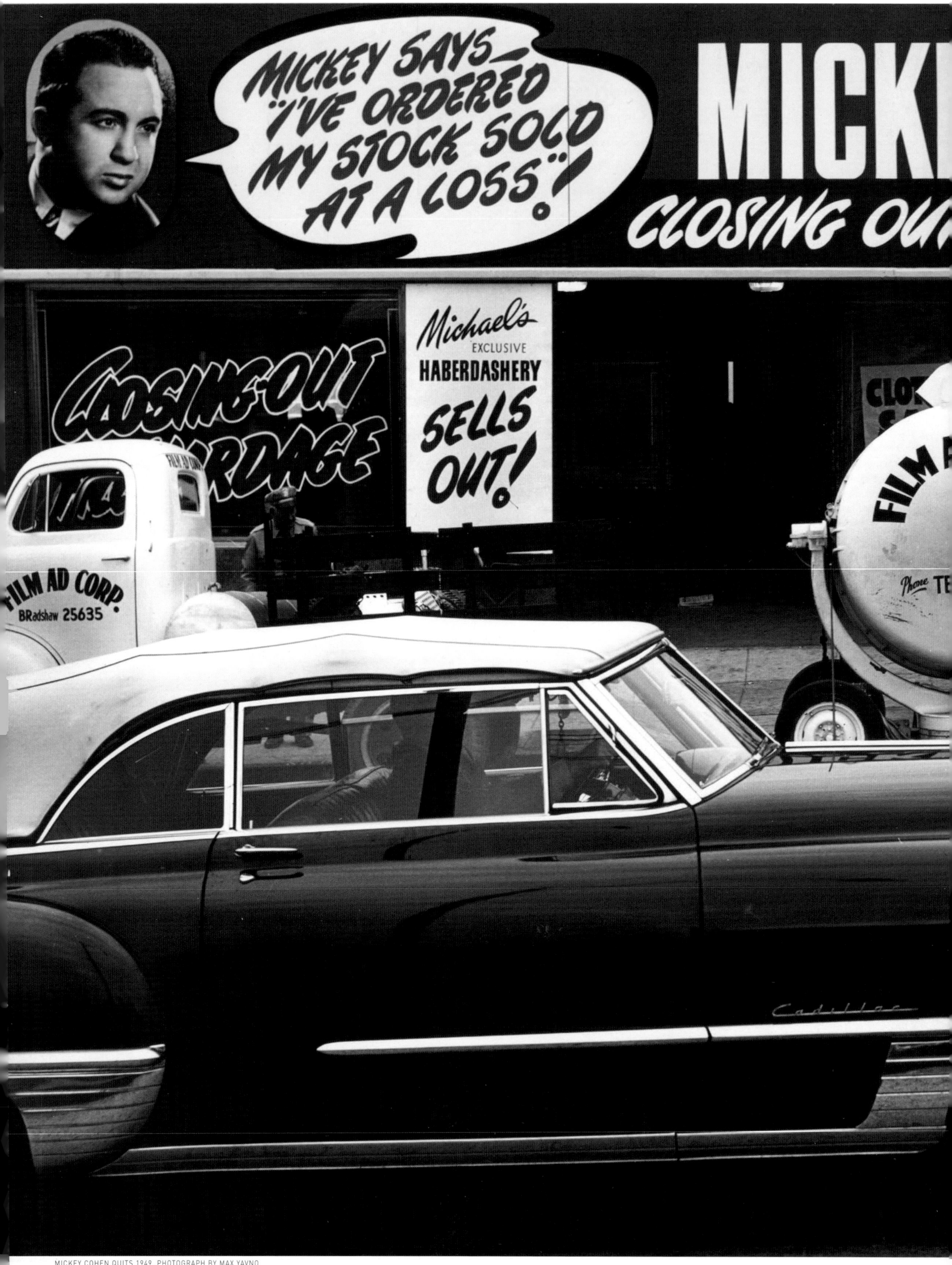

MICKEY COHEN QUITS, 1949. PHOTOGRAPH BY MAX YAVNO

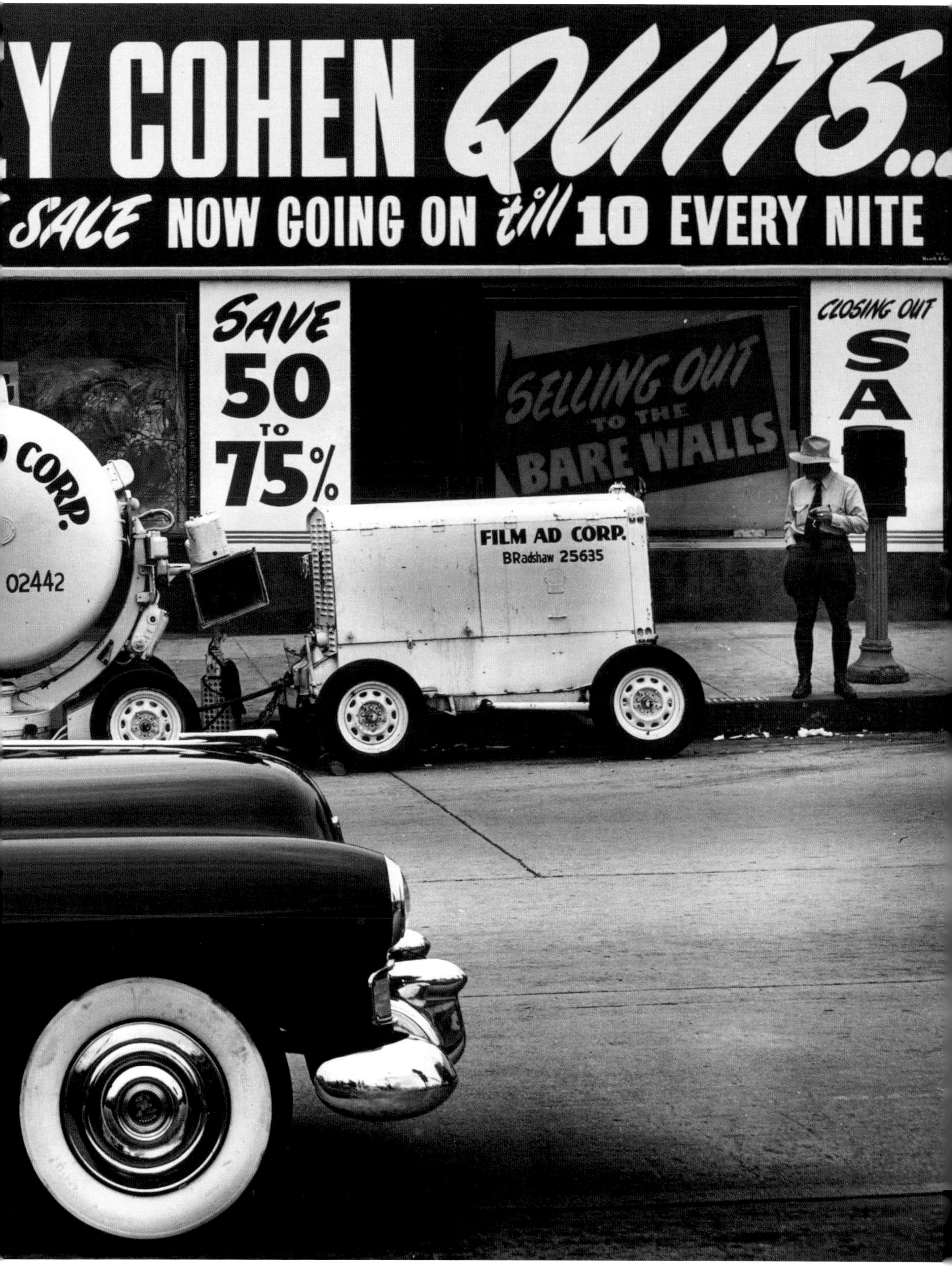
Y COHEN QUITS...
SALE NOW GOING ON till 10 EVERY NITE
SAVE 50 TO 75%
SELLING OUT TO THE BARE WALLS
CLOSING OUT
S
A
CORP.
02442
FILM AD CORP.
BRadshaw 25635

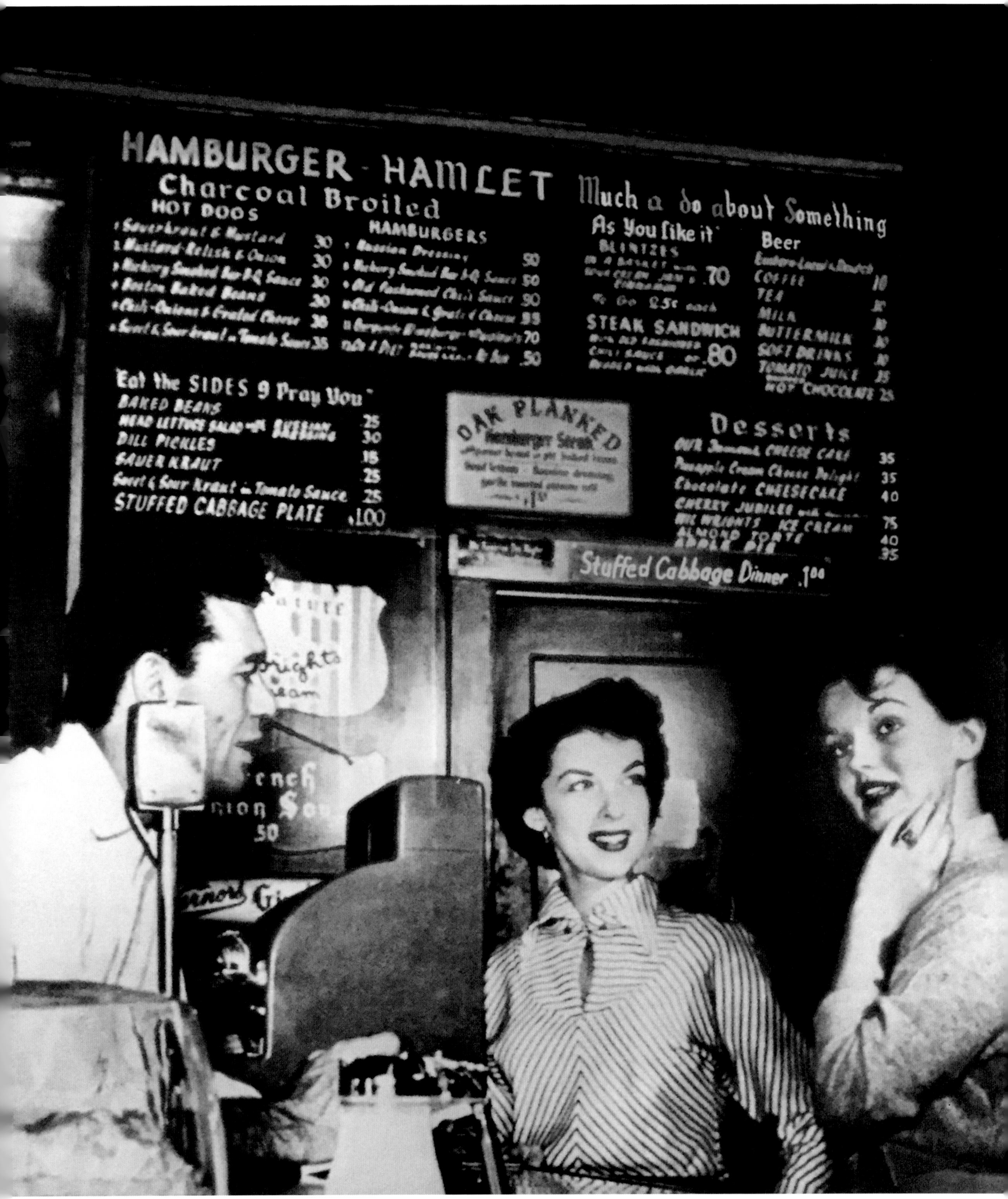
HAMBURGER HAMLET
Charcoal Broiled
Much a do about Something
HOT DOGS
HAMBURGERS
As You Like it
BLINTZES
Beer
COFFEE
TEA
MILK
BUTTERMILK
SOFT DRINKS
TOMATO JUICE
HOT CHOCOLATE
STEAK SANDWICH
Eat the SIDES 9 Pray You
BAKED BEANS
DILL PICKLES
SAUER KRAUT
STUFFED CABBAGE PLATE
OAK PLANKED
Desserts
Chocolate CHEESECAKE
ALMOND TORTE
APPLE PIE
Stuffed Cabbage Dinner

Hamburger Hamlet

Give Me the No. 17, Rare, with a Vanilla Shake

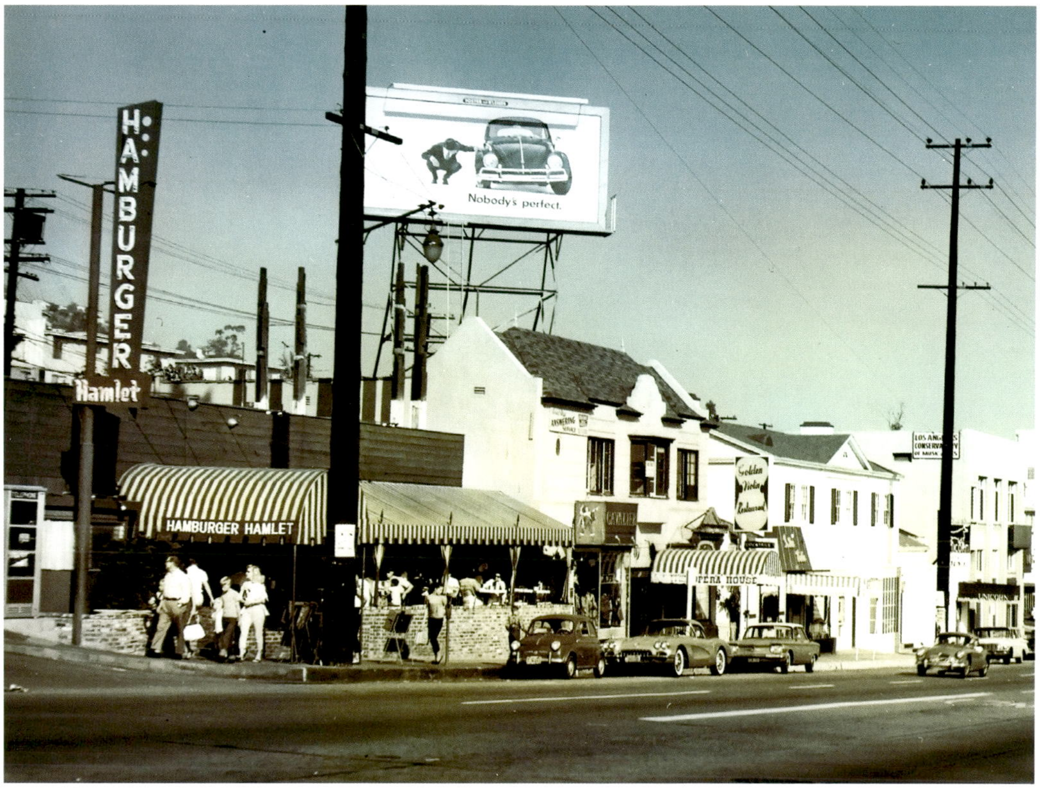

The first Hamburger Hamlet was located at the corner of Sunset and Hilldale. The Lewises prepared some of the signature dishes in their kitchen at home. Even after the couple achieved great success, some pot pies were still made at home, but by then were driven to the restaurant in a Rolls-Royce.

There was a time when every resident of L.A. seemed to champion a favorite Hamburger Hamlet, and within it a favorite red booth, a favorite hostess, and a favorite dish. The subject is very personal, so let me talk about my choices and my Hamlet. In reverse order, my favorites were the Emperor Henry burger (a lethal, heart valve–crippling caloric concoction named in honor of Rex Harrison), Frances Davis, and a booth next to the windows on Doheny Road in the Hamlet that was at the western edge of the Sunset Strip.

Most weekdays, clutching three newspapers, I would stroll a half block from my condo to the Hamlet at noon and be greeted by Frances. She was also a singer, dancer, and delightful raconteur. And her face graces the jacket cover of my favorite album by her former husband, Miles Davis, part-time scoundrel, monster, and soaring genius of jazz. And rarely was there a day when some certified celebrity wasn't on-site, easily slipping into a remarkable crowd of families, tourists, and office workers. Hamlets were so celebrated and successful in Los Angeles that they soon began to pop up across the country.

The Hamlet arrived in 1950 when Warner's contract player Harry Lewis (he achieved some fame in *Key Largo*, playing with Humphrey Bogart and Edward G. Robinson) decided to trade the Klieg lights for a gourmet hamburger stand. On his first date with Marilyn Friedman, he told her of his ambition. The couple was soon scouting locations and found one at Hilldale and Sunset on the Strip. At about the same time, they also managed to get married, and she became Marilyn Lewis.

← Harry Lewis and his wife, Marilyn Friedman Lewis (right), started out greeting patrons at the cash register under the Hamburger Hamlet menu board. Marilyn came to Los Angeles from Cleveland, hoping to become a costume designer. She eventually became a fashion designer.

As it happened, the Lewis marriage was facilitated by the famous. Sammy Davis Jr., Tony Curtis, and Jeff Chandler ran the restaurant for Marilyn and Harry so they could drive to Vegas to get married.

Harry bet his $3,500 life savings on hamburgers. But just before opening, the Lewises were out of cash and in hock to the gas company, which threatened to turn off their service, dooming their future. Marilyn, a dealmaker, found the building's meter reader, offered him free meals forever if he would look the other way, and, well, the gas stayed on.

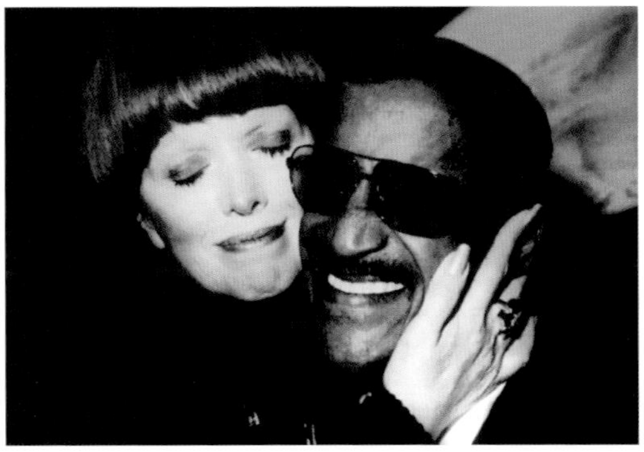

Harry was the operations guy. A son said he could have thirty sizzling patties on the grill and cook each one precisely to order. And he was a hawk on the restaurant floor, constantly scanning the room for any shortfall in performance.

Marilyn, an ambitious young woman who had hitchhiked to L.A. from Cleveland, was the idea person. She ran the menus, the promotion, and the style. There was a keen focus on quality comfort food, well served. It all clicked.

The décor was club-like, with dark, stately wood paneling, simple chandeliers, and overstuffed red-leather booths and chairs at the tables. The walls featured framed charcoal drawings of the clientele or Hollywood street scenes, film industry memorabilia, and panels of lines from Shakespeare.

← Marilyn Lewis with Sammy Davis Jr., a friend and customer.

Hamburger Hamlet was a significant success—the customers were packed in, and glad to have a place to sit. Illustrations of celebrated clientele adorned the walls.

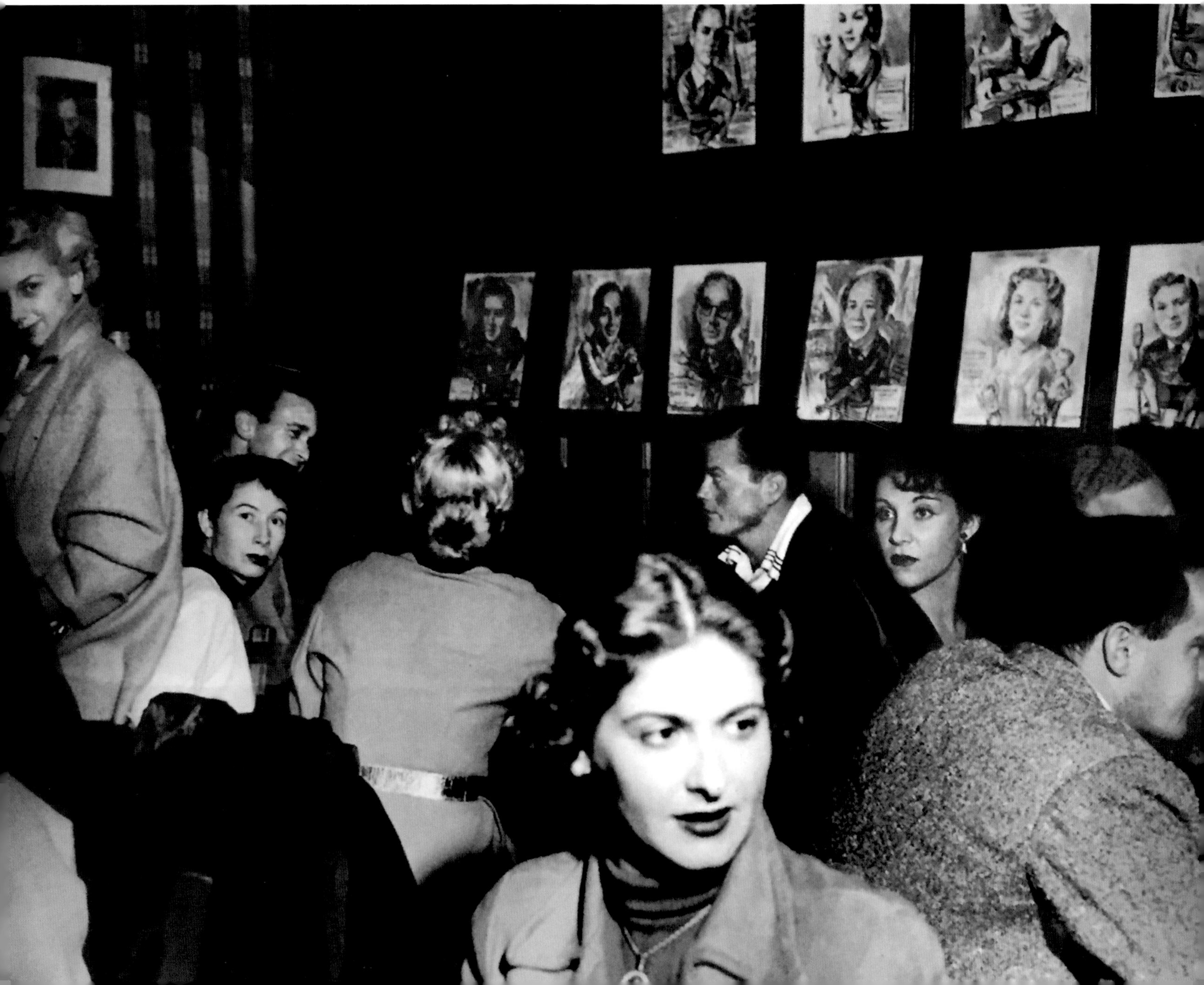

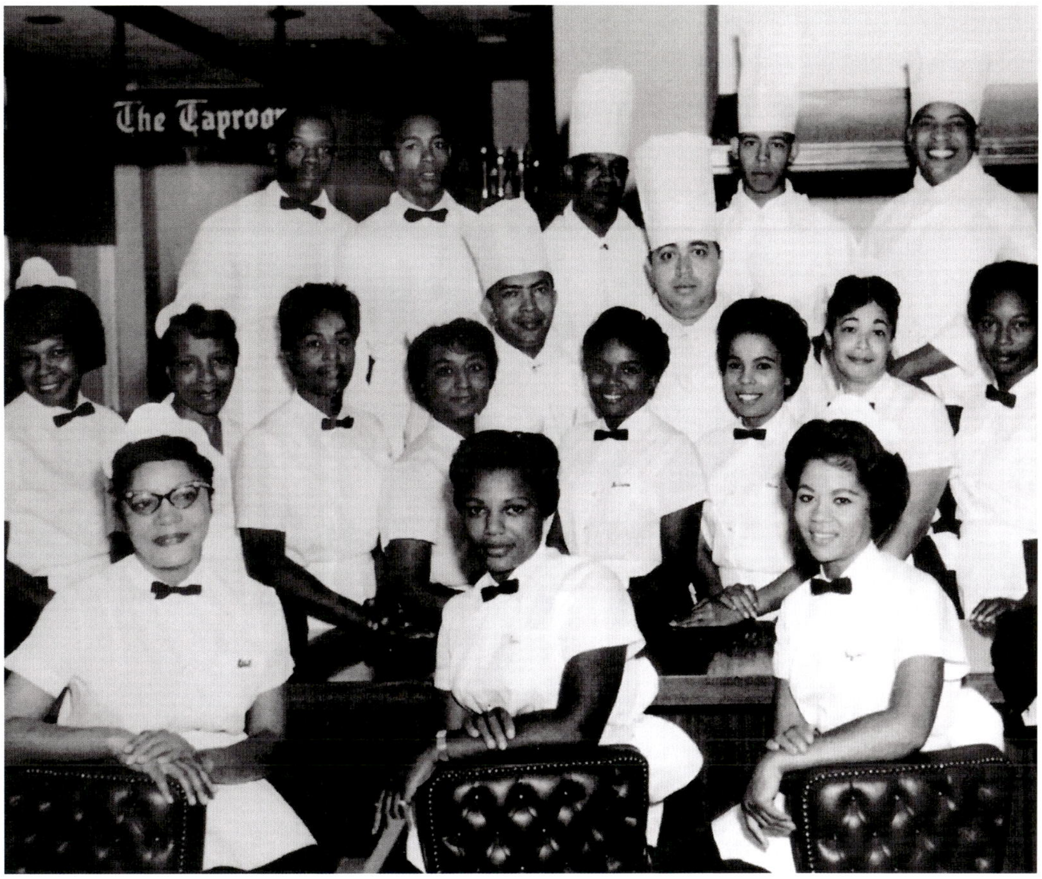

The Lewises hired many African Americans to work in the kitchen, and in the early days, the waitresses were exclusively black. When public transportation stopped because of the civil uprising in an African American neighborhood, the Lewises hired vehicles to bring their employees to and from the restaurant. As time passed, the hiring practices came under scrutiny for reverse discrimination, and eventually the wait staff was integrated.

The couple became local celebrities. And Marilyn fueled her creative side by developing a fashion design business that enjoyed success. In the fashion business, she was known as Cardinali. Dyan Cannon wore a Cardinali jumpsuit on her first date with Cary Grant. Nancy Reagan opted for a vibrant floral print Cardinali dress when she was First Lady of California. Somehow, Marilyn also managed to produce two successful film documentaries.

Marilyn fueled her creative side by developing a fashion design business that enjoyed success. In the fashion business, she was known as Cardinali. Dyan Cannon wore a Cardinali jumpsuit on her first date with Cary Grant.

The business was sold in 1987, though the family quickly created a new restaurant, Kate Mantilini, on Wilshire in Beverly Hills. Intent on sharp, modern architecture, Marilyn handpicked the now-renowned-but-defunct Morphosis team of Michael Rotondi and Thom Mayne (who would go solo and eventually win the Pritzker Prize) to design the restaurant—and the couple's own home at the beach. The food, while as eclectic as the architecture, played second fiddle to the design, but made Kate Mantilini a clever combination of comfort and deconstructivist sophistication.

Eventually, Kate Mantilini closed. As did every single Hamlet; at its peak, there were twenty-four. These days, there is no shortage of hamburgers on the Sunset Strip, from the irresistible, classy burger at the Sunset Tower to the dishy chili cheeseburger at Carney's railroad car across the street. Eventually, everyone in L.A. seemed to have found his or her Hamlet favorite. Consider a burger with chopped peanuts and bleu cheese. Where else but on the Strip? ■

Harry Lewis passed away in 2013, after running the tightest hamburger ship ever. He was ninety-three. When Marilyn Lewis died in 2017, her obituary credited her with creating the gourmet hamburger. She's shown here with Brett Doherty, who spent six years working for the Lewises.

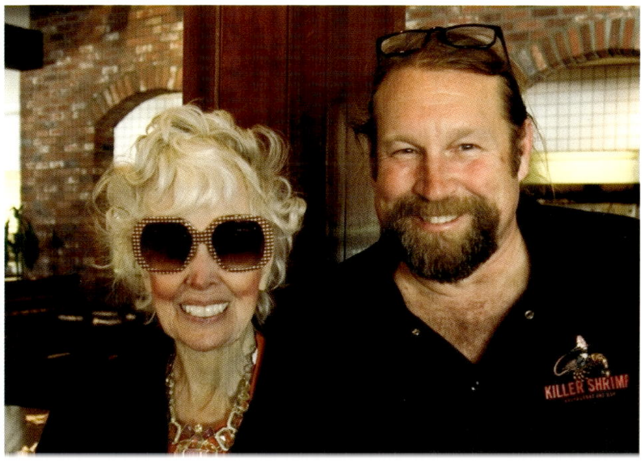

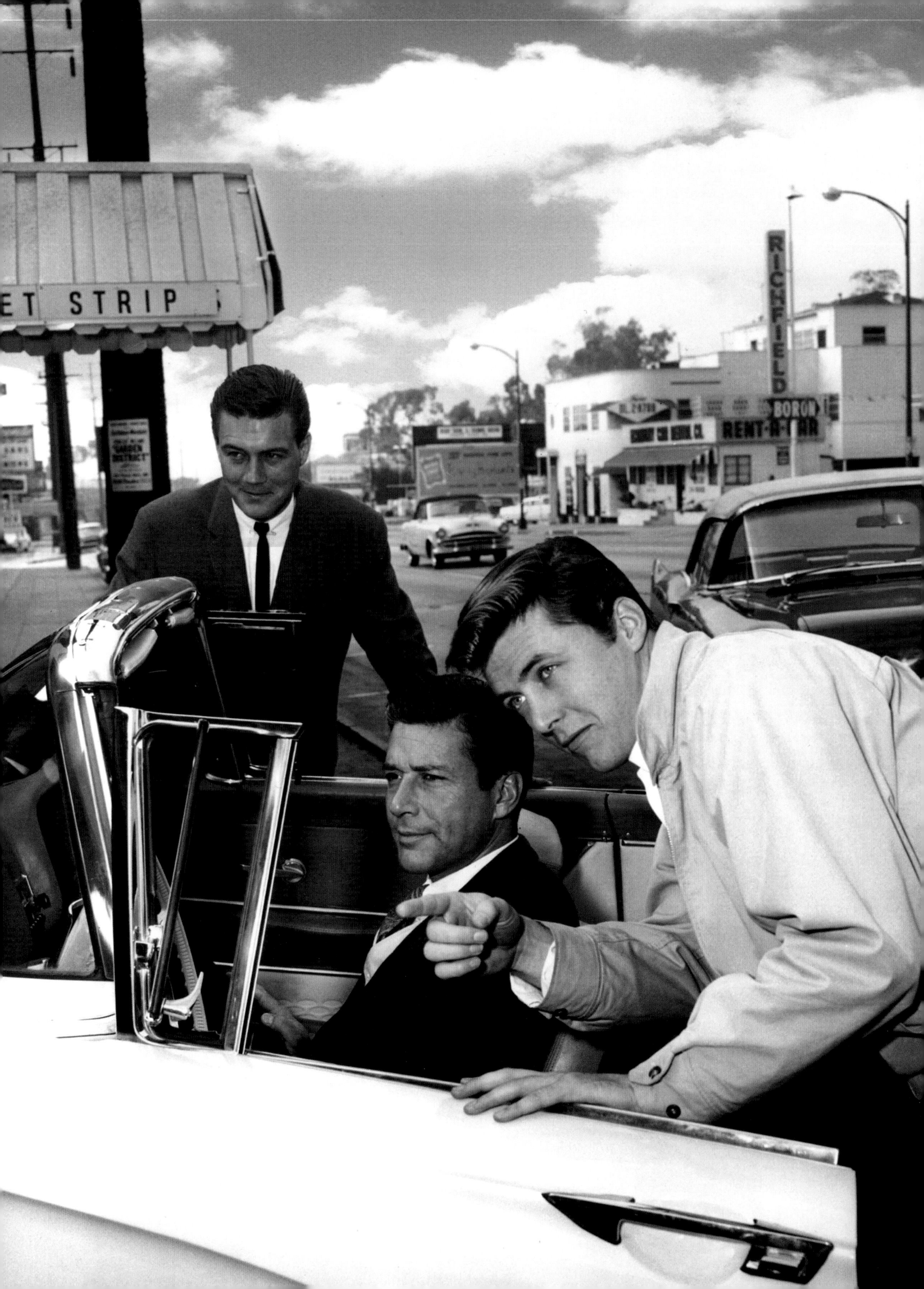
ET STRIP
RICHFIELD
BORON

77 Sunset Strip

The Most Famous Address that Never Existed

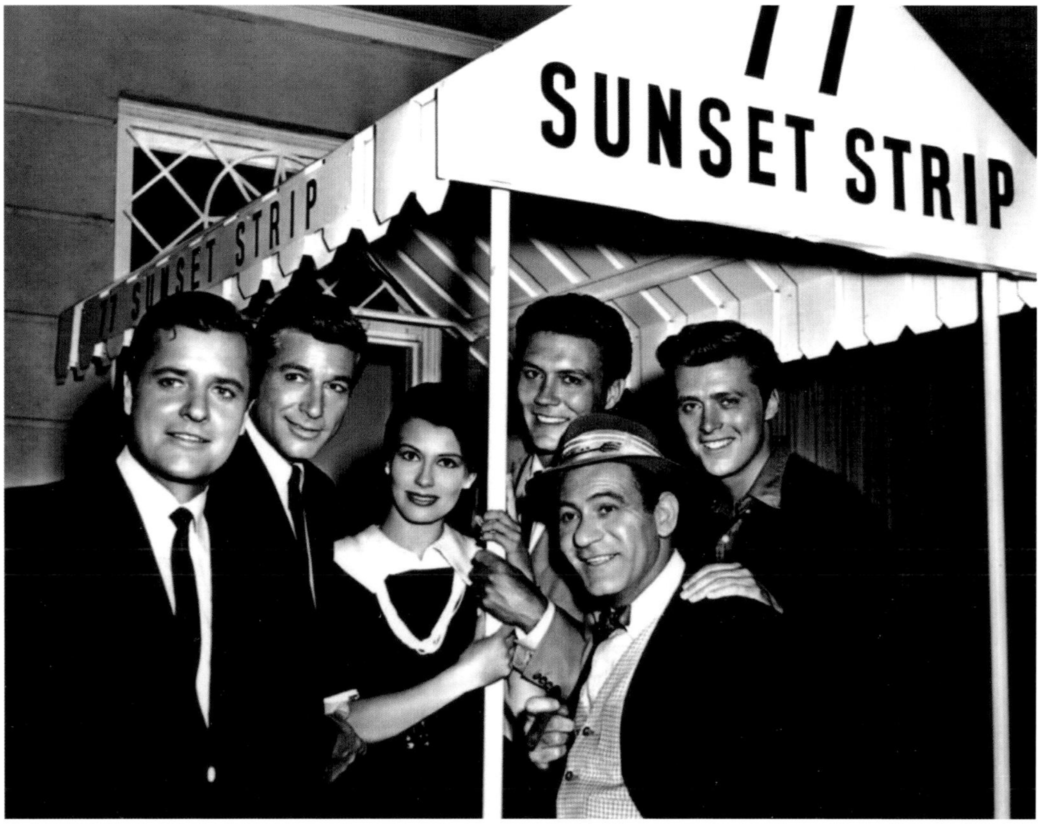

The entrance to 77 Sunset Strip (of course that wasn't a *real* address) was devoid of charm or efficiency, but crowded under it, on an apparently pleasant day, are the television stars who made the address world famous: from left to right, Richard Long, Efrem Zimbalist Jr., Jacqueline Beer, Roger Smith, Louis Quinn, and Edd "Kookie" Byrnes.

There they were, after a half-century, cheerful, resolute, smart. The guys of *77 Sunset Strip* were back at work, solving a case, in black and white, on an appropriately small television monitor in a media center in Beverly Hills. It seems this young San Diego girl, cute but insufferably petulant, on the verge of inheriting a large fortune, was making her way to the Sunset Strip in pursuit of a groovy and giddy life. Oh, by the way, she also witnessed a dreadful murder. In pursuit of her are two sinister men, a cagey conniver and his beefy goon in a suit so tight you can almost hear the seams splitting. They have a devious scheme for separating the innocent lass from her heavy dollars—and from a seat testifying before a murder trial jury.

To the rescue? That car-park lothario of the Strip, Gerald "Kookie" Kookson III, who shuffles vehicles in what is the real-life parking lot of Dino's (yes, as in Martin) Lodge, while emulating the two private detectives next door at #77. Efrem Zimbalist Jr. and Roger Smith play the detectives Stu Bailey and Jeff Spencer, Bailey a former agent of the OSS (the WWII forerunner of the CIA) with an Ivy League PhD, Spencer a former government agent with a law degree. Both good at judo.

ABC put the Warner Bros. show on the air in 1958, accompanied by a finger-snapping, energetic theme song. Needless to say, there was no #77 on the Sunset Strip.

← *77 Sunset Strip* created a weary catalog of publicity stills featuring the stars looking somewhat engaged. Here, Edd Byrnes was the official pointer, referencing "something out there" to the vaguely interested Roger Smith, left, and Efrem Zimbalist Jr.

ABC put the Warner Bros. show on the air in 1958, accompanied by a finger-snapping, energetic theme song. Needless to say, there was no #77 on the Sunset Strip. The actual address of the show's famed parking lot was 8524 in those days, and the office, real-life home to the Mary Webb Davis modeling agency, was 8532. Although the site has been consumed by a large hotel that looms over the sidewalk and Strip, some tourists—and not a few Angelenos—still break into the *77 Sunset Strip* theme song when they pass the iconic point.

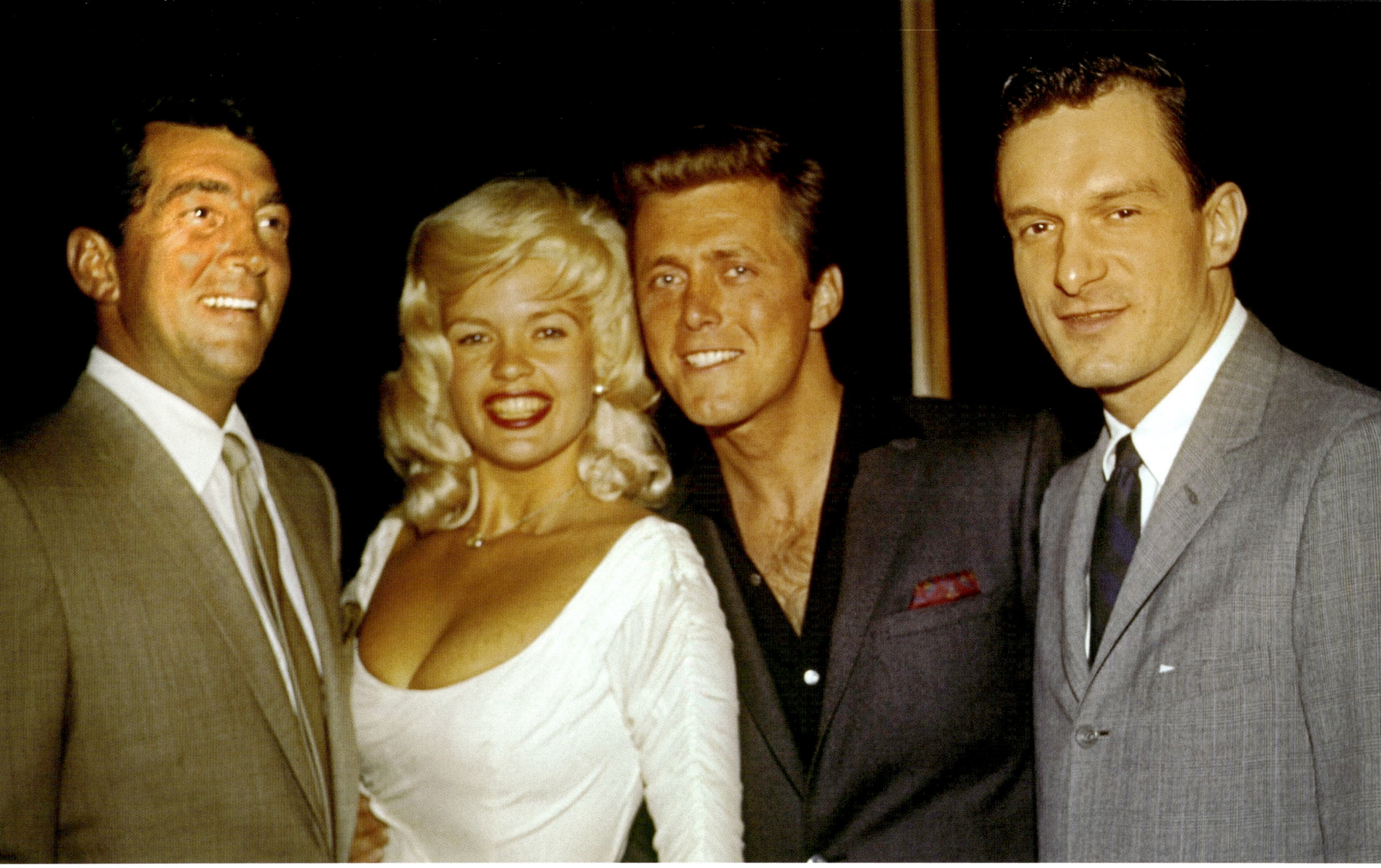

Jayne Mansfield was a surprisingly capable actress who ultimately was identified more for her physique and unrelenting publicity than her performance skills. She fell into the category of "blonde bombshell." Mansfield is seen here with Dean Martin, Edd Byrnes, and Hugh Hefner.

In the show's pilot episode, Kookie, played by Edd Byrnes, is, of all things, a vicious, irredeemable serial killer. It being television, the audience loved him. So when the series began its remarkable run, which lasted until 1964, Kookie shows up as a spiffy, high-energy character playing off the snobbish detectives he wants to emulate. He was utterly cool, decidedly hip, and had a penchant for grooming his pompadour. By 1959 Byrnes had become such a heartthrob that he and a very perky Connie Stevens ended up with a breathy Top 40 single called "Kookie (Lend Me Your Comb)" and even appeared on Dick Clark's *American Bandstand* to plug it. Years later, Roy Huggins, the creator of the show, described Kookie in the pilot as "Charles Manson with a comb," hardly an appropriate love interest for besotted teenage girls. But there was no explaining away the fact that Kookie returned to the Strip after he was headed to the electric chair. Instead, Zimbalist broke down the fourth wall and appeared out of character at the top of the second episode to guide viewers: "This week," he said, "we'll just forget that in the pilot [Kookie] went off to prison to be executed."

If *77 Sunset Strip* ever had a real victim, it was Dino's Lodge, which probably would have been preserved as a national landmark had its address really been #77.

The show thrived and energized a faltering ABC prime-time schedule. It defined the action/adventure/detective format. The popularity of *77 Sunset Strip* inspired several series featuring smart private eyes with quirky sidekicks working in unique, trendy locations: *Hawaiian Eye*. *Bourbon Street Beat*. *Surfside 6*.

For all the inherent silliness, the show was remarkably creative. And its success and cachet resulted in guest appearances by notable actors such as Roger Moore, Ellen Burstyn, Diane Ladd, Keenan Wynn, Jim Backus, Ida Lupino, George Jessel, Peter Lorre, and even Dodger pitcher Sandy Koufax. Huggins had a stellar TV track record that started with *Maverick*, even before *77 Sunset Strip* appeared, and subsequently contributed to other huge hits like *Rockford Files* and *The Fugitive*.

If *77 Sunset Strip* ever had a real victim, it was Dino's Lodge, which probably would have been preserved as a national landmark had its address really been #77. Martin's cocktail lounge/restaurant

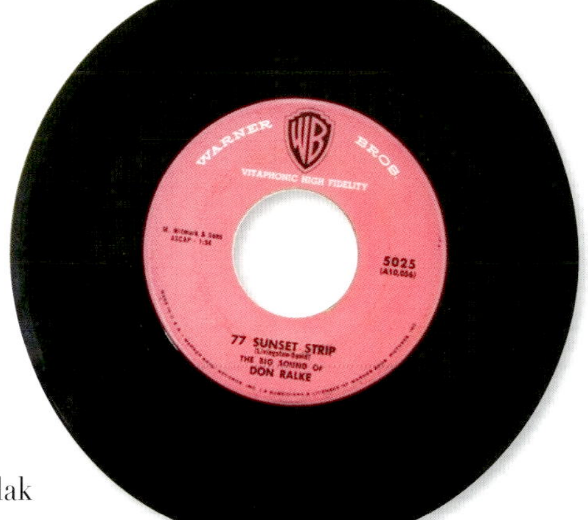

The theme song for the series became a hit, one of the most recognizable songs in television history.

attracted an elite Hollywood crowd. The building's exterior, seen frequently in the television show, carried a sign featuring a caricature of Martin's face. Film and television critic Shawn Levy recalled that "Dino's Lodge was immensely popular, serving homestyle Italian food and grilled entrees in a wood-paneled atmosphere meant to replicate the great roué's den."

But when *77 Sunset Strip* clicked, fans from the sticks flocked to the Strip and to Dino's. The players and agents and writers suddenly found themselves competing for seats with tourists from Nebraska aiming Kodak Brownies at anyone who looked vaguely familiar. The celebrities took flight, Dino's degenerated into a prosaic tourist trap and lost its luster. And then Martin ended up in acrimonious litigation with his partners. He summed up his restaurant experience in two words: total regret. By 1962 he pulled out entirely.

Because of unrelated litigation, *77 Sunset Strip* hasn't been seen in homes for decades. A pity. Rene Reyes, director of public programs at the Paley Center for Media, agrees: "The moment you heard that iconic theme song, you knew the adventure and glamour of the Sunset Strip was entering your living room."

It still feels that way, even in black and white, on a tiny screen, in Beverly Hills. ■

For a time, Dino's Lodge enjoyed a classy reputation, drawing Hollywood elites to a gracious room with an extensive menu ($6.75 for a New York sirloin steak was pricey for the time). But its exposure on *77 Sunset Strip* drew a tidal wave of tourists that washed away the horrified regulars and turned the place into a decidedly déclassé tourist trap.

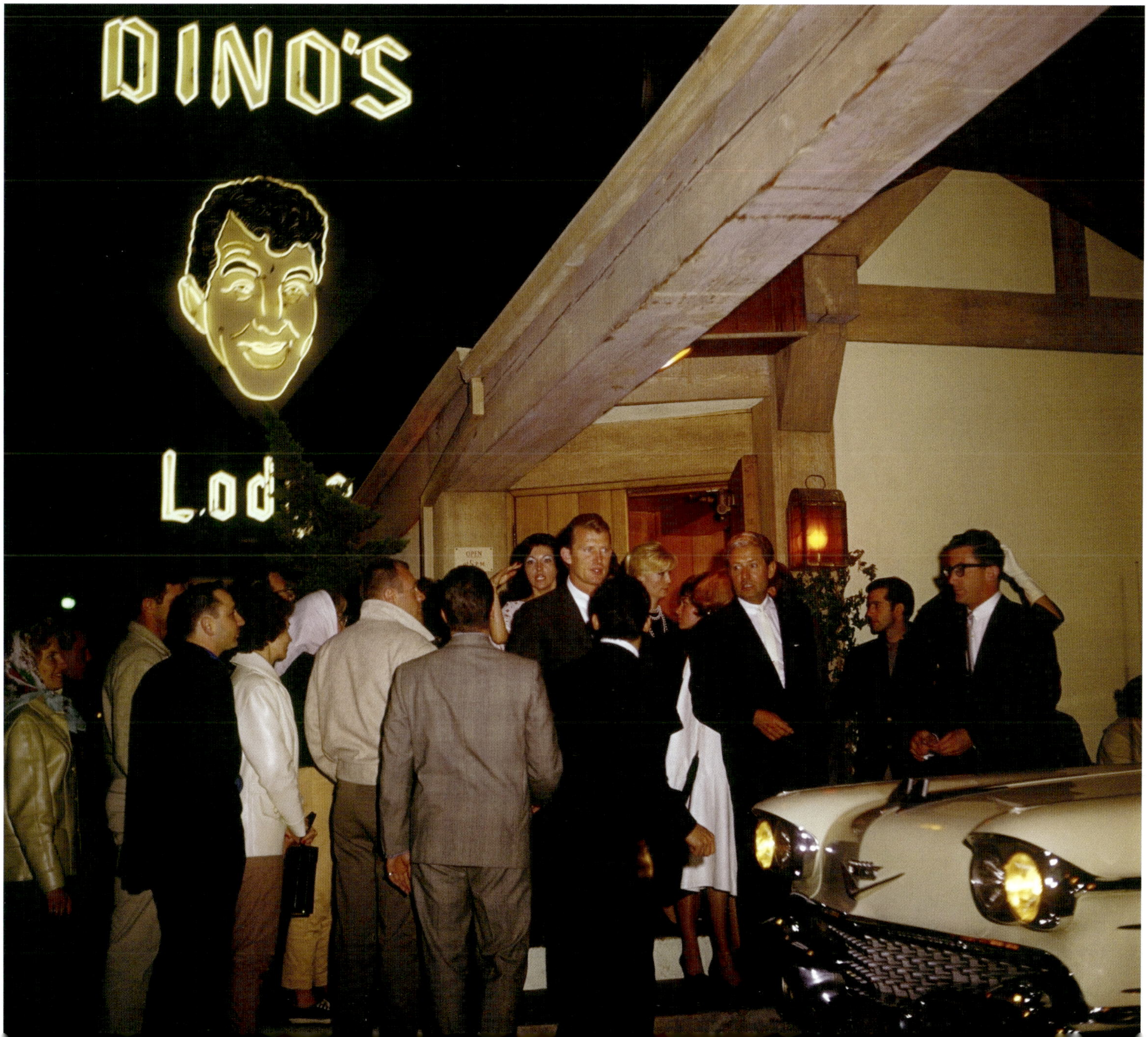

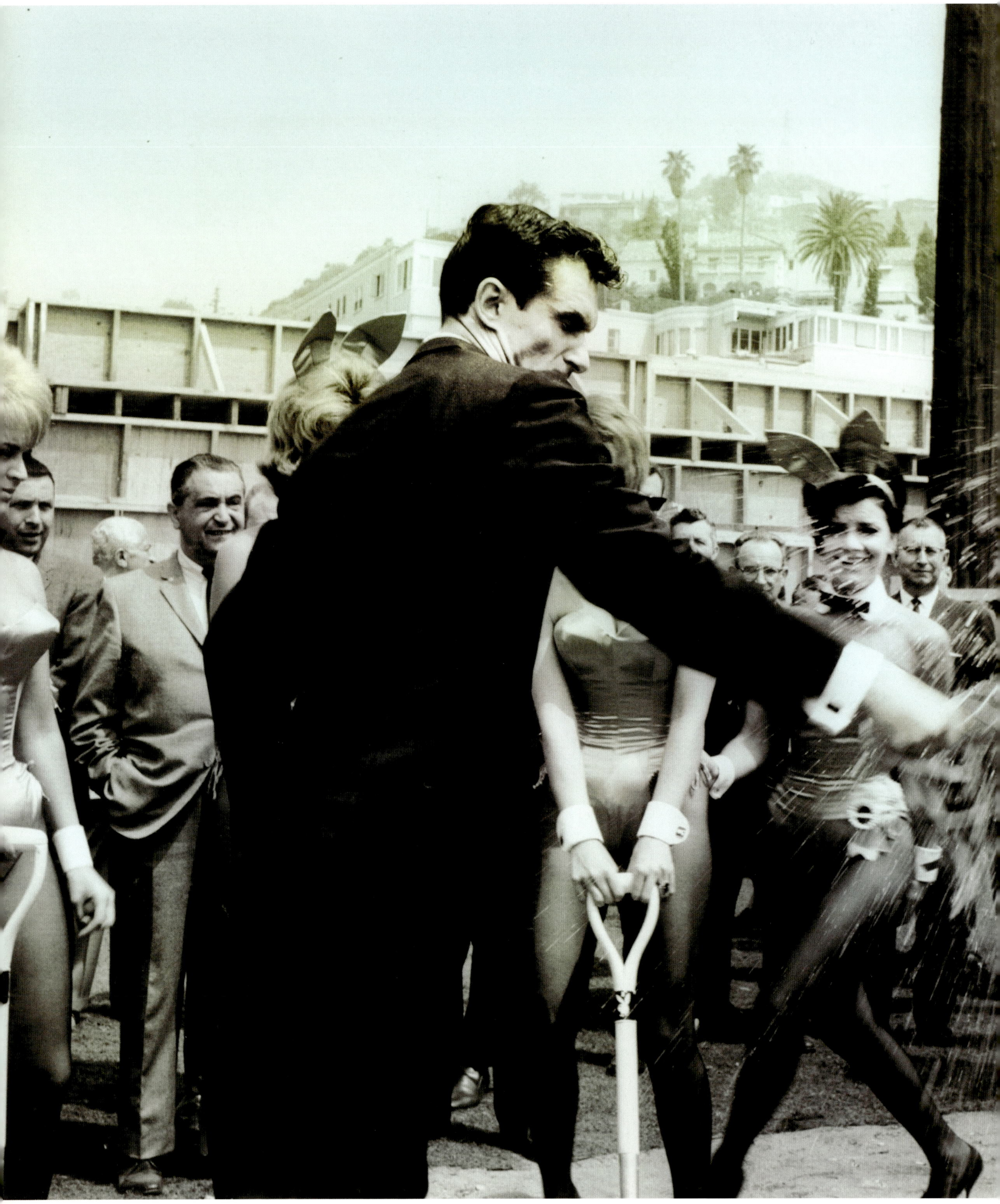

The Playboy Club

Join the Vanguard for $25

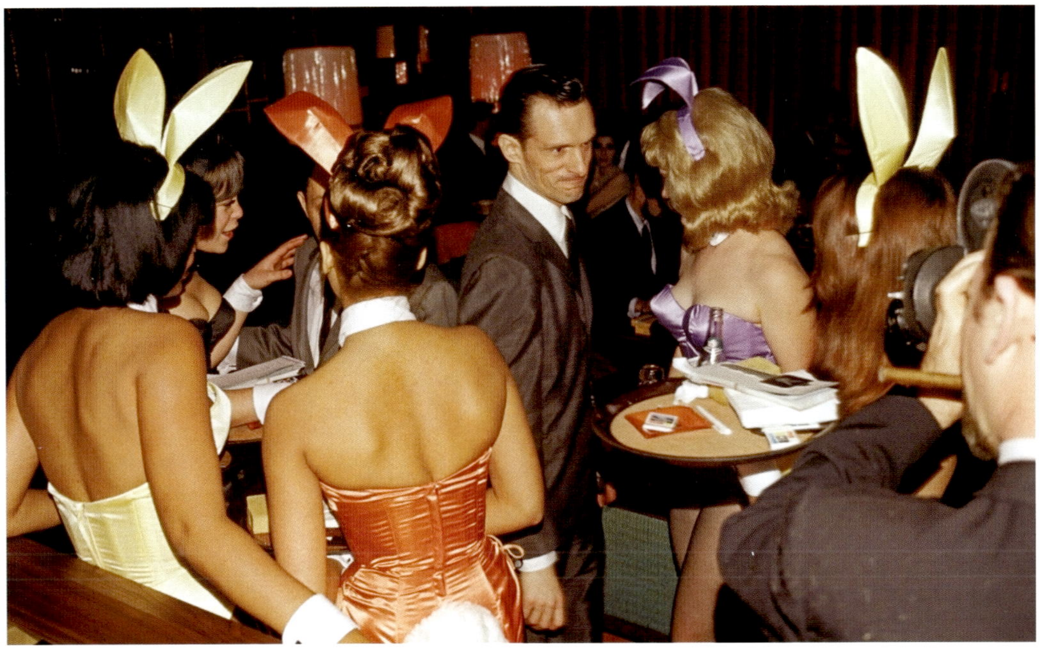

For years, Hefner seemed to travel outside the mansion with a colony of bunnies, very often in their signature costume. A former Bunny-of-the-Year offered her getup for sale: $3,999.99.

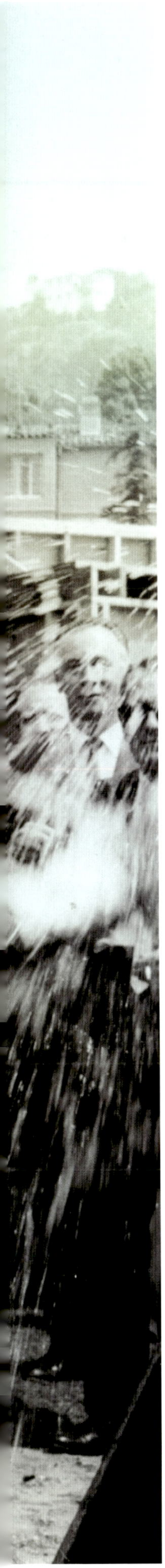

In 2011, NBC premiered a thankfully short-lived primetime dramatic series called *The Playboy Club*. For fogeys with memories that stretch back a half-century or so, the show seemed tinny and inauthentic. But more troubling, it was mortifying. Back then, did men actually believe that women in cleavage-enhancing bunny suits with cottontails and flopsy blue-satin rabbit ears, serving drinks in a smoke-filled club room, were sexy? Well, live with it—they did.

In his heyday, Hugh Hefner perfectly captured what was on the minds of young men as they fumbled their way into adulthood and identity and careers and, perhaps most important, sex. Hefner articulated and illustrated all this in his *Playboy* magazine, which debuted in 1953, well before the first club opened in Chicago in 1960 and another followed on the Sunset Strip in 1964.

Back then, did men actually believe that women in cleavage-enhancing bunny suits with cottontails and flopsy blue-satin rabbit ears, serving drinks in a smoke-filled club room, were sexy?

It seems absurd to a modern cognoscenti, but the magazine and clubs constituted a transformational moment. The publication of the first edition of *Playboy* was a watershed moment. There was life before *Playboy* and life after. But for a young, middle-class man in 1953 America, life would never be the same. When he got his first subscription to the magazine, still in its discrete brown wrapper, he had come of a new age. A good part of that was Hefner's remarkable creativity and empathy for young males. Add to that his skill at fighting censorship and rejecting public condemnation and religious recrimination. Conservative critics assailed Hefner's core philosophy, with William F. Buckley describing it as a "sort of a hedonistic utilitarianism."

← Hugh Hefner cracks a Champagne bottle at the groundbreaking for the Playboy Building, which opened in 1964 on the Strip at 8560 Sunset. Playboy Enterprises is long gone from the spot, but it is, and no doubt always will be, the Playboy Building.

But there was more to the *Playboy* philosophy, many acknowledged. Some gave credit to Hef for helping to liberate women, taking their bodies out of the porn rags and into the pages of a magazine that not only worshipped these beauties' goddess style, but added some intellectually stimulating articles. Some early feminists railed against the clubs. Gloria Steinem, who went undercover as Bunny Marie Ochs for an article on the clubs, deplored the Bunny identity and role, calling it demeaning to women. She also considered the clubs themselves "profoundly tacky." All the attention

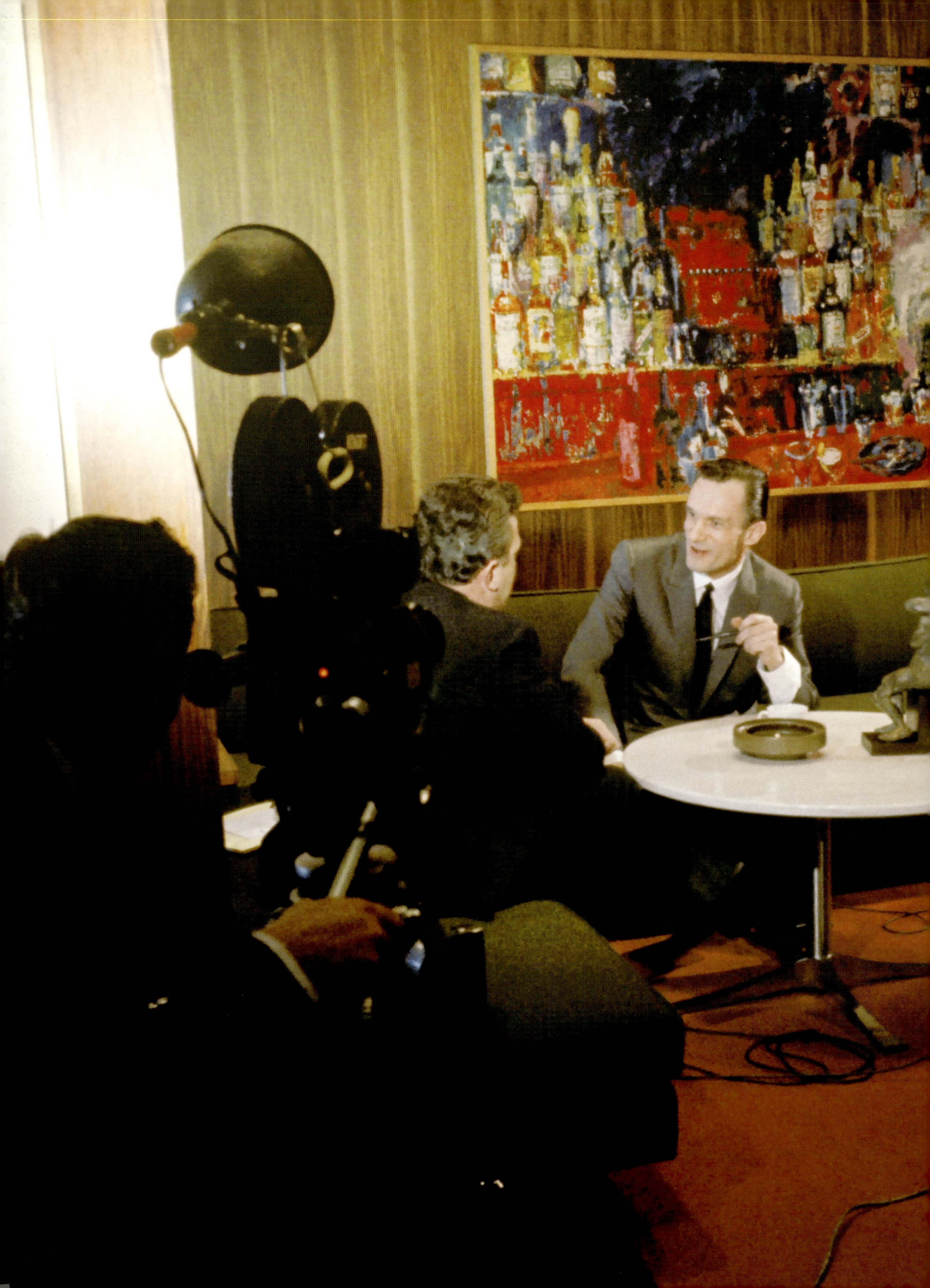

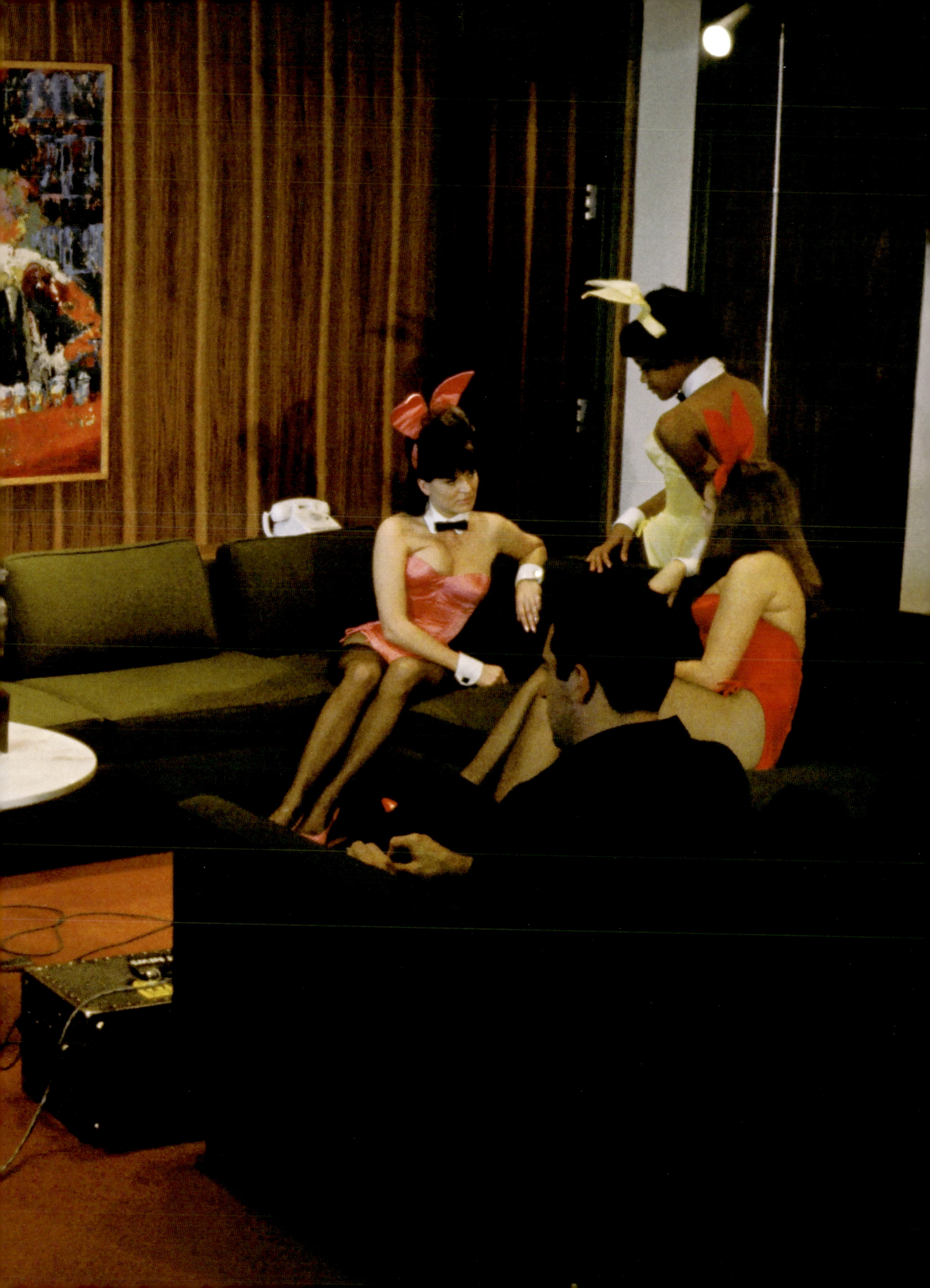

← *Overleaf*
Hefner hosted two television series over the years. Both confirmed his wisdom—or good fortune—in initiating his career with a magazine and not a television show. He was awkward on camera, and Playboy culture itself didn't translate well to a then-stodgy medium, overseen by a fuddy-duddy Federal Communications Commission. Hefner's appreciation helped contribute to the success of artist Leroy Neiman, whose work dominates the wall.

meant Hef kept getting richer. The bunny ears and cotton tails were eventually relegated to logos and the clubs, and before long women were as welcome at the tables as men.

Hefner was an articulate and forceful proponent of the sexual/social revolution that swept through the late 1950s and 1960s. He was probably delighted when the executive director of the Kinsey Institute that studied human sexuality told *Time* magazine that "Hefner's genius is that he has linked sex with upward mobility."

Hef also was a proponent for civil rights, the social acceptance of homosexuality, and he became outspoken about women's liberation, despite being perceived by many as an exploiter of women. His message found traction. The magazine circulation peaked at seven million. There were 230,000 Playboy Club members, who were known as keyholders. To Hefner, the clubs were an extension of the concept developed in the magazine: "to bring to life many of the [magazine's elements]. . .good food and drink, pretty girls, good entertainment."

The Playboy Club on the Strip occupied the first four floors of the Playboy Building at 8560 Sunset, just east of the Sunset Plaza shops and restaurants. There were no Chicago or Los Angeles "versions" of the Playboy Club. The clubs that spread across the country were fundamentally identical in design and attitude, ensuring that a man presenting his twenty-five-dollar membership key would always be admitted to a familiar Playboy Club environment.

Hefner was an articulate and forceful proponent of the sexual/social revolution that swept through the late 1950s and 1960s.

It was probably inevitable that Hefner and the Playboy headquarters would eventually relocate from Chicago to Los Angeles. Initially, Hefner created a Los Angeles pied-à-terre (with a rotating circular bed, of course) in the Playboy Building's penthouse. And later, as Chicago turned frigid in more ways than the weather, he closed the Windy City mansion, purchased a Holmby Hills mansion (a castle, by most standards at the time), and became an Angeleno.

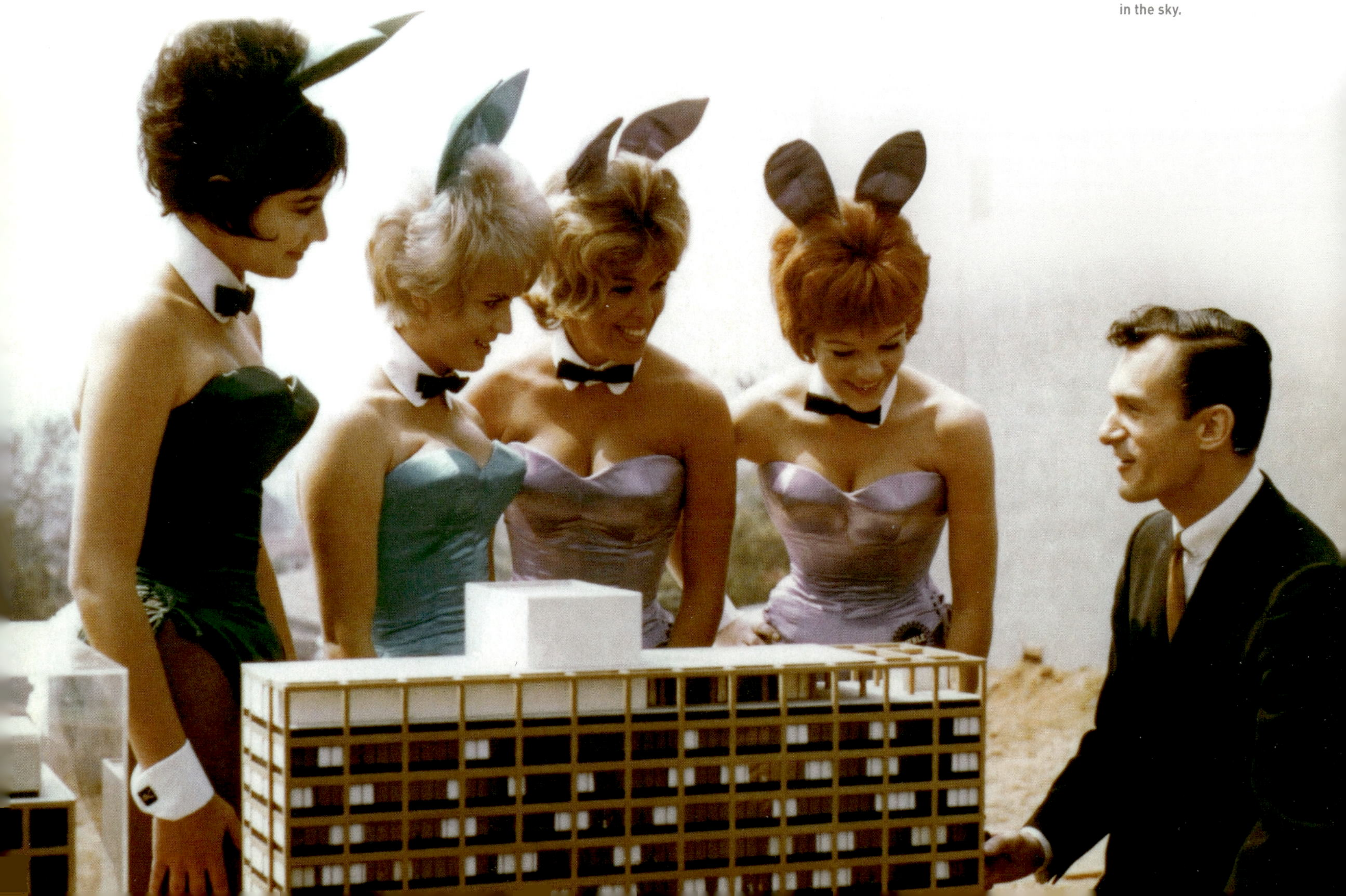

While Hefner relished the joys of his building on the Strip, he bought in 1971 for $1.1 million a 21,987 square foot Gothic Tudor castle in the prestigious Holmby Hills neighborhood of Los Angeles. He decorated twenty-two rooms with all the toys a "playboy" could want. Before he died at age ninety-one in 2017, the mansion sold for $100 million, and he continued to rent it back for a million dollars a year, until he went to the great playground in the sky.

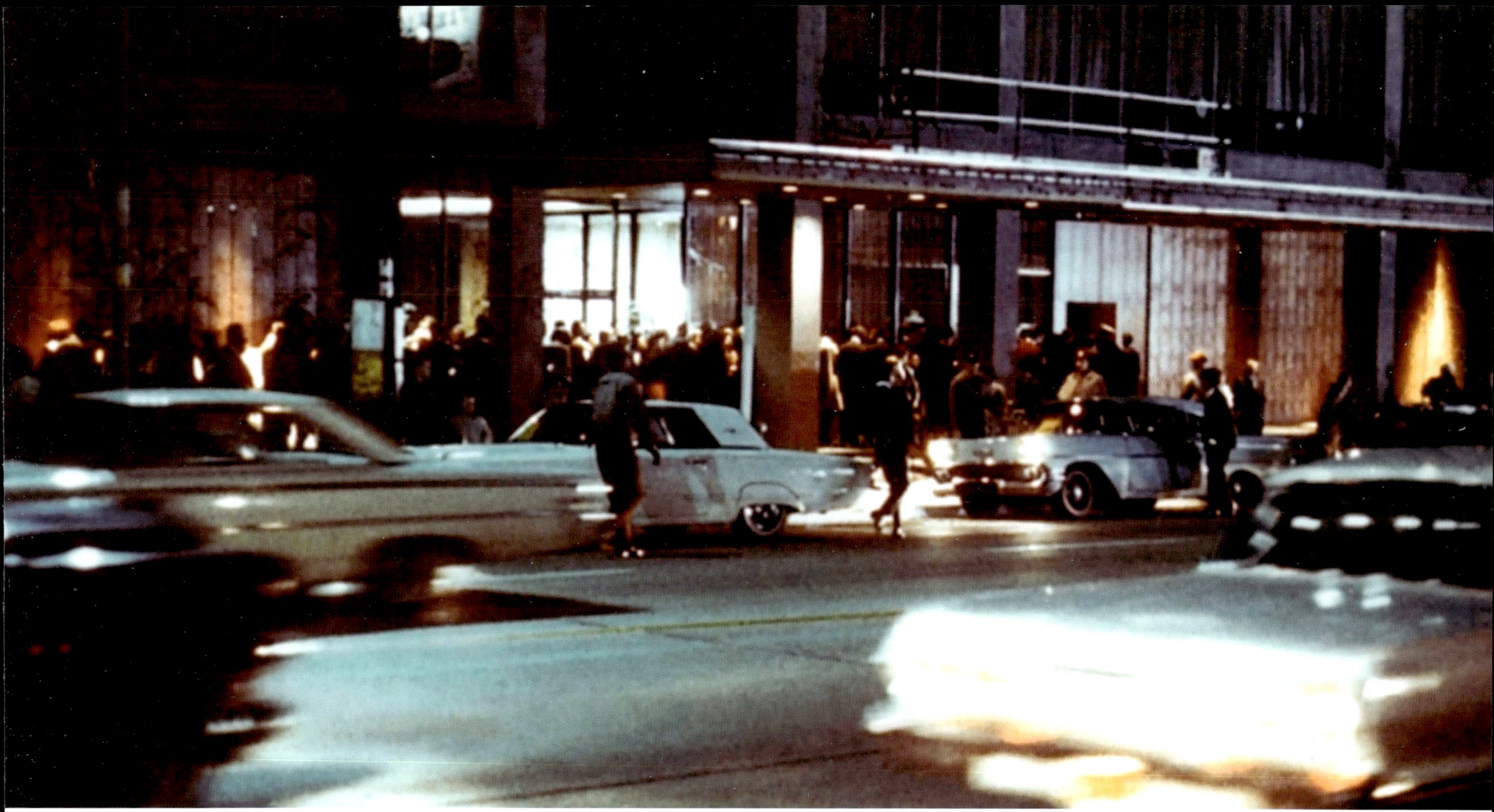

The Playboy Club had a gala opening night/New Year's Party on December 31, 1964. Headliners were comedian Milton Berle and Hugh O'Brien, star of television's *The Life and Legend of Wyatt Earp*, and actress Shirley Jones, in white ermine.

"Hollywood itself is a magnet," Hefner said in the fascinating documentary entitled *The Sunset Strip*. "It has great feminine appeal, sexual appeal, and the Strip is the personification of that.... The Strip had its own personality, and it certainly dramatically changed decade to decade. It evolved but always reflected what was going on."

Eventually, the magazines and clubs seemed to lose that sense of what was happening. A rougher, less-sophisticated crowd joined the clubs, undermining the sense of exclusivity. A bunny from the New York club told *Vanity Fair* that while walking one day in New York City a sooty worker on the back of a bilious garage truck began yelling at her using her bunny name. She had waited on his table the prior night at the club. When the clubs lost their cachet, Hef folded them after what was—for nightclubs—a remarkably long lifespan.

Rather rapidly, the magazine lost its brio. Society, rapidly spinning off new voices and issues and indulgences, moved out ahead of the Playboy ethic, which began to feel outdated, a relic frozen in time.

Then, rather rapidly, the magazine lost its brio. Society, rapidly spinning off new voices and issues and indulgences, moved out ahead of the Playboy ethic, which began to feel outdated, a relic frozen in time. With one of the world's most famous logos (created in '53 in about ten minutes by the magazine's art director), *Playboy* now is active in merchandising here and abroad. After a brief experiment with no nudity on its pages, the magazine retreated to its bare roots.

Hefner himself conceded little to age. He managed to embody a frail incarnation of that Playboy persona—even well into his eighties. Some old fans admitted to experiencing a certain cringe factor to the old rake and his Bunnies who were about sixty years younger than he. One night at a Strip steakhouse, he came through the door with several young women from the mansion. A whirl of sneering jokes drifted down the bar, most from young turks with a cynical attitude about anything over forty. But the codgers, easing their arthritis and apprehensions with therapeutic pricey bourbons, were tolerant, a bit understanding of it.

And then one day, he was gone. Hefner defined the Playboy life. People may quibble about whether the results were for the better or worse for society. For women. For men. But with his philosophy, he accomplished something notable and had a voice in how life is lived today. ■

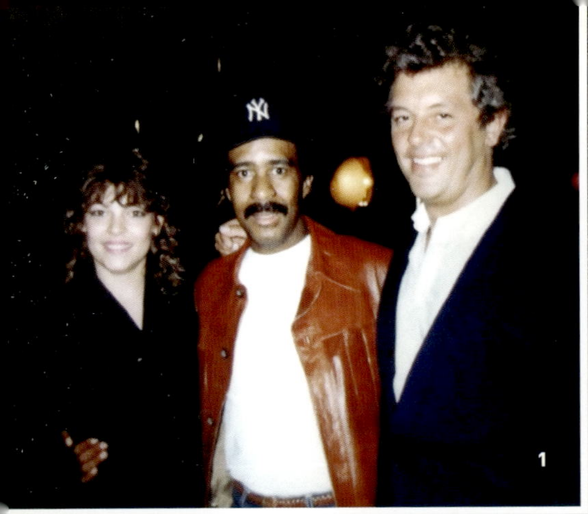
1

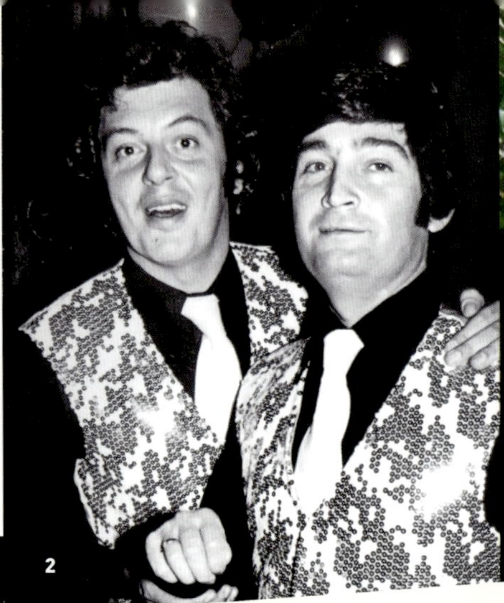
2

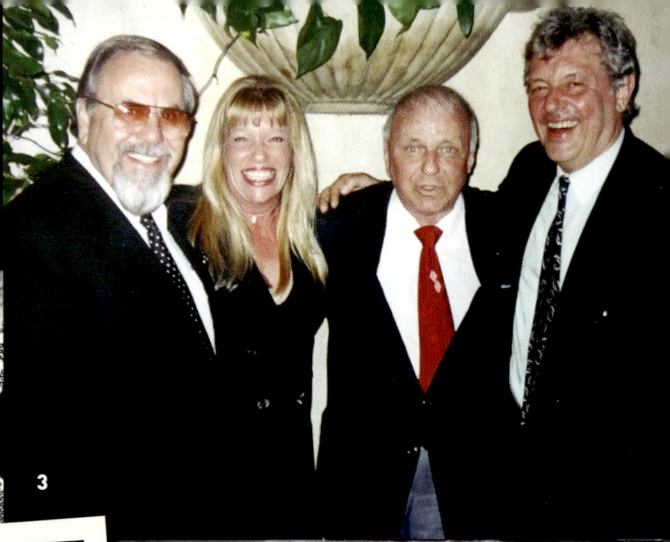
3

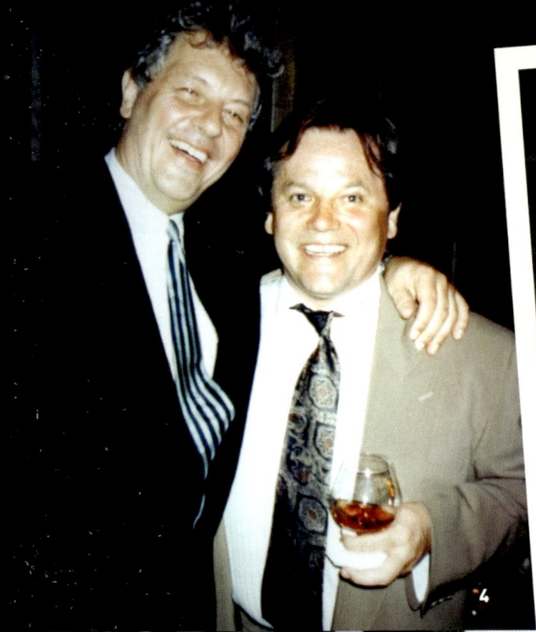
4

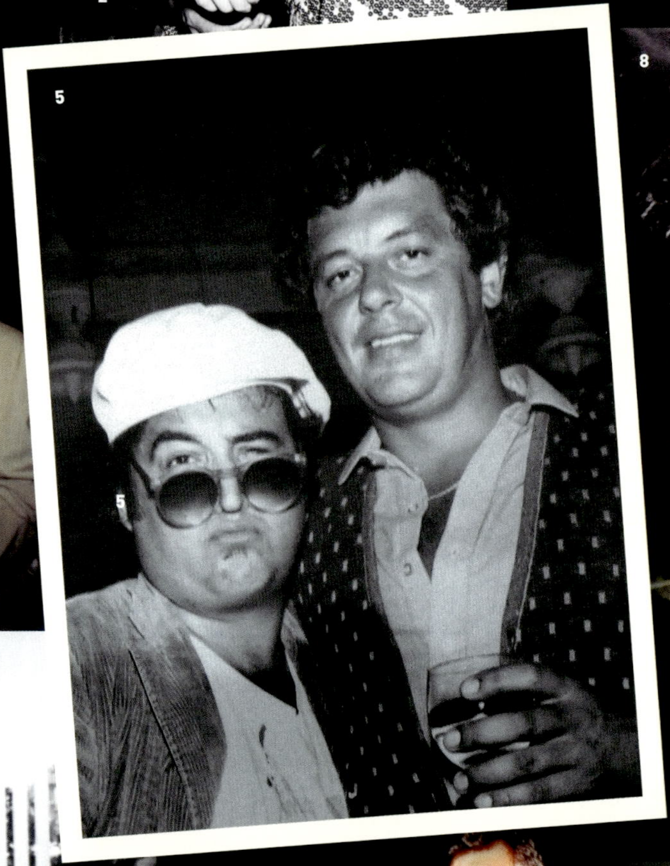
5

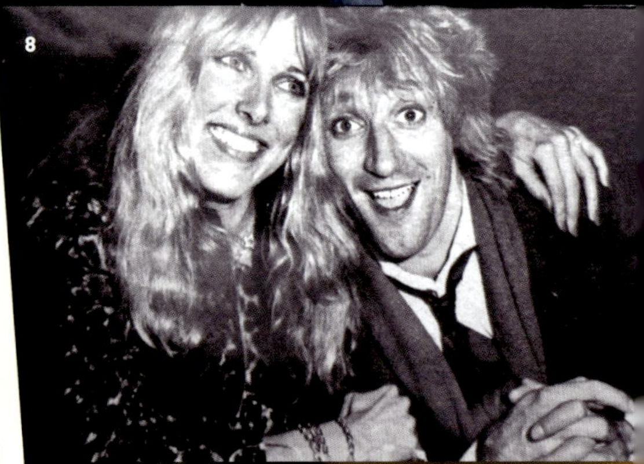
8

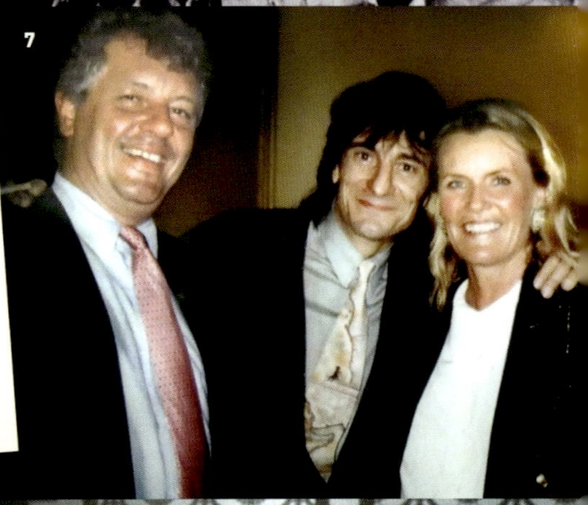
7

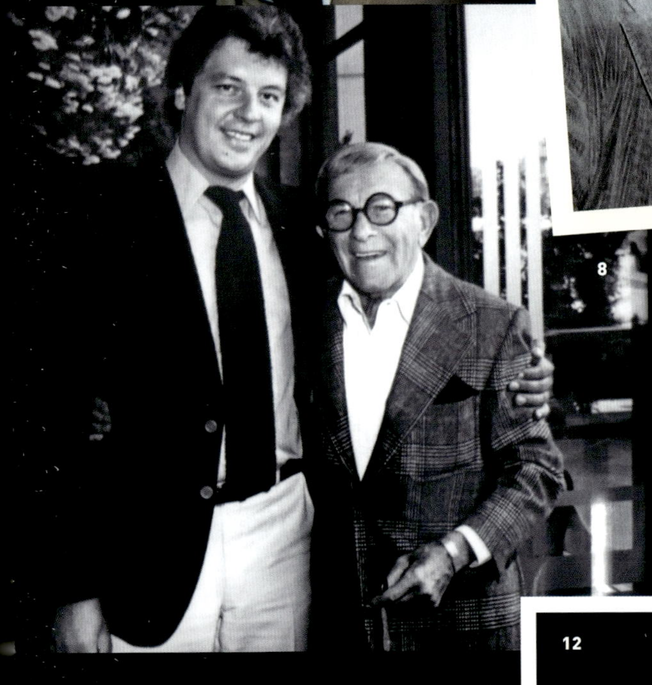
8

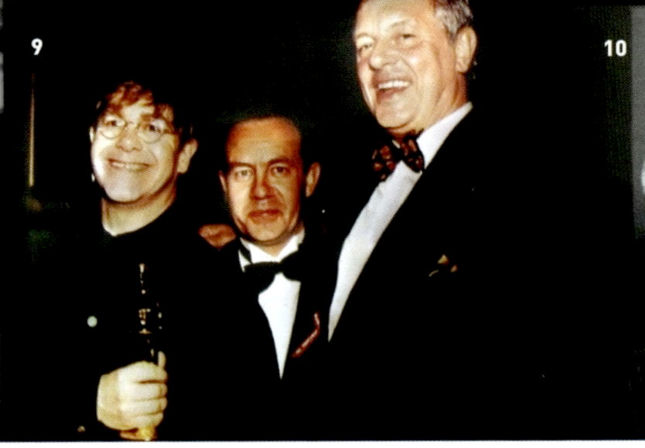
9

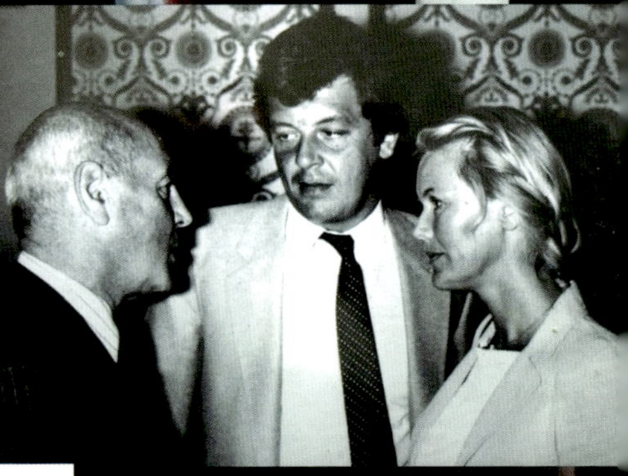
10

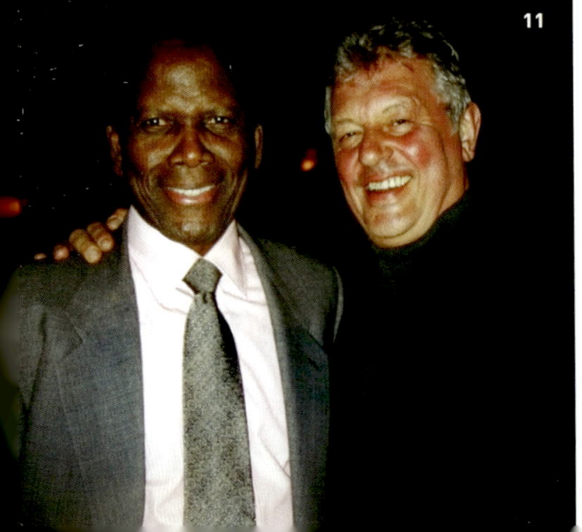
11

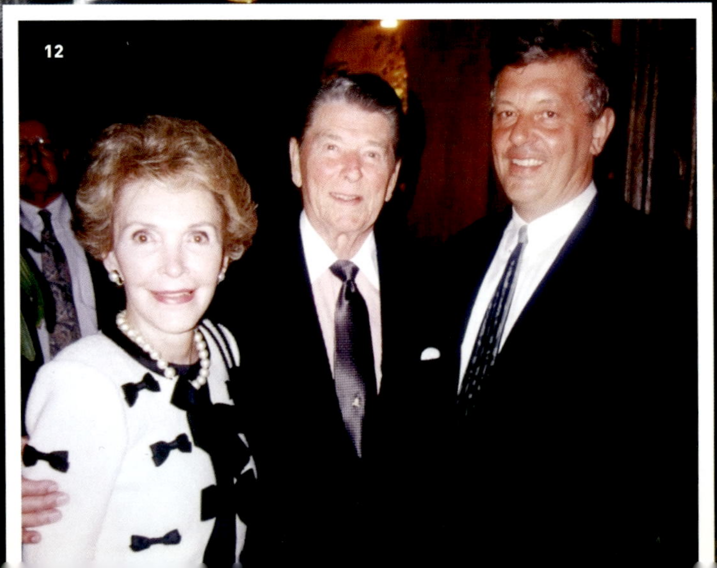
12

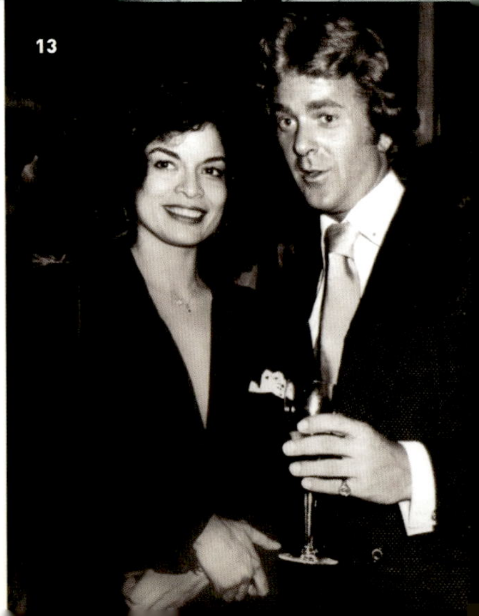
13

Le Dôme

Eddie Kerkhofs's Celebrity Central

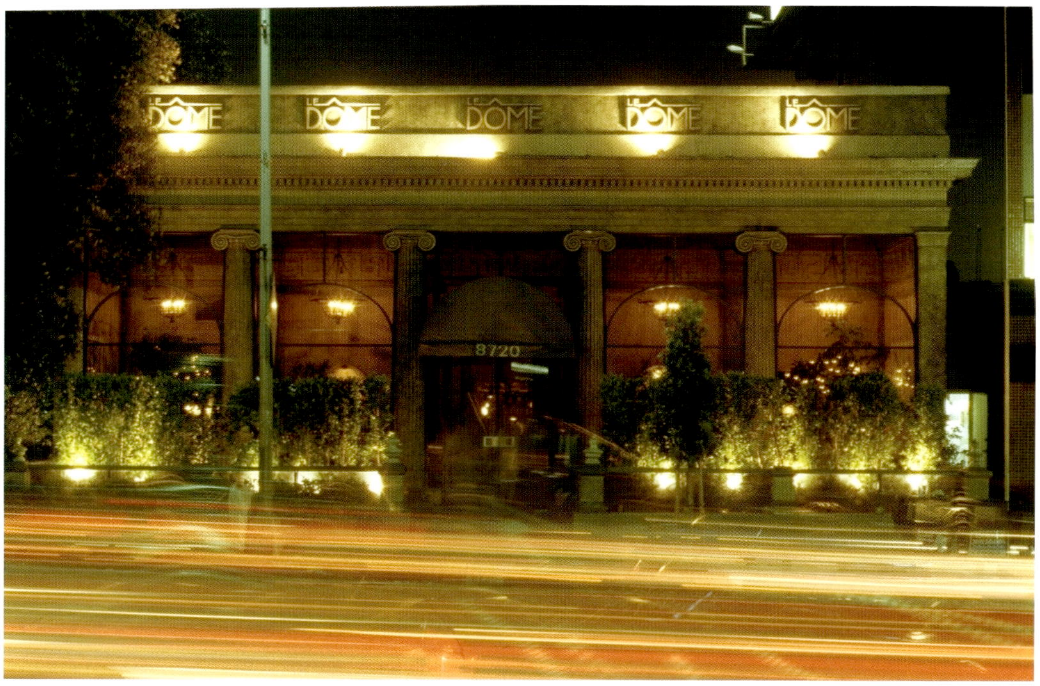

Le Dôme, which stayed open until 1 a.m. in a town notorious for closing early, fast became a glittering hot spot on the Strip for a late-night crowd of Hollywood stars. The building once housed designer William Haines's studio.

←
Le Dôme, with famous financial backers like Rod Stewart and Elton John, attracted a steady stream of A-list celebrities from the worlds of music, film, and a few society stragglers. The restaurant's founder Eddie Kerkhofs made it into snapshots with most of them. Here's Eddie with:
1. Stephanie Haymes and Richard Pryor (center);
2. co-founder Michel Yhuelo (right);
3. George Schlotten (left), Michèle Ritz, and Frank Sinatra (center right);
4. Wolfgang Puck (right);
5. John Belushi (left);
6. Alana and Rod Stewart;
7. Ronnie Wood (center) and Eddie's wife Britt Kerkhofs;
8. George Burns (right);
9. Elton John (left) and Bernie Taupin (center);
10. Baron Philippe de Rothschild (left) and Britt Kerkhofs;
11. Sidney Poitier (left);
12 Nancy and Ronald Reagan (center); and
13. Bianca Jagger and Ross Benson.

Le Dôme was one of those restaurants where you remembered the scenes. Not just the jaunty vulgarity of a soused rock musician or the baleful hubris of a faltering mogul, but the personal ones. The inspiration of a beautiful but badly disabled actress who defined courage by just getting to the bar. The fraught breakup of a long but sadly freighted romance. And one night, most vivid, sensing the mood of the dining room change—freeze, actually—like the first jerk of a modest earthquake. Ronald Reagan had entered the room—brown suit, ruddy cheeks, the pol smile, walking purposefully towards a party in the back. And every clawing aspirant in the room looking at this presence thinking the same thing: there he is, Hollywood's greatest success story, a play-by-play baseball announcer for an obscure Iowa radio station who came to Catalina to cover the Chicago Cubs spring training camp, became an actor, and ended up the president of the United States who won the Cold War. Top that.

Le Dôme was the creation of Eddie Kerkhofs, a Belgian who completed hotel and restaurant school in Brussels and came to America for apprentice work in a lobster joint outside Boston. A famous American politician who owned the real estate arranged for Eddie to apply for a green card. According to Eddie, neither realized a green card applicant was susceptible to the American military draft. In those dire Vietnam days, the local draft board had minimal interest in lobster chefs but a high priority for sturdy young men who could carry an M16 while wading through lobster-free rice paddies.

Eddie's boss told the draft board the young man was absolutely critical to his business and, besides, he had worked so hard he had no time to learn English. "He's not smart," the boss said, "but he can cook."

Well, no and yes.

Eddie and the war never coincided, and he landed on Hollywood Boulevard with fifty bucks in his pocket and, far more important, knowing a fellow Belgian who co-owned chic Le Saint Germain restaurant on Melrose. Eddie went on the payroll, paid his kitchen duty dues, worked as a waiter, and was soon suited up as the general manager. Gregarious, smart, and ambitious, Eddie later found some core investors for a new restaurant of their own. Rod Stewart, Elton John, and Peter O'Malley were among fifty investors who put up $3,500 each in exchange for $5,000 in food. With that, an A-list of buddies, bankers, and investors worked up an appetite of their own. One, a highly successful radio operator, put up $700,000 for a ten percent share. The team opened Le Dôme at the Sunset Plaza area of the Strip, just several doors west from where the fabled Trocadero once stood. But these were lean times on the Strip, and the most lucrative business seemed to be printing For Lease signs. With its constellation of heavy hitters, Le Dôme opened to what Eddie, only twenty-eight years old at the time, modestly calls "great fanfare." Los Angeles was a notoriously early-to-bed town, so Eddie stayed open late. "Every place closed at ten, except the hamburger joints. We decided to go French brasserie like the historic Le Coupole on the Boulevard du Montparnasse. And stay open until one."

The customers came in three shifts, like clockwork: the six-to-eight, upscale, cocktail crowd. Then the eight-to-ten diners, frequently in coat and tie, the ladies with jewels. And finally, the upscale rock 'n' rollers rolled in late, along with people who had been to the Bowl or the Greek or the clubs. "The late, after-the-concert crowd included the Stars. The Entertainers. And they all had entourages," Eddie said, checking his watch, as if he was hoping to see that old gang again.

Le Dôme became the contemporary descendent of the famous clubs that once illuminated the Strip. It had quality and flair and personalities. And just enough edge to generate a tangible sense of a somewhat unpredictable energy. Eddie was able to exclude the Strip's cadre of poseurs, riffraff, and sponges, but the core crowd was not without a sense of spontaneity. Rod Stewart, in his autobiography, noted that "given the clientele and its tastes, the downstairs bathroom at Le Dôme rapidly became a sort of romper room for the ingestion of mood enhancing substances and, occasionally, sexual dalliances—between-course intercourse, as it were."

"Given the clientele and its tastes, the downstairs bathroom at Le Dôme rapidly became a sort of romper room for the ingestion of mood enhancing substances and, occasionally, sexual dalliances—between-course intercourse, as it were."

—ROD STEWART FROM *ROD / THE AUTOBIOGRAPHY* (2012)

In that same memoir, Stewart explains some of the perks of being an investor in an elegant restaurant—you can start a food fight, or at least you think you can:

> "One night I had a big table at Le Dôme for members of the Exiles (my football team) and Dudley Moore tried to get my attention across a crowded room by lobbing a pork chop at me. The most almighty food fight ensued, possibly the worst I have been in: a blizzard of meatballs and mixed vegetables. The scene appalled even the normally equable Eddie. He had a fit and banned us both on the spot. We were soon back, though."

Despite food fights and emotional fiascoes and sometimes astonishing self-indulgence, Le Dôme was a comfortable and classy restaurant, favored by the Reagans and other Hollywood royalty like the Michael Douglases and Sidney Poitiers, not to mention image-conscious agents and music executives.

"It started in 1977, and we sold in 2003," Eddie recalls. "I was like a little kid coming from the farm. To me it was all a dream." The elegant building with its faux French façade has since served a variety of restaurants, none of which achieved similar status.

Eddie Kerkhofs moved on, with a new partner, Silvio De Mori, to establish a small bistro with a smart crowd on the edge of Beverly Hills. He travels extensively with his wife, a former international airline flight attendant, and they live up one of the swank canyons above Hollywood Boulevard on three tranquil acres. Decades earlier their home served as the dormitory for a bizarre cult that was supported by its own Sunset Strip restaurant whose sign read: The Source. ■

→
Eddie Kerkhofs and friends, in snapshots from his private archive. Here's Eddie with:
1. Roger Waters;
2. with the Le Dôme staff;
3. Rod and Alana Stewart;
4. the main dining room;
5. Gregory Peck (left), Kirk and Anne Douglas (center);
6. in the bar;
7. Britt Kerkhofs (left), Whoopi Goldberg;
8. Rod Stewart (left) and a big bottle of Lynch-Bages;
9. Sammy Davis;
10. Michael Lipman (left), Barbara Bach and Ringo Starr;
11. Rod and Rachel Stewart.

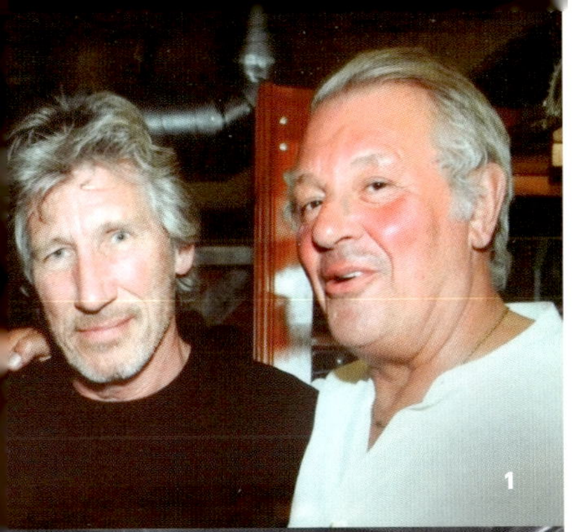
1

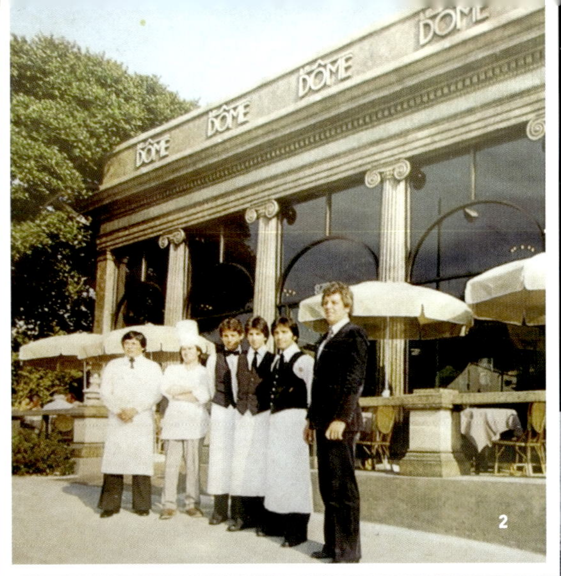

2

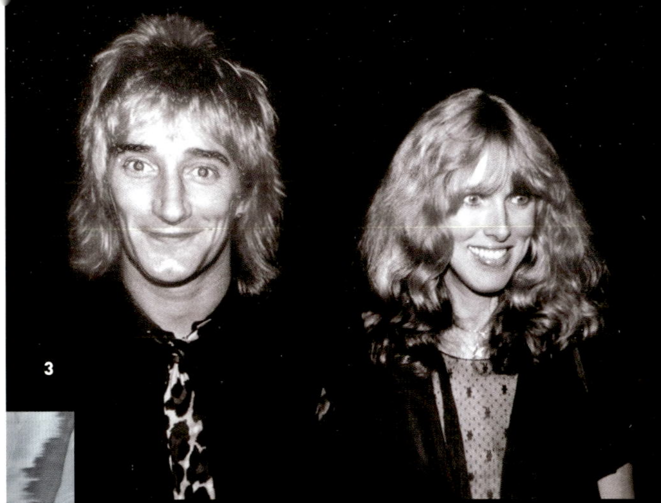
3

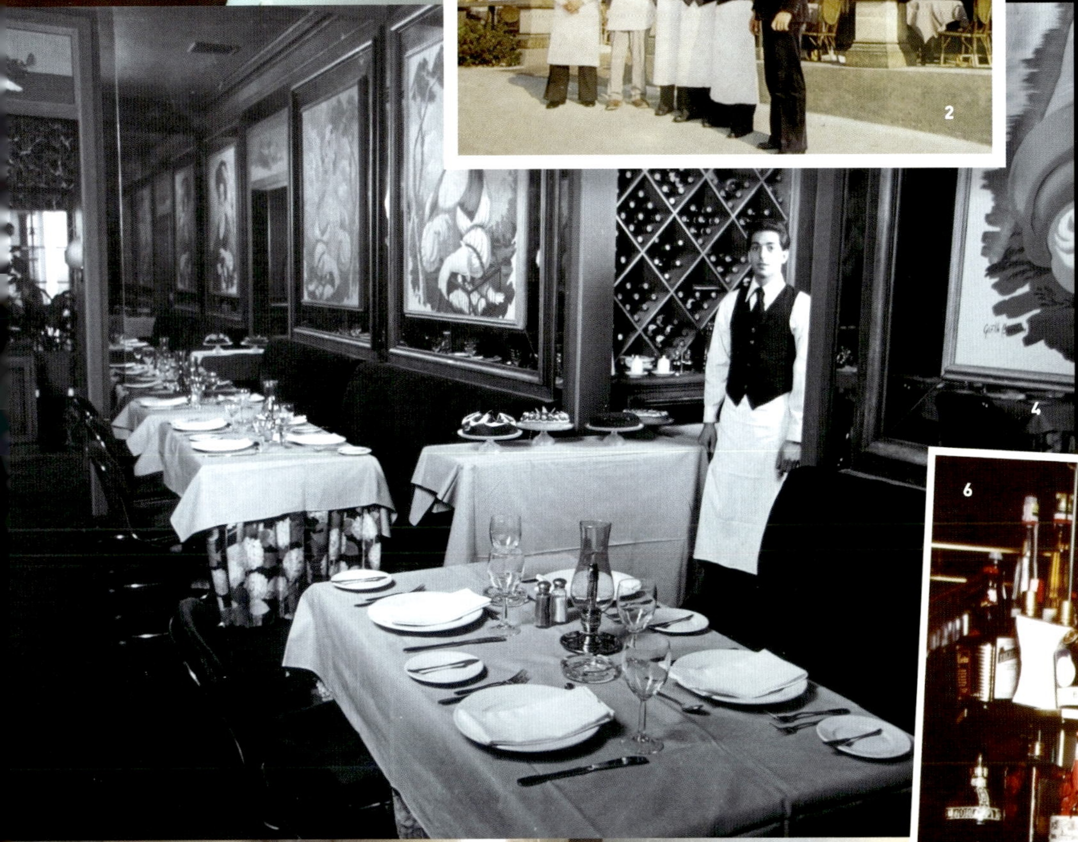
4

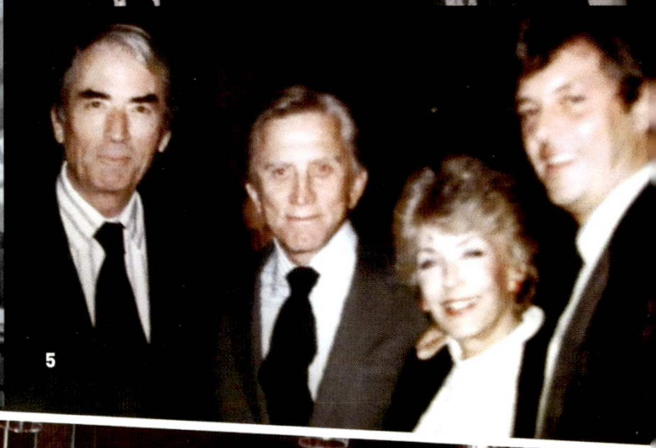
5

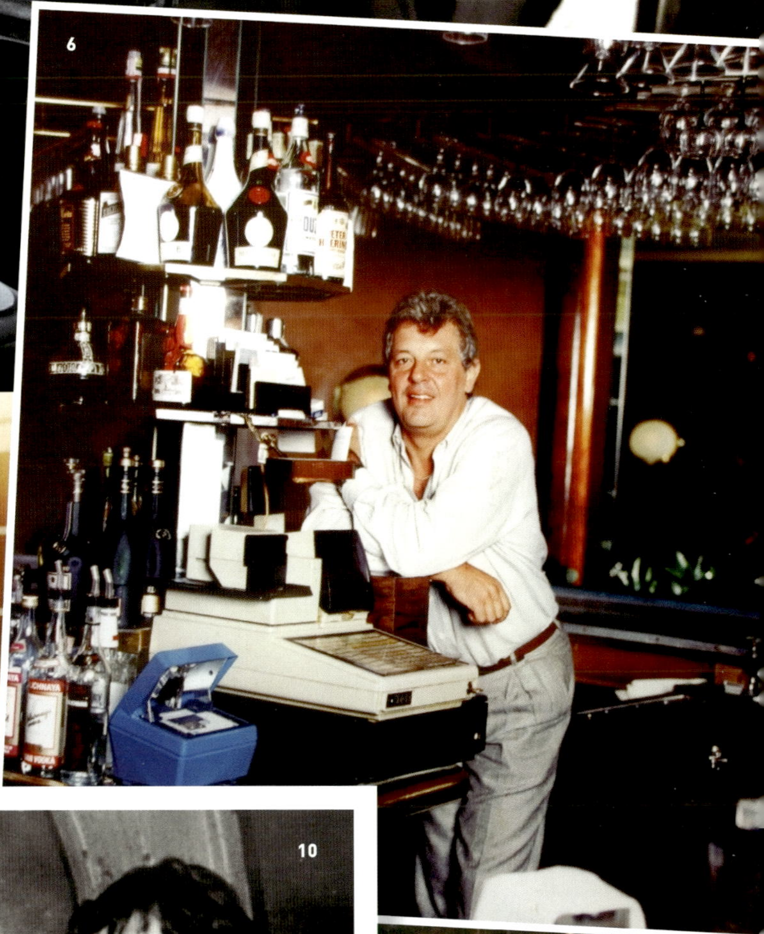
6

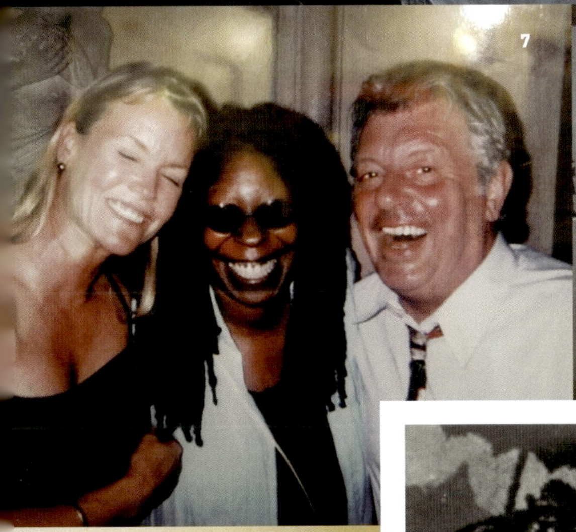
7

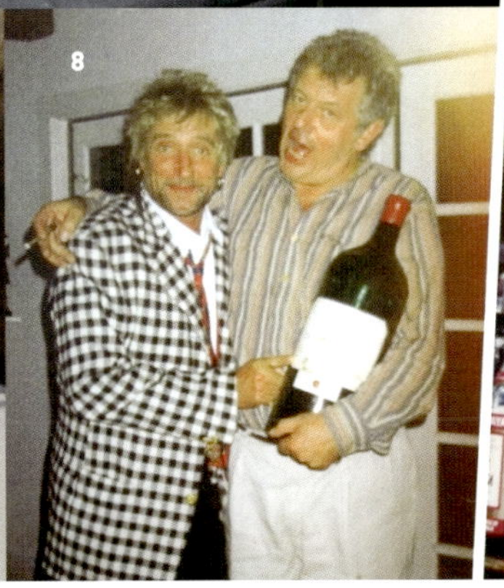
8

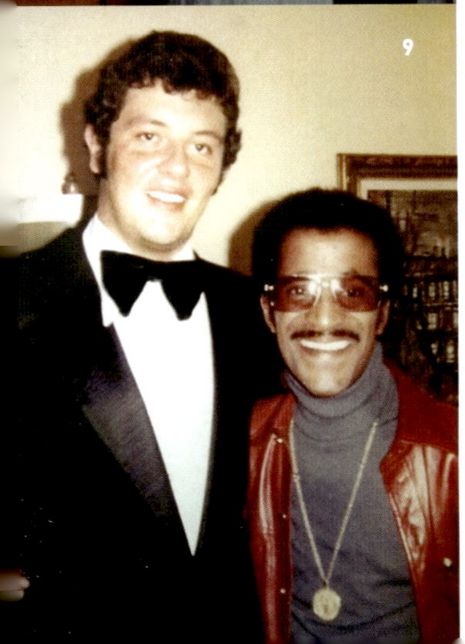
9

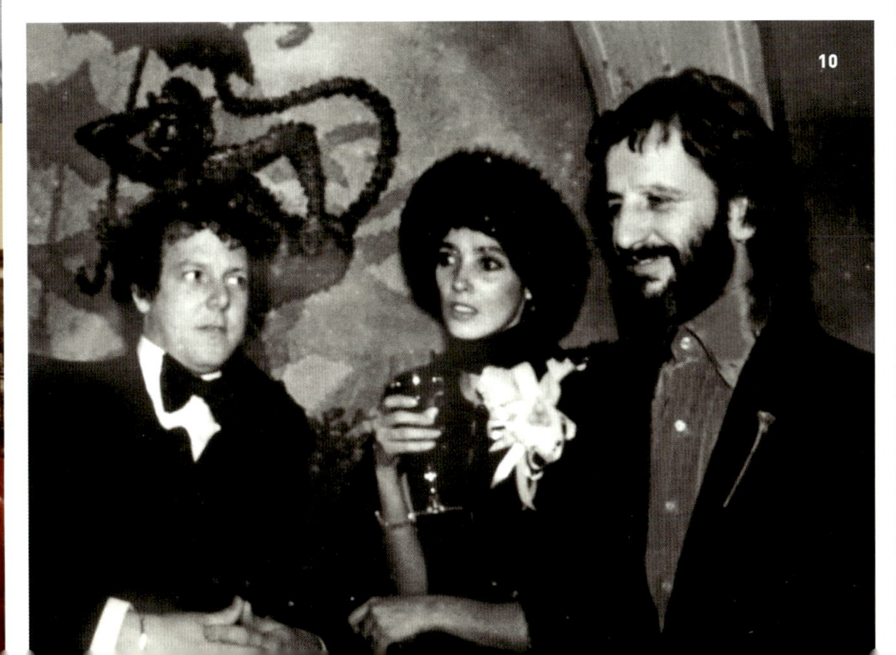
10

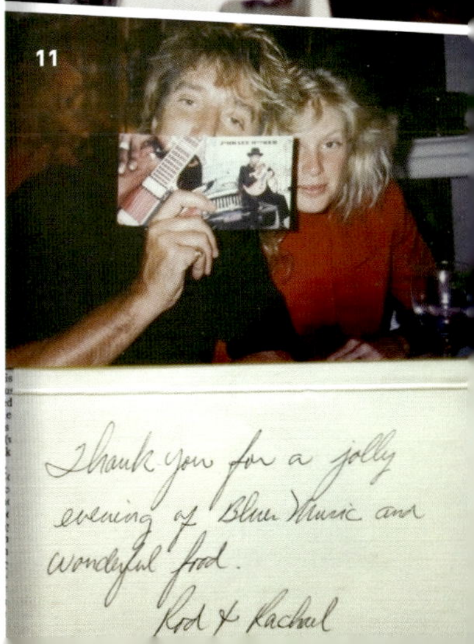

11

The Source

Nutters, Dreamers, and Mushroom Salads

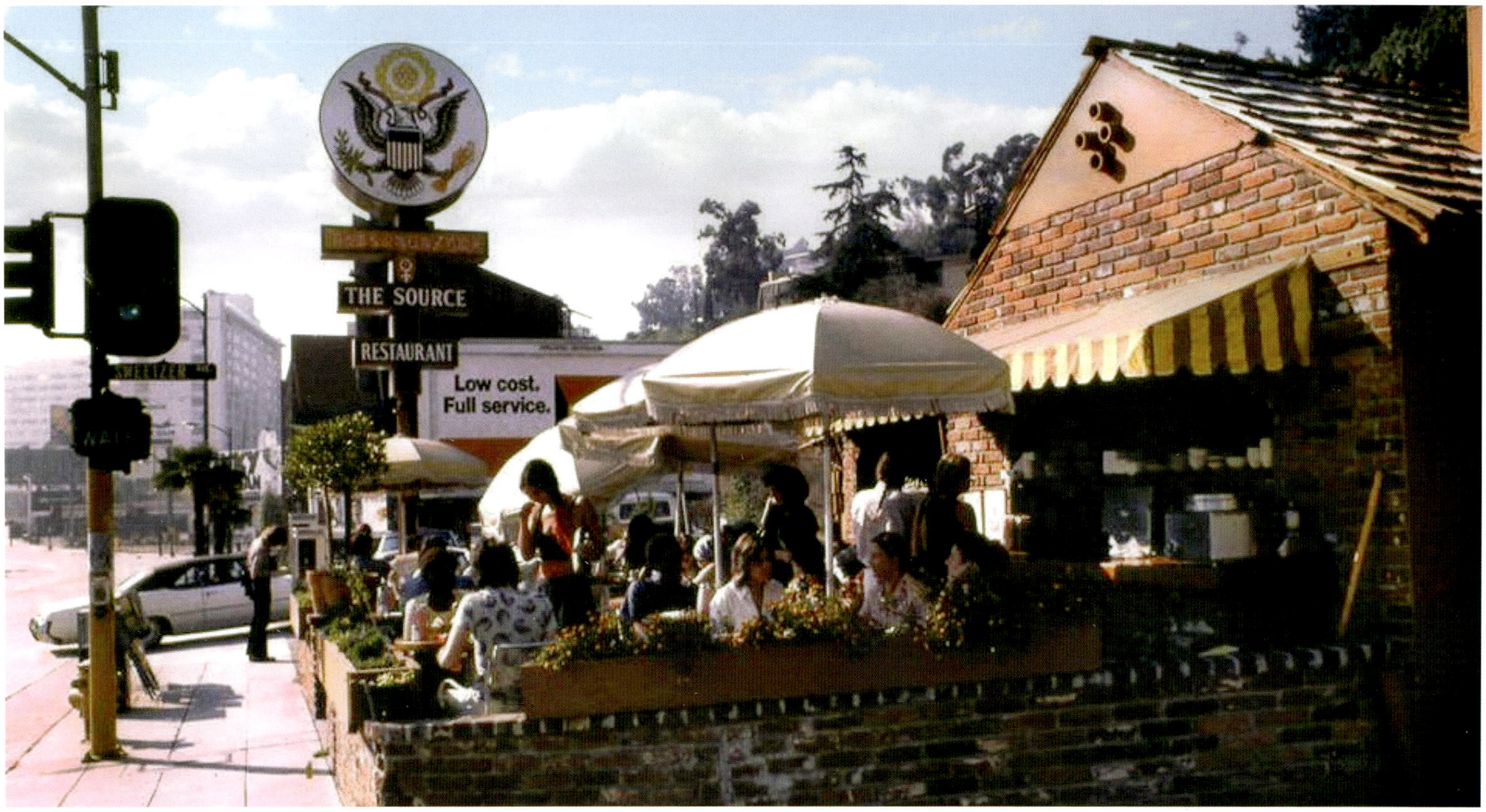

The Source looked like just another sidewalk restaurant on the Strip, but film fans knew it as the location for a memorable scene in the 1977 Woody Allen/Diane Keaton film classic, *Annie Hall*. Far left, the guru/owner of the Source, one-time actor Jim Baker, is seen in a still from his audition tape to play Tarzan. He didn't get the role, so he created a real-life leading role for himself in his own cult.

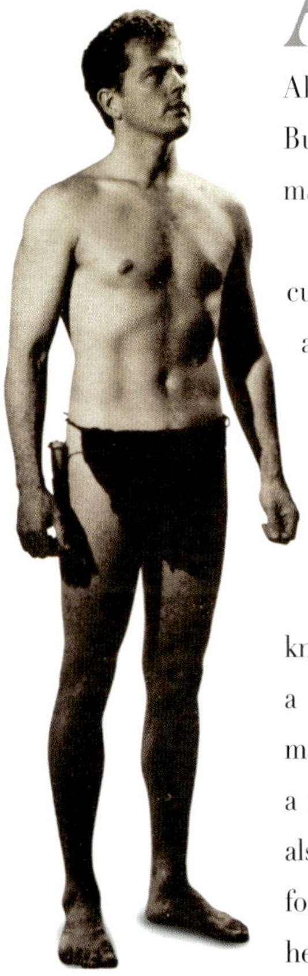

Alvy Singer and Annie Hall, those emotionally incompetent and befuddled characters in the 1977 Woody Allen comedy that bears her name, were seen taking lunch in a Sunset Strip restaurant called the Source. The dithering and angst of the Woody Allen and Diane Keaton characters was bewildering to a large segment of the American public. But their flakiness was clearly established when Alvy ordered a lunch of "alfalfa sprouts and mashed yeast" as he sat on the Source's patio.

Only in California. And only on the Strip. And only in a restaurant created by an outlandish cult that took the restaurant's name as its own and, for a few years, operated in a realm of astonishing New Age delusion.

The Ohio steel town where I grew up viewed this New Age California as suspiciously foreign. In a world of catfish, fried chicken, and the most leaden German cooking, "sprouts and mashed yeast" could quickly rise to the level of a cunning Leninist plot.

But as it turns out, appallingly so, the founder of the Source was born and raised in Ohio. Jim Baker, ultimately known as the Source's Father Yod, was, among other things, a masseur, a World War II combat veteran, a champion martial arts combatant, an operator of a body-building gym, a restaurateur, and a failed sandals store entrepreneur. He also was a flop in his cinematic ambition to be cast as Tarzan of the Apes (an unsurprising aspiration for many Ohioans). There was, however, a certain amount of flummery in his lore, particularly the claim he shot down thirteen or so attacking Japanese planes from the deck of his sinking ship in the Pacific.

Only in California. And only on the Strip. And only in a restaurant created by an outlandish cult that took the restaurant's name as its own and, for a few years, operated in a realm of astonishing New Age delusion.

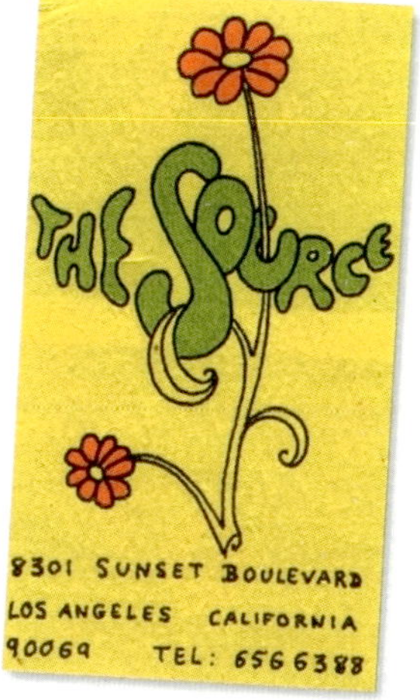

Baker was larger than life, a strapping, handsome, and engaging man. During his time on the Strip he also killed two men, one over the treatment of a mongrel dog (killed the man with his bare hands) and the other over an affair with a married women whose outraged husband allegedly came after Baker who was in his apartment on the Strip. Baker killed that man with either a gunshot or a karate blow, depending upon which lethal action came first. It was also reported that Baker bragged about robbing banks when his endeavors were short on cash.

Baker ran three restaurants during his culinary period on the Strip, the most famous being the Source, which was an early and popular health food restaurant. There were claims that it was a favorite of Marlon Brando, Julie Christie, John Lennon, Warren Beatty—even Greta Garbo—and a host of other "with it" celebrities of the day. The waitstaff included mostly fit and attractive young men and women, who ultimately formed the nucleus of the Source, the spiritual commune-turned-cult. Baker, who had been flitting about with assorted yogis and mystics and occult types (hardly in short supply during the '60s), began to design and implement his own spiritual force. He leased what was presumed to be an old Harry Chandler family mansion (fifteen bedrooms, supposedly) in toney Los Feliz, recognized by Baker's followers (dressed in blindingly white robes and turbans) as the Mother House.

There were claims that it (the Source) was a favorite of Marlon Brando, Julie Christie, John Lennon, Warren Beatty... and even Greta Garbo...and a host of other "with it" celebrities of the day.

LA Weekly described the core belief practices there as a "rigorous program of spiritual [activities] involving elaborate breathing techniques (beginning with a single six-second hit of 'sacred herb' at three in the morning), cold showers, radical shifts in gender roles, yoga, chanting the Tetragrammaton, natural home birth, magical visualization, Aleister Crowleyian ego suppression rituals, and tantric sex."

The creed of Crowley, an English flake who took the magical name Frater Perdurabo (claimed to mean Brother, I Shall Endure to the End), failed to limit the ego of Father Yod. Yod was given to wearing flashy white suits, traveling around the city in his blue Rolls-Royce, and surrounding himself with very young, attractive followers.

With his sturdy build, long hair, and rich white beard, Father was a commanding presence. Presumably, the Chandler family didn't renew the Los Feliz lease. As the Source's in-house historian named Isis Aquarian (*nee* Charlene Peters, and one of Father Yod's fourteen wives) recalled: "I imagine the sight of a hundred young people living in one house all wearing white and following around a man who looked like Moses, might have made some of the neighbors nervous."

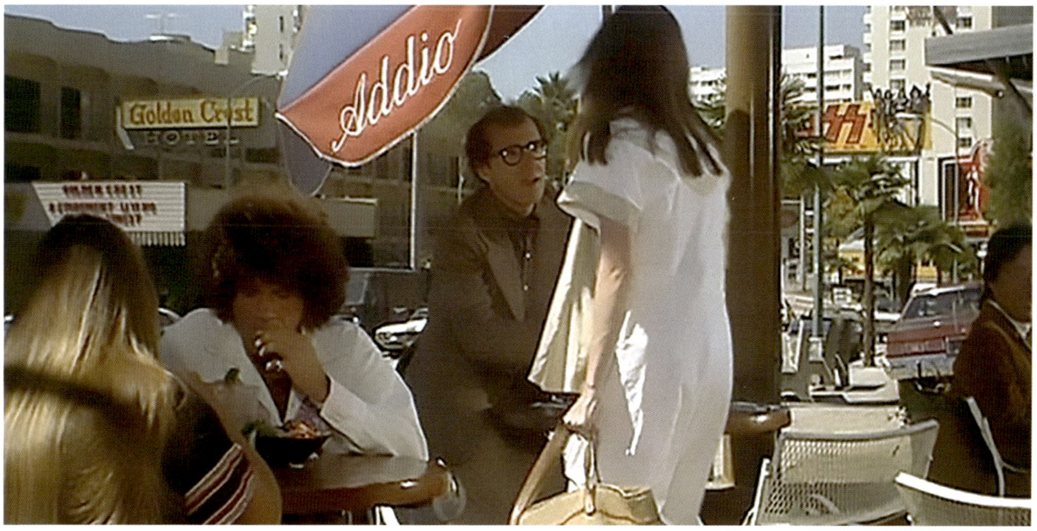

Between scenes at the Source. That classic meal on film produced one of the more frequently quoted lines in American film. Speaking of Los Angeles, Woody Allen as Alvy Singer says "I don't want to move to a city where the only cultural advantage is being able to make a right-hand turn on a red light."

Overleaf →
The women of the Source assembled around a Rolls-Royce for a promotional photograph—not for the Rolls, but for a record album. Note the number of children and pregnant women. That's Baker peeking out the door behind the ladies and their offspring, undoubtedly exhausted.

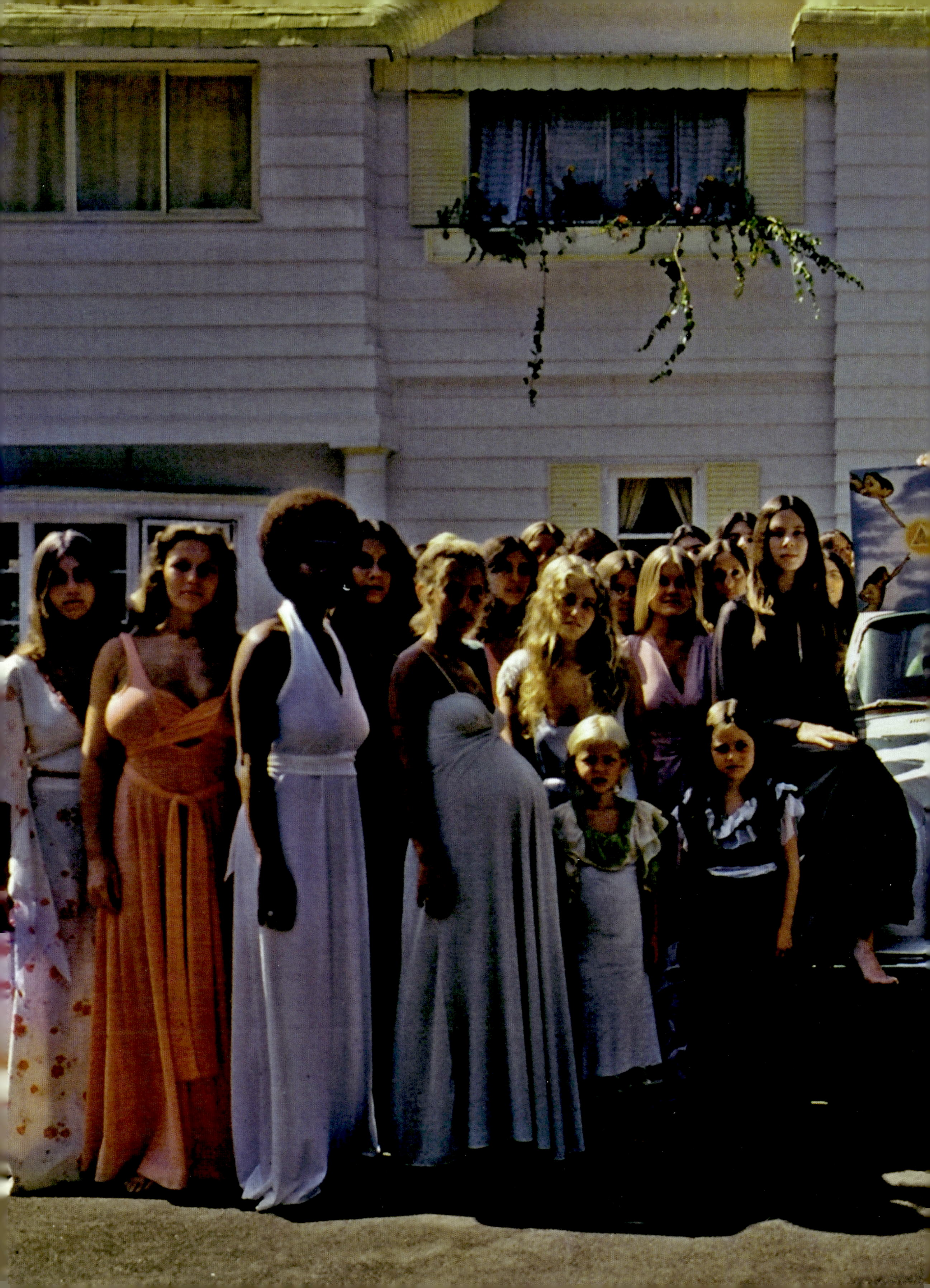

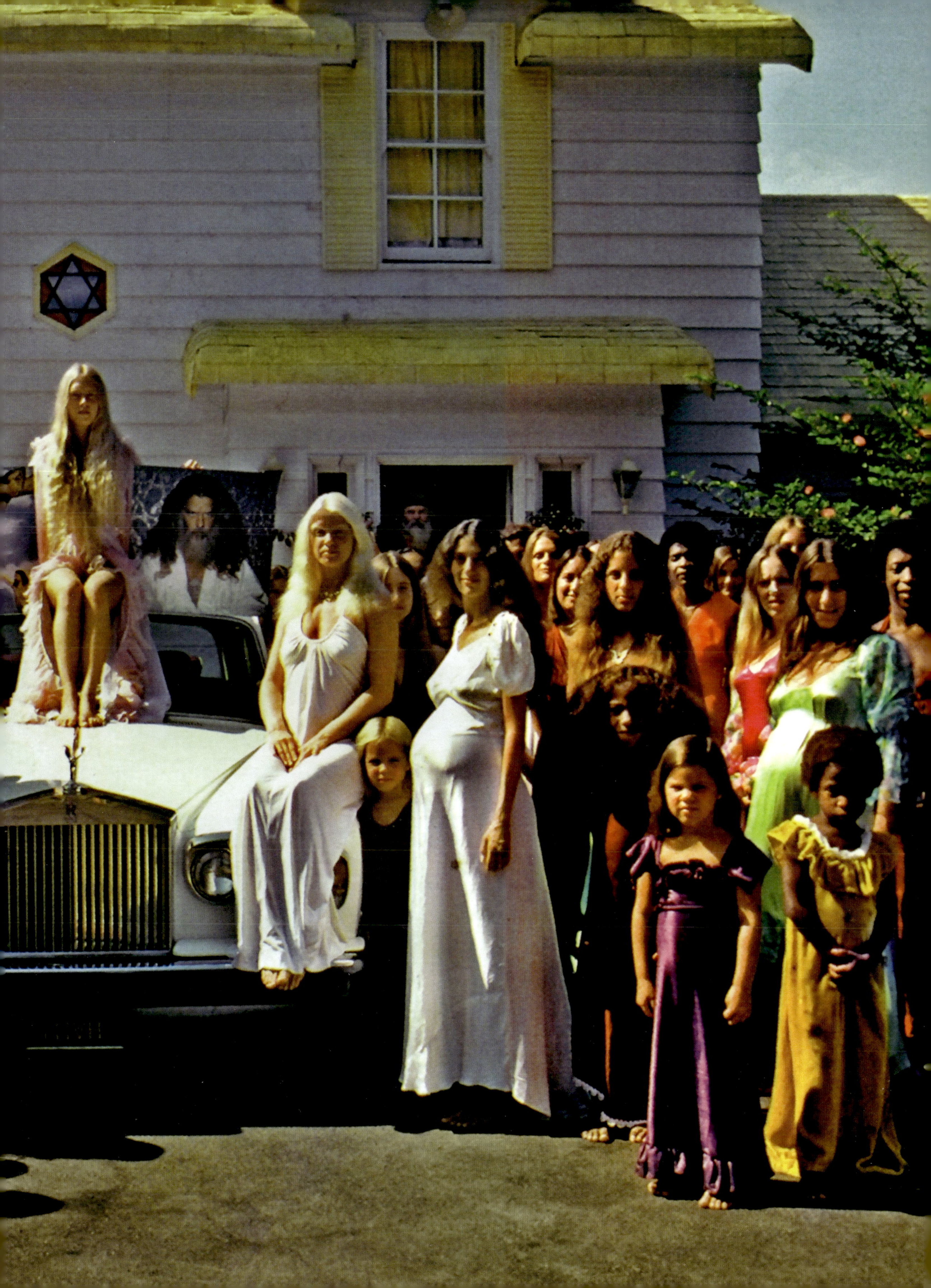

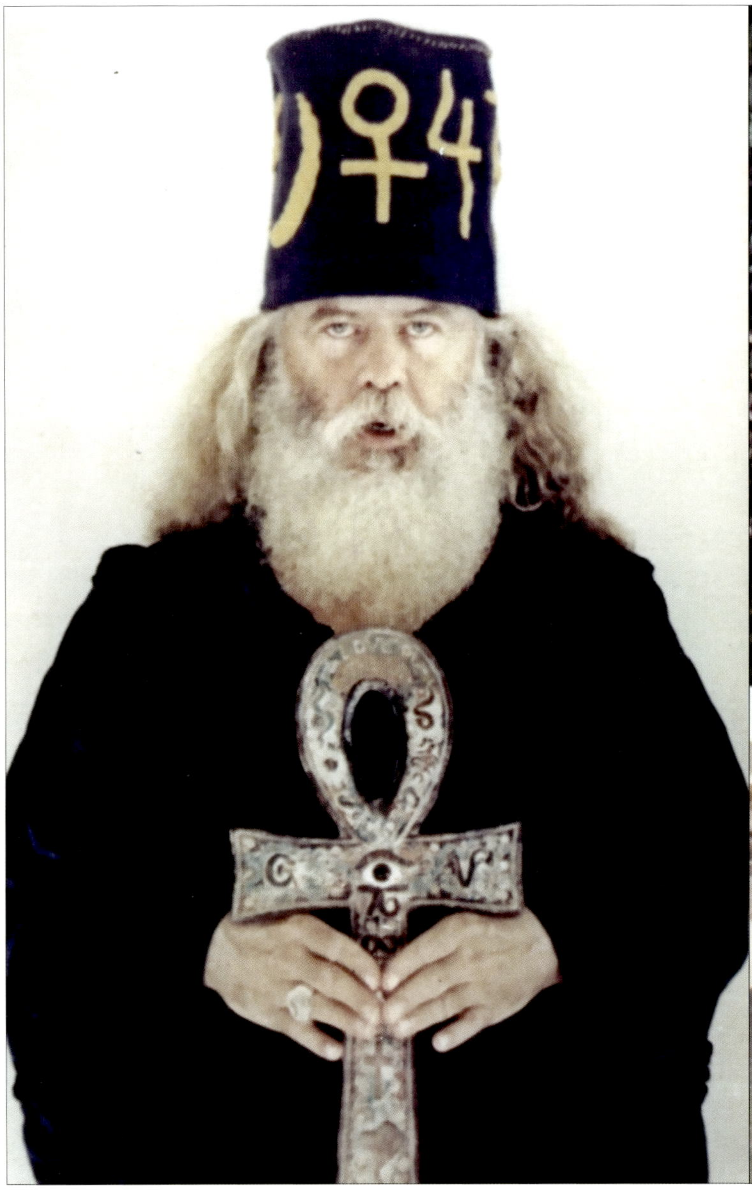

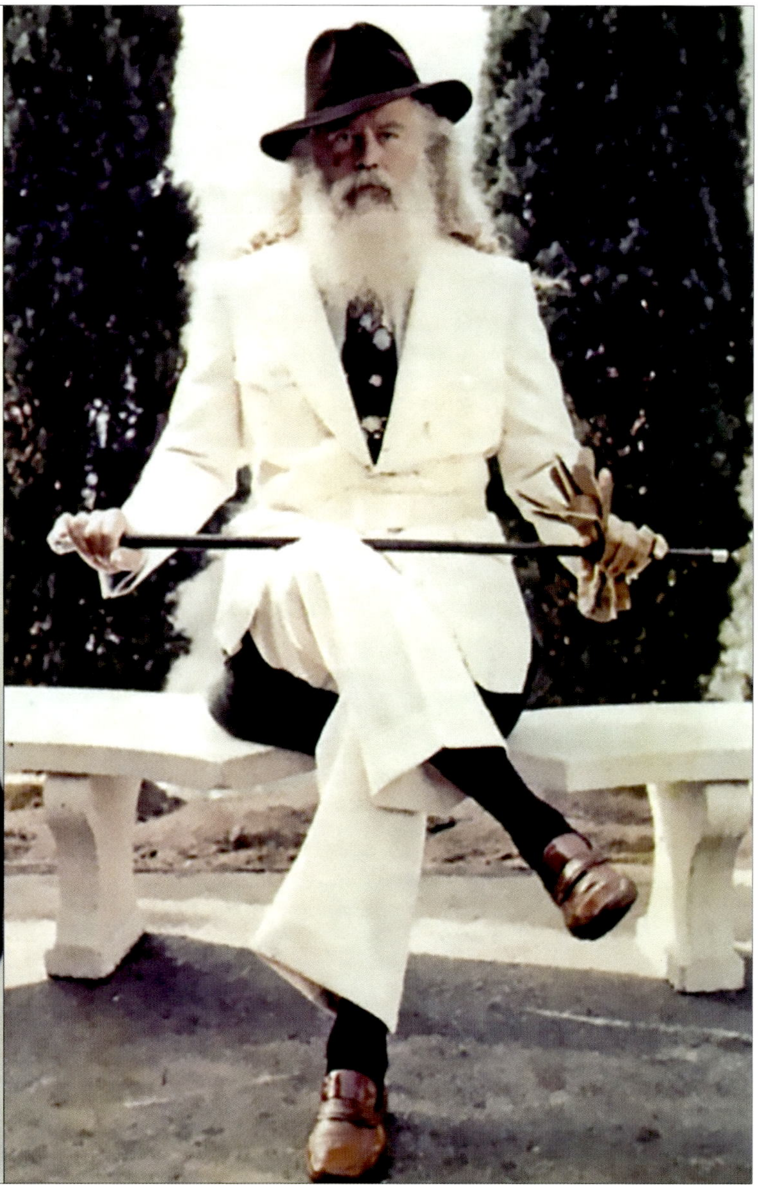

Baker had two images as Father Yod. One, in his stunning costume of leadership, with all its mystical symbols of spiritual consequence, and the other, his off-duty garb, a sartorially precise white suit and raffish fedora.

But money was not a problem for the cult. One member recalled that they took the day's receipts from the restaurant and just spent it. Sometimes at Chasen's. "Father had the Rolls-Royce and we all would get really nice clothes, with somebody dressed up like a chauffeur, and drive to Beverly Hills," explains a Family member cum restaurant manager named Omne, as Aquarian relates in the pages of her sympathetic tell-all, *The Source: The Untold Story of Father Yod, Ya Ho Wa 13, and The Source Family*. On one occasion they claim to have gone into Chasen's when California's governor Ronald Reagan was dining there. "(We bribed) the maître d' to sit us next to (Reagan). The women—looked like faeries because they wore nightgowns with camisoles. (They had) bare feet and hair down to their asses, and they were all under thirty. So three of them would walk in with three guys, dressed in German velvet robes with big heavy belts and jewelry and sandals and long hair and beards," and sit down next to Reagan. Unfortunately, there is no record of the governor's reaction. Or why Chasen's ever let these bizarre people through the door.

"Father (Yod) had a Rolls-Royce and we all would get really nice clothes, with somebody dressed up like a chauffeur, and drive to Beverly Hills."

The family, with more than a hundred members, then moved up Nichols Canyon into a house built by Catherine Deneuve, who some say kept a couple of leopards in backyard cages. Deneuve and the cats were long gone, but the faithful lived in the house and elaborate tent structures spread around the property. The Source was now administered by thirteen women. Father Yod (soon to elevate himself to the designation of YaHoWha) had fourteen wives. One gets the sense here of a presumably therapeutic volume (for some) of tantric sex, if not just plain sex, as the tribe drifted towards polygamous arrangements. That proved upsetting to many in the congregation at a time when the whole package was reportedly dismaying law enforcement authorities. There were hints of investigations..

With the internal problems, and the potential for public ones, the Source took leave for Hawaii. It was not, for many, a haven. And YaHoWha, with no hang-gliding experience, decided one morning to take flight. He soared off a cliff with a hang glider and pretty much dropped like a rock, suffering fatal injuries. There is debate as to whether it was basic stupidity, a drug-induced stupor, an accident, or a suicide.

YaHoWa, with no hang-gliding experience, decided one morning to take flight. He soared off a cliff with a hang glider and pretty much dropped like a rock, suffering fatal injuries.

With his passing, the group eventually faded away. Many of the members have stayed in touch, generating a lot of written and film/video material about the Source. At a recent reunion, observers noted how "normal" many of the attendees now seemed to be—a bit touchy feely, but part of the broad mainstream. One wonders if there weren't some who slipped away and drove by the Mother House, Nichols Canyon, and the now decidedly secular cantina. Under the Johnny Depp castle. ■

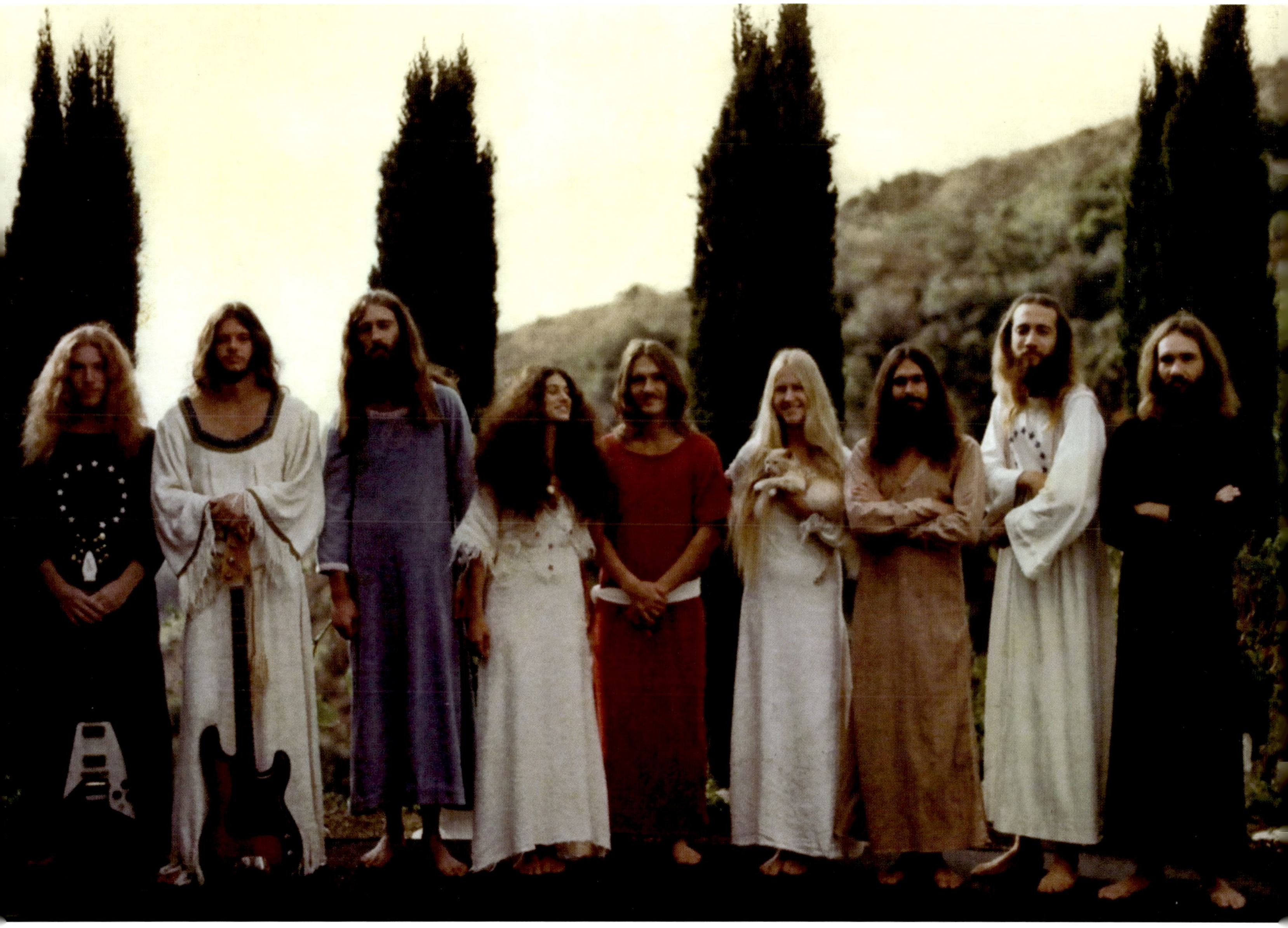

When Father Yod's robed disciples posed for a photo with the Hollywood Hills in the background, the resultant image struck biblical notes.

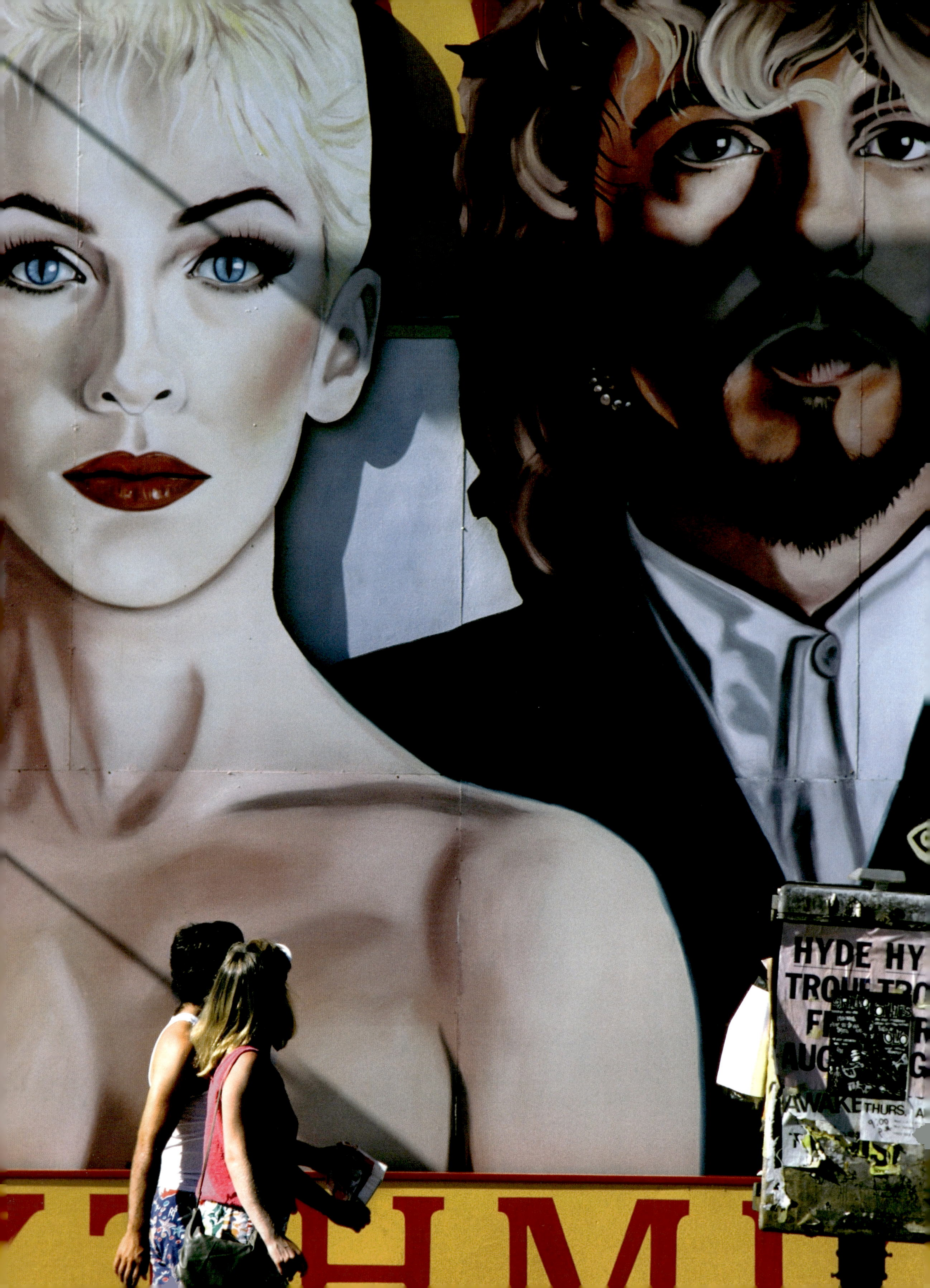
HYDE HY
AWAKE THURS,

Tower Records

Symbol and Center of an Era

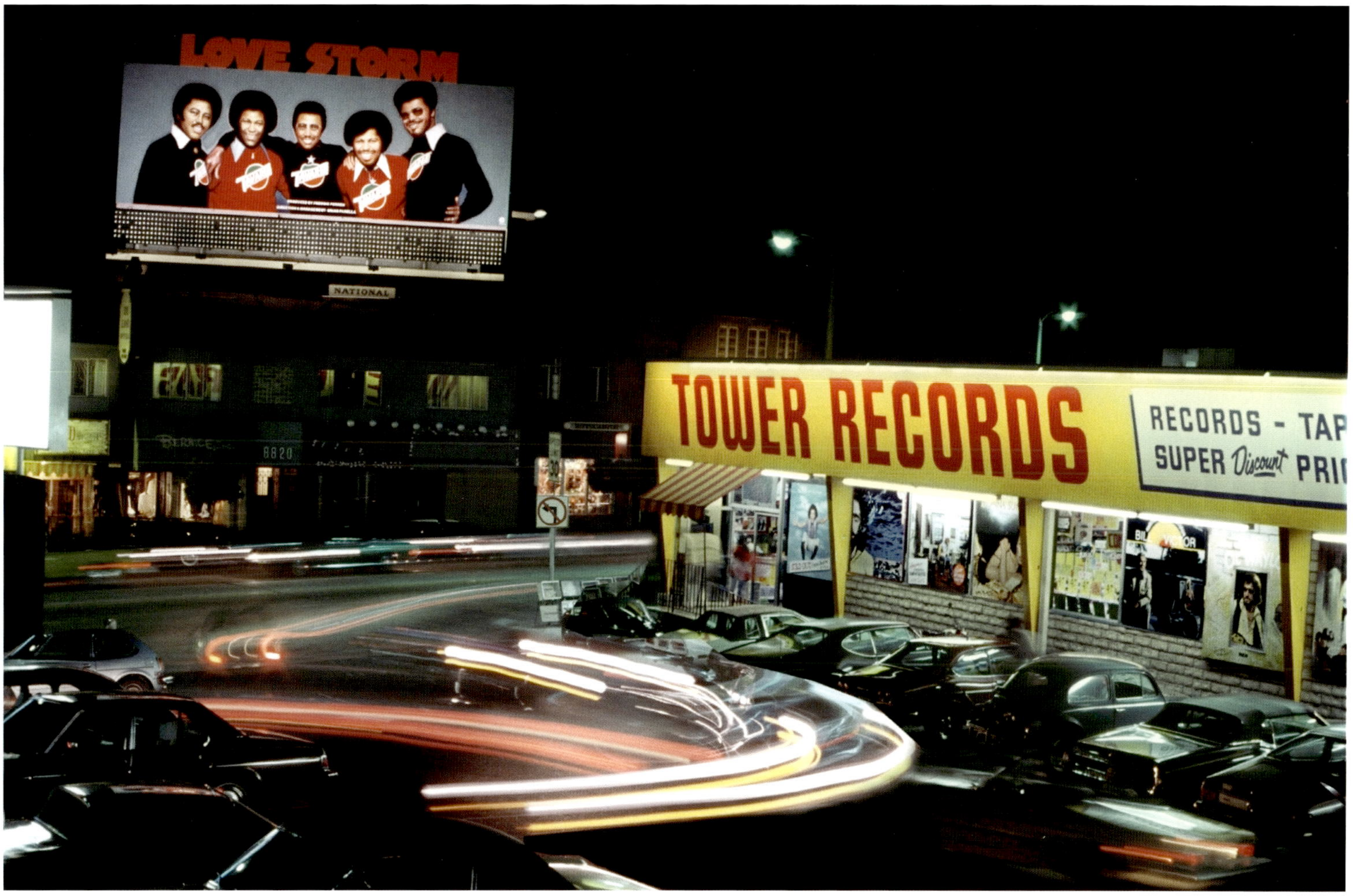

Tower Records, on the Sunset Strip, an icon of its era, was popular both with fans and the musicians playing in nearby clubs thanks, in part, to its late hours. 1977.

← A Eurythmics billboard celebrates the British rockers Annie Lennox and David A. Stewart, who were popular both in the U.S. and across the pond. To promote new releases, Tower commissioned painters to create temporary artwork that showcased the album covers, and soon became its own unique billboard on the Strip.

The most doleful sight along the Sunset Strip is the old Tower Records store, a shell from another age, a symbol of the most joyful and precious and triumphant days of rock 'n' roll.

There was a time when John Lennon admired the store so much that he recorded the voiceover for a Tower commercial. In Lennon's days, one could park in front of Tower Records, and release the kids to disappear through the glass doors into the hypnotic world of their music and cultural identity. With them occupied, it was easy to wander out for some of the other wonders of the Strip—a coffee and grilled cheese at Duke's, a CD at the small but encyclopedic Tower Classical music store, a bottle of a smart Cabernet and two robusto cigars at a grungy but handsomely stocked liquor store with no known name—and still have time to select some books and magazines at Book Soup. And then, back to extricate the kids from Tower.

There was a time, in fact, when John Lennon admired the store so much that he recorded the voiceover for a Tower commercial.

It was an extraction. Kids rarely left Tower with enthusiasm. For them, and the other adherents of rock 'n' roll, and all its creative variants, the seemingly encyclopedic collection of music was the true center of the universe, a place of discovery, of revelation, the archival evidence of music's powerful presence in their lives.

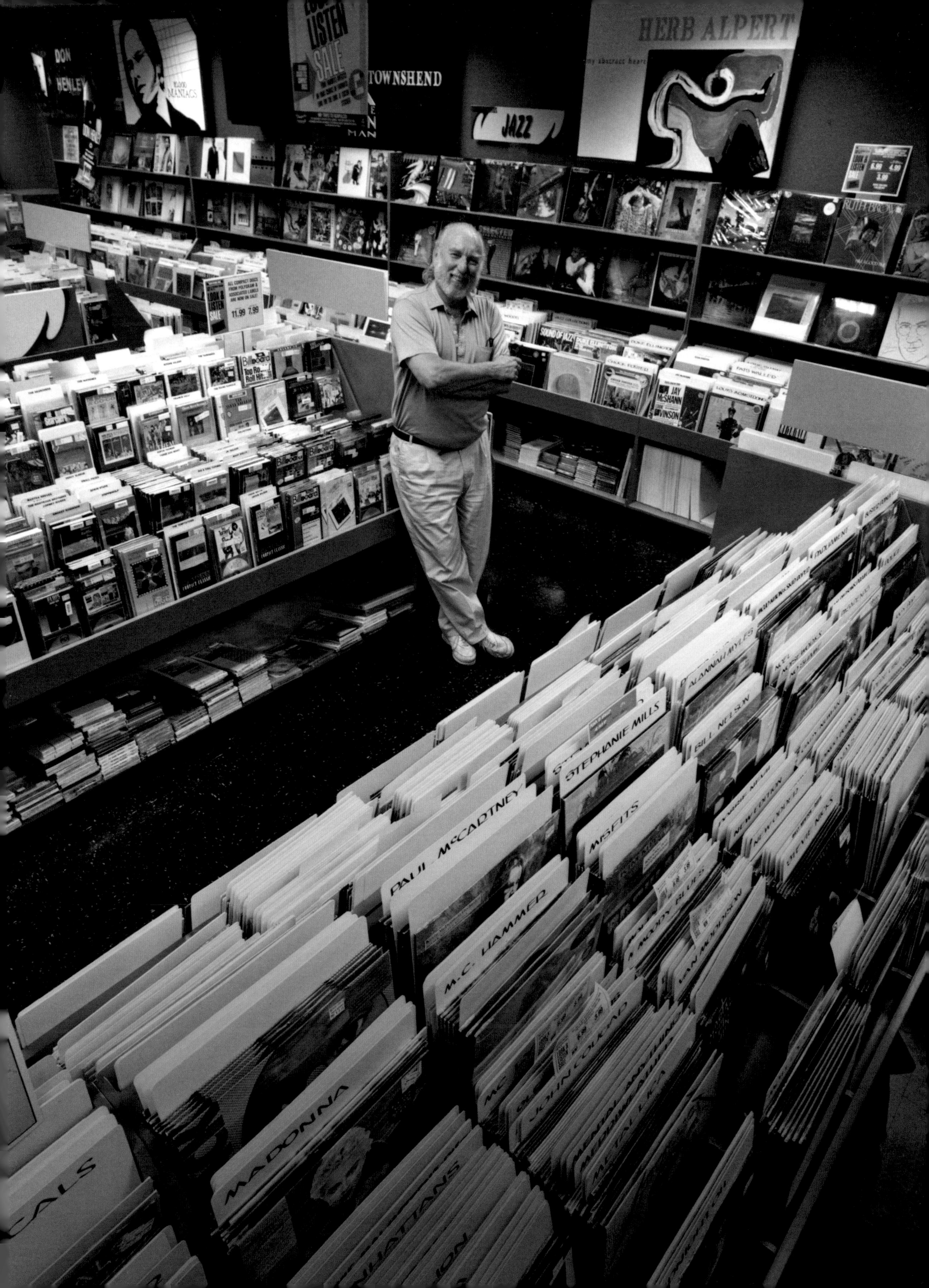
HERB ALPERT
DON HENLEY
10,000 MANIACS
LISTEN
SALE
TOWNSHEND
JAZZ
PAUL McCARTNEY
STEPHANIE MILLS
ALANNAH MYLES
BILL NELSON
MADONNA
JOHN COUGAR

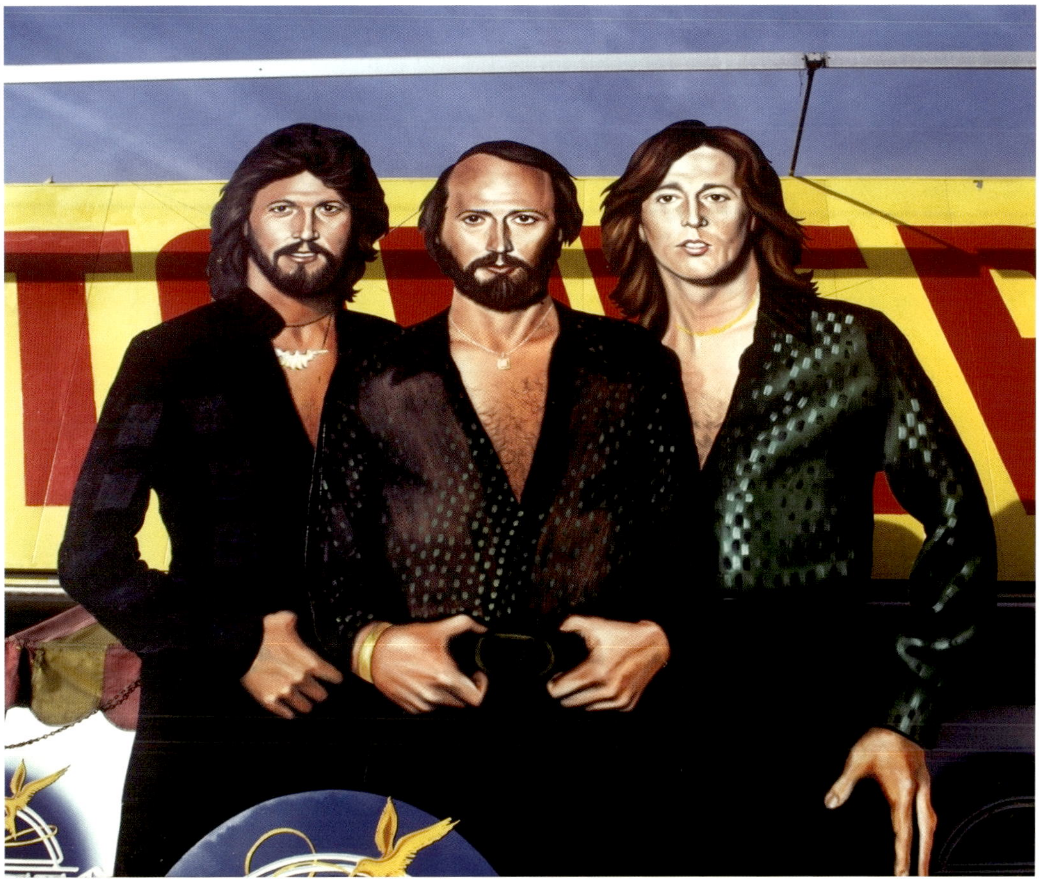

A large cut-out billboard displayed in front of Tower promoted the Bee Gees—brothers Barry, Robin, and Maurice Gibb—and their 1979 release, *Bee Gees Greatest.*

It was also a club where people of all ages and backgrounds, of all perceptions of taste and knowledge, could mingle with comfort and respect. And the staff, disheveled, harried, but always attentive and accessible, knew their business. One writer recalled checking out some CDs and overhearing two nearby men talking with great sophistication about nuances of British rock. She looked over to see who they were. Indeed, a store clerk was casually chatting with David Bowie. Tower was that kind of place.

The legendary store started in the most unlikely of places: Sacramento. In 1960, no one associated the then-stodgy California state capital with the creation of a brand that served the fiercely independent, aggressively non-establishment music world for decades. Sacramentan Russ Solomon, born in 1925, was the son of a druggist. At a young age, Russ began selling music out of his father's store, and with the help of a relative adept at carpentry, eventually created his own little music store.

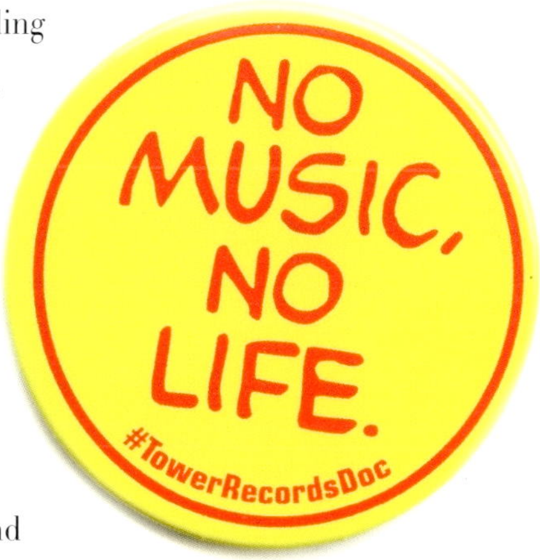

Solomon made all the right moves in defining a store that not only sold the music of his time, but also respected that music. And he hired people devoted to that organizing principle. Yet nothing indicated that he had created the first of a powerhouse chain of music stores that would expand around the world, from Sacramento to San Francisco to the Strip—in 1971—to New York and then on to places like Dublin, Hong Kong, Tokyo, and beyond. By 1999 Tower was reported to be a billion-dollar corporation, and yet still somehow felt a bit downhome. A Sacramento intersection featured Tower Books, Tower Music, and a Tower Theatre. Eventually there were 189 stores in thirty countries; everywhere Tower was linked to the music and the musicians.

←
Russ Solomon takes advantage of a rare quiet moment at the Sunset Strip Tower store, 1979. It is next-to-impossible to drive down Sunset past the site without feeling an acute nostalgia for hours and days spent roaming the aisles, discovering new sounds and artists, and sensing a kinship with other shoppers.

One of its most well-known fans was Elton John, who, when in Los Angeles, would visit the Strip store on Tuesday mornings to check its newest stock. "It was a ritual," he told actor and documentary filmmaker Colin Hanks. "And it was a ritual I loved. I mean, Tower Records had everything. Those people knew their stuff. They were really on their ball. I mean, they just weren't employees that happened to work at a music store. They were devotees of music."

Hanks, son of actor Tom Hanks, spent several years producing a documentary about Tower, *All Things Must Pass* (2015), a loving celebration and, ultimately, an overdue obituary. The stores, which ran from 1960 to 2006, were finally decimated by new technologies of music and the growth of discounters.

"Tower Records had everything. Those people knew their stuff. . .They just weren't employees that happened to work at a music store. They were devotees of music."

—**SIR ELTON JOHN** FROM DOCUMENTARY *ALL THINGS MUST PASS* (2015)

In recalling the place, Hanks said, "Tower sort of helped pave the way for your identity. For lack of a better phrase, music makes people—where you sort of latch on to music as a way of identifying yourself or your tribe. I got that at Tower Records."

And so did a lot of other people.

As for Solomon, he retired in Sacramento and developed his interest in photography. Perhaps the most symbolic sight along the Sunset Strip, the old Tower store still bears the red-and-yellow sign. It's repainted to add an air of authenticity—a vivid tribute to the days when music was what mattered. ■

→ This hand-painted image of David Lee Roth adorned Tower to promote his album *Eat 'Em and Smile* in 1986.

Overleaf → Dolores Drive-in, shown here in the 1940s on the site that ultimately housed Tower Records. It was first home to Simon's Drive-in from 1935 to 1945. Post Dolores, came Jack's on the Strip Drive-in, in the 1950s. The building was demolished in the mid-'60s, making way for music stores, none more iconic than Tower.

Brian Wilson of the Beach Boys is featured on the Sunset Strip side of Tower with a large picture, part of the promotion of a solo record/album (1988).

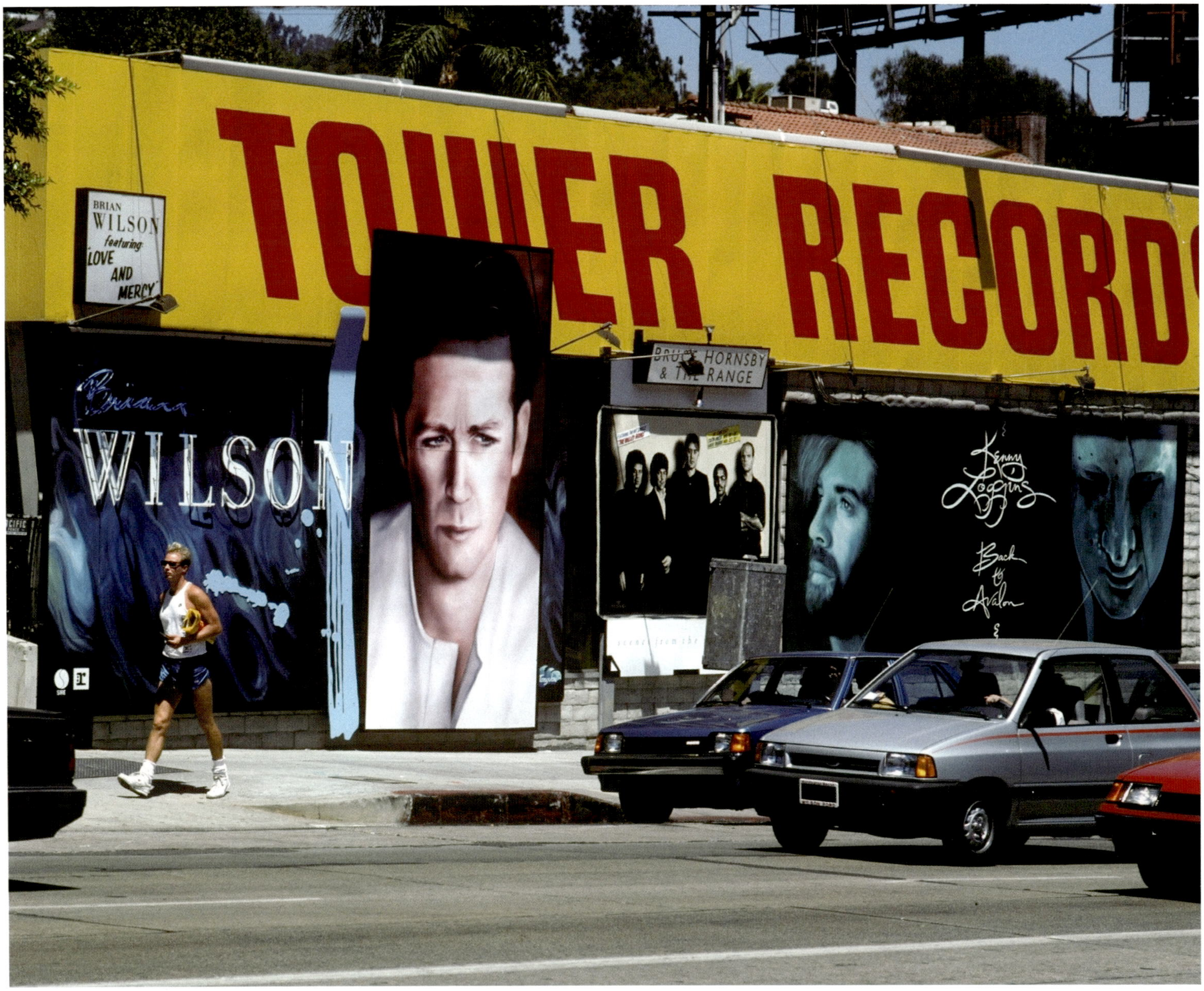

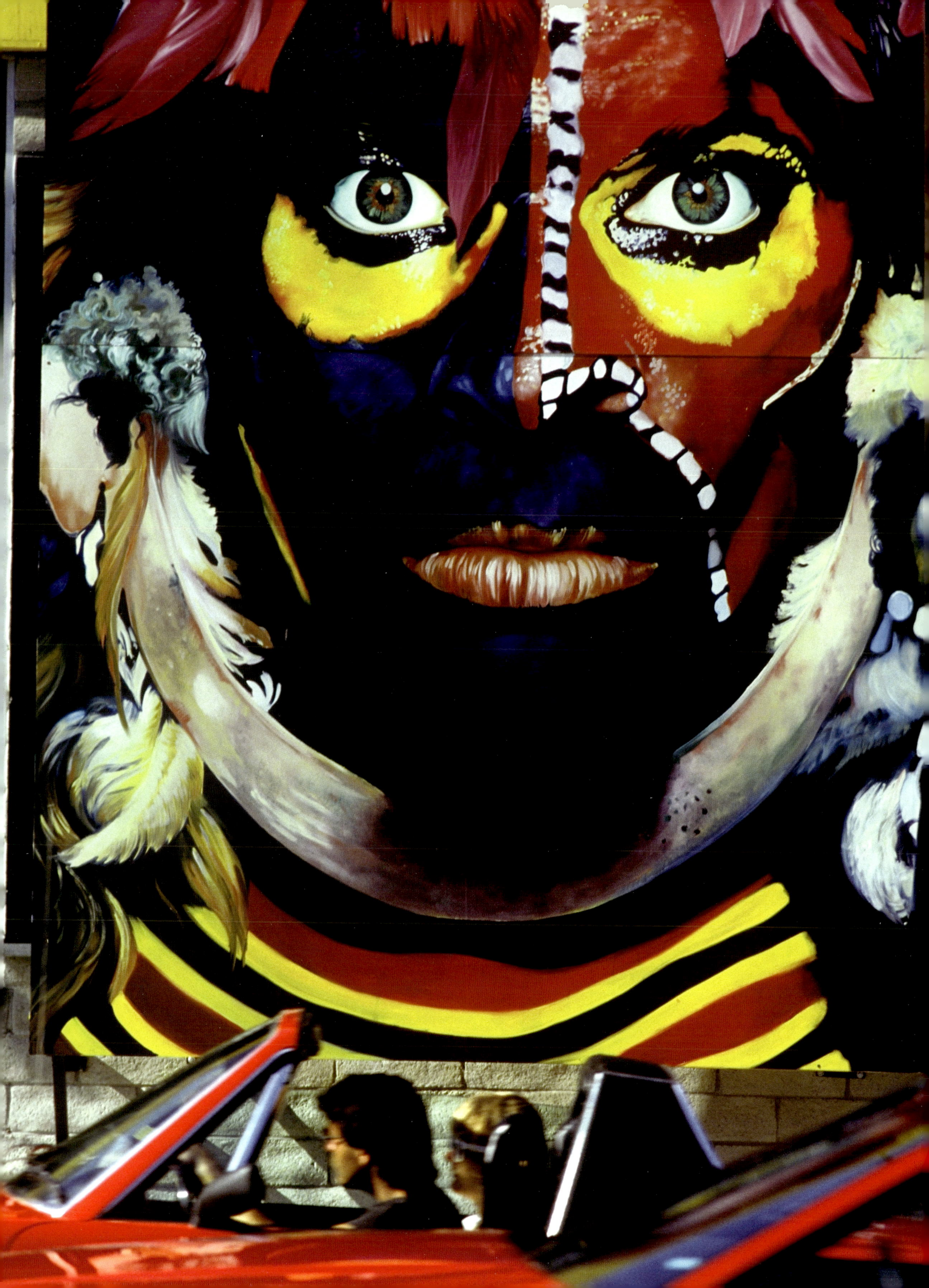

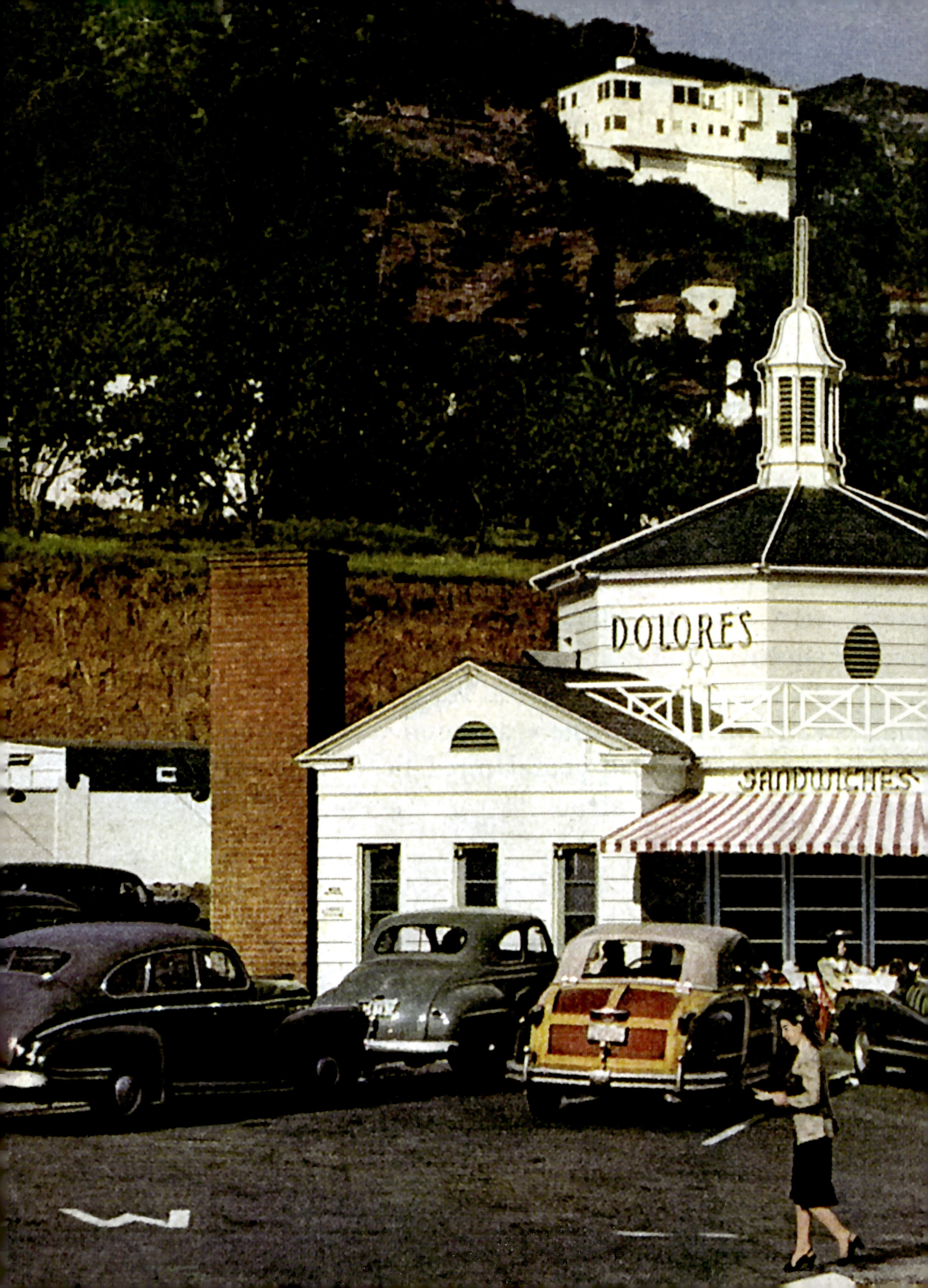
DOLORES
SANDWICHES

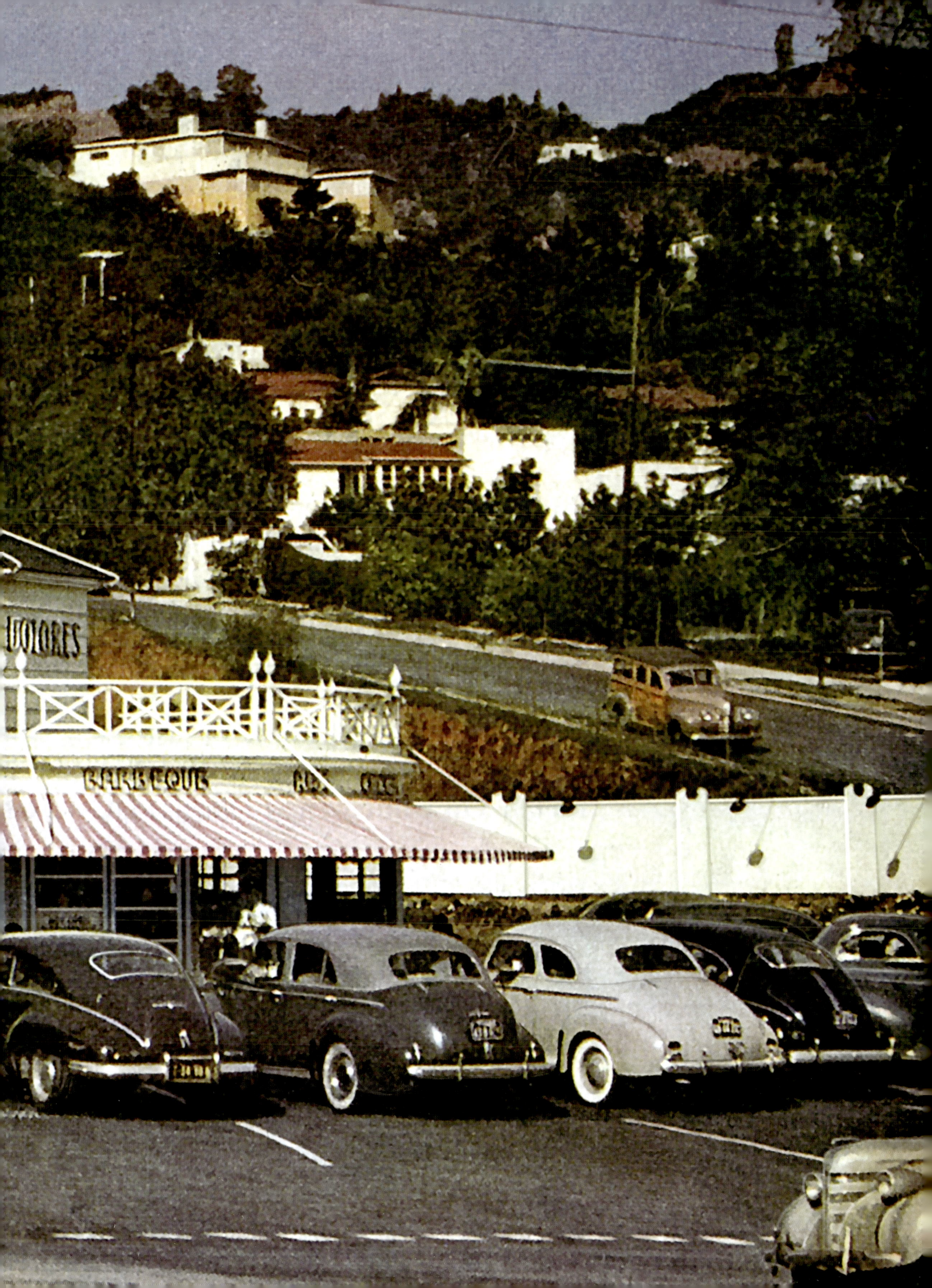
DOLORES
BARBEQUE

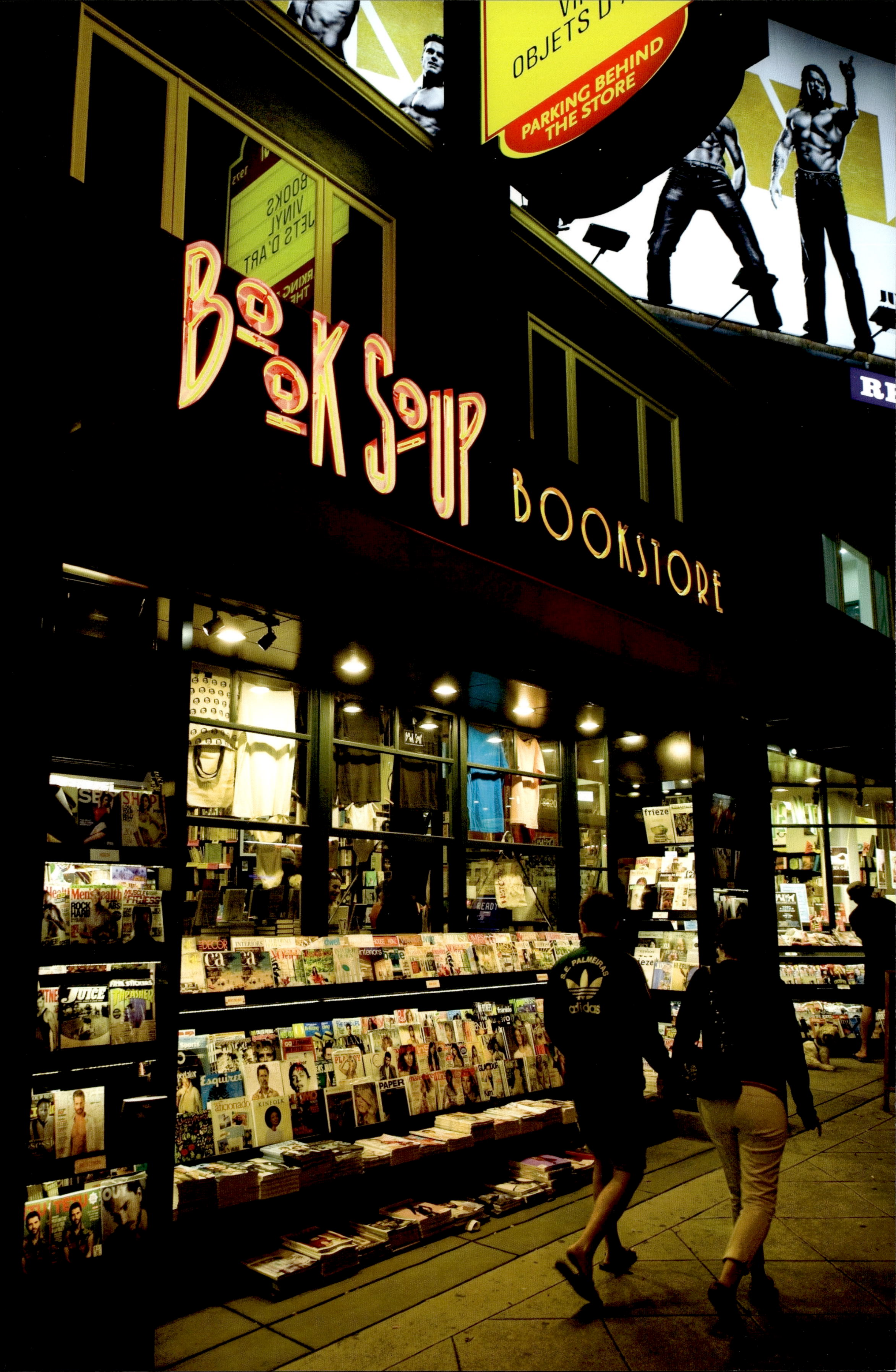
OBJETS D'A
PARKING BEHIND THE STORE
BOOKS
VINYL
JETS D'ART
BOOK SOUP
BOOKSTORE

Book Soup

A Book Lover and his Legacy

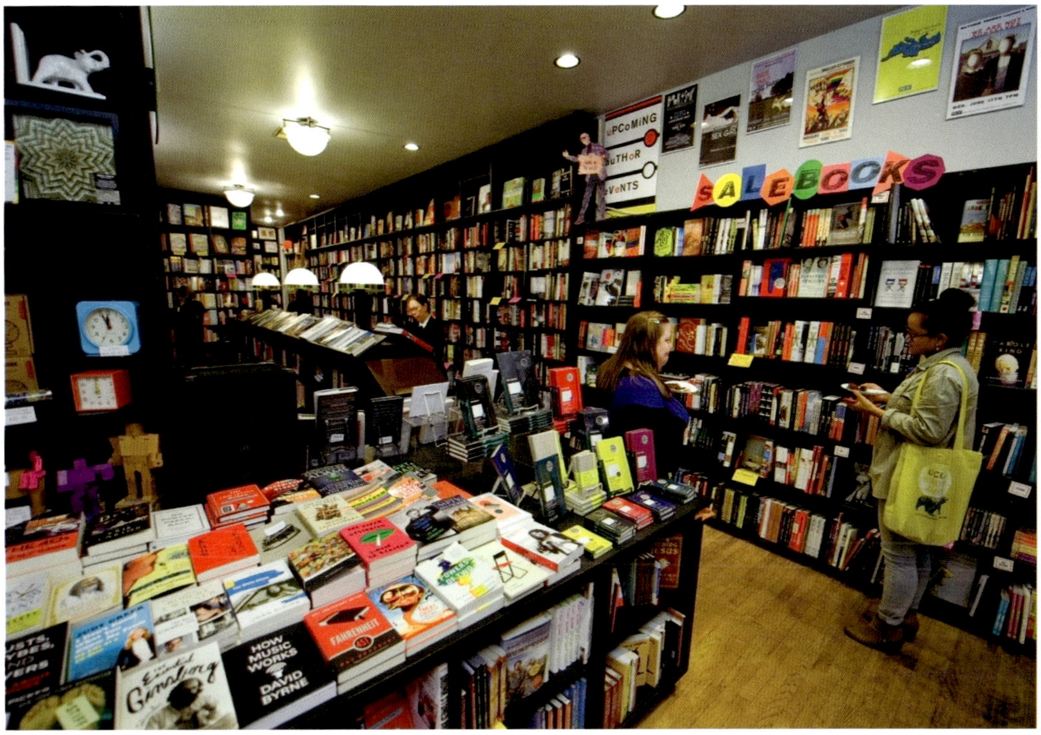

Book Soup, a warren of books and magazines that provides instant immersion into knowledge and amusement, is also a site for celebrity watching. The only bookstore on the Strip, it has withstood the tests of time and technology.

The Sunset Strip is hardly known for celebrating the cerebral.

Over the decades, a vague sense of smart could be seen in its snappy hotels and nightclubs. And those cagey gangsters and shady promoters were not without creative juice.

But no smash-nosed henchman ever cruised the Strip trying to buy a good book for gangster Mickey Cohen to enjoy at bedtime.

In 1975 two UCLA grad students put together some cash and decided to break the mold. They opened a bookstore on the Sunset Strip in what Dickens would describe as "a sleeve of a room," recalled by old-timers to be squeezed between a strip joint and a head shop. Very trendy for the time.

> **Glenn Goldman, who was the personification of Book Soup, imagined an old-fashioned bookstore with very modern sensibilities. He loved books. And respected readers.**

Hardly an overnight success. Partner Glenn Goldman, who became the personification of Book Soup, imagined an old-fashioned bookstore with very modern sensibilities. He loved books. And respected readers. It was not uncommon, when cashing out a couple of books, for him to sidle up and politely inquire why you selected those two books. And would you kindly report back on them when you were next in the store.

He was serious about books, so serious that when sales dwindled, and the cash flow plummeted, he moved into the store. Yes, to live there.

Goldman's Book Soup was located on a street trending to the seedy. And the punks and rockers stalking the Strip were far more interested in the sidewalk culture and the clubs than an aspiring bookstore. But Goldman persevered. The iconoclast believed there were plenty of books that could be sold to the eclectic population living in an area with Beverly Hills to its west, Hollywood to its east, the Hollywood Hills to its north, and a dynamic gay community coalescing all around. it would just take some time.

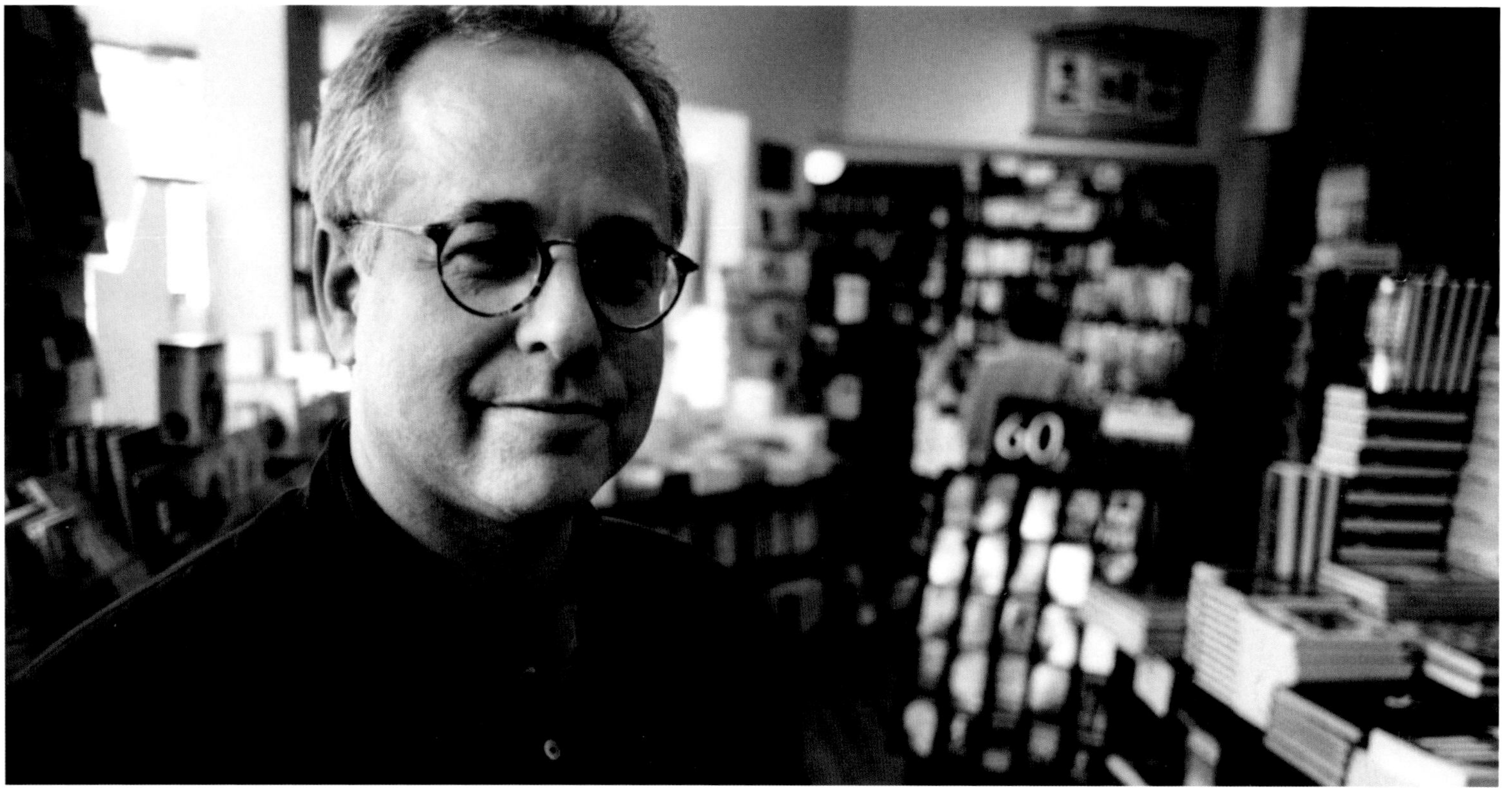

In 1975, Glenn Goldman had a dream that many—if not most—thought was folly: to open a bookstore on the seedy, downright nasty, Sunset Strip. He went on to build a store that is a haven for all things "book." Goldman kept the flame alive in good times and bad and established a loyal audience for his eccentric—and mind-boggling—bookstore.

He was right. Picking books for that crowd would be tricky. But Goldman did it. Art books. Architecture. Memoirs. Music. Fashion. Fiction of all persuasions and the ribald tell-alls. And bring in the authors for casual lectures. Put their names on the marquee outside. The hipsters, the fans, and most of all, the readers followed. And so did the sales.

The shelves overflowed. The piles of books started collecting on the stairs and the floor, on every available space. The subjects expanded: from the Treaty of Guadalupe Hidalgo to the latest lurid variations of *Hollywood Babylon*, from the most mind-numbing, but oh-so-hip literary novel to a sophisticated analysis of American film cinematography, to the politics and sociology of all things West Hollywood, American, Earthly. For his store, Goldman asserted no topic was too big or too small.

After one staff meeting, two employees went into Goldman's office and declared, "You have to stop buying books! We're out of room." With an impish smile, he said to his colleagues: "But I'm the book buyer. That's what I do. I buy books."

And he did. If it was in some way relevant to the neighborhoods, to the Industry, to Los Angeles, to the human spirit, he bought it. He was, after all, the ultimate book man.

So you can find in Book Soup an incredible, idiosyncratic selection of knowledge and fun and discovery. To a layman, the stock shows a bias to entertainment, social and political issues, innovation, relevant fiction, and all things media. It is not a selection for a Costco crowd. But the store was and is not above a dramatic buy. On one occasion a $10,000 book, *Commedia Dell'Arte*, proved irresistible. The post-Goldman management knew the book "was a celebration of everything Glenn believed in. It was the perfect Book Soup tome. Over the top. Sexy. Beautifully designed. And somewhere out there, in the Book Soup universe there would be a buyer.

That person soon came through the door: one of the world's most famous rock stars, and an avid Book Soup customer. He bought the book. Needless to say, many of the store employees refer to him by his first name, but always prefaced by the honorific title Sir bestowed by Her Majesty the Queen. (Bookstores are compulsive about protecting their customers' reading tastes, but in this case, rest assured, the Book Soup people are not referring to a former Beatle.)

In the 1980s the store was relocated to a larger site a few blocks east, across from the old Tower Records, in or close to a commercial area once occupied by the Utter-McKinley Mortuaries. (Ironically, almost adjacent to the mortuary was the haberdashery and office of gangster Mickey Cohen. Whether Utter's provided any "courtesy" discounts for Cohen's fallen colleagues or adversaries is unknown.)

After Goldman's untimely death at age fifty-eight in 2009, the store was purchased by the Pasadena bookstore, Vroman's. The Book Soup back office went modern, but the shelves maintained their unique charm, the steps kept their piles of books, and the whole place never lost its empathy for the customers.

The management, employees, and long-term customers recall Goldman with respect and fondness. And his marvelous wit. When British Prime Minister Margaret Thatcher attempted to ban an exposé book by a former spy, Goldman ran an ad in *Private Eye* declaring: "Banned in Britain. Available in America." And when J.D. Salinger was living as a near-hermit in New Hampshire, and not publishing any new work, Goldman had a small sign at a counter declaring "Special orders for new Salinger book." Of course, there was no such book.

At a time when so many quality bookstores have shuttered, Book Soup continues to defy the Internet discounters. At any given time, it has sixty-five thousand titles on hand.

Prudery was never in the Book Soup vocabulary. It had "full frontal" in its erotica section far before the Internet made it mundane. There were even Book Soup condoms for sale. But to the somewhat more than casual observer, the store's erotica was devoid of inhibition but always possessed at least some relationship to a quality bookstore justification. As a Vroman executive said, "This ain't your mother's bookstore."

At a time when so many quality bookstores have shuttered, Book Soup continues to defy the Internet discounters. Not to mention defying the harsh realities of how many books can be crammed, stocked, or leveraged coherently/safely into a relatively small store (about sixty-five thousand). Goldman created a store which is, as one person terms it, a great equalizer. Customers sort of check their credentials at the front door. There are no pretensions. It is perhaps one of the few bookstores with a self-declared, credible tagline. "Bookseller to The Great & The Infamous."

With high-end hotels and condos and retailers settling and resettling onto the Strip, the new wave of well-heeled residents and visitors strolling the Strip will further boost the popularity and economics of Book Soup. Decades ago, Glenn Goldman got it right. There was, surprising to many, a place on the Strip for something cerebral. ■

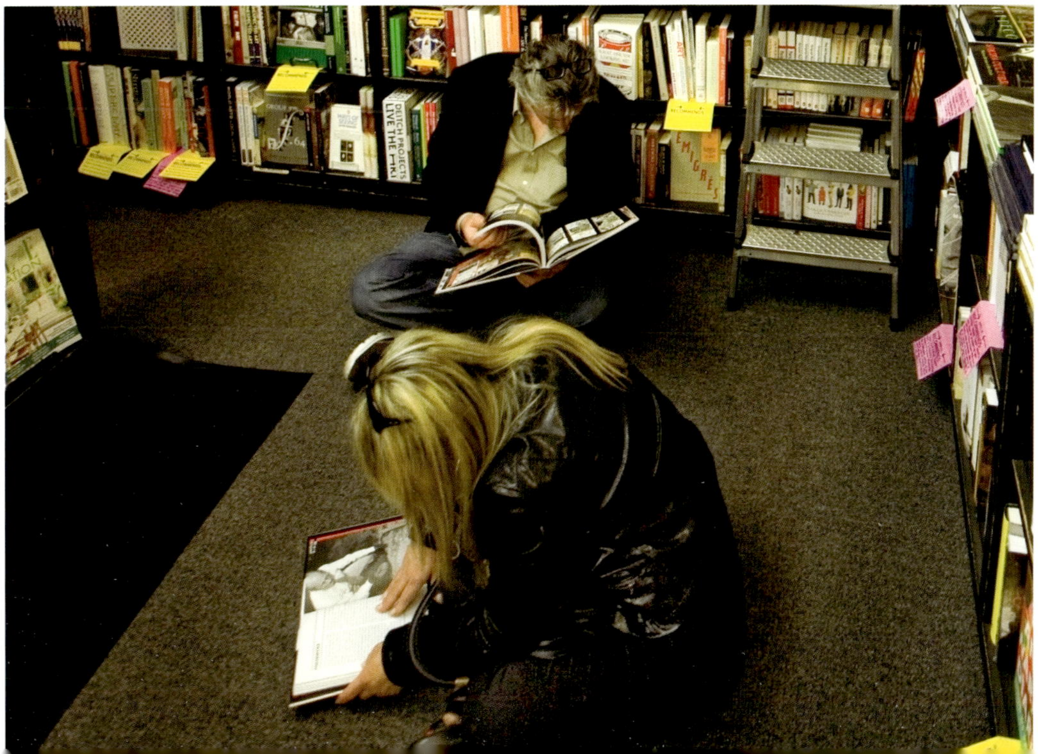

Books. Masses of intriguing and seductive books. A casual walk through the store can easily burn hours with more than sixty-five thousand enthralling titles that demand attention and respect.

Spago

California Cuisine. . .and a Pizza Revolution

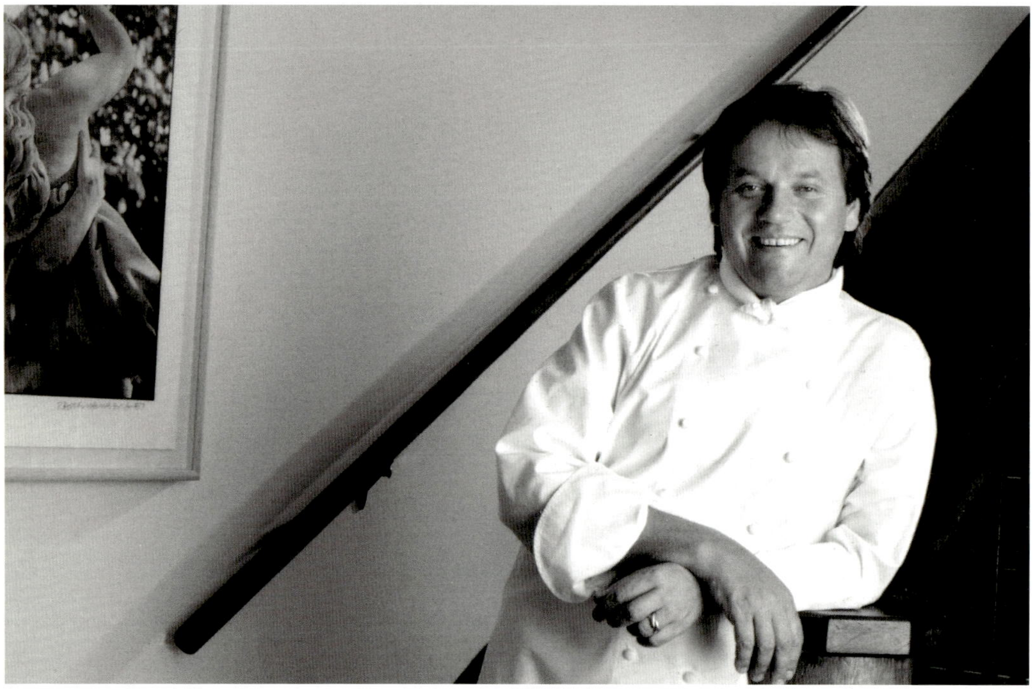

Wolfgang Puck, here in 1988, has a lot to smile about. From his native Austria to the Hotel de Paris in Monaco to Maxim's in Paris to Los Angeles as chef of the famed Ma Maison, Puck built a reputation for fine food. But when he opened a pizza parlor, he redefined pizza pie.

It was easy to be intimidated by Spago, the legendary restaurant once perched on a hill slightly above the Sunset Strip. You turned north at the old Tower Records and continued until dead-ending at a shabby mob of paparazzi and a fleet of gleaming Phantoms and Corniches.

Spago was the creation and domain of Wolfgang Puck, the gracious owner/chef who helped define California cuisine—along with his then-partner/wife, the diaphanous Barbara Lazaroff. What was so daunting? The crowd. Self-congratulatory. Clubby. Cliquish. And why not? They, the core clientele, were wizards of the entertainment business. And Puck had parity, an equally gifted creative and business force who, decades after Spago's Sunset Strip debut, looms large in food lore.

Puck once described the basic qualities of his restaurant's appeal: "local products, freshness, simplicity, lower prices, less solemnity, and no truffles." (The inevitable imitators, and there have been many, unfortunately embraced solemnity with ballooning prices and wearisome blizzards of truffles). Wolf created this congenial and decidedly informal atmosphere with Lazaroff's astonishing décor, rooted in a style best described as Cucamonga patio modern. But what mattered was good food and great company. It was a room of peers, filled out by fawning foodies and civilians anxious to be in proximity to the elevated. Puck himself was the center of this universe, a premier world-famous chef long before cable television began pressing out celebrity chefs with the frenetic enthusiasm of the Franklin Mint issuing new coins.

Puck himself was the center of this universe, a premier world-famous chef long before cable television began pressing out celebrity chefs with the frenetic enthusiasm of the Franklin Mint issuing new coins.

Spago was not without its moments of drama. One of the more outlandish occurred one night in June 1987 when the Los Angeles District Attorney Ira Reiner was dining inside with his wife, Diane Wayne, and two children. Ignoring the Rolls and Porsches, three gunmen decided to steal a rather humdrum, standard-issue Buick. Unfortunately for them, it was the DA's standard-issue Buick. In it was Reiner's flabbergasted investigator/bodyguard/driver Henry Grayson, who was suddenly a

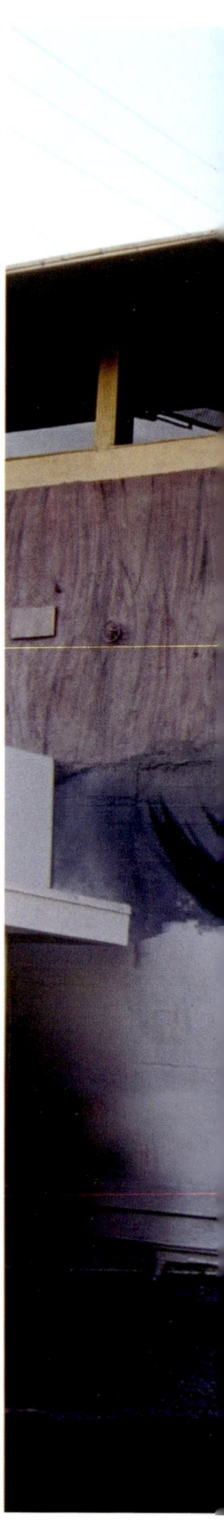

hostage and could understand the pair discussing in Spanish whether or not to kill him.

When the folly of all this became clear to even the malefactors, the decidedly unwise guys abandoned the Buick, and Grayson made his own exit. The hoodlums were soon arrested and awarded ample jail time to reflect on their careers, if not their taste in automobiles.

Puck eventually opened a new, flashy Spago in Beverly Hills, and not long after, shuttered the Sunset Strip restaurant. While hardly an architectural marvel, the building that housed Spago was in its day easily visible from the Strip and perceived as a place of class and vitality. Without Puck inside, it became a forlorn, blocky structure, a scruffy has-been, rapidly deteriorating, waiting for some bankable swell with a grand idea.

But it is difficult to imagine any idea topping Spago on the Strip. ■

Spago on the Strip is long gone, having relocated to, where else? Beverly Hills. Thus Puck added the word Hollywood to the Strip spot to differentiate the two. No need. It was the Sunset location that turned hipsters into Puck's loyal fans, and Puck into a household name (no credit given to Shakespeare).

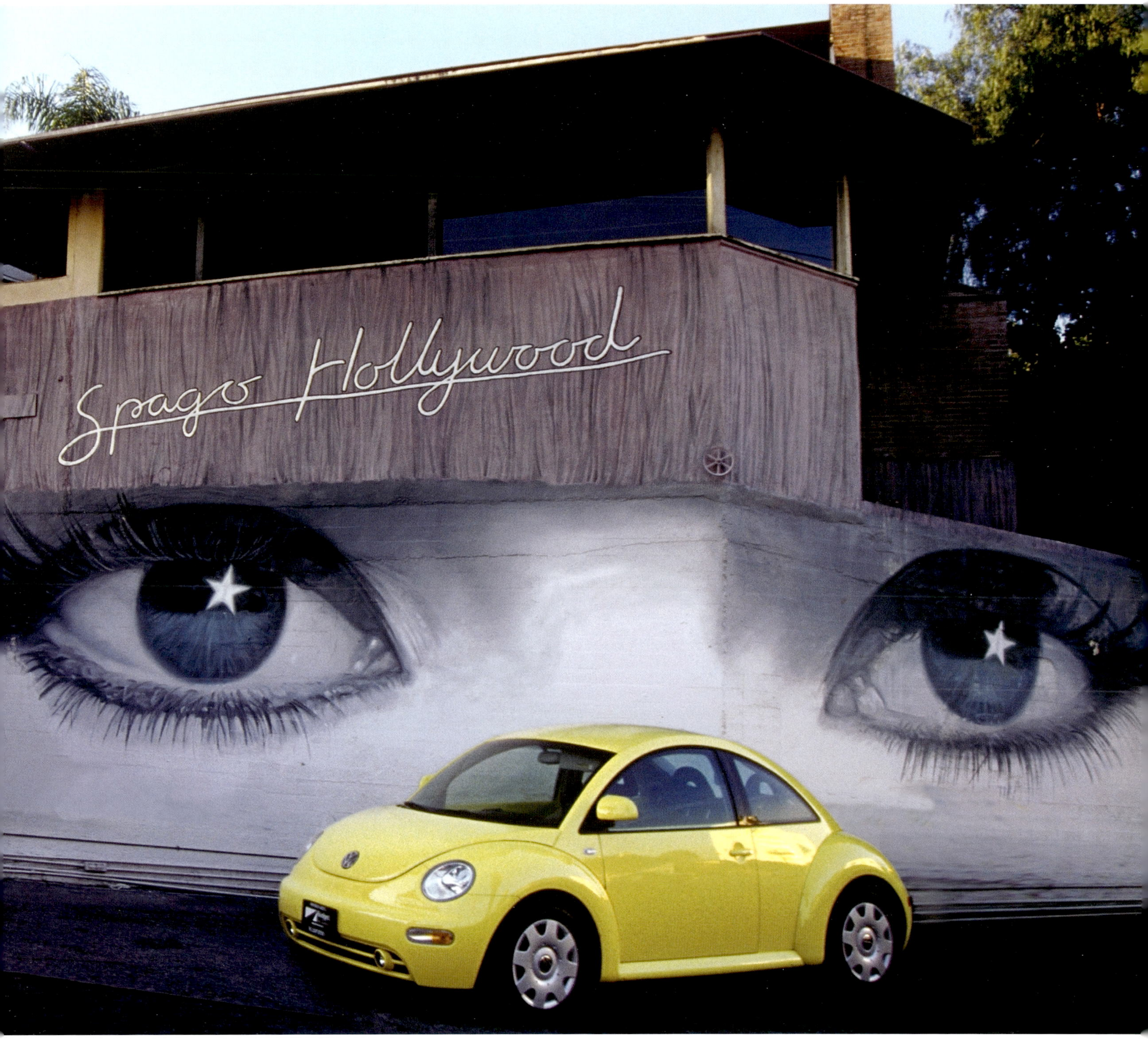

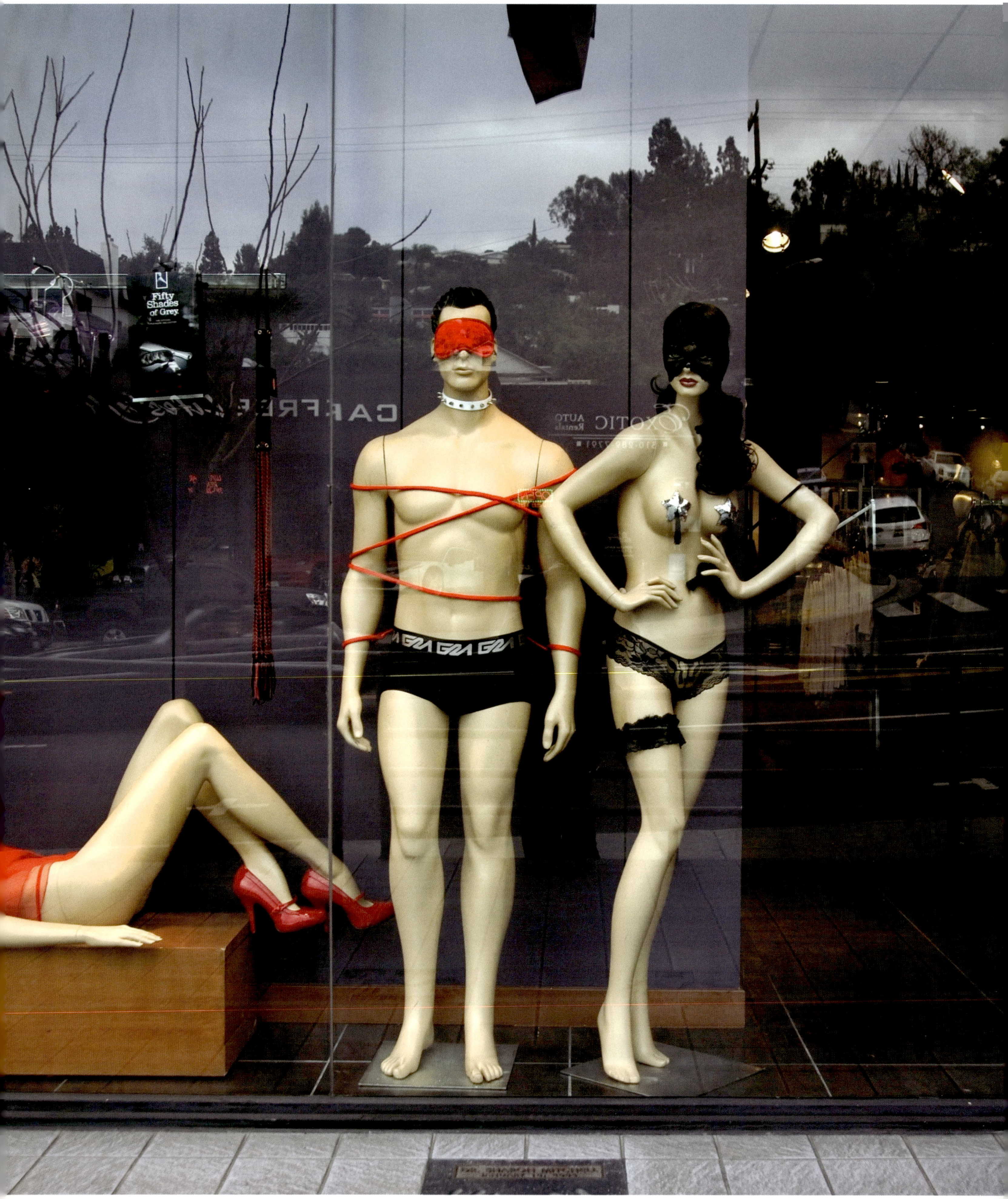
Fifty Shades of Grey.

Sex on Sunset

Where Subtlety is Not an Asset

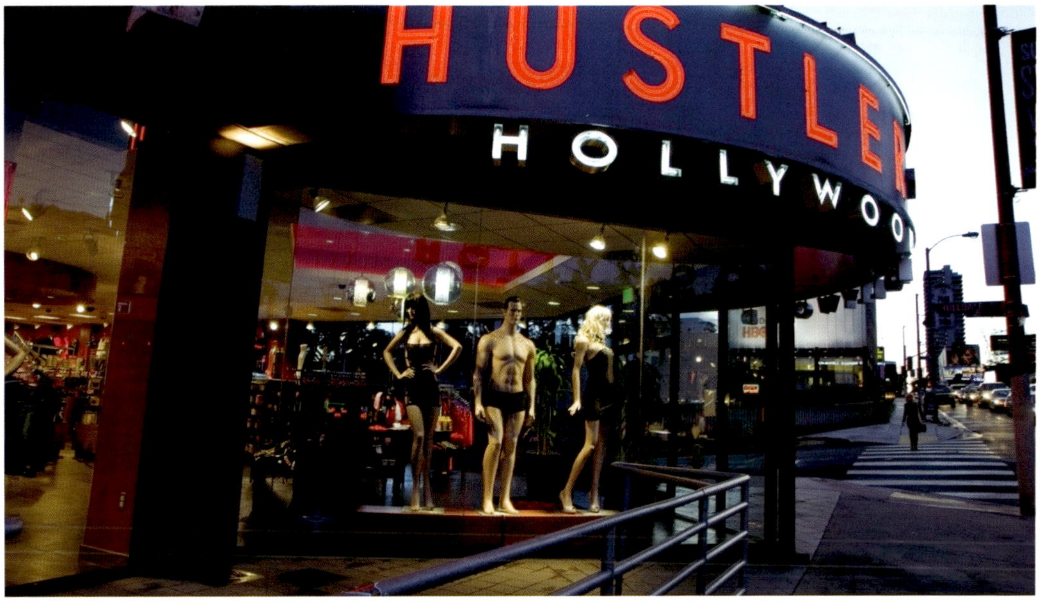

The Sunset Strip, never given to subtlety or temperance, was the longtime location of Larry Flynt's Hustler Hollywood store, a remarkable sexual souk, opened in 1998. It evolved into a chain of the stores, including one on Hollywood Boulevard.

Before the Internet, before crafty young boys could outmaneuver their parents and access a world of perpetual lust on their iPhones, a boat-sized automobile navigated the Sunset Strip, a vessel that constituted a mobile form of teenage titillation—or perhaps, illumination. It was a white Lincoln Continental stretch limo, and painted on it was a lush naked woman. She was not anatomically correct—well, not precisely—but resplendent in her seductive repose. The car turned left from the Strip onto North Doheny Drive and up the hill, almost to the summit. Parked in front of the delightfully embellished residence of Larry Flynt, founder of the *Hustler* empire, that car and that woman were symbols of everything an adolescent male might want. Occasionally, late on early summer evenings, cohorts of young boys would laboriously pedal their bikes up the staggeringly steep hill to gaze in awe before this vehicle of fleshy revelation.

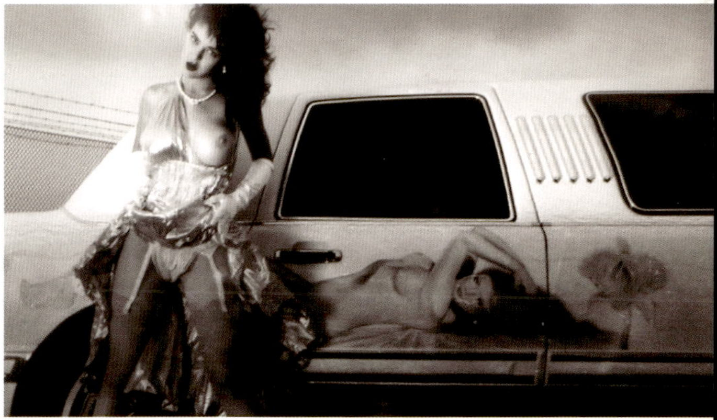

Hustler Founder Larry Flynt frequently was seen traveling along the Sunset Strip in a stretch limousine featuring—on both sides—a large, vivid, anatomically detailed drawing of a woman.

The Sunset Strip, for all its vulgarian indulgences, never really sold sex. While hardly ascetic, the Strip is, appropriately, all foreplay. The sex is just out of sight. Behind the front door of a brothel. Masked by a hotel's sensualities of design and expensive cotton sheets and sultry history. Inside the securely closed door of a restaurant's restroom. And the institutional coquetry of the bars and music halls and clubs is scripted foreplay. And a strip club feels as irrelevant on the Strip as a hardware store or a bridal gown shop.

If there was anything on the Strip that was unrelentingly lucid and point-blank direct in your face about sex, it was—what else?—the Hustler Store. Beginning in 1998, it stood on the Strip as the ultimate emporium of boutique carnality, a testament to the heroic scale, the sheer lasciviousness of mating sex with mercantilism. It wasn't some seedy little dive shop with obfuscated windows and signs that say Adults Only Gifts; no this was sex toys for fun, for everyone. Years ago, the Hustler store seemed dominated by DVDs, artfully arranged in a kind of a libidinous Dewey Decimal System.

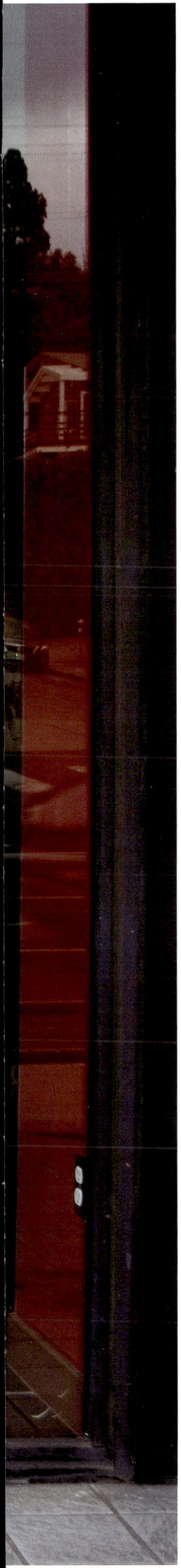

←
The Hustler Store became famous for a stupefying range of prurient apparel, lubricious potions, and mechanical devices of, at times, alarming utility.

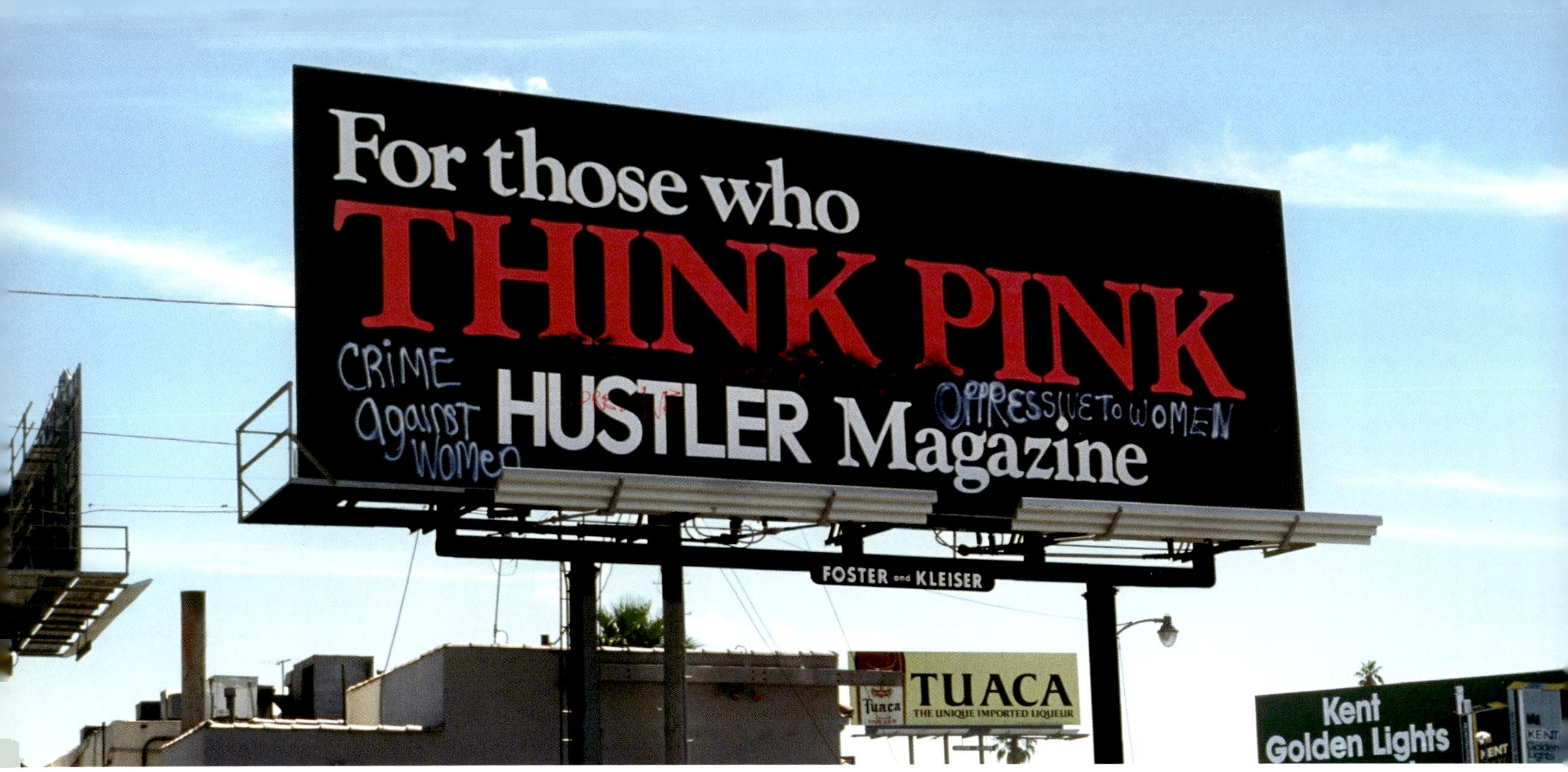

In 1978, this controversial Hustler billboard loomed above the Sunset Strip, prescient of things to come in the twenty-first century. Blunt, to say the least, the offensive advertisement was protested by a women's group that deemed it a "crime against women" and "oppressive to women."

Fantasies and desires were labeled and stocked in racks of precise definition. No vague hints here. No curtains of modesty to shield the faint of heart. Only the true debauchee could scan those shelves without occasionally recoiling in shock and exclaiming, "You've got to be kidding!"

The store addresses sex in its most fundamental and, occasionally, astonishing forms. Today, the most familiar of all that is seen on television, sequestered up in those four-digit channels. And Hustler is certainly in the cable market, claiming to be the largest supplier of adult product to the cable channels of the world.

Now, the store seems dominated by fanciful clothing, or hints of clothing, and an awe-inspiring array of presumably sex-enhancing objects. Forget the $1,995 spanking chair (structurally, a bit mystifying, but one assumes in compliance with relevant federal consumer safety standards). Who knew there were so many mechanical enhancements to a human delight that seemingly thrived for millennia without batteries? Most memorable perhaps is a 24-karat gold-plated object ($3,900) of such graceful, pleasing, aesthetic design ("sexual jewelry [with] floral motifs reminiscent of the Belle Époque") that it could well be displayed in a museum store's Christmas collection of best stocking stuffers, advanced as a novel knickknack for a living room coffee table. Just don't accidentally flip the switch.

Out of obvious necessity, Flynt is deeply schooled in the First Amendment and politics, insightful about creating and managing businesses, and perhaps as a result, adroit at making money.

The Charles Henry Harrod of these stores is Flynt, who emerged from a destitute county in Kentucky ("we didn't have two food stamps to rub together") to build, without one shred of embarrassment or mortification, a robust pornography empire (*Hustler* magazine, the historic cornerstone of the business, is still making money—barely, he notes—in a lucrative world of digital porn). If he had been born in Fairfield County to an Ivy League family with an account at Brown Brothers Harriman, he could conceivably be a Harvard MBA today and chairman of a Fortune 500 company jetting in his Gulfstream G650ER to Bilderberg. He did not take the Harvard route; he didn't need to; Larry Flynt is very smart. Law Review smart.

Sitting at breakfast in the Peninsula Hotel on the edge of Beverly Hills, he talks softly, devoid of pretense, with a slight Appalachian lilt to his voice. Out of obvious necessity, he is deeply schooled in the First Amendment and politics, insightful about creating and managing businesses and, perhaps as a result, adroit at making money. Considering his chosen field, nothing has come easily to Flynt. Being from Magoffin County is one thing, but being gunned down by the definitive American lunatic/shooter Joseph Paul Franklin, quite another. Over approximately three years in the late 1970s, Franklin murdered fifteen men, women, and children. He also wounded many more, including the famed lawyer and civil rights figure Vernon Jordan (1980) and Flynt (1978), who has used a wheelchair ever since the madman shot him.

Flynt's current business focus is the Hustler Casino, and moving deeper into the gambling industry. Flynt himself is a blackjack player of legendary skill, capable of playing three hands simultaneously with a starting stake of fifteen thousand dollars on each. He is no longer a gambler when it comes to his retail operation. With the Strip housing designer brand boutiques selling thousand-dollar shoes and the clothes to go with them and signs pointing toward less humor and more serious fashion, he has sold—at a nifty profit, he notes—the Sunset Hustler store site (as well as his office building on Wilshire Boulevard). The store, one of thirteen across the country, is destined for the Hollywood and Highland tourist denizen, where there is far more foot traffic.

Flynt himself is a blackjack player of legendary skill, capable of playing three hands simultaneously with a starting stake of fifteen thousand dollars on each.

And what will replace the Hustler store on the Sunset Strip? Rumors have swirled that Gwyneth Paltrow and some associates will replace the Hustler structure with an English-styled private club, perhaps one based on a London establishment that years ago enjoyed the membership of Charles Dickens and Anthony Trollope. But when this book went to press, no confirmation was available. Could the store with a Porn Hall of Fame Sidewalk (Ron Jeremy, Marilyn Chambers, Flynt himself, and others of equal renown), in the great tradition of the Sunset Strip, morph into something radically different, a posh club of faux Sloane Rangers with tans, arguing the relative merits of Cumberbatch vs. Redmayne, or what will it take to finally muffle those nettlesome Scots?

The arrival of a fogey establishment and the Hustler store moving to the more boisterous Hollywood Boulevard are indicators of the Strip moving upscale. And, of course, there are no testosterone-driven boys peddling up the hill to view that embellished, illustrative limousine. "I helped a lot of young people get through puberty," Flynt says with humility. And a touch of nostalgia. ■

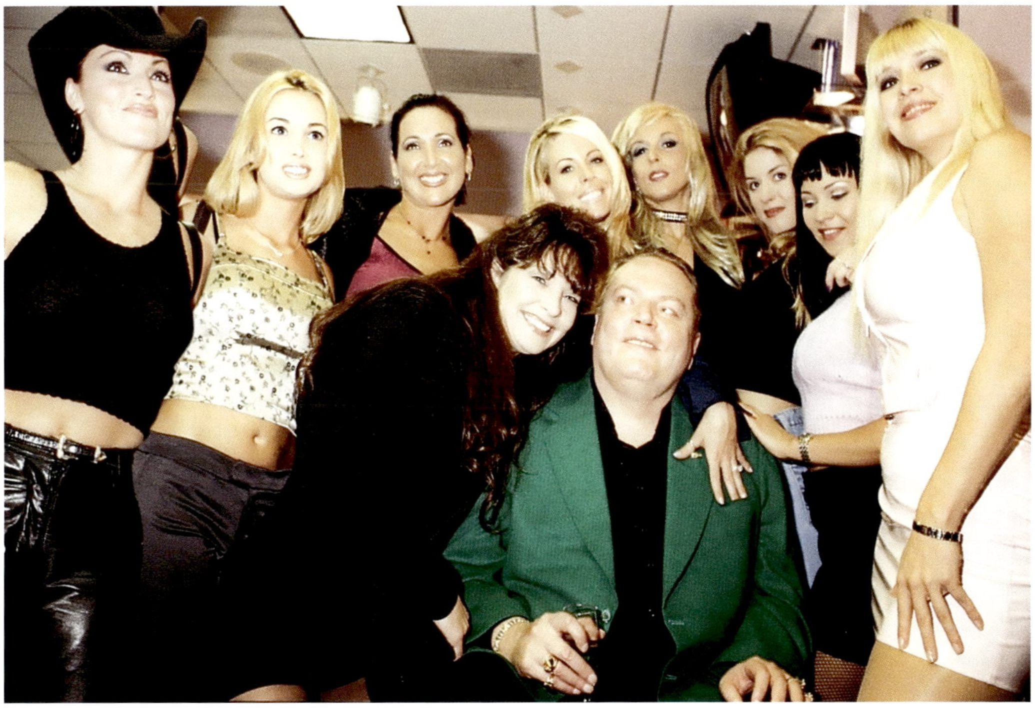

The Hustler store-opening in 1998 brought dread to the few fusty people living in West Hollywood. But for Flynt and his fans, it was another major step in expanding a brand and commercializing the product that had brought him success. . .sex.

Ed Ruscha

He Captured the Soul of the Strip

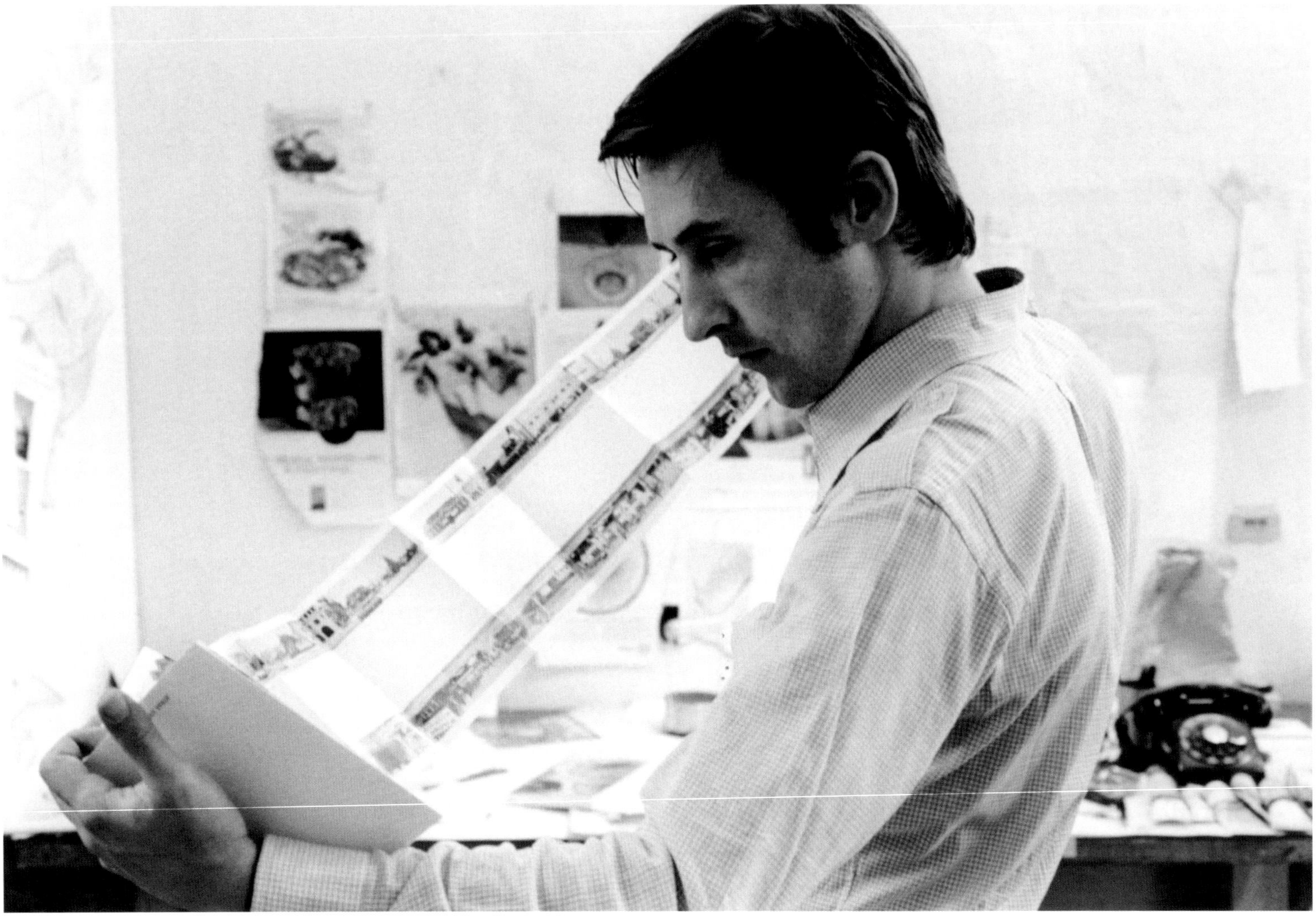

RUSCHA UNFOLDING EVERY BUILDING ON THE SUNSET STRIP, 1967. © JERRY McMILLAN/COURTESY OF CRAIG KRULL GALLERY

Artist Ed Ruscha unfolds the accordion-like pages of his 1966 book *Every Building on the Sunset Strip*, which both documents and pays homage to L.A.'s most fabled boulevard—he captured the soul of the street. Original first-edition copies of the book are considered to be pieces of art in book form.

His photographs of city streets have become important historical documents. So, too, for the Sunset Strip.

A used bookseller on Amazon once offered a signed, first-edition copy of Ed Ruscha's 1966 book, *Every Building on the Sunset Strip*, for $9,500. To create the work for his book, Ruscha, one of the most esteemed modern artists, mounted a Nikon in the bed of a pickup and photographed—in sequence—every building on the Sunset Strip.

Ruscha is perhaps the most Angeleno of all the Los Angeles artists. A filmmaker, photographer, painter, and printmaker, he's created a remarkable and voluminous body of celebrated work, and a great deal of his work relates to his L.A.

But Ruscha determined this documentation had to unfold a story like no other in the city. So he assembled the photographs in a book whose pages unfurled accordion style, implying that the storefronts and restaurants and hotels that composed his Strip could not for a second be separated, not even by the turn of a page. The artbook generated much buzz in the world of photography, a major innovation in the genre of street photography. To a person who routinely travels the Strip, the images are an occasionally shocking look over the shoulder at another era, a time increasingly unrecognizable. ■

The musicians were coming on strong in the late 1960s, old-timers were fading from the scene, and the street conveyed a patina of fatigue, a creeping urban dinginess. With the exception of the music clubs and a few classic buildings, it looked very much like the outer edge of Phoenix or Bakersfield. Only the shadows and neon and chaos of the night could elevate most of the street to an aura of excitement. Barely.

A half century and a new millennium later, the Strip is on an azimuth to a high end, dramatic future. Better? That can provoke a debate. The Strip is increasingly a corporate creation, its future keyed to the interests and indulgences of an upscale, uptown, credit card crowd. Big buildings. Big display windows. Big design. Big transactions. Big crowds. All the "big" is riding on a core belief in a sumptuous tomorrow, of deep pockets and mercantile dreams realized—the same dreams that brought forth the Strip in the first place. Dreams still evidenced in the old Strip landmarks that have survived for decades.

The Strip is best when you can feel the now but also sense a nostalgic wind at your back, a breeze nudging you into the future. The Strip's legitimacy requires at the very least a cranky respect for the past. Gentrification works only if history—including some of the grit and hustle and silliness—survives. The Strip will keep its integrity only if there is enough pluck in its character to give an earthy finger to the parvenu swells and planners flocking to the future. The tanning salons and hamburger joints and seedy saloons should find a niche in the shadows of the oh-so modern buildings and the modish hotels and the next big-name designer shops.

The new Sunset Strip is betting on success. If there is a continuing sense of the Strip's history—the raison d'etre of the Strip—and if the new places and faces live in proximity with memories of Billy Wilkerson and Mickey Cohen and the Byrds and last call at Le Dôme, the odds are positive.

Overleaf →
A steady stream of cars speeds west at rush hour seemingly oblivious to a Sunset Strip that is drastically reinventing itself for the 21st century.

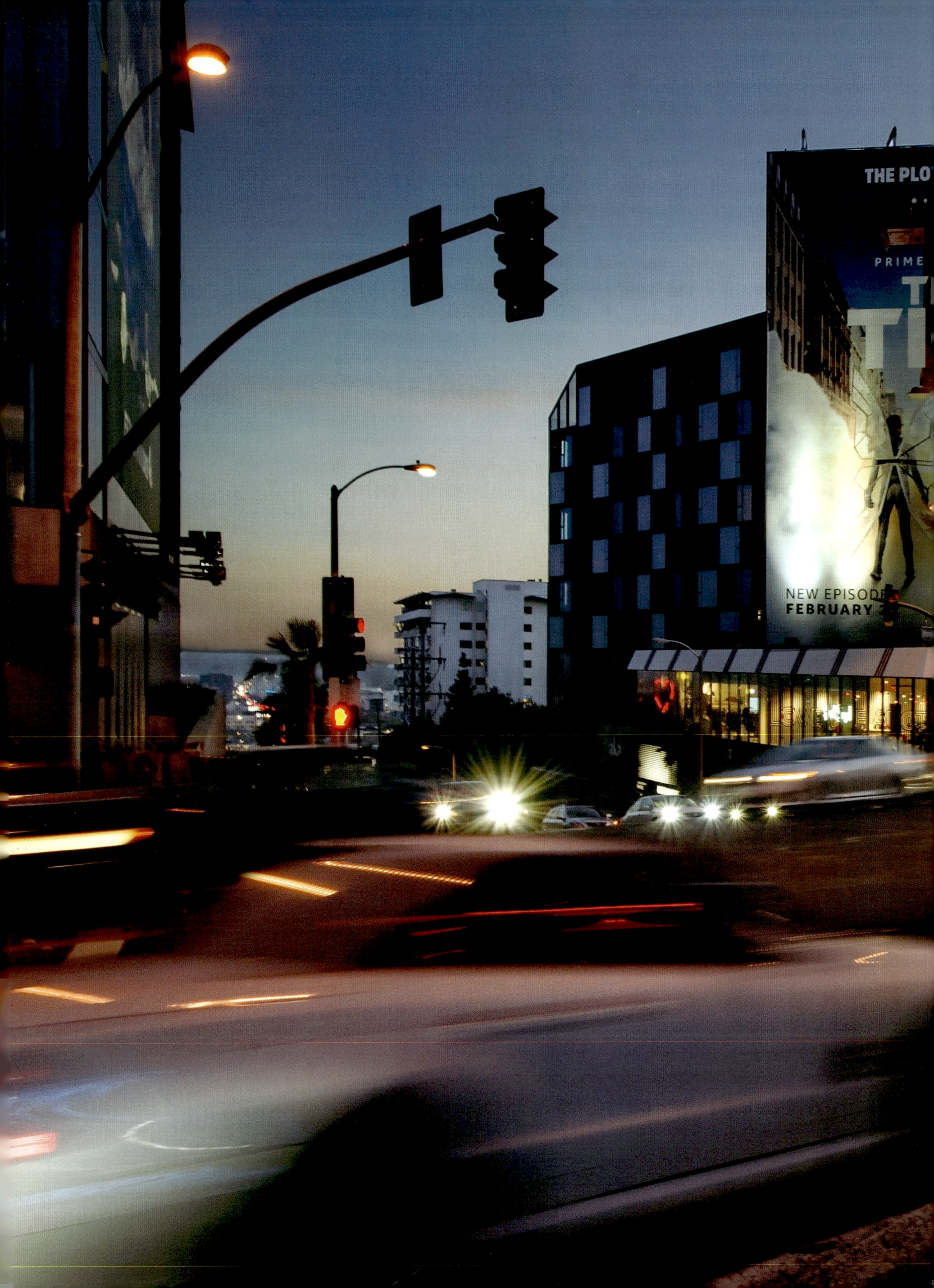
PRIME
FEBRUARY

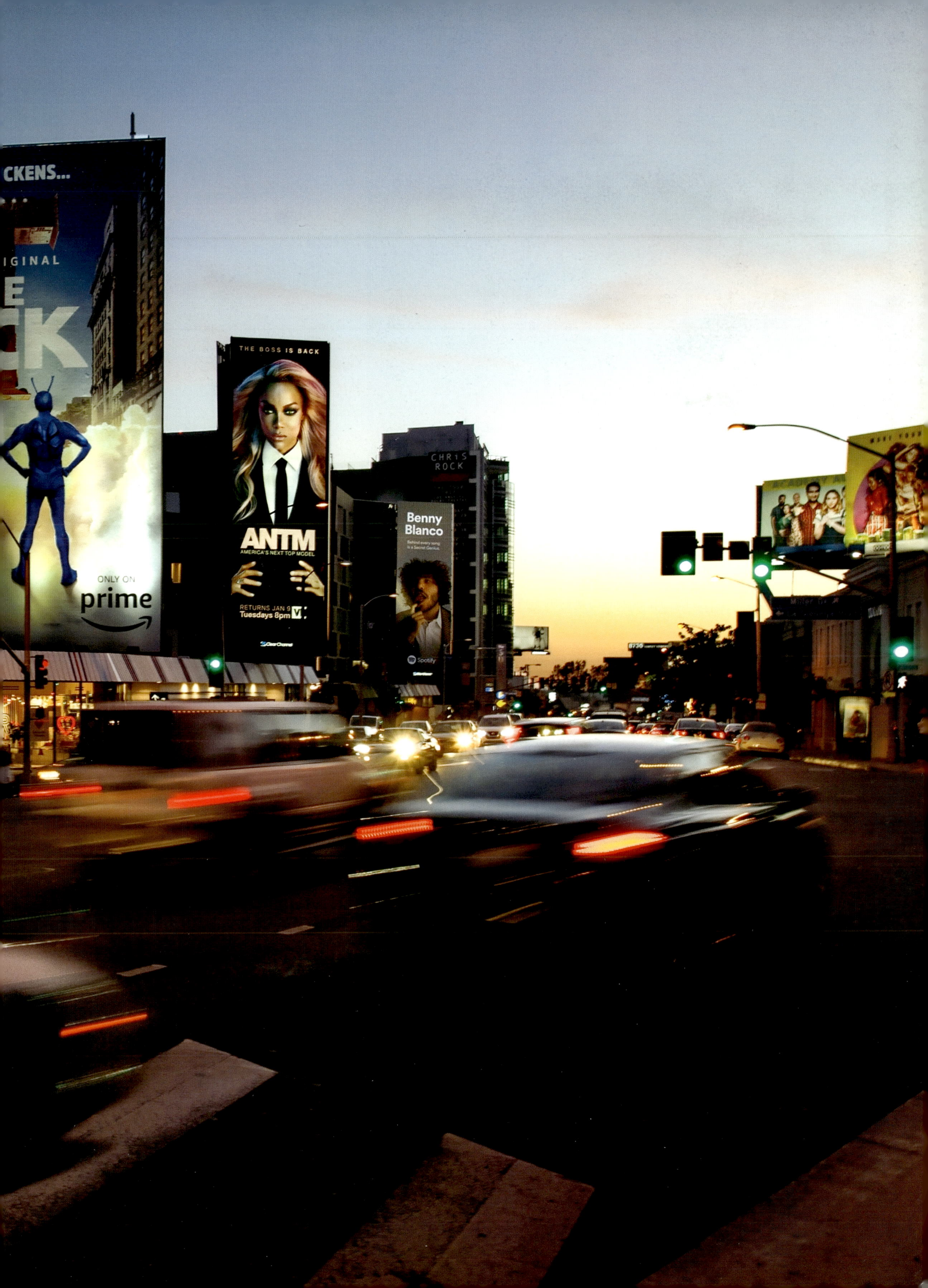
CKENS...
IGINAL
THE BOSS IS BACK
ANTM
AMERICA'S NEXT TOP MODEL
RETURNS JAN 9
Tuesdays 8pm
ONLY ON
prime
CHRIS ROCK
Benny Blanco
Spotify

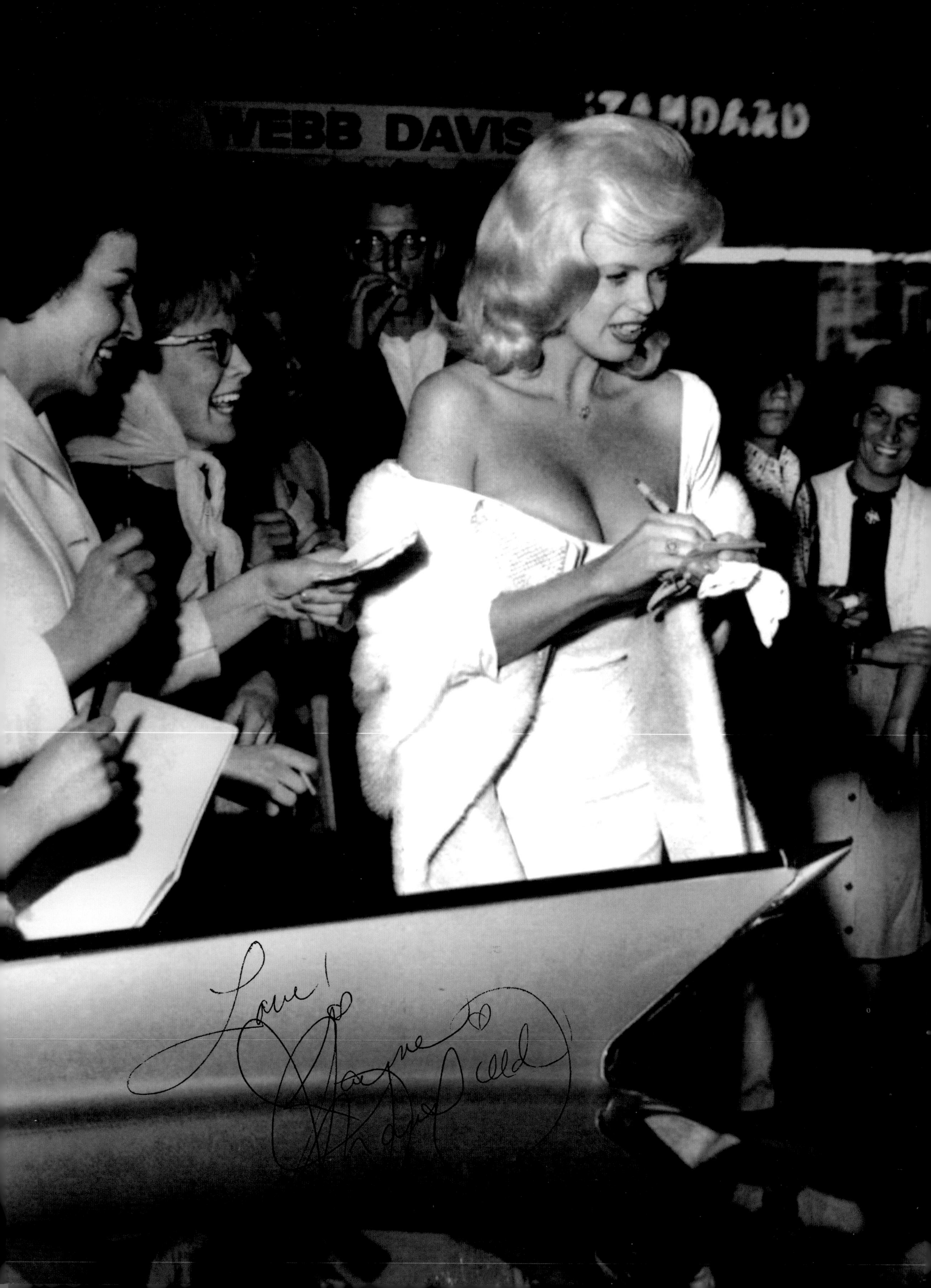
WEBB DAVIS
Love!

ACKNOWLEDGMENTS

Books that convey a story through a marriage of words and images are by nature collaborative.

Since this book examines the Sunset Strip through both a historical and contemporary lens, it required the skills and assistance of many talented people to complete. We thank those who went out of their way to help in its creation.

A very special thank you to Kate Kelly who was there at the beginning when the idea for this book was just taking shape and made many invaluable contributions.

Our deep gratitude to Marc Wanamaker for preserving and sharing historic photographs of the Sunset Strip that have helped us to illustrate this book.

We also want to thank the following people for contributing their time and resources: Isis Aquarian, Sean Berios, Brett Doherty, Alison Duke, Karen Figilis, Larry Flynt, Frank Gehry, Jaguar Heritage USA, Hulya Karadeniz, Cheryl Lodinger, David Loehr, Mary Mallory, Stephen D. Martinez, Jean Mathison, Francis S. Montgomery II, Charlene Peters, and Dick Wells & David Janzow.

We remember and thank the late Phyllis Kirk Bush, for her long-ago introduction to Eddie Kerkhofs of Le Dôme, who generously opened his archive and memory bank to us.

We are also grateful to Paddy Calistro and Scott McAuley, who embraced this book from the beginning and brought to it and us their creativity, motivation, and astonishing patience. We are proud to see our book added to the library of books Angel City Press has published about Los Angeles, its history, culture, and people.

Finally, a special thanks to Robert Behr and Cindi McIntosh Behr for use of their rare 1965 Austin Healey 3000 Mk III for our cover photography, and to our model, Courtney Saladino Gurney.

—VGS, RL, and FE

← Jayne Mansfield signing autographs next to her 1960 pink Cadillac. She died in a car-truck collision in 1967 at the age of thirty-four. By that time she had become a star of theater, film, and television. She married three times, had five children, and was a popular *Playboy* magazine playmate. She was also known, perhaps renowned, for her exceptionally voluptuous figure. Those curves caught the eye of Emmeline Snively and her agents at Blue Book Modeling Agency, who had helped Norma Jean Dougherty become Marilyn Monroe. Mary Webb Davis, whose sign is blazing on The Strip, was a competitor of Miss Snively. Webb Davis models were considered to be more "refined" than the beauties who emerged from Blue Book. Jayne made a point to sign autographs, thanking her fans for making her a star.

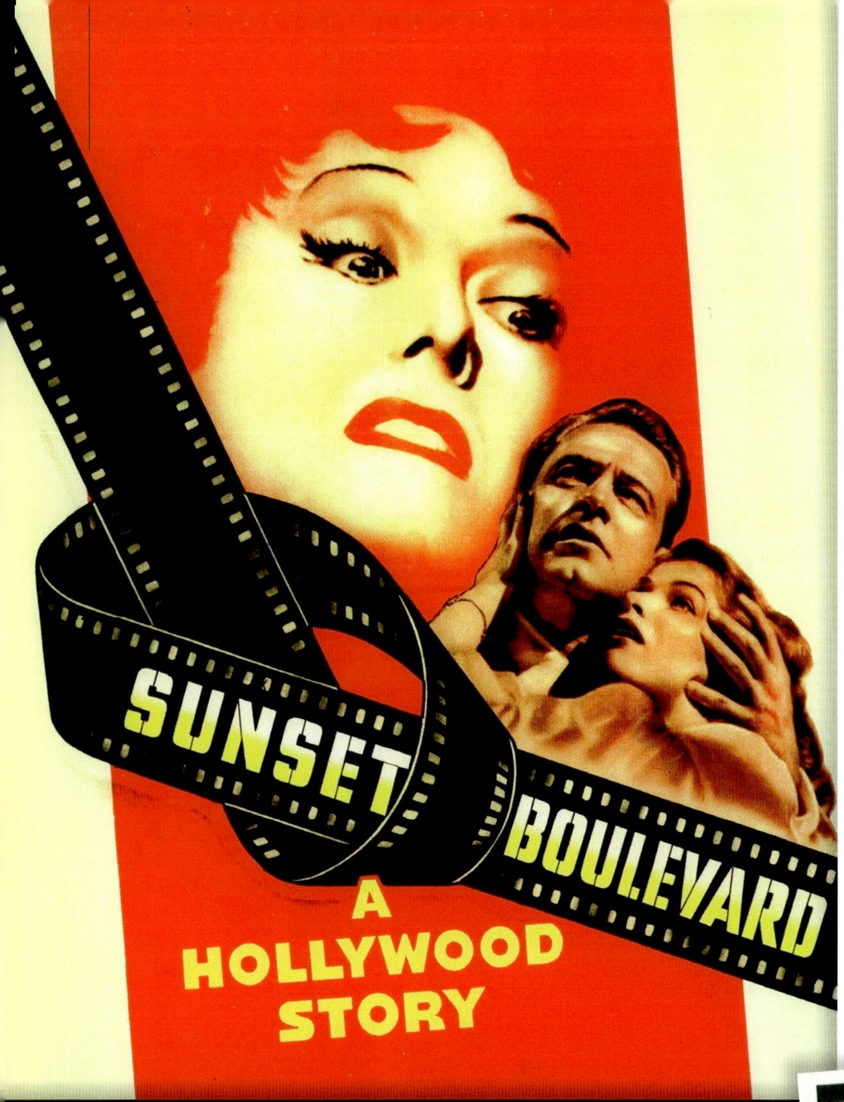
SUNSET
BOULEVARD
A
HOLLYWOOD
STORY

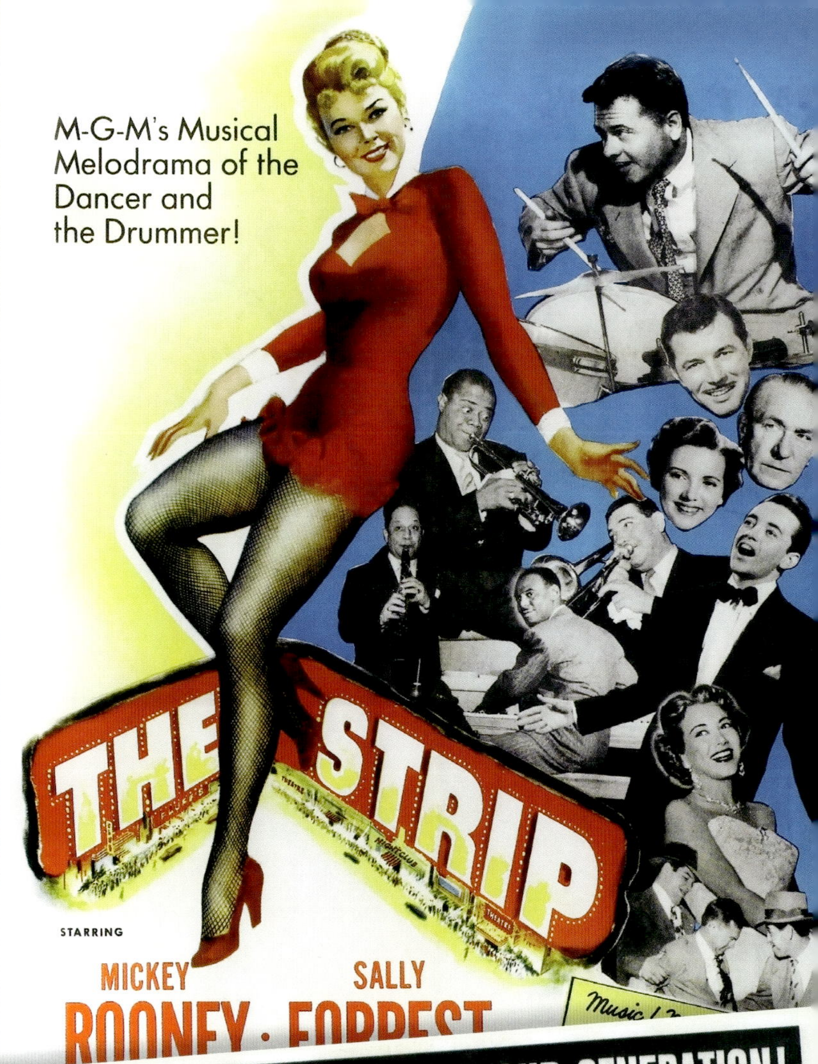
M-G-M's Musical
Melodrama of the
Dancer and
the Drummer!
THE STRIP
STARRING
MICKEY
SALLY

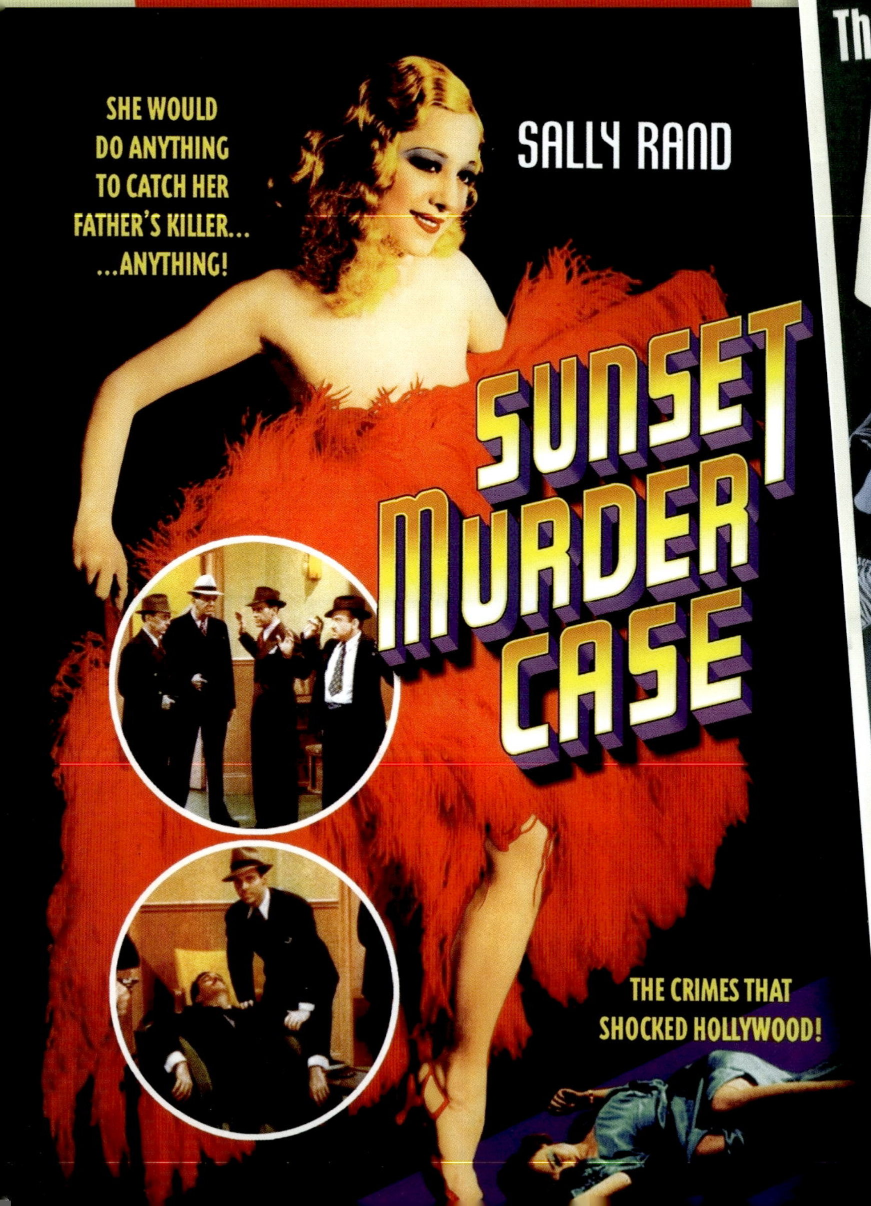
SHE WOULD
DO ANYTHING
TO CATCH HER
FATHER'S KILLER...
...ANYTHING!
SALLY RAND
SUNSET
MURDER
CASE
THE CRIMES THAT
SHOCKED HOLLYWOOD!

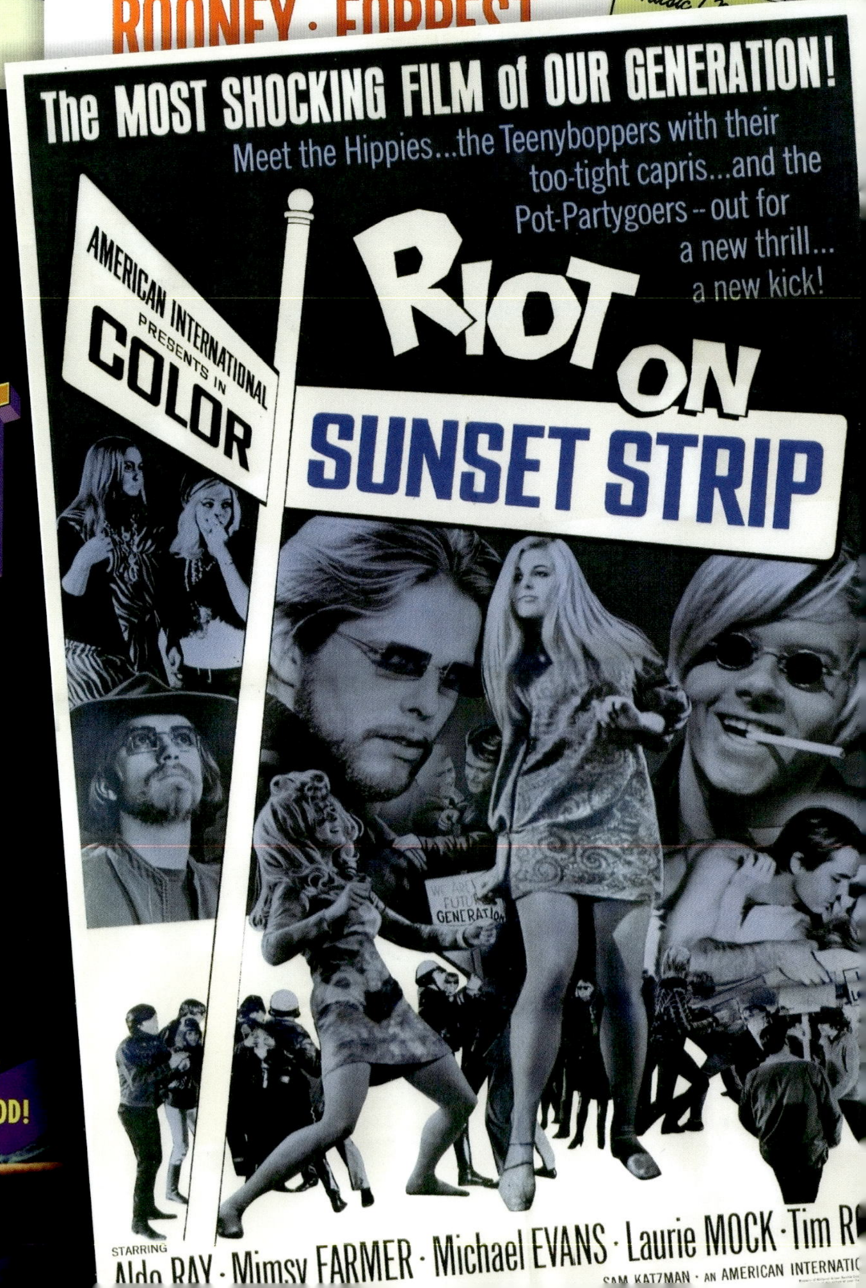
The MOST SHOCKING FILM of OUR GENERATION!
Meet the Hippies...the Teenyboppers with their
too-tight capris...and the
Pot-Partygoers -- out for
a new thrill...
a new kick!
AMERICAN INTERNATIONAL
PRESENTS IN
COLOR
RIOT ON
SUNSET STRIP
STARRING
Aldo RAY · Mimsy FARMER · Michael EVANS · Laurie MOCK

PHOTO CREDITS

The authors and publisher are grateful to the following sources for permission to reprint the images on the pages listed. For any further information, contact the publisher.

Academy of Motion Pictures Arts and Sciences, Margaret Herrick Library **28, 42, 57, 70,101**; MGM Special Collection **101**; Marc Wanamaker Collection **102**

Isis Aquarian/The Source Archives **142–147**

Berend Archives/Frans Evenhuis **44** (left), **68** (top right), **72, 73, 92–93, 96, 97, 103, 114** (top), **126, 129, 131** (top), **154–155, 170, 174**

Bison Archives/Marc Wanamaker **2–3, 4–5, 6–7, 8–9, 43, 45, 51, 52, 68** (top left), **69, 78–79, 80, 82–83, 90, 123, 176**

Book Soup **158**

California State University Northridge Department of Geography Map Library **Endpapers**

Center for Creative Photography, University of Arizona Foundation **120–121** Photo by Max Yavno/©1988

Center for Sacramento History **150**

Brett Doherty/Hamburger Hamlet **122, 124, 125** (top)

Alison Duke **160**

Everett Collection **39, 62, 64, 65, 91, 104, 112** (top right), **128**

LFP Inc. **163** (bottom), **165**

Gehry Partners **44** (right) and **46–47** Rendering 2016 by Visualhouse, each © 2016 Gehry Partners

Getty Images **109** Jon Brenneis; **66** Michael Ochs Archives/Photo by Earl Leaf

Hollywood Photographs/Bruce Torrence **38, 56, 85, 95,106–107,108**

Jaguar Heritage USA **10–11, 175**

James Dean Museum **86–87** Photo by Frank Worth

Kate Kelly **68** (matchbox), **71** (top) **76**

Eddie Kerkhofs **138, 141**

Robert Landau **1, 14–15, 32, 36, 48, 49, 53, 54, 55, 58, 63, 71, 76, 77, 125** (bottom),**139, 148, 149, 151–153, 156, 157, 159, 161-163** (top), **164, 168–169**

Los Angeles Public Library Photo Collection **34** Photo by Paul Chinn, **40–41, 81** Photo by Herman Schultheis, **105, 114** (bottom), **115, 119**

Los Angeles Times Photographic Archives (Collection 1429), Library Special Collections, Charles E. Young Research Library, UCLA **30–31, 59, 60, 88-89, 110–112** (top left), **113, 116–117, 118**

Mary Mallory **84**

Jean Mathison **99** (top)

Jerry McMillan/Craig Krull Gallery, Santa Monica, California **166**

Photofest New York **61, 98, 99** (bottom), **100**

Playboy Enterprises, Inc.**130, 131** (bottom), **132, 133, 134–135, 136, 137**

University of Southern California/USC Special Collections **75**

USC Libraries. California Historical Society Collection, 1860-1960 **24**

Dick Wells/David Janzow **68** (center; bottom), **91** (bottom), **127, 172**

Willie Wilkerson III **94**

←
Clockwise from top left: The 1950 film noir classic *Sunset Boulevard* directed by Billy Wilder indelibly etched the street's name into popular culture by recounting a darkly cynical tale of fame, decadence, ambition and greed in the "behind-the-scenes" world of Hollywood movie making.

The Strip has always been a great backdrop for trouble, at least on the big screen. Mickey Rooney returned to MGM after a three-year absence to star as a jazz drummer who falls in love with a gangster's moll. *The Strip* (1952) was filmed on location with interior shots at the clubs Mocambo and Ciro's. The movie's hit song, "A Kiss to Build a Dream On," was nominated for an Academy Award.

Riot on the Sunset Strip (1967) is a low-budget counter-culture exploitation movie set during the 1966 Sunset Strip riots and was produced and rushed into theaters within four months. The film's budget was a paltry $250,000 but it managed to yield a box-office return of over one million dollars.

Sunset Murder Case (1938) stars burlesque dancer Sally Rand posing as a stripper who gets work in a nightclub where she believes her father was murdered. . .and she wants revenge! The poster's tagline explains it all.

INDEX

Dolores Drive-in, famous for its barbeque chicken and milk shakes of course (1950s).

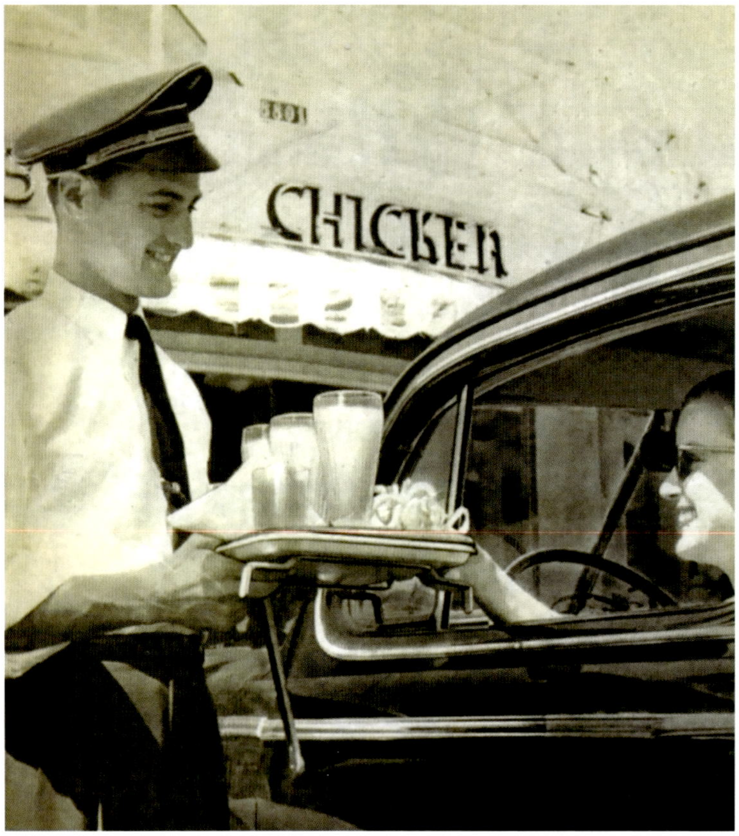

William Lyons (right) just sold Clark Gable a new X120 at the Hornburg Jaguar dealership (1950).

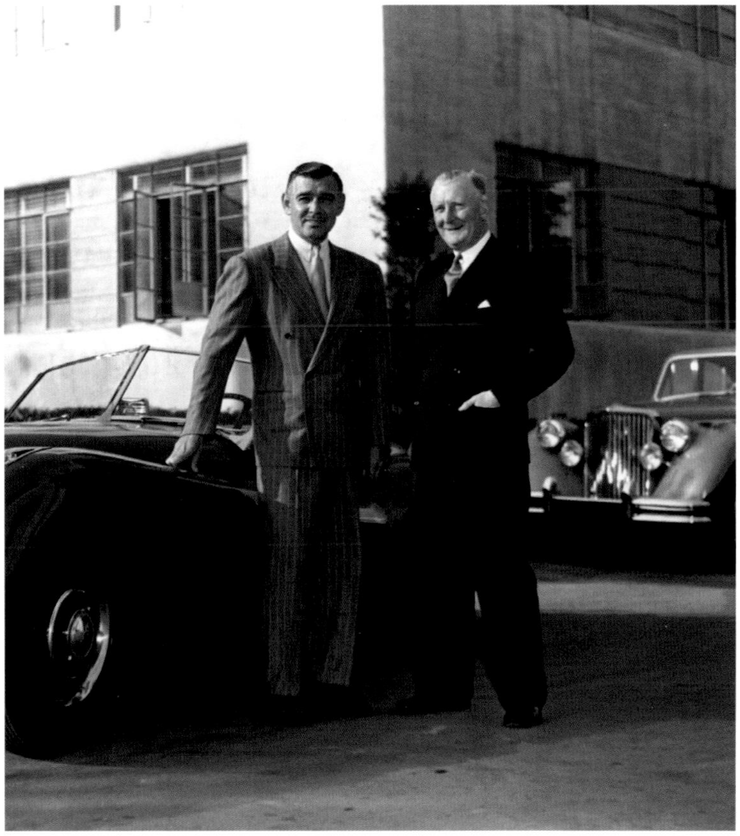

Selling maps to movie star homes in 1946.

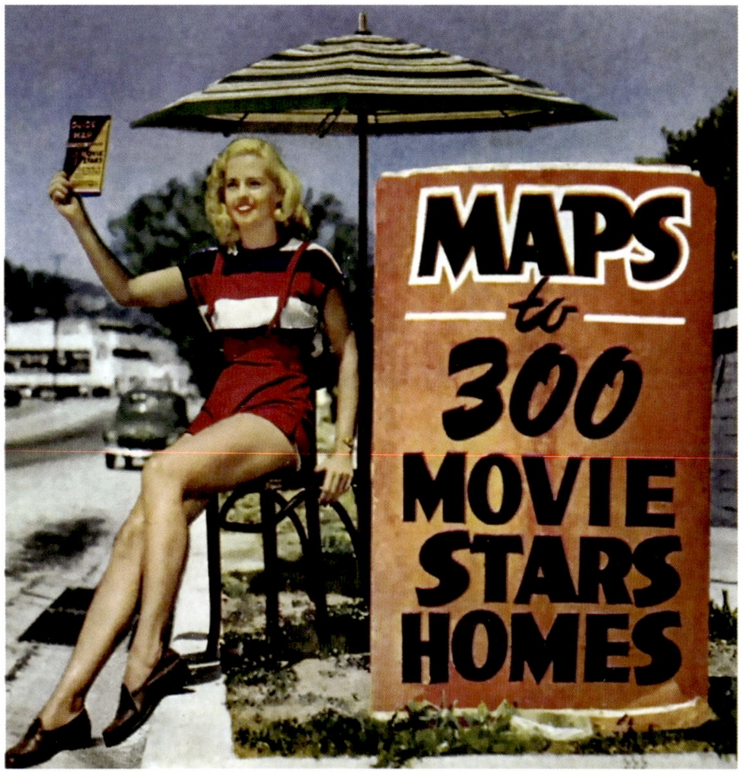

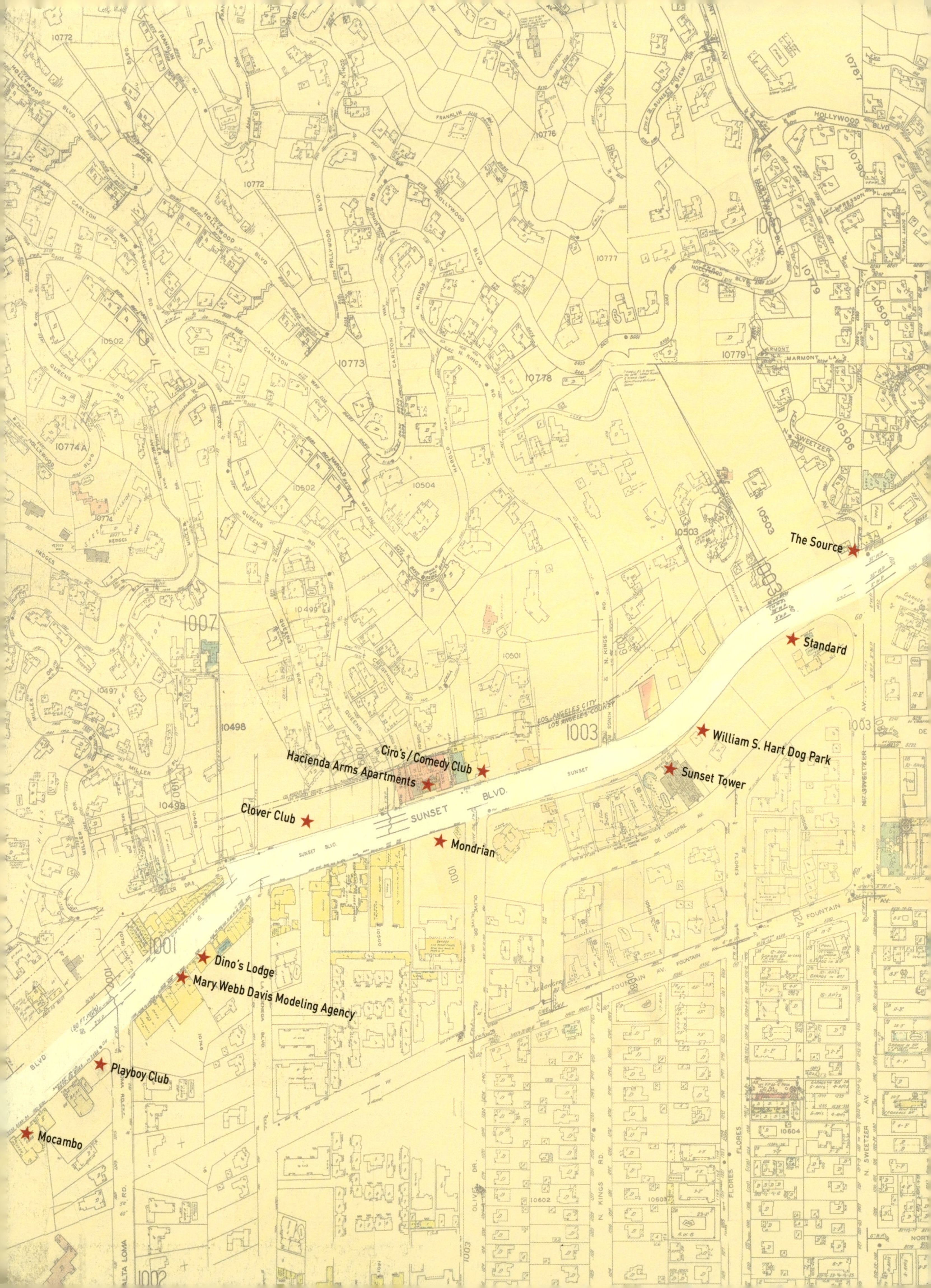
The Source
Standard
William S. Hart Dog Park
Sunset Tower
Ciro's / Comedy Club
Hacienda Arms Apartments
Clover Club
Mondrian
Dino's Lodge
Mary Webb Davis Modeling Agency
Playboy Club
Mocambo
SUNSET BLVD.